International Strategies and Techniques
for Future Local Government

International Strategies and Techniques for Future Local Government

Practical Aspects towards
Innovation and Reform

Marga Pröhl (ed.)

Bertelsmann Foundation Publishers
Gütersloh 1997

Die Deutsche Bibliothek – CIP-Einheitsaufnahme

International strategies and techniques for future local government :
practical aspects towards innovation and reform / Marga Pröhl (ed.). – Gütersloh :
Bertelsmann Foundation Publ., 1997
Dt. Ausg. u.d.T.: Internationale Strategien und Techniken für die
Kommunalverwaltung der Zukunft
ISBN 3-89204-275-6
NE: Pröhl, Marga [Hrsg.]

© 1997 Bertelsmann Foundation Publishers, Gütersloh
Responsible: Dr. Marga Pröhl
Translation: Britta Schleicher
Editors: Margit Sommer, Dr. Ulrich-Christian Pallach
Copy editor: Sabine Stadtfeld
Production editor: Kerstin Stoll
Cover design: HTG Werbeagentur, Bielefeld
Logo design: Christiane Rasche-Hellmann
Typesetting: Jung Satzcentrum, Lahnau
Print: Rosch-Buch Druckerei GmbH, Scheßlitz
ISBN 3-89204-275-6

Contents

Preface 7

Introduction 11
Marga Pröhl

Phoenix: Alternative Service Delivery Strategies 17
Heather E. Campbell, Susan J. Perkins, Frank Fairbanks

Hæmeenlinna: Enhancing Citizen and Community Participation ... 75
Krister Ståhlberg

Public Participation in Municipal Life:
The City of Quebec in the North American Context 103
André Beauchamp, Jean Dionne

City of Neuchâtel: From the Reform of the Local Management
Structures to the Concept of Partnership 131
Monika Dusong

Tilburg: Competition in Local Government 149
N. G. Maij

Bertelsmann Foundation: Comparative Performance Measurement –
A New Type of Competition between Local Governments 183
Bernd Adamaschek, Gerhard Banner

Christchurch: Culture Change in the Staff Organisation –
An International Perspective.............................. 209
Mike Richardson, Ian Brooks

Braintree: Our Aim is Quality............................. 249
Tony Bendell, Louise Boulter, Robert Atkins

Farum: Strategic Planning at the Local Level in
a Decentralized Public Sector............................. 291
Palle Mikkelsen, Leif Frimand

Christchurch: Strategic Planning in Local Government –
A Practitioner's Perspective 327
Mike Richardson

Delft: The Use of Information and Communication Technology
by Local Authorities – An International Perspective 357
*Piet Severijnen, Arre Zuurmond,
Mirjam Kalverda, Joy Ramsamoedj*

Human Resources Management in the City of Duisburg 407
*Winfried Lappé, Elke Holzrichter, Günter Grygiel,
Gabriele Nakonz, Robert Tonks*

Appendix 449

Preface

Our epoch is characterized by permanent societal change. This has altered the conditions bearing on the success of social orders. Conserving traditional achievements is no longer the paramount goal of society. Instead, the objectives are a higher level of well-being, education, equity and offering chances to individual people to freely shape their own lives. The systems that make up our social order must take into account this change of the framework conditions and have to be adapted accordingly. New solutions have to be found, amongst others, for reshaping the economy, political life, science, health care, and public administration. Also, our way of thinking is in need of fresh impulses concerning values and intellectual orientation. The lack of common standards will impede concerted action of society as a whole, a topic worth considering. The Bertelsmann Foundation confronts these challenges and systematically engages in modernizing the above-mentioned systems.

In former times, centralism and thinking in hierarchical terms did their share in coping with society's problems. Now that many traditional premises are no longer valid, these principles have lost their original meaning. The tasks today's society has to master are too complex and comprehensive by far. They require continuous evolution. Therefore, the question arises what kind of systems of social order we need to successfully meet present day challenges. We have been taught by the past that big hierarchical organizations are not capable of bringing about change by themselves. However, flexibility and the openness to intrinsic innovation are important requirements which the structures of any future polity will have to fulfill. To reach this objective, it is necessary that individual people be at liberty to form their own ideas and that responsibility be delegated. Only thus can we gain new insight into how things may work better.

It is this system which I have introduced in the Bertelsmann company and – it does work. As an entrepreneur, one must get an opportunity to really make mistakes and to learn from them. This line of thinking is not only valid regarding managerial tasks, it should also come to prevail in our polity. It is no longer sufficient for the state to only pursue the aim of guaranteeing public order and conformity to law in its actions. That is why in public administration as well, more leeway has to be given and responsibility be devolved. The risk is not uncontrollable. In any case, in order to fully exploit the employees' potential, responsibility has to be passed on to them. And they well possess the necessary faculties for this. They have been educated to act as autonomous beings and to think independently, and they wish to make use of their talents. Even at the bottom rank of hierarchy, individuals want to feel that their work makes sense. Public servants ought to be able to say: "We enjoy our work." Incidentally, this is the prerequisite for making them think about how to do things even better and find new approaches – and in doing so to consult the citizens.

Being able to measure the output achieved is a necessary condition for delegating responsibility. Only in this way can the citizens and those in charge verify to what extent the work done by public servants contributes to effectivity and efficiency in public administration. In free enterprise, the exchange of goods in an open market is the guarantor for this. However, competition and market structures are what public administration is deficient in. All the same, achievements may also be measured there. Transparency of public administration performance is made feasible by modern management techniques and planning and reporting systems. And it does work – as the City of Phoenix/USA has demonstrated in an exemplary manner. Beyond that, performance criteria, performance comparisons and benchmarking help to stimulate competition and to measure efficiency. If municipalities lay open the data from performance comparisons, citizens are also provided with a fact-based platform for democratic opinion building. For the first time, they are able to judge their administration's quality.

In order to arrive at this type of evolution in public administration, we need to follow new roads and be prepared to accept the risk. In Germany, the ebb in public finances has made action such an urgency as to arouse evolutionary courage. Municipalities have already begun to experiment. It would be erroneous, however, to believe that we are able today to replace old regulations by new ones. For the time being, it would be of great help to modify old regulations in order to give municipalities the chance of learning.

Early success must not induce us to underestimate people's inertia and their insistence on the status quo. It is, first of all, the politicians who hesitate in their task of modernizing the administration. Their objection is that a democracy pursues other goals and needs other procedures than does free enterprise. Thus, a major obstacle to the process of modernization consists in making politicians understand that new approaches endanger neither the principle of conformity to law nor the principle of equity. Politicians' resistance also stems from their having "grown up" with quite another kind of leadership technique. Therefore, they must be made to grasp the fact that these new principles of leadership and controlling do not present an unjustifiable risk vis-à-vis the society. It is a risk that can be contained.

In Germany, some progress is being made: the Saarland, for instance, an entire *Bundesland*, has announced its readiness to reform its local authorities. Things have really started moving. Even in problem areas of local government such as the cultural activities department, the Bertelsmann Foundation has succeeded in informing customers, evaluating achievements and controlling activities in such a way that the work done by this department can be aligned with the very diverse needs of citizens.

The 1993 Carl Bertelsmann Prize "Democracy and Efficiency in Local Government" has considerably contributed to this success. At that time, we did look for the best-governed city via an international research effort – and we found this city. We learned that problems which we still have to solve for Germany have been mastered elsewhere on our globe. There was a lot we were able to learn from the award winners Phoenix/USA and Christchurch/New Zealand, but also from other municipalities nominated. These new insights have had their effect on our country as well as on others. We have also come to understand that the international exchange of experiences amongst specialists and practitioners in the field of administration is well suited to promote developments in local government.

That is why the Bertelsmann Foundation established the "International Network for Better Local Government" in April 1995. Its members are the ten communities nominated for the Carl Bertelsmann Prize in 1993. By its expertise, its knowledge and an on-going dialogue, this group will assist in making new developments come about in a suitable manner.

I am convinced that we help to further evolution in our day – which is especially important in Germany where many citizens complain that business cannot go on as usual. And they are quite right in this. Through its actual involvement and through an international exchange of experiences between active administrators, the Bertelsmann Foundation will point out new ways, in cooperation with other countries and communities. The International Network enables us to significantly contribute towards rendering administrations more stable, more citizen-oriented and more innovative. Things can be changed, even if we live in a period of wide-spread stagnation. I am confident that our method will be successful.

Reinhard Mohn

Introduction
Marga Pröhl

In the last few years the modernization of local government has become a central issue. More and more local authorities are in the process of reforming their city halls from within. The objective of these reforms is to secure the efficiency of the cities for the future. With these modernisation approaches the municipalities are responding to changing societal background conditions: Scarcer financial resources, increasing demands of citizens on public services as well as the wish of public service staff for more responsibility have called into question the efficiency of the traditional bureaucratic system of public administration. The buzz word "The City as a Service Company" indicates the direction in which the development is supposed to be going. A stronger business management orientation is designed to achieve more efficiency, customer satisfaction and employee motivation in public administration. At the same time, all reform efforts are dedicated to answering two overriding questions. Firstly, how can local government provide the services needed by the citizens even more effectively in the future? And secondly, what kind of organization does local government need so that it can be shaped and further developed in the future?

Especially in other countries municipalities can already look back on long years of modernization experience. In the early nineties when hardly anyone in Germany was thinking about reforms along the lines of "New Public Management" cities abroad were already experimenting with new management and organization models. Within the framework of the 1993 Carl Bertelsmann Prize on the subject of "Democracy and Efficiency in

Local Government" the Bertelsmann Foundation therefore looked for innovative concepts and model solutions in Germany and abroad. An international working commission developed a number of criteria for the research, an abbreviated version of which merits inclusion at this point:
1. performance under democratic control,
2. citizen and customer orientation,
3. cooperation between politicians and the administration,
4. decentralized management,
5. controlling and reporting,
6. employee potential and
7. capacity for innovation and evolution secured by competition.

Ten municipalities that turned out to be particularly innovative were nominated for the prize. These were Braintree (England), Christchurch (New Zealand), Delft (Netherlands), Duisburg (Germany), Farum (Denmark), Hæmeenlinna (Finland), Neuchâtel (Switzerland), Phoenix (USA), Quebec (Canada) and Tilburg (Netherlands). After an extensive examination of the municipalities by consultants on the spot the cities of Phoenix, USA, and Christchurch, New Zealand, were jointly awarded the prize.

In order to be able to promote the international learning process and exchange of experience more continuously and systematically in the future the Bertelsmann Foundation established an international network for the reform of local government in April 1995. Members are the cities nominated for the 1993 Carl Bertelsmann Prize. In these cities the city manager or a representative whom he trusts actively Cooperate with the network. Other members are the Bertelsmann Foundation itself and the Local Government Centre for Management Studies, Cologne (Kommunale Gemeinschaftsstelle = KGSt).

The objective of the network is to further develop existing administrative reform concepts by way of an active exchange of experience among public administration practitioners. The network members do international research to find successful examples of reform efforts, discuss reform concepts and strategies and examine them as to their successful implementation. The Bertelsmann Foundation supports the network financially and organizationally. The members of the network presented the results of their work at a symposium on the premises of the Bertelsmann Foundation in June 1996. The results of this first working cycle are contained in this publication. They are not such that any theories could be derived from them. Instead, different strategies and model solutions as used by the network members and other cities are to be described to provide both practice-oriented examples of and possible approaches to the strategy development of other cities.

In 1995/1996 the members of the network worked on the following issues:
– *cultural change in local government*
   In the course of the last decade the organization culture in local authorities has changed all over the world. How did this change come about? How was it initiated and implemented? What are the consequences of this change? Christchurch has set itself the task of investigating the experience that network cities have gained with cultural change and, in doing so, of providing support to other local authorities. Christchurch's own experience has also been included in this report.
– *quality management*
   Improved efficiency and stronger customer orientation can be attained only by way of sustained quality management. "Braintree District Council" is a leader in the development of quality management systems in public administration in Great Britain. This chapter will give a general introduction to the subject of quality management, discuss the special features of quality management in public administration and elaborate on the quality management concept as implemented at Braintree. The quality management concepts of the network cities will be portrayed and analyzed.
– *employment of information and communication technology*
   Modern information and communication technology offers more and more new possibilities for organizations. It is one of the most important resources for the improvement of municipal services. The Dutch city of Delft will investigate the extent to which local authorities are using the new developments of information and communication technology. The use of information and communication technology is analyzed on the basis of the example of Delft, an international survey and three case studies.
– *requirements and concepts of personnel management*
   In addition to a change in the administration culture and new forms of organization the modernization of public administration requires mod-

ern and comprehensive personnel management. The city of Duisburg will shed some light on the changing background conditions of personnel management, analyze new instruments of personnel management and explain its own strategic personnel management concept. The critical success factors for efficient personnel management under changing background conditions will finally be defined.

- *citizen participation*

  The citizen is not only the customer for the services provided by the local authority but also the principal ordering them. Citizen participation can therefore exert a positive influence on the municipality's legitimacy as well as on its quality and efficiency. The subject of citizen participation was dealt with by the cities of Hæmeenlinna, Quebec and Neuchâtel. Hæmeenlinna reports about the results of a piece of international research among the network cities. Quebec focuses on the North American continent and gives a detailed description of its own approach. At Neuchâtel the idea of citizen participation is part and parcel of the city's comprehensive concept of partnership. The city explains this notion of partnership and how citizen participation was embedded in this concept.

- *alternative service strategies*

  Changes in background conditions have led to the collapse of the traditional service strategies that were based on the state's monopoly. A number of different alternative service strategies have been gaining ground in the last few years. Phoenix has been looking for alternative approaches to service delivery in the North American context and describes successful case studies.

- *competition*

  Competition is the driving force behind innovation and evolution. Lack of competition in local government has led to a situation where the innovation potential of the cities could not be exploited to the full. However, in the last few years competitive elements have increasingly been introduced into local authorities. Tilburg gives an overview of the different ways of implementing competition in local government and also describes cases of limited competition in municipalities. In Germany and the USA the cities measure and compare their performance and derive from this possible improvement measures for their own organizations. This inter-community performance comparison, providing surrogate competition as it does, constitutes a comprehensive approach to increasing efficiency in public administration. The concept of inter-community comparison as well as the commonalities and differences between the German and the American approach are portrayed and analyzed by the Bertelsmann Foundation.

– *strategic planning*

Because of the more and more rapid societal change, strategic planning is becoming increasingly important in the field of public administration. Strategic planning puts local authorities into a position of building up and nurturing success potentials and of employing resources in a target-oriented fashion. Christchurch describes its own experience with strategic planning and passes on some practical hints on the subject to the reader. The Farum local authority describes the Danish model and explains the strategic planning concept of the city of Farum.

Phoenix: Alternative Service Delivery Strategies
Heather E. Campbell, Susan J. Perkins, Frank Fairbanks

Executive Summary 19
1. Introduction 22
2. Intergovernmental Cooperation 24
    2.1 City of Scottsdale, Arizona Partners with Scottsdale School District 26
    2.2 City of Portland and Multnomah County, Oregon Progress Board 29
    2.3 Chesterfield County and Chesterfield School District, Virginia 31
    2.4 City of El Cajon and La Mesa, California Traffic Services .. 34
    2.5 Lessons Learned 35
    2.6 Conclusions 36
3. Public-Private Cooperation 37
    3.1 City of Palo Alto, California, and Digital Equipment Corporation 39
    3.2 Downtown Phoenix Partnership, Inc. 41
    3.3 America West Arena, Phoenix, Arizona 43
    3.4 City of Phoenix Partners with Waste Management of Arizona (WMA) 45
    3.5 Lessons Learned 47
    3.6 Conclusions 49
4. Privatization/Competition 49
    4.1 City of Phoenix, Arizona Public-Private Competition Program 52

    4.2 City of Indianapolis, Indiana Competition and
Privatization Initiatives 56
    4.3 City of Long Beach, California Golf Courses............ 58
    4.4 Lessons Learned 59
    4.5 Conclusions....................................... 60
5. Decentralization and Enterprise Strategies 61
    5.1 Decentralization................................... 62
    5.2 Enterprise Activities 66
    5.3 Lessons Learned 68
6. Summary and Conclusions 68
Literature... 70

Executive Summary

The environment for government is changing. The changes are fueled by increased citizen distrust of government and a rising tide of belief that government is inefficient. In this environment, the traditional government service delivery strategy, bureaucratic monopoly, breaks down. Various alternative service delivery strategies look appealing.

This paper presents case studies of situations where alternative strategies were tried and worked. The alternative service delivery strategies presented in detail are intergovernmental cooperation, public-private cooperation, and privatization/competition with a brief discussion of decentralization and enterprise strategies. In each section, we begin by discussing the scholarly literature on the technique. For each case, we describe:
- the problem to be solved,
- the proposed solution and how it was developed,
- implementation issues, and
- measures of success.

We end each section with lessons learned.

The intent of the paper is to present ideas for making positive change. The guiding questions for the paper are: 1. Under what circumstances are alternative service delivery strategies successful? And: 2. What special benefits do alternative service delivery strategies have to offer?

Intergovernmental cooperation

Intergovernmental agreements are formal arrangements in which governments pool resources. Case studies include the following cooperative efforts:
- city and school district build and operate a joint-use library,
- City-County Progress Board develops and collects data on joint benchmarks,
- county and school district combine fleet management,
- two cities combine street and traffic lighting resources.

Intergovernmental Cooperation seems to be an appropriate alternative service delivery strategy when governments have similar needs or interests. Financial pressures were present in most of our case studies. Flexibility was required of participants, as well as the ability to relinquish their former level of control over operations. Benefits included service level improvements and cost savings.

Public-Private Cooperation

Partnerships involving governmental and non-governmental entities take many forms and coalesce for various purposes. They work well for economic development and can also allow enhancement of service levels through sharing of resources. Case studies include the following public-private partnerships:
- city and private corporation provide on-line computer query capability to citizens,
- government-business partnership enhances city downtown,
- sports franchise and city provide downtown sports facility,
- city and private firm have a reciprocal transfer station waste disposal agreement.

The case studies illustrate the importance of clearly defining responsibilities and understanding the environment in which each entity operates. These partnerships all resulted in benefits to each party and the community as a whole.

Privatization/competition

This section discusses the value of using competition in selecting a service provider for the delivery of government services. Case studies discussed include:
- City of Phoenix Public/Private Competition Program,
- City of Indianapolis Competition and Privatization Initiatives,
- City of Long Beach Golf Course Privatization.

Circumstances surrounding the adoption of this alternative service delivery strategy differ in each of the cases studied, but each of the cities clearly assumed new risks in experimenting with this service delivery approach. Phoenix and Indianapolis use a competition program – each believing that the best way to determine who should provide service can be decided through competition. Long Beach was interested in contracting-out its golf course operation. Cities report cost reductions, revenue increases, and service level improvements.

Decentralization and enterprise strategies

This section presents two strategies we find particularly interesting. Decentralization can be performed entirely within the public sector while enterprise activities take place within the market sector. Case studies discussed include:
– locational decentralization: City of Phoenix Juvenile Curfew Program,
– decision making decentralization: City of Phoenix Employee Involvement Strategy,
– enterprise strategies: San Diego and Los Angeles, California Government Stores.

The examples illustrate that creativity, whether in moving services to where the demand is, making better use of employee resources by enhancing their participation, or in selling publicly-owned products, can enhance government's ability to meet social needs.

Summary

The driving force behind alternative service delivery in government is citizen demand for better, more responsive, and more efficient service. Since resources available to governments are limited, providing services at a lower cost can mean the government can provide more or better services. Further, certain techniques can actually enhance revenues, allowing more service provision.

After reviewing the case studies in this paper, our conclusion is that alternative service delivery strategies are most likely to be successful, first, in an environment where risk-taking is encouraged. Another ingredient that was present in most of the case studies was the willingness to relinquish some control formerly claimed by the bureaucracy. Third – and partly compensating for the second – a clear articulation of goals and responsibilities of each party is necessary at the outset to ensure that service is delivered in a timely and effective manner. Fourth, common to all alternative service delivery methods is the need to involve individuals outside the organization.

1. Introduction

Citizens' relationships to their governments are changing. These changes are fueled by increased citizen distrust of government, and a rising tide of belief that government is inefficient. Along with these attitudes, citizens are increasingly reluctant to support tax increases and in some cases are calling for tax decreases. Twenty-one of the fifty U.S. States cut taxes in 1994. Cities have not been as quick to lower taxes, but they are feeling pressure to provide more service without tax increases. Over 43 percent of cities responding to a 1994 National League of Cities survey reported real dollar reductions in capital spending (Reason Foundation, 1995). In addition, as consumers, people expect high-quality products and services that change rapidly in response to customer demands. These expectations have carried over to the public sector. These attitudinal changes are so prevalent that a central policy goal of President Clinton's administration is "reinventing government."

In this environment, the traditional government service delivery method, bureaucratic monopoly, breaks down. Instead, governments must find alternative delivery strategies that increase service quality, responsiveness, and citizen trust while decreasing – or at least holding constant – costs.

An International City Manager Association (ICMA) nationwide survey of municipalities and counties (conducted in 1992) indicated that change is occurring. Responses were received from 1504 municipalities and counties. The primary factors for organizations considering alternative service delivery were fiscal pressures, either from external forces (such as decreases in Federal funding supplied to lower levels of government) or internal attempts to cut costs (to improve efficiency). Internal attempts to cut costs were a factor for 91 percent of the municipalities that used alternative strategies; external pressures were a factor for 55 percent of the municipalities. Less frequently cited factors included political climate, mandates, and unsolicited proposals made by other organizations. Despite tighter fiscal constraints, there was little evidence to indicate that local governments are discontinuing services (Miranda and Andersen, 1994).

Though bureaucratic monopoly is low risk, there is much evidence it is not low cost. Consequently, alternative service delivery strategies are especially sought to provide services while decreasing costs (Miranda and Andersen, 1994, p. 26). Various options are being tried, including decentralization, citizen/customer empowerment, public-private Cooperation, volunteerism, intergovernmental Cooperation, and privatization/competition. These options illustrate how "local governments have adjusted their structures and modes of operation to develop from the traditional local authority to a modern, democratically controlled public service company" (Bertelsmann Foundation, 1994, Vol. 1, p. 11).

The intent of this paper is to present ideas for making positive changes. Focusing on the three areas of intergovernmental Cooperation, public-private Cooperation, and privatization/competition, and briefly discussing decentralization/enhanced employee involvement and enterprise strategies, this paper presents case studies of situations where alternative strategies were tried and worked. The analyses do not always allow generalizations about what strategies work best, or the average quantities that can be saved; in many cases, use of these strategies is too new or too intermittent to allow generalization. Instead, this paper is intended to unleash creativity by presenting some good practices. Experience in this century suggests that experimentation is crucial to keep up with the rapid pace of change.

This paper is organized into four sections, one for each of the four alternative strategies we emphasize. Cases of alternative service delivery strategies were identified from published sources (sources are listed at the end of the paper), and then people who had been involved were asked to fill in details (because the authors are in Phoenix, Arizona, it was easier to get pertinent information for Phoenix-area cases, so that area is over-represented). We selected case studies designed to illustrate our guiding questions for this paper:

1. *Under what circumstances are alternative service delivery strategies successful?* and
2. *What special benefits do alternative service delivery strategies have to offer?*

In each section, we begin by discussing the scholarly literature on this technique (if we were able to identify any), and then present case studies. For each case, information permitting, we describe:
– the problem to be solved,
– the proposed solution and how it was developed,
– implementation issues, and
– measures of success.

We end each section with lessons learned.

2. Intergovernmental Cooperation

Intergovernmental agreements are formal arrangements in which at least two governmental entities pool resources to deliver designated services. The "pooling" may be in the form of shared responsibility, employees, expenditures, and resources; or 100 percent of the responsibility carried by one entity with monetary payments made by the other as compensation for services received.

In an article published in 1993, the case is made for local governmental units to Cooperate more effectively through the use of interlocal or intergovernmental agreements (Fundis et al., 1993). According to Fundis, "Three criteria are needed for such Cooperation: [it] (1) must be voluntary, (2) must be [controlled by] the governmental bodies, and (3) must preserve the identities of the existing units of government" (ibid., p. 47). Fundis et al. (1993) give several reasons why this Cooperation occurs:

1. Problems do not respect political boundaries (e.g., flood control, water supply).
2. Economies of scale can result in efficiency, cost sharing, and affordability of services and equipment.
3. Cooperation can be a defensive strategy to prevent state or federal assumption of a local function or to discourage the formation or growth of special purpose districts; and
4. Interdependence of local units in an area may require or foster Cooperation.

Identifying "communities of interest" may be an effective way of determining services to consolidate. Many current governmental structures were designed for another time. They were created when the typical city existed by itself in a largely rural unpopulated area. Now "cities" are actually metropolitan regions with a proliferation of overlapping governmental jurisdictions: municipal and county governments, school districts, transit authorities, state and federal regional offices, etc. Making bigger governments by consolidating and abolishing entities is not the answer. Too much energy can be spent on "territorial wars" while nothing is accomplished, and larger bureaucracies tend to be sluggish and inefficient. Starting with problems people care about and finding ways to use regional resources will allow measurable progress (Barnett, 1994, p. 11).

Some services lend themselves naturally to intergovernmental consolidation. Economies of scale can lead to significant savings when purchasing is done as a group. An expansion of the group size results in benefits and savings in health, life and liability insurance and employee assistance programs. Consolidating equipment management provides greater efficiencies in facility use, labor, site management and upkeep. Group fuel purchases and storage can have significant savings when only one site needs to be certified to meet all state and federal safety and environmental regulations. County-wide 911 (a phone number designated nationwide for emergency services but paid for locally) is now seen as an affordable alternative that avoids the duplication of services. Combining and sharing technical training for certification classes (police and fire) can result in time and dollar savings for governments. Independence is giving way to practicality. "We want our own services" has been replaced by "We are all in this together" (Fundis et al., 1993, pp. 98–99).

Table 1: Percent of respondents reporting using intergovernmental cooperation for seven service types

	percent of cities surveyed
mental health	67 percent
child welfare programs	63 percent
tax assessing	51 percent
transit systems	49 percent
title Records/mMap maintenance	44 percent
alternative tax bill processing	38 percent
sewage collection and treatment	33 percent

Source: Miranda and Andersen, 1994

Intergovernmental Cooperation is increasing in popularity as a method of delivering services. A 1992 ICMA survey indicates the use of Cooperative arrangements is becoming more common and embraces a wide variety of services (see table 1).

Following are four in-depth examples of intergovernmental Cooperation. The Portland-Multnomah example is especially interesting in showing how governments can join together to create community-wide comparative performance measures.

2.1 City of Scottsdale, Arizona Partners with Scottsdale School District

In 1988, the City of Scottsdale (population 173,000) and the Scottsdale School District decided to establish a joint-use library. A partnership between the two entities was not new since they had successfully Cooperated in the past to provide recreation programs.

Problem statement – Scottsdale library partnership

In this case, a problem did not exist, but an opportunity presented itself that two government organizations decided to use to both of their advantages. The City of Scottsdale was interested in opening a branch library in the northern part of the city. They had sufficient funding but did not own any land in the desired area. They saw an opportunity to combine forces with the school district since the local school district already possessed land where a high school was to be built plus they also had $33 million in bond funding available for the construction of the school. In the district, public schools always include school libraries.

Proposed solution

A District Administrator approached the City of Scottsdale. The City of Scottsdale conducted some research and discovered that other joint library projects had been successfully completed. Approximately one year of negotiations were conducted before a final intergovernmental agreement was signed by both parties. This agreement specified the various rights and responsibilities of each party in regards to the capital portion of the project, start-up costs, operating expenditures and daily operations.

Implementation issues

This type of arrangement was new to both the school district and the city. As such, one of the first implementation issues was contingency planning in case the agreement did not work out to both of their satisfactions. They devised the agreement and asset purchases so that the assets could be easily split in the event that the agreement failed and the two entities decided to part ways. Under the agreement, the school district provided and paid for all construction costs associated with the library. The City funded the furnishings and fixtures for the library and all personnel. The cost of books was split 60/40 city/school district. In this way, if the partnership did not work out, the building could be left at the school and the City could remove its assets.

Developing accountability for operations was the second issue. They decided to write the contract to specify that the library be operated by the City as a branch library located on a school campus. No school district staff are employed at the library. This arrangement has the benefit of maintaining clear accountability since the City and its employees are fully responsible for operations.

The third implementation issue dealt with the proposed sharing of operating costs. They decided that operating costs could be shared. The library has a total of 18 staff members. Since the school district would normally staff a library with one librarian and two library aides, the district pays the equivalent amount toward the joint library's expenses. Ongoing book purchases are funded using the City's usual book budget of $ 115,000 per city library offset by a contribution by the school district equal to the district's annual book budget of $ 9,900 per school library. Thus, total annual book costs to the City are $ 105,100.

Another implementation issue dealt with developing a design that would be acceptable to both parties. In order to encourage use by the general public, the school was designed so that the library has its own entrance at the front of the building. (Normally school libraries are entered from the school and are open only during school hours.) This design feature allows the public to visit the library without having to walk through the school and allows longer hours. The library also has its own parking lot separate from the school's.

A final implementation issue dealt with operating hours for the library. Traditionally, school library hours are open far less than City branch library hours. To accommodate student schedules, the library opens at 7:00 am during the school year unlike other branch libraries which open at 10:00 am. Because of these additional early morning hours, the library is not open on Sundays like other branch libraries; however during the school year it is open for 71 hours per week, which is seven hours more than the main library, 11 hours more than other branch libraries, and 26 hours more than school libraries. During the summer, the joint use library hours are reduced to 56 per week.

Project implementation began in 1988. However, the school district put the project on hold for two years in the fall of 1993 because of uncertainty as to school demographics since the school was being built in a new and rapidly-growing area. This delay was also a logical move from the standpoint of the City because the area's population was not yet large enough to sustain a branch library. In the fall of 1995, the school and the library opened.

Measures of success

This experiment was so successful that the City and School District have agreed to participate in another joint-venture library.

Both parties saved on capital costs. Based on a 10,000 square-foot library (the usual size of a Scottsdale branch library) construction and design costs would have been $ 1.3 million. The School District saved approximately $ 1.2 million on interior fixtures and furnishings. Total capital cost to build the 18,000 square-foot, 50,000 volume joint-use library was $ 2.5 million. There are also ongoing savings in operating costs.

Service levels are improved. As mentioned above, the library is able to offer extended hours to City of Scottsdale residents. The school district is able to offer students a more extensive collection of books, access to online research, and connection to the Internet and Worldwide Web (Register, 1996).

2.2 City of Portland and Multnomah County, Oregon Progress Board

The Progress Board was created in September 1993 under the direction of Ms. Vera Katz, Mayor of Portland (population 517,000) and Ms. Beverly Stein, Chair of Multnomah County (population 626,000) Board of Commissioners. It evolved from *Portland Future Focus,* an ongoing program designed to implement a strategic vision for the city (created by Mayor Bud Clark in 1991), and the Multnomah County 1989 *Visions* project which created a long term plan for the county.

Problem statement

While both the City and the County had participated in strategic planning efforts, none of the efforts had led to ongoing change and improvement, or Coordination of any type between the two entities. Since Portland comprises 75 percent of the County, there are large overlapping interests, populations, and problems.

Proposed solution

Long term strategic planning efforts by the city and county culminated in the creation of the Portland-Multnomah Progress Board. Through focus groups, thousands of citizens came together over five years to describe their vision and to set benchmarks. The benchmarks reflected the citizens' vision for the future. Goals were set to describe the community that government, businesses, non-profit organizations and citizens wanted to help build. The Progress Board, consisting of community leaders, was designed as a means for the County and City to jointly focus their benchmarking efforts on common goals as a means to improve their community.

Five major areas of focus were selected and benchmarks were developed relating to each of those areas. The focus areas are (1) the economy; (2) education, children and families; (3) environment and quality of life; (4) governance; and (5) public safety.

Implementation issues

A major implementation issue related to obtaining relevant feedback from several community groups. The effort was time-consuming. The benchmarks (measurements used to address pressing problems) were developed between September, 1993 and January, 1994 with the assistance of the community groups and other interested parties.

Another implementation issue related to the availability of the benchmark information. In January, 1994, selection of the benchmarks was complete; however no data were collected until the end of the year, and then only a few were available. In the meantime, things have improved. Currently, the Progress Board has defined 76 benchmarks and collected data for 59 of these.

Consistency of data is an implementation issue, as is collecting the information in a manner that is useful to the people that will be using the data. A research analyst employed by the Board measures the benchmarks. This is done by establishing contact with key individuals who can provide the relevant data and, in many cases, collaborate on the measurement process. Measurement is not consistent across all of the benchmarks. For some benchmarks, only one type of data is available while for others numerous types are available (Harris, 1996).

Measures of success

The project is so new that measures of success are not yet available. The Progress Board has determined the indicators they will use to judge the success of the project. These indicators are (1) Government use of the benchmarks and (2) Community use of the benchmarks (Harris, 1996). Of course there is anticipation that knowledge will be a precursor to improvement, but the current focus is on developing and using the benchmark information. The data are broken down to the neighborhood level whenever possible so that the benchmarks have relevance throughout the community. This breakdown allows neighborhood leaders to identify problems specific to their areas (Harris, 1996).

2.3 Chesterfield County and Chesterfield School District, Virginia

Chesterfield County, Virginia (population 254,000), developed an agreement with the local school district to share the cost of fleet maintenance.

Problem statement – Chesterfield county and school district

Chesterfield County has experienced rapid growth during the past several years. The rapid growth within the county resulted in increased service and funding requests from a variety of County departments causing increasing fiscal pressures. A particular area of concern involved the public schools, which had become overcrowded as a result of this growth. In an unusual arrangement, the County Board of Supervisors had budgetary control over the schools and the associated School Board, although the schools operated independently of the County Board. Budget hearings conducted by the Board of Supervisors became more and more contentious as the schools requested additional funding.

Proposed solution

A tax increase was not viewed as a solution to the school's fiscal problems because the elected officials feared public outcry. Instead, a team was assembled to look for areas of service duplication and inefficiency within the county and school district. A review of fleet maintenance operations suggested the potential for consolidation in the servicing of the school and county vehicle fleets.

Implementation issues

One implementation issue was obtaining accurate cost-accounting information for decision making. Prior to the review of fleet maintenance, there was no analysis or cost tracking to determine the per-unit cost of operation. A cost-accounting system was implemented to track the cost per mile to operate vehicles in the fleet. Since 1992, with the implementation of new fleet management policies described below, operating costs have decreased $.05 per mile, saving the county and school district a combined $ 400,000 based on 8 million vehicle miles (12.8 million kilometers) per year.

Another implementation issue related to combining the two fleet maintenance facilities. The result of the joint review led to the school fleet being placed under control of the county. The school board was reluctant to agree to this transfer of control unless there were some safeguards in place to insure the quality of service provided. Therefore, a contract between the school board and the county was developed which specified service levels to be provided for school buses. This is a three-year contract and is reviewed annually to determine whether predetermined service levels have been met.

Measures of success

A preventative maintenance system has been instituted where there was none previously. Service consolidation has led to a reduction in the total number of vehicles needed for the county and schools as a whole.

Several productivity improvements occurred. Prior to the policy change, mechanics were stationed at remote locations each morning and evening with a van loaded with spare parts, in order to ensure that children arrived at schools or homes on time. If a school bus broke down, one of these mechanics would be nearby to repair the vehicle where it was stranded. However, a review of maintenance history showed that the buses broke down so infrequently that the costs far outweighed the benefits. A total of eight mechanics were assigned to perform this duty, and it was determined that a total of 40 mechanic hours per day were spent at these assigned locations, but the mechanics rarely performed any actual maintenance work. This method of fleet management has been discontinued. Instead of stationing mechanics at remote locations, if a bus breaks down a replacement bus is driven to pick up the children. The faulty bus is later towed. Three mechanic positions were eliminated.

Another example of productivity savings dealt with vehicle fueling. Three staff were dedicated entirely to refueling vehicles. The team reviewing fleet maintenance operations determined that these positions were not necessary if vehicle drivers performed the refueling. Closing a district service center, and reducing the number of refuellers and mechanics led to personnel savings of $ 200,000 annually (Perry, 1996).

2.4 City of El Cajon and La Mesa, California Traffic Services

El Cajon (population 100,000) is located 10 miles east of San Diego in San Diego County, California. San Diego is a city of approximately 1 million.

Problem statement – cooperative traffic services

Since El Cajon is situated near a large city, it experiences the heavy traffic volume of that city. The County of San Diego provided street light and traffic signal services for all cities in the county until the late 1970s. At that time, the service was contracted to a private business and administered by the county. San Diego County was not particularly concerned about the cost of the service as it merely passed the cost on to the surrounding cities. A competitive process was not used to bid the contract and the county had little concern about whether or not El Cajon and the other cities were satisfied. Further, the county charged the cities a fee to administer the contract and this was unacceptable to El Cajon.

Proposed solution

In the early 1980s, El Cajon decided to jointly contract for street light and traffic signal maintenance with the nearby City of La Mesa (population 53,000). This eliminated the administrative charges from the county and allowed the cities to have direct control over their service levels.

Measures of success

This arrangement proved to be so successful both in terms of service and cost that a total of five cities in San Diego County [El Cajon, La Mesa, Poway (population 44,500), Santee (population 53,000) and Lemon Grove (population 24,000)] now jointly contract for these services. A unique aspect of the arrangement between the cities is that while the contract is bid for service to all the cities, each city is responsible for administering and monitoring contract performance for its own area.

Ed Krulikowski, City Traffic Engineer for the City of El Cajon, reports that the unit cost of service has actually decreased each time the contract has been bid due to increased competition and improvements in service efficiency. El Cajon has saved 30 to 40 percent compared to the previous arrangement administered by San Diego County.[1] Savings are about $ 50,000 annually for El Cajon. The total service area has 250 traffic signals and 5,000 street lights (Krulikowski, 1996).

2.5 Lessons Learned

Following are some potential pitfalls and benefits from using government Cooperation as an alternative service delivery strategy.

Potential pitfalls

- Time must be invested in preparation of an intergovernmental agreement.
- Specification of contract requirements may be difficult or time-consuming since, for example, quality measures often are not used by single entities.
- Loss of control may result for one or both of the partners.

Benefits

- Cost savings and
- service level improvements.

Intergovernmental Cooperation seems to be an appropriate alternative service delivery strategy when governments have similar needs or inter-

---

[1] This situation supports a point, made later in the paper, that it is competition, not the publicness or privateness of a service provider, that results in cost efficiencies.

ests. This was the case in all the agreements studied. Financial pressures were present in three of the four cases presented – particularly for Chesterfield County and El Cajon. Usually, entering into an intergovernmental agreement required each entity to give up some control it had formerly enjoyed, including adjusting specifications to suit more than one entity (such as in the Scottsdale Library example). The City of El Cajon actually changed from relying on one entity not of its choosing (the County) to others. This case shows that governments relying on each other is not necessarily intergovernmental Cooperation. Intergovernmental Cooperation only occurs when both parties take an active interest in the service provided.

Service-level improvements were common in the cases we studied. Only Portland and Multnomah did not report any cost savings, but their driving goal was to improve product quality and savings were not an issue. Therefore, this case study was unique.

According to Scottsdale officials, the success of the joint venture between the City of Scottsdale and the Scottsdale School District was dependent on each party's willingness to invest time in the preparation of a detailed intergovernmental agreement that established project goals and the rights and responsibilities of each entity. To produce this agreement, open communication was imperative and it laid the groundwork for continuing relations between both parties. Both parties learned that innovation and a willingness to change go a long way in establishing a working partnership. Another factor contributing to the success of a project of this magnitude is that it was undertaken in a political and community climate that allowed risk-taking and innovation and welcomed cost reductions.

2.6 Conclusions

National research provides some insight into developing successful intergovernmental Cooperative agreements. The Docking Institute of Public Affairs at Fort Hays State University, Kansas, has identified the groundwork necessary for successful restructuring services through intergovernmental agreements. According to them, four preliminary issues need to be resolved:

1. Consensus formation – Identifying and utilizing key local leaders to "sell" the opportunities and savings that are expected from the service consolidation helps build consensus.
2. Political constituent support – Despite their personal beliefs, leaders still have to be able to defend their actions/votes to their constituencies and to the media. A sound plan with explicit Cooperation of other societal or governmental sectors greatly facilitates this process.
3. Organizational structure creation – Some form of organization has to be agreed upon to implement or manage the change.
4. Recognition of potential barriers – Recognizing potential barriers such as financial front-end costs to begin a consolidated service project, historical antagonisms that exist between the governing bodies, and concern about loss of community or institutional identity (Fundis et al., 1993).

The case studies we used illustrated the importance of points (3) and (4). While the first two points were not apparent in these case studies, organizations planning to implement this alternative service delivery strategy should also consider those issues in advance of implementation.

3. Public-Private Cooperation

Public-private Cooperation, particularly for the furtherance of economic development goals, is becoming increasingly recognized as an effective alternative service delivery strategy. In fact, the first chapter of the influential book *Reinventing Government* (Osborne and Gaebler, 1992) focuses on public-private partnerships, and a survey of the membership of the American Economic Development Council indicated a substantial increase – to about 1/3 – in development organizations that are formed with both business and public resources (Kolzow, 1994, p. 5). Public-private ventures can combine strengths of both sectors, including flexibility, accountability, continuity, and socially-desirable investment, along with pooled resources greater than would be available to either alone

(O'Looney, 1992; Kolzow, 1994). Further, analysis indicates that public-private partnerships can be effective tools for economic development in both rural and urban settings (Larkin, 1994).

In general, the strengths of private sector organizations are efficiency and responsiveness, while public sector strengths include accountability and a social/public welfare focus. International competition is increasing pressures on the public sector to "become more flexible in order to get the job done" (O'Looney, 1992), but rigidity is one of the great weaknesses of bureaucratic monopoly. Additionally, involving private leaders can promote continuity because they are not disrupted by elections as public leaders may be (Kolzow, 1994). Joint ventures can allow investment which is politically difficult for purely public entities (*ibid.*), and which is not profitable for purely private ones. Overall, combining the two can allow an optimal mix of flexibility, continuity, and accountability (O'Looney, 1992; Kolzow, 1994; Larkin, 1994, p. 7) along with the ability to "... interweave scarce public and private resources in order to achieve [a] community's goals" (George Latimer, Mayor of St. Paul, Minnesota; quoted in Osborne and Gaebler, 1992, p. 27; see also Kolzow, 1994).

In particular, public-private partnerships are frequently used to further economic development goals. As stated by Kolzow, "the purpose of a planned economic development effort is to influence private sector decisions for the benefit of the community" (1994, p. 4). Nonetheless, public-private Cooperation has much to offer the business community as well (Kolzow, 1994, p. 4). There is evidence that public-private partnerships can be effective either in urban or rural settings (Larkin 1994). For example, Goldstein and Luger (1992) studied 120 "research parks" (organizations that combine academic, state or local government, and commercial entities) located in 44 American states, and found that those in rural areas led to modest economic growth and development (cited in Larkin, 1994, p. 8). Manufacturing networks, rarely used in the United States but much more frequent in other industrialized countries, can offer clear benefits such as worker training, technology transfer, cost reduction, and access to new markets. However, "there is little likelihood that private firms will create enough networks on their own," so government has an important role in helping them form (Larkin, 1994, p. 8).

The following cases detail some examples of successful public-private partnerships, including two that focus on increasing citizen services rather than the more common goal of economic development.

3.1 City of Palo Alto, California, and Digital Equipment Corporation

The City of Palo Alto, California (population 56,000) is situated near Stanford University and is in the heart of "Silicon Valley." The residents of the region are primarily academicians or have jobs relating to computer technology and tend to be comfortable using computer technologies. One computer networking group estimated that 50 percent of citizens of the area have access to computers (Pound, 1995).

Problem statement

A committee composed of City, school district and business representatives considered methods to provide City and school district information to citizens. Since many citizens were computer-literate, there was strong demand for City government information, but the City did not have funding or expertise available to provide such access.

Proposed solution

Digital Equipment Corporation, an information technology company, agreed to pay an annual license fee for access to the City's rights-of-way for running a fiber optic line to serve its own sites and to run a second fiber-optic line for the City's exclusive use at no additional charge. The City and Digital developed a partnership to address the City's information needs. The cable links City Hall and Digital's Network Systems Laboratory. In February 1994, the City of Palo Alto established a mini-network of information with an Internet link and Worldwide Web user interface, becoming the first city in the United States to establish full Internet capabilities.

Implementation issues

The first implementation issue was acquiring sufficient hardware and software for public access. The city did not have funding for workstations. A phased approach was taken (and is still being implemented). The network, in operation since April 1994, was established by donations of hardware and software from Digital; Hewlett Packard, a computer hardware company; and a local electronics store. The local electronics store donated two personal computers that were placed in Palo Alto City Hall for the public's use and Hewlett Packard donated a laser printer for use with these computers.

Maintaining data on the server was another implementation issue. The City of Palo Alto assumed responsibility for data maintenance. Putting the server in place took less than one year to complete but the information offered on the server continues to grow and evolve. In addition to City information, information from the Chamber of Commerce, Palo Alto Historical Association, the Palo Alto Unified School District and the Palo Alto Medical Foundation is available on the network. City information includes City and government history, City codes and procedures, pictorials of City Council members, downtown maps, lists of local attractions, hotels and restaurants, and CalTrain train schedules. Currently, some city permit approvals are posted on the server. Eventually, a citizen seeking a building permit, for example, may be able to apply for the permit on-line.

As with any new service, publicity was required to notify citizens. Palo Alto issued press releases to inform the public about the network and published the e-mail address of the City Council. A special "Feedback" box solicits comments and questions from the public. These comments are distributed to Palo Alto council members and the city manager for appropriate follow-up.

Measures of success

The partnership between Digital and Palo Alto allowed the City to join the information superhighway and offer its citizens, and others, another way to access data about City government at their convenience.

The Chamber of Commerce offers local businesses the opportunity to advertise on the server. These businesses have realized increased sales prompting new businesses to join the server and advertise their services. Some of the initial increased sales were due to timing: the server came online prior to the area hosting the World Cup Soccer Tournament in 1994. International visitors were able to use the network to reserve rooms at Palo Alto hotels, for instance, introducing Palo Alto businesses to a new client segment.

The number of inquiries to the network is approximately 1 200 per day. The network is managed by the City-Wide Information Network Committee (a committee that reviews city-wide information issues, software and hardware needs, etc.) and receives many information requests daily. Future plans include additional public terminals in the public libraries to accommodate interested citizens (Pound, 1995).

3.2 Downtown Phoenix Partnership, Inc.

The International Downtown Association is located in Washington, D.C. Its mission is to maintain the vitality of inner cities by promoting investment in retail, cultural, and other entertainment businesses to create a vibrant city center (Mullen, 1996). The City of Phoenix and the Phoenix Community Alliance asked the International Downtown Association to perform a comprehensive assessment of the downtown Phoenix community.

Problem statement

The research concluded that a Coordinated effort was needed to manage investment and future efforts in downtown Phoenix. Criminal activity in downtown was a problem. Another threat, common to large U.S. cities, was that most of the downtown workers left the area at night and frequented businesses in neighborhoods near their homes. This made it difficult for downtown businesses to stay viable (Mullen, 1996).

Proposed solution

The Downtown Phoenix Partnership, Inc., a nonprofit organization whose mission is to create and maintain a vital downtown Phoenix, was created in 1990 as a result of this recommendation. The Partnership focuses on a 90-block area (1.5 square miles). It receives most of its funding from assessments on the non-residential property owners within those 90 blocks. Assessments range from $ 300 to $ 100,000 per year, based on use and linear frontage (size and accessability to main thoroughfare). These property owners include for-profit business enterprises as well as government entities. Additional funding for the partnership is also derived from corporate donations (Mullen, 1996).

The Partnership's Board of Directors, composed of City leaders representing various Downtown entities (both public and private), provides a voice on issues relating to Downtown Phoenix. It also determines funding priorities, develops the Partnership's annual budget ($ 1.2 million in 1996) and work programs, and oversees the implementation of the work plan. The budget and work plans are also reviewed by the downtown property owners and the City Council. The Partnership fosters Cooperation among various parties, including local, county, and state governments, businesses, corporations, employees, property owners, and cultural and nonprofit organizations.

The Partnership's work program focuses on five areas (Security, Marketing, Transportation, Streetscape, and Administration). The Partnership is also involved in zoning and development issues that affect the downtown.

Measures of success

Since its establishment in 1990, downtown sales and property tax revenues from trackable sources have increased. According to the Partnership, total downtown sales in 1989 were $ 56.8 million and in 1995 they grew to $ 114 million (Reagor, 1996). At the same time, major crimes in downtown have decreased (Mullen, 1996).

3.3 America West Arena, Phoenix, Arizona

Facility development can involve any number of participants working together to construct a needed community facility. The participants can benefit economically as well as by providing a facility that enriches the community.

Problem statement

Downtown Phoenix experienced significant redevelopment in the 1980s, but it lacked a major entertainment facility to attract large numbers of citizens and visitors on a regular basis. Without such a facility, business development was hindered and community pride in the downtown area was low (Kearney, 1996). At the same time, the Phoenix Suns of the National Basketball Association (NBA) were looking for new revenue streams (from high-profit box seats and fixed advertising signage). The Suns were tenants in an aging facility (seating and amenities not up to NBA standards) that offered limited opportunities for revenue enhancement because box seating and fixed signage did not exist and could not be incorporated into the facility due to its age.

Proposed solution

Seeing an opportunity to meet both parties' needs, the City and the Phoenix Suns agreed to jointly develop the 20,000-seat America West Arena. The Arena is owned by the City and operated by the Phoenix Suns. Development and construction of the facility were funded and managed jointly. The City contributed $47.8 million; the Suns contributed $52 million. The City's participation in the project was funded by a one percent increase in the hotel/motel tax and a two percent tax on short-term vehicle rentals. The Phoenix Suns sought their own long-term bonded debt.

Implementation issues

The first implementation issue was the negotiation of an appropriate contract. It was not easy for the City and the private company to come to an agreement on terms to build and operate a facility when neither one of the entities had any previous experience. Coordinating the private-sector need to make a profit with the public-sector need to provide service to citizens was difficult – resulting contracts need to be very lengthy and specific.

Cost overruns, when they developed, were not appropriate for the public agency to incur – the private-sector party was responsible for covering cost overruns. Ongoing management of the facility was assumed by the private sector firm, the Phoenix Suns. Accustomed to operating as a business, it is sometimes difficult for them to deal with the public disclosure (accountability) responsibilities of a government.

Measures of success

The City of Phoenix Community and Economic Development Department reports that Arena events attracted nearly two million people to the downtown district during the first two years of operation (the arena opened in June 1992). This attracted new restaurant and retail development. Over 30 restaurants and retail establishments opened after the first year of operation. The Arena itself generated about $ 500,000 in sales tax revenues for the City, and the estimated economic impact of five conventions held at the Arena during that time period was $ 25.6 million. Economic benefits arise from convention businesses causing restaurant use, motel, rental car, and miscellaneous purchases.

For the Phoenix Suns, the Arena has brought new revenue streams from box seats, advertising, concessions and ownership interest in new affiliated sports franchises that play in the arena (such as the Arizona Rattlers arena football team). The City benefits by receiving a fixed operating fee which increases by three percent each year and a percentage of net revenue after payment of Phoenix Suns debt service and payment to a replacement fund (projected to reach approximately $ 360 million over the first 30 years of operation). The City also receives $ 21–25 million in sales tax revenue from food and concession sales in the arena (we could not quantify how much of the sales tax revenue would have been received anyway at the old facility, but the majority is new revenue due to new eating and drinking establishments such as cappuccino bars and food franchises such as Pizza Hut).

3.4 City of Phoenix Partners with Waste Management of Arizona (WMA)

Solid waste management today is complicated by rising populations and environmental regulations. Such pressures encourage cooperation to handle the challenge of providing reliable solid waste services while being sensitive to the environment. Increasingly, solid waste management involves public-private agreements through which each party benefits while working to reduce the waste stream and mitigate the effects of waste and its by-products.

Problem statement

Several waste management companies approached the City of Phoenix Solid Waste Division with a proposal to allow the City to use their waste disposal/transfer facilities when it was convenient for the City to do so. Excess capacity was available at the private facilities, and the companies were also interested in using City facilities since City facilities were closer to some of their customers (the City is a very large geographic area of 464 square miles). The Solid Waste Division evaluated the proposals and realized that, while the companies' facilities may sometimes be closer, resulting in transportation savings, the cost charged by the companies, per ton, for dumping at these facilities was higher than the City's cost to dispose of trash at its own facilities.

Proposed solution

The City proposed an agreement that would be fee-neutral to both parties. Waste Management of Arizona (WMA), one of the companies that approached the City, agreed to a reciprocal agreement to utilize each other's existing and proposed disposal/transfer facilities.

Implementation issues

One implementation issue included developing an agreement that would result in cost savings to both parties. The agreement specifies that the City of Phoenix and Waste Management each will use the other's landfill or transfer station when it is most economical for each individual operation. The agreement establishes a minimum exchange of 2,000 tons per month. Charges for any tonnage not part of the ton-for-ton exchange are $ 21.00 per ton at one of WMA's facilities and $ 11.00 at its other facility.

Another implementation issue was operational. Foreign traffic (trucks and trailers not belonging to the operator of the facility) would increase at the facilities. Operations would be slowed if this traffic did not move out of the facility as rapidly as the trucks belonging to the operator. To solve this problem, the agreement specifies a maximum vehicle turnaround time at each facility of no longer than fifteen minutes.

Measures of success

The agreement results in shorter hauling times and quicker turnarounds for trucks. The shorter distances help extend vehicle life, reduce maintenance, and decrease air pollution emissions. Savings from the agreement are estimated between $ 400,000 and $ 500,000 per year for the City's Solid Waste Division. Savings for Waste Management are not available to us, but they indicate that the agreement saves money for them, also (Henning, 1995).

The agreement is for four years with the option of extending an additional three years. Since the agreement with WMA was signed, the City of Glendale, Arizona, a suburb of Phoenix, convinced by the success Phoenix achieved, signed a similar agreement with a term of four to six years.

3.5 Lessons Learned

Following are potential pitfalls and benefits from using public-private Co-operation as an alternative service delivery strategy.

Potential pitfalls

- Different incentives, goals, and constraints for public and private entities;
- difficulty specifying the level of quality required – contract negotiations are lengthy.

Potential benefits

- Revenue increases for both public and private entities;
- service level improvements;
- more interesting and economically healthy communities;
- increased efficiencies.

Partnerships form for a variety of reasons, but generally these alliances perform some function that, without participation by more than one organization, would not produce the same results. Such alliances have become more common as governments have been forced, through a combination of declining (or flat) funding along with increased service demands from citizens, to unite with others to provide solutions to today's problems. Some private sector organizations have been motivated to enter into partnerships with governmental entities by a desire to improve the community while improving their business. Some have been motivated by self-preservation or the need to comply with governmental regulations. Other reasons for forming partnerships abound.

The cases studied are examples of successful partnerships. Each party's area of responsibility was clearly defined. Whenever several entities are involved in a program, the likelihood of miscommunication or omission rises. To combat this phenomenon, frequent communication is essential to avoid mistakes and misunderstandings. Also important is an understanding of the environment in which each party operates. For example, in the City of Phoenix partnership with the Phoenix Suns, the public organization needed more time to receive permission to participate in the project because political approval was required. Results of financial operations were disclosed to the public – a practice the private entity was not accustomed to experiencing. It is best to identify and plan for these conditions before entering into a partnership, to avoid confusion and frustration later.

The most promising partnerships are those that result in tangible benefits to each party while benefiting the community. One possible benefit (though not illustrated here) of partnering with the private sector is that tax increases can be reduced or forestalled by providing services in alternative ways.

For governments hoping to enter the computer age, some lessons Palo Alto shared are particularly appropriate. In Palo Alto's case, Digital installed the security system that prevents unauthorized entry and serves as the expert in maintaining the network. The system is very complicated and the city would rather build in-house expertise for such a critical function. Palo Alto staff suggests that any city undertaking this type of effort ensure that the staff maintaining the system have the training necessary to adequately service the network, or, in lieu of this, select software that is user-friendly and requires less technical expertise to maintain. Palo Alto also recommends, for the sake of convenience and ease of communication, that whatever agency a city may contract with to design the layout of its Home Page be physically located in the same area. Finally, Palo Alto suggests that, as city departments become interested in producing their own page of information to add to the system, their pages be edited centrally to maintain a consistent organizational appearance.

3.6 Conclusions

The development literature on public-private Cooperation offers several guidelines for success, including the following:
- an environment that encourages entrepreneurial, risk-taking, behavior (Kolzow, 1994),
- networks of key groups and individuals in all sectors (Kolzow 1994),
- the minimum number of accountability mechanisms, strategically placed to ensure ethical behavior (O'Looney, 1992, p. 21),
- patient and careful analysis (Sears and Reid, 1992, cited in Larkin, 1994), and
- mutual respect that transcends negative stereotypes both public and private leaders may have about each other (Larkin, 1994).

In some countries, certain social or legal structures (such as German co-determination laws) may insure that some of these conditions are met (O'Looney, 1992). In others, such as the United States, these conditions cannot be taken for granted and must be worked on. Our case studies indicated that sometimes governments and private entities can have the same goals and similar requirements – such as the Downtown Phoenix Partnership – an entity composed of both government and private sector organizations. In other cases, goals may be completely different, but the desired outcome is the same. For example, the goal of the Phoenix Suns organization was to improve their facilities and improve revenues while the goal of the City of Phoenix was to improve the downtown area and its tax bases, but the desired result was the same – a multi-purpose arena. In the examples given, the public entities and the private entities both gained.

4. Privatization/Competition

"Privatization" means very different things in the United States than it does internationally. Our national government owns and operates very few enterprises. The United States, in fact, ranks second from the bottom (just slightly higher than Japan) among industrialized societies in the percentage of gross domestic product for which government spending accounts. Other countries such as Great Britain, Portugal, New Zealand and Mexico, have sold state-owned enterprises like the telephone service or national airlines to the private sector; this is sometimes called "de-nationalization." The United States has less to de-nationalize, so when we speak of "privatization" we often mean contracting-out discrete services to the private sector (DiIulio/Kettl, 1995), or demonopolization allowing *competition* (Weimer/Vining, 1992, p. 148). As stated by DiIulio and Kettl, "The great lesson of the nation's now lengthy experience with privatization is that it is *competition*, not the publicness or privateness of a program, that drives costs down and performance up." (DiIulio/Kettl, 1995, p. 26) This is supported by research in public policy analysis (see, e.g., Weimer/Vining, 1992, Chapter 7), which finds that *contestability*, or the possibility of competitive pressures, brings efficiency and, in particular, lower costs. The key is to inject those competitive forces into services provided by governments.

Contracting is becoming a popular alternative service delivery strategy. The Mercer Group, an Atlanta-based management consulting firm, conducted a survey of 120 local governments in 34 states in 1987. Preliminary results of its 1995 update to the survey show that contracting has greatly increased in popularity (see figure 1, Reason Foundation, 1995).

Nationwide, service levels after contracting for services seem to be good. A 1989 survey by the National Commission for Employment Policy found that 72 percent of local officials rated the quality of their contracted services "very favorable," and 10 percent "slightly favorable," while only 13 percent rated them "slightly unfavorable," and five percent "very unfavorable." The same study found that contracting saved local governments 15 to 30 percent (Osborne and Gaebler, p. 89). The goal of private sector service delivery is to save money and improve quality of service. Generally speaking, citizens believe that government organizations are wasteful, while market competition promotes efficiency. Although anything *can* be contracted, knowledgeable people often draw different conclusions about what *should* be contracted.

In this chapter we present three case studies: (1) City of Phoenix Public-Private Competition Program, (2) City of Indianapolis Competition and Privatization Initiatives, and (3) City of Long Beach Golf Courses privatization. These three case studies are diverse in scope. The City of Phoenix discussion focuses on a competitive process where contracting is only one of two possible outcomes. Here, the true situation is one of competition/contestability. The City of Indianapolis discussion includes both services contracted without competition and services submitted to competition. The Long Beach example includes only one service – golf course operations – which the city determined should be contracted-out.

Figure 1: Percent of respondents contracting public services, by type

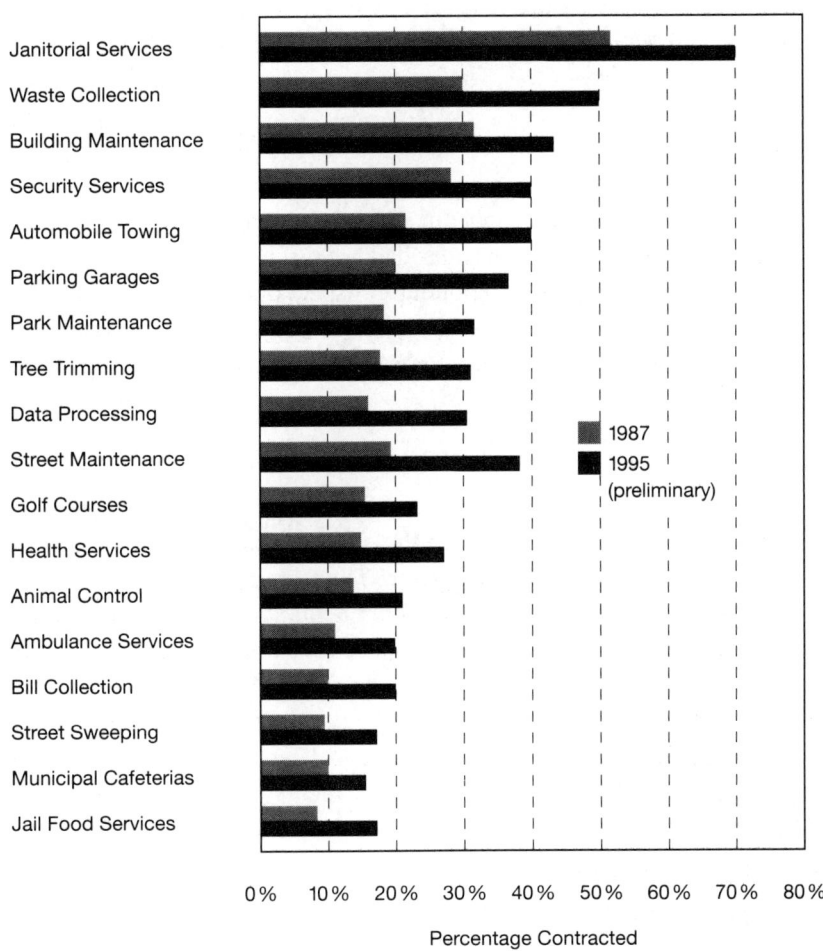

Source: Mercer Group

4.1 City of Phoenix, Arizona Public-Private Competition Program

The City of Phoenix (population 1.2 million) was a pioneer in fostering competition between the public sector and the private sector. Phoenix invented the public/private competitive process in 1979. While the City also contracts for many services, their competition program includes only those services where City forces compete against the private sector to determine who should provide service. The City has used the process to determine service delivery providers for 14 service areas as diverse as refuse collection and public defender services (City Auditor Department, 1995).

Problem statement

The competitive process arose from severe economic conditions that occurred in 1979. General tax revenues had not reached the level forecasted. The City was faced with the unpopular prospect of cutting services to the public. Private firms approached Phoenix's City Council and promised cost savings if they were awarded contracts to provide particular services.

Proposed solution

Phoenix officials chose to compare the City cost of service with private sector costs in a sealed bid competition. The technique was developed as an experiment to see if cost savings could actually occur without a negative impact on service levels. Performance levels were specified in contracts and then City forces were asked to compete on the same specifications as the private bidders. The decision was made to use City avoidable costs in the City bid (i.e. costs that can be isolated and removed from the City budget, not "soft" costs that the City incurs regardless of who provides the service). Once all sealed bids were opened, the City Council selected a service provider.

Implementation issues

The first implementation issue was to develop procedures for the competitive proposal process. The process itself is similar to the traditional purchasing process except that a proposal from a City department is solicited. When a City department is bidding on service delivery, additional steps are necessary to maintain the integrity of the process. The City Auditor's office takes two additional steps to establish the credibility of the in-house proposal: a pre-bid certification of the City proposal and a post-implementation audit of the selected service provider (whether or not the City is chosen).

Implementation involves developing detailed contractor specifications. When the City is selected to provide service, these specifications become a "performance contract" with City management. If the City does not provide the service, contract monitoring becomes an important City responsibility. It is necessary to develop a reliable monitoring system. Without good specifications, it is difficult to monitor contract performance.

Another major implementation issue relates to placement of employees when private providers are chosen. Because the City of Phoenix values its employees, this was of key concern. When the City is experiencing growth, employee reductions in one area are not a major issue because employees can be placed in other positions, but when growth slows, steps are taken to minimize layoffs: the City plans in advance of the bid advertisement to freeze similar positions and hire new employees on a temporary basis so that permanent employees will not be at risk of losing their jobs. Some employees are usually hired by the contractor.

Measures of success

A new way of doing business evolved. Initially, the City found that the private sector could provide the service at a cost lower than the City could match. Since then, however, the situation has changed. According to Frank Fairbanks, the City Manager of Phoenix, "Through the years we learned to streamline operations, to reduce costs, to modernize equipment and empower employees to harness their best thinking. Now we compete head-to-head with the private sector and about 50 percent of the time we are successful in procuring the contract. No matter who wins [the specific competition], our taxpayers always win because our performance standards emphasize service quality as well as cost. Quality is guaranteed in these contracts by the measurement of specific performance standards throughout the life of the contract." (Bertelsmann Foundation, Vol. 2, 1994, p. 114)

Table 2: Summary of actual cost savings/avoidance Life-to-date June 30, 1995

	$
Aviation	
Airport landscaping	1,000
Nursery/plant maintenance	14,400
Fire	
Emergency transportation	2 898,000
Billing and collection services	467,000
Housing	
Low-income housing maintenance	23,000
Senior housing management	72,000
Neighborhood Services	
Lot Maintenance	6,700
Parks, Recreation and Library	
Median maintenance	470,000
Public Works	
Refuse collection	17 113,000
Landfill operation	7 711,000
Street Transportation	
Street sweeping	36,000
Street repair	109,000
Landscape maintenance	409,000
Water Services	
Water meter repair	176,000
Wastewater instrument calibration	105,000
Total	**$ 29 611,000**

The City of Phoenix measures cost savings as well as customer satisfaction to determine whether or not the effort to change service delivery methods has been successful. Overall, the City has realized documented savings of $29 million over the past 15 years from competitive bidding of services (City Auditor Department, 1995). Table 2 summarizes the cumulative savings by department and service area.

Refuse collection is an example of a service area where costs have actually decreased – even in nominal terms – over the 15 year period, while holding quality constant. Figure 2 illustrates the cost per house per month from the first competition in 1979 to the most recent competition in 1992. One line shows figures unadjusted for inflation. The more dramatic line adjusts for inflation. Customer satisfaction actually increased slightly during this time period. For example, customer service surveys indicate that in 1985, the ratings for refuse collection were 7.5 on a scale of 1 to 10 with 10 the most satisfied. In 1993, ratings were 7.9 for the same service (Behavior Research Center, 1993).

Figure 2: Refuse collection

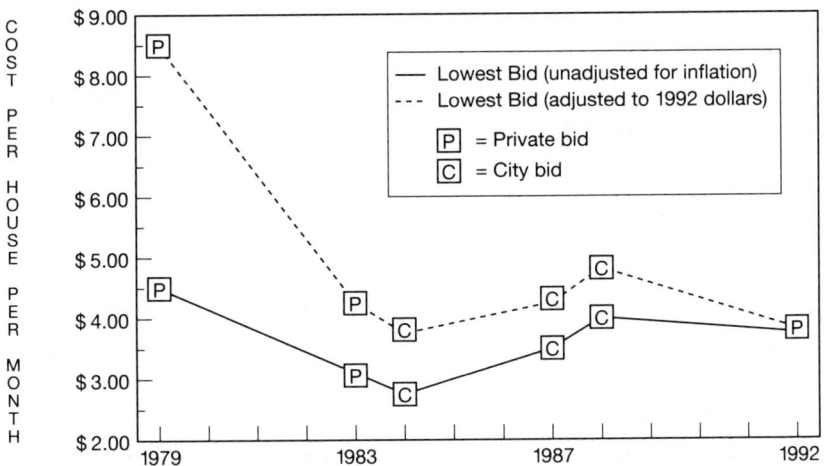

4.2 City of Indianapolis, Indiana Competition and Privatization Initiatives

The City of Indianapolis (population 767,000) is a leader in the effort to introduce competition into the provision of local government services. Since taking office in 1992, Mayor Stephen Goldsmith has used competition in several service areas.

Problem statement

Mayor Goldsmith was elected to office in 1991 based on his promise "to increase efficiency and reduce the cost of local government" (City of Indianapolis, 1996). This was popular because it was an economic necessity for Indianapolis. The City faced tough competition from seven relatively low-tax counties that surround Indianapolis. Every time Indianapolis tax rates went up, it increased the incentive for families and jobs to head for the suburbs. Initially an advocate of "privatization," a policy of transferring City services to private contractors, Mayor Goldsmith quickly came to realize that "privatizing in itself is not valuable; monopolies, public or private, are inefficient, so the key is to create a marketplace for municipal services" by fostering competition between City departments and private contractors (Broder, 1993).

Proposed solution

Mayor Goldsmith determined that the solution would be to put free market forces to work in his city government. To guide the effort, he established the Service, Efficiency, and Lower Taxes for Indianapolis Commission (SELTIC) in 1992. SELTIC's goal is to improve government services and make them more efficient, decrease costs, and eliminate waste by opening up government services to competition. The SELTIC commissioners are nine of the most entrepreneurial members of the Indianapolis business community. They form study teams of four-to-seven members to examine specific areas.

SELTIC meets only when necessary and does not issue reports. Instead, the group makes specific recommendations to the Mayor, who then arranges to have the proposals presented and debated in a public forum. The proposals concern specific areas that the commissioners believe would benefit from either a competitive proposal or some other approach to decrease costs.

Implementation issues

Indianapolis identified the following key implementation issues:
- Markets must be analyzed to determine if there is adequate potential competition. Indianapolis refers to this effort as "analysis of congenial market place." If adequate competition does not exist, the service will not be submitted for competition.
- First-line supervisors within the area submitted to competition are often more antagonistic than the labor union. Their jobs are often the ones eliminated by restructuring for competition.
- Political support is needed from the Mayor for each specific area. Support is sought from other council members.
- Assuring financial accountability may be a problem. If the area submitted for competition is not currently using Activity-Based Costing (ABC), implementation of ABC is put on a fast track.

Measures of success

The commission has opened scores of government services to competition. The 1995 budget indicates that tax rates are frozen for the sixth straight year and forecasts a surplus, even though in 1992 the Mayor inherited a budget that was $20 million short.

The cumulative cost savings are impressive: $6.5 million in 1992, $12 million in 1993, and $27.6 million in 1994. These savings enabled the City to increase the amount of money spent on public safety to one-third of the City budget in 1995 (an all-time high). Increasing the emphasis on public safety was a priority for the citizens of Indianapolis.

Since Indianapolis is a strong believer in small government, one of their measures of success is reducing the number of government employees. They have been very successful in that (5140 employees in 1991 to 3870 employees in 1995). The City of Indianapolis determined that the majority of this reduction is due to their competition and privatization initiative. Employees were absorbed readily in the private sector, since unemployment in the community is very low (3.2 percent) (Olsen, 1996).

4.3 City of Long Beach, California Golf Courses

The City of Long Beach (population 482,000) owns five golf courses. Until 1984, all the courses were operated and maintained by City employees.

Problem statement

The City's general fund provided about $2.5 million in annual support over and above user charges to golfers. Nonetheless, the courses were poorly maintained and deteriorating. Fees to the public were low compared with the fees charged by other golf courses. The City Council rarely supported fee increases, which were viewed by citizens as tax increases.

Proposed solution

The City decided to contract operation of the courses to American Golf Corporation (the largest golf course management company in the world).

Implementation issues

The most sensitive issue dealt with the elimination of City positions. To avoid layoffs, city employees were moved into other positions in the City, and positions were reduced through attrition.

Another implementation issue was developing contract specifications – a very tedious process. City officials found that they had to enlist the help of front-line employees to develop specifications for the contractor since they had no idea what performance specifications should be. For example, should the grass be cut to 1 inch or 1/2 inch? City staff feel that the maintenance contract is still not as strong as they would like it to be (Hester, 1996).

Measures of success

The results are impressive. Long Beach measures success using both cost and service-level indicators. Long Beach no longer provides general fund support to the courses; instead, it receives $ 2.5 million annually in lease revenues. City expenses related to the golf operation, such as contract monitoring, are relatively minor.

The golfing public is very happy with the condition of the courses. The contract monitor has comment cards at the golf courses that ask patrons to rate the service and course condition. Last year, approximately 500,000 rounds were played at the five courses; customer complaints totaled 279 during the same period. User fees are set using a market study; this keeps them comparable with the marketplace (Hester, 1996).

4.4 Lessons Learned

Following are potential pitfalls and benefits from using competition/privatization as an alternative service delivery strategy.

Potential pitfalls

– Decreased number of employees – requires careful advance planning;
– specification of contract requirements – may be difficult to specify the level of performance required.

Potential benefits

- Cost savings,
- revenue increases and
- continuing or increasing levels of customer satisfaction.

The circumstances surrounding the adoption of this alternative service delivery strategy differ. In Indianapolis, a strong political leader took office promising dramatic efficiency improvements. In Phoenix, financial challenges encouraged the government to find an alternative way to deliver service, and in Long Beach, the City was tired of subsidizing a special interest (golfers) at the expense of other taxpayers. Two things are similar: (1) all cities faced undesirable fiscal conditions, and (2) the cities were willing to risk the unknown (competition or private service providers) rather than continue with the inefficiencies of their bureaucratic service delivery methods.

4.5 Conclusions

Long Beach indicated that the private sector was able to make service improvements that the public sector could not make. Their experience accords well with a standard result in the economics literature that, along with the benefits of contestability (mentioned above), helps explain why privatization/competition can be such a beneficial alternative strategy. Economic analysis indicates that, when a good is provided as a common or public good, it will be over-consumed, there will be under-investment, and eventually the Tragedy of the Common will result (in the Tragedy of the Common, each individual behaving rationally will destroy the common good to the detriment of all). As suggested by the Coase theorem, the allocation of property rights results in the socially-optimal level of consumption and investment (see Weimer and Vining 1992, pp. 61 and 149). Contracting-out a common good, as Long Beach did with its golf courses, gives the private entity incentives both to minimize costs (to increase its own profits) and to husband the good.

The Long Beach experience also highlights the effects of political realities. The political process resulted in money spent on higher citizen priorities such as public protection and youth recreation programs at the expense of special interests such as golf. While this does not make economic sense from the standpoint that $ 1 invested in an enterprise such as golf may return $ 1.50 to the City for other uses, whereas $ 1 spent on public protection or youth recreation programs will not generate an economic return, it is a political reality. An elected group of officials will not be able to spend money on an enterprise, no matter what the return, if the citizenry is calling for more money to be spent in high-priority areas. By contracting-out, the good was moved from the political arena to the market arena.

Phoenix and Indianapolis attribute their success with their programs to the injection of competition into what was otherwise a monopoly. Other cities (Charlotte, Cleveland, Milwaukee, Chicago, Philadelphia, and New York) seem to agree since major competition efforts are underway in those cities (Reason Foundation, 1995).

5. Decentralization and Enterprise Strategies

Due to space limitations, this paper concentrates on three alternative service delivery strategies: intergovernmental Cooperation, public-private Cooperation, and privatization/competition. These three present a continuum: from strategies that are closer to tradition because they are located entirely in the public sector, through hybrid strategies, to strategies that are located in the market sector. Viewed in this way, these three can be said to span the universe of possible strategies. In addition, these three were chosen because there is both research and experience demonstrating potential pitfalls and the proven ability to increase efficiency. However, there are many other alternative service delivery strategies that the creative government can try (see Osborne and Gaebler, 1992, Appendix A for many examples). In this section, we briefly discuss two additional strategies that we find particularly interesting: decentralization, and enterprise activities. Decentralization can be performed entirely within the public sector, while enterprise activities take place within the market sector.

5.1 Decentralization

Decentralization strategies move away from rigid, control-oriented models of governance into more flexible models. The flexibility can be in bringing services to the community, or in enhancing employees' control over their tasks. Such strategies have the potential to increase governmental responsiveness, citizen trust, employee commitment, and cost-effectiveness.

In decentralization, responsibility for performance is moved as far downward in the organization as possible, changing the organizational concept of front-line employees from street-level *bureaucrats* to street-level *leaders* (Vinzant and Crothers, in press). Simply moving service provision from a single, central location to several different locations can increase citizen access. Further, in full-fledged decentralization, functional departments are given product-oriented budgets (as well as latitude in using them) and move toward becoming increasingly independent entities within the overall strategic structure of the local authority. This allows the local authority to adjust to economic and social conditions that differ between areas (Bertelsmann Foundation, 1994). Further, enhancing involvement so that employees have more control over their jobs – including the option of taking risks – increases commitment and leads to better efforts (Lee and Cayer 1994, pp. 93–94)

Here we present two case studies from the City of Phoenix, one which demonstrates locational decentralization, and the other which describes decentralization of decision making authority through enhanced employee involvement.

Locational decentralization – City of Phoenix Juvenile Curfew Program

The Phoenix Juvenile Curfew Program outstations services for curfew violators through an innovative juvenile crime prevention program conducted jointly by the Parks, Recreation and Library Department and the Police Department.

Problem statement

Curfew violations were rarely enforced, as processing required a trip to a downtown location, taking officers away from more serious crimes. Gang violence was escalating and minors were on the streets at late hours. The Mayor of Phoenix strongly supported a stricter curfew program as a means to prevent innocent youth from becoming injured or dying. Even when police officers took the time to drive to a central location and file charges, there was not a suitable facility to detain the minors while they waited for an adult.

Proposed solution

A stronger Curfew Ordinance was enacted, and a decentralized curfew enforcement program was implemented at four sites throughout the city. The Parks, Recreation, and Library Department offered the use of some of their recreation centers to process juvenile curfew violators and offer intervention assistance.

Implementation issues

Obtaining funding for the program was an issue. The departments combined their budget resources to pay for staff and operating facilities and located State funding for crisis intervention and family counseling. The departments determined that it was not cost effective to maintain all four sites, and experience showed that one site could be eliminated. The departments now operate three sites.

Measures of success

At the end of March, 1996, a total of 13,077 youths were cited for curfew violation. In 1994, Police data indicated that 79 percent of the juveniles did not re-offend and 18 percent received counseling services.

The Police Department indicates reduced criminal nighttime activities by juveniles. Since the program began, violent crimes (homicide, sexual assault, robbery, aggravated assault) have been reduced by ten percent. The Police Department also reports a slight decrease in the proportion of juveniles as victims of violent crimes.

Decision making decentralization – City of Phoenix employee involvement strategy

Problem statement

The City of Phoenix leadership wanted to emphasize quality and customer satisfaction in the organization. Both community planning and corporate strategic planning processes identified quality and customer focus as vital to the organization's success. The City had strong management systems, but many employees felt that past initiatives to increase customer satisfaction or improve productivity mainly focused on cutting resources. Phoenix needed a strategy that clearly conveyed the organization's interest in quality and customer satisfaction, a way for people to understand what was changing and why the changes were being made, and an environment that would lead employees to support the change.

Problem solution

Phoenix researched the problem and found that the literature on quality suggested that enhanced employee involvement would build the sense of ownership and the commitment that were needed to achieve organization-wide quality and to sustain results over the long run. Therefore, the city chose to decentralize/delegate approaches to developing quality and customer satisfaction.

Implementation issues

A decentralized approach to direction-setting was new for the City, and the use of time was always a concern. The enhanced involvement process felt slow at times, and there were instances where the decentralized, bottom-up approach of involving employees in direction-setting had lost momentum. Maintaining the organization-wide goal, keeping the employees convinced that this new direction was not just a fad, and preventing the focus on quality from becoming an isolated program were constant concerns.

Many different forms of involvement were employed. Several surveys were taken of City employees to see if they agreed that a focus on quality and customer satisfaction was the appropriate organizational direction. Fortunately, employee response was strongly in favor of these goals. Next, we requested employee assistance in defining quality and developing an overall model for the City. Employee task forces were created to develop specific plans for awards, training and program design.

Measures of success

During the 1990s, the general public's approval of government has declined (Lee and Cayer, 1994). Also, the early 1990s were difficult economic times for City employees; there were periods without pay increases and a reduction of 500 positions (out of 11 500). It is all the more noteworthy, then, that during this time both City employees' and residents' satisfaction, as measured by surveys, improved. In response to the question, "How satisfied are you with the overall performance of the City in providing services to Phoenix residents?," 81 percent of our citizenry answered either "satisfied" or "very satisfied" (City of Phoenix, 1996).

In response to the question, "Overall, is the City of Phoenix a good place to work?," City employees responded positively 97 percent of the time (City of Phoenix, 1993).

5.2 Enterprise Activities

Most of the alternative service delivery strategies we have discussed focus on the goals of cost-saving and service improvements, though some also result in enhancing available resources. To manage effectively in a resource-scarce environment, state and local governments should explicitly consider both sides of the financial picture: revenues as well as expenditures. In many cases, governments have resources that are valuable in the marketplace. Enterprise (profit-making) activities such as the sale of products, services, or expertise are an alternative revenue source for governments (Mercer, 1992). Enterprise activities can include user fees, selling expertise, and selling products. For example, San Diego, California sells training and management consulting, and earned revenues of $ 150,000 in the fiscal year ending June 1994 (Quality Report, 1995). The New South Wales, Australia Road and Traffic Authority developed a complete road-management system – comprised of software and hardware for both active control and maintenance – and succeeded in licensing it to several cities world-wide, including Hong Kong (Gross 1994).

Here we present some examples from California. In a creative, and even humorous way, two entities succeeded in generating revenues by selling surplus products and name-recognition. These examples show that governments may have valuable collateral resources they rarely consider.

San Diego and Los Angeles, California government stores

Problem statement

The state of California was particularly hard-hit by a recession, leading to budget reductions for many programs. In addition, local governments often have surplus property to dispose of.

Proposed solution

Both San Diego City (population 1.2 million) and Los Angeles County (population 9.7 million) decided to raise extra revenue by selling products that capitalized on name-recognition and peoples' positive attitudes toward local governments.

The Los Angeles County Department of Coroner has a store and a mail-order catalog called "Skeletons in the Closet." They sell such things as toe-tag key chains, beach towels with a police chalk-outline of a body, and boxer shorts (men's underpants) emblazoned with the word "undertaker." Since October of 1993, gross sales have been $ 20,000 per month.

The City of San Diego sells surplus street signs (at $ 20–$ 75 each), banners from city events, antique street lanterns, manhole covers, used parking meters (at $ 40 each), fire hydrants ($ 325 apiece), and firefighter gear (State and Local Government, 1995).

Implementation issues

Government entities selling products or services in the marketplace can encounter several barriers: (1) government ventures competing with private business can lead to charges of unfair competition, (2) local authorities may lack legal authority to advertise, market, or sell, (3) generally some investment capital must be used, (4) city employees are not trained to perform such activities (Lemov, 1994).

The last issue can be solved by contracting with a professional merchandiser. Under San Diego's contract, the contractor receives 18 percent of the first $ 100,000 of sales and ten percent thereafter (Lemov, 1994).

Measures of success

The Los Angeles Coroner has been able to use profits from its store to support a program to sensitize teenage drivers to the consequences of drunk driving.

The San Diego City Store was started with $ 100,000 in seed money to be paid back in three years. However, the store returned the entire sum in the first six months of operation (Lemov, 1994).

Many other cities, including Chicago, Illinois and Tempe, Arizona are opening government stores.

5.3 Lessons Learned

The two types of strategies discussed in this section are quite different. Nevertheless, all cases illustrate that creativity, whether in moving services to where the demand is, making better use of employee resources by enhancing their participation, or in selling publicly-owned products, can enhance government's ability to meet social needs.

6. Summary and Conclusions

The driving force behind alternative service delivery in government is citizen demand for better, more responsive, and more efficient service. Since resources available to governments are limited, providing services at a lower cost or pooling resources can mean governments can provide more or better services. Common are stories of increasing service demands and decreasing dollars. Local governments are actively dealing with the question, "How can we deliver service cheaper, faster, and better?". As our City Manager related at the Bertelsmann Symposium in 1993, "I once heard a Formula One driver tell a reporter on television: 'It's not good enough to simply meet last year's best times. If we are not going faster than last year, we are falling behind. Everyone else is going faster.'" We need to instill this same competitive spirit into all of our government operations. We need to surround ourselves with managers and employees who will take risks, who will set high performance standards, who will fight bureaucracy, who will put customers first and find their greatest enjoyment in stretching a tax dollar to its limits. Like driving Formula One, there are real risks but there is also the excitement of the challenge and success.

Our first guiding question for this paper was: *Under what circumstances are alternative service delivery strategies successful?*

Governments were eager to share their experiences, including lessons they had learned along the way about what was right and what was wrong with each approach. After reviewing the case studies in this paper, our conclusion is that alternative service delivery strategies are most likely to be successful, first, in an environment where risk-taking is encouraged.

A second ingredient that was present in most of the case studies we examined was the willingness of the bureaucracy to relinquish some control.

Third – and partly compensating for the second – a clear articulation of goals and responsibilities of each party is necessary at the outset to ensure that service is delivered in a timely and effective manner. Particularly when transferring to a new service delivery method, outcomes should be specified or all parties may be disappointed. Therefore, measurement systems, agreed upon by all parties at the outset, are an important component of any alternative service delivery strategy. These measurement systems provide objective feedback on whether the service is meeting its intended purpose.

Fourth, common to all alternative service delivery methods is the need to involve individuals outside the organization. This requires Cooperation among groups that may have vastly different perspectives and methods of achieving the desired output. Finding a method of communicating and meeting the goals of these various groups is important. All four of these points were supported by both literature and case studies we reviewed.

Our second guiding question was: *What special benefits do alternative service delivery strategies have to offer?*

The answer to this question is: better service, service delivery at a lower cost, and/or enhanced revenues. Examples of cost savings are prevalent throughout the case studies. While the public entities do not have a profit goal, they enjoy cost savings that they can pass on to their citizens through reduced taxes or increased service levels in other programs.

Service level improvement can be found using the Portland-Multnomah example – they believe that their combined efforts will result in a better, more useful product. Long Beach, Phoenix, and Indianapolis experienced dramatic service-level improvements by using contracting (Long Beach) or competition (Phoenix, Indianapolis). Using private-sector expertise, Palo Alto was able to develop a high-quality service for its citizens that they could not have provided otherwise. By decentralizing, Phoenix was able to create a service that did not *in fact* exist before. Long Beach and the California cities involved in enterprise activities were able to generate revenues.

It seems fitting to end this paper with a lesson common to all of the cases we studied – there must be a willingness on the part of the organization to reach out and experiment with new service delivery methods. Often, this involves risk-taking on the part of the governmental unit and relinquishing control of a particular program in order to better serve its citizens. But, as President Franklin Delano Roosevelt said, "The country needs... the country demands bold, persistent experimentation. It is common sense to take a method and try it; if it fails, admit it frankly and try another. But above all, try something..."

Literature

Barnett, Camila Cates (1994), "Challenge, We Need New Ways to Govern New Kinds of Cities," Governing, December.
Behavior Research Center (1993), City of Phoenix Community Attitude Survey, August.
Bertelsmann Foundation (1994), Carl Bertelsmann Prize 1993: Democracy and Efficiency in Local Government, Volumes 1 and 2.
Broder, David S. (1993), "A Mayor Shows Gore's Team the Way," The Washington Post, August 25.
City Auditor Department (1995), City of Phoenix Public/Private Competitive Process Overview.
City of Indianapolis (1996), The Indianapolis Experience: A Small Government Prescription for Big City Problems.
City of Phoenix (1996), Organization Improvement.
City of Phoenix (1993), An Overview of Organizational Change.

Cranford, John (1995), "A Guide to Award-Winning Technology," Governing, January.

Di Iulio Jr., John J. and Kettl, Donald F. (1995), Fine Print: The Contract with America, Devolution, and the Administrative Realities of American Federalism, The Brookings Institution, Washington D.C.

Flanagan, Jim and Perkins, Susan (1995), "Public/Private Competition in the City of Phoenix, Arizona," Government Finance Review, June.

Fundis, Ronald J., Gould, Jr., Lawrence, Hoy, Donald A., and Morin, Arthur L. (1993), "The Interlocal Agreement: A Tool for Efficient Resource Pooling and Regionalization," Kansas Governmental Journal, February.

Goldstein, H. A. and Luger, M. I. (1992), "University-Based Research Parks as a Rural Development Strategy." Policy Studies Journal, 10.

Gross, N. R. (1994), "Lccensing the Public Sector's Intellectual Property: The SCATS Experience," Australian Journal of Public Administration 5 (2/June).

Harris, Kathleen (1996), Research Analyst, Portland-Multnomah Progress Board. Telephone interview, April 25.

Henning, Bruce (1995), Solid Waste Disposal Engineering Administrator, City of Phoenix, Arizona. Telephone interview, September 25.

Hester, Phil (1996), Manager of Parks Bureau, Long Beach, California. Telephone interview, April 15.

Kamensky, John M. (1996), "Role of the 'Reinventing Government' Movement in Federal Management Reform," Public Administration Review, Vol. 56, No. 3, May/June.

Kearney, Brian T. (1995), Business Development Administrator, City of Phoenix, Arizona. Telephone interview, May 2.

Kolzow, D. R. (1994), "Public/Private Partnership: The Economic Development Organization of the 90s." Economic Development Review, Winter.

Krulikowski, Ed (1996), City Traffic Engineer, City of El Cajon, California. Telephone interview, May 1.

Larkin, R. G. (1994), "Public-Private Partnerships in Economic Development: A Review of Theory and Practice." Economic Development Review. Winter, pp. 7–9.

Lee, D. S. and Cayer, N. J. (1994), Supervision for Success in Government: A Practical Guide for First Line Managers. Jossey-Bass, San Francisco.

Lemov, P. (1994), "Balancing the Budget With Billboards and Souvenirs," Governing, October.

Martin, Bret (1996), American Golf Corporation, Santa Monica, California. Telephone interview, April 17.

Mercer, J. L. (1992), Public Management in Lean Years: Operating in a Cutback Management Environment. Quorum Books, Westport, Connecticut.

Miranda, Rowan and Andersen, Karlyn (1994), "Alternative Service Delivery in Local Government, 1982 – 1992." The Municipal Year Book 1994 International City/County Management Association, Washington, D.C.

Mullen, Margaret (1996), Executive Director, Downtown Phoenix Partnership, Phoenix, Arizona. Telephone interview, May 6.

O'Looney, J. (1994), "Public-Private Partnerships in Economic Development: Negotiating the Trade-off Between Flexibility and Accountability." Economic Development Review, Fall, pp. 14–22.

Olsen, Tom (1996), Director of Enterprise Development, City of Indianapolis, Indiana. Telephone interview, May 1.

Osborne, David and Gaebler, Ted (1992), Reinventing Government: How the Entrepreneurial Spirit is Transforming the Public Sector. Plume, New York.

Perry, Tim (1996), Equipment Management Supervisor, Chesterfield County, Virginia. Telephone interview April 29.

Platt, Suzy and The Library of Congress (1989), Respectfully Quoted: A Dictionary of Quotations Requested from the Congressional Research Service, Library of Congress, Washington, D.C.

Plunkett, Stephen R. (1996), American Golf Corporation Fact Sheet, Santa Monica, California, May 13.

Pound, R. (1995), Information Technology Manager, Palo Alto, California. Telephone interview, August 30.

Quality Report (1995), "San Diego's Entrepreneurial Centre Learns Business Ups and Downs." Public Sector Quality Report. 3 March.

Reagor, Catherine (1996), "Downtown doubles its sales since 1989." The Arizona Republic, May 3.

Reason Foundation (1995), Privatization '95, Los Angeles, California.
Register, Judy (1996), Library Director, City of Scottsdale, Arizona. Telephone interview, April 17.
Sears, D. W. and Reid, J. N. (1992), "Rural Strategies and Rural Development Research: An Assignment." Policy Studies Journal, 20.
State and Local Government (1995), Management and Administration, MGT-14
Stern, William M. (1994), "We Got Real Efficient Real Quick," Forbes, June 20.
Vinzant, J. and Crothers, L. (in press), "Street-level Leadership: Rethinking the Role of Public Servants in Contemporary Governance." American Review of Public Administration.
Weimer, David L. and Vining, Aidan R. (1992), Policy Analysis Concepts and Practice, Prentice Hall, Englewood Cliffs, New Jersey.

Hæmeenlinna: Enhancing Citizen and Community Participation
Krister Ståhlberg

Executive Summary 76
1. Introduction 78
2. Local Governmental Development Policy
   and Public Participation. 80
3. Some General Observations on Citizen
   and Community Participation 84
4. Citizen Participation and Community Involvement:
   Some Examples 88
5. Conclusions and Future Challenges 95
Literature. 99
Appendix 100

Executive Summary

This paper discusses examples of citizen and community participation in the cities of the Bertelsmann network.

Local government is above all being judged against two criteria: legitimacy and efficiency. Recently, possibilities for participation have been considered to be of increasing importance. For this, there are quite a number of reasons, observed from the citizens' point of view as well as from that of the local government. In particular, participation is discovered to be a "public resource," apt to improve public services and decisions, the use of which is becoming a must seeing that a growing number of tasks and problems have to be faced with diminishing resources.

In this situation, the network cities have elaborated distinctive procedures and techniques – reflecting the diversity of tasks and challenges. Local politics and participation are in fact "local." At the same time, all cities have in common that they explicitly guarantee citizen participation. Insofar as this political decision is theory-based, three approaches may be distinguished in the debate on local government reform: liberalism, managerialism, and communitarianism. These approaches offer differing answers to the questions concerning the citizen's role, the function of and the possibilities of his participation, the kind of empowerment, the desired structures and finally the intellectual basis. Practically speaking, these three approaches will not be found in a "pure" form although there are preferences specific for each country.

The cities within the international network, Braintree (UK), Christchurch (New Zealand), Delft (Netherlands), Duisburg (Germany), Farum (Denmark), Hæmeenlinna (Finland), Neuchâtel (Switzerland), Phoenix (USA), Québec (Canada) and Tilburg (Netherlands), have submitted 102 case descriptions on participatory mechanisms used or projects implemented. On the one hand, their evaluation confirmed our findings on the above-mentioned motives for and trends toward greater citizen involvement in communal activities. Beyond that, further insight into present practices and problems of local government reform could be gained:
- All cities stressed the importance of continuous "customer" surveys on the basis of an explicit customer orientation.

- There is a dividing line between representative democracy and "small-scale" democracy within communities with its neighborhood and customer orientation, concerning the range of citizen empowerment and their involvement.
- Projects relating to a certain district or to the users of a specific service are to be most frequently found. The micro-level, i.e. narrowly defined groups, and the macro-level, i.e. an entire community, are much more rarely represented.
- Everywhere there were difficulties in mobilizing and motivating citizens. In the first place, it was important to identify a suitable segment of the community.
- At present, most projects on citizen participation are initiated by the authorities. It will take quite some time before an important number of like initiatives are to be found on the citizens' side.
- Freedom of choice and consumers' rights, viz. elements of the liberal approach, have been underrepresented as elements of citizen participation concepts up to now.
- There is a wide gap between potential and factual citizen participation.
- Efforts for systematically retrieving information from current projects on citizen participation are likewise underdeveloped. This is not to say that the available data are not highly interesting.

Finally, concrete projects from the above-mentioned cities are presented, some conclusions are drawn and future challenges identified, amongst others:

- A certain trend toward bottom-up initiatives can be discerned. At least, citizens are increasingly being consulted and involved in the early stages of political projects at local level.
- Cooperation presupposes participation even in the planning stage. This also serves to better understand the validity of different points of view within the citizenry.
- In the future, cross-sectoral cooperation of different authorities will become even more important. Often, burning problems of the communities cannot be coped with unless there is such cooperation.
- The criteria for measuring the success of certain projects need to be further developed, especially because growing citizen participation may in the beginning lead to growing discontent.

- In a paradoxical fashion, citizen participation may tend to favor those groups advantaged from the beginning whereas problem groups and marginalized groups will find it difficult to gain access in the first place. A future challenge will consist in integrating such groups.
- Finally, it must be noted that citizen distrust toward politics and authorities has increased, with interest in political issues remaining very great. Thus, continuously involving citizens in the decision making on public affairs will continue to be a challenge.

1. Introduction

Generally speaking government is judged against two sets of criteria: efficiency and legitimacy. These are in some periods perceived to be, at least to some extent, in conflict with each other and the values are accorded varying weights. In the 1960s and 1970s values of legitimacy and community participation were important. In the 1980s efficiency was more important. The 1990s seem to be a period in which the importance of participatory values is growing, but it also seems to be a period in which the concern is explicitly over the balance between both legitimacy and efficiency.

The purpose of this presentation is to review examples of citizen and community participation in cities participating in the International Network for Better Local Government, sponsored by the Bertelsmann Foundation. Data on which this paper is based, has been collected into a case bank which will be made generally available in order to facilitate the diffusion of good participatory practices (see appendix).

Attitudes today toward participation do not seem to be as ideologically infused as they were some decades ago. Citizen participation and community involvement are approached in a more practical manner. Participation is seen not only as a value in itself, but also, and perhaps even predominantly, as a way of improving public services and public decision making. Consultative participation is seen as an important mechanism for guaranteeing quality management, whilst acceptance of and the perceived quality of decisions can be enhanced through joint problem solving by community groups within traditional local decision making. Real devolutive participation can be seen as fostering public responsibility within close communities. Thus, a first message is that *participatory mechanisms are not judged solely as values in themselves, they are seen as instrumental to public services and public decision making as well.*

Another clear impression that is conveyed by the roughly 100 participatory cases that have been submitted by the cities within the network, is that *local participation is genuinely local.* Both the purposes of participatory mechanisms and the substantive issues that are dealt with vary from one city to another, although, of course, similarities can be found as well. Participatory arrangements nevertheless seem to be deeply embedded in local and national culture as well as in local structural preconditions. There is not one or a few participatory prescriptions to be made, but rather a repertoire of participatory mechanisms to choose from according to local situational considerations.

A third point to stress is that there seems to exist *an increased awareness of the necessity to use citizen participation and community involvement as a means to solve local problems.* Inner city redevelopment projects, urban rootlessness with concomitant social problems, vandalism and unemployment, and simple fiscal stress, all represent challenges which are increasingly met by means of deeper public involvement in decision making and in implementation of local policy. Disregard of public involvement has a price-tag attached to it.

Finally, a fourth general message of this paper is that, despite all the participatory variation that can be found, *all cities seem to pursue an explicit policy of ensuring community involvement in public services and in public decision making.* This involvement extends beyond the mere formal requirements of representative democracy. Thus the public is perceived of as a resource to be used in the pursuit of better services and a more responsible local community.

2. Local Governmental Development Policy and Public Participation

In the present debate on local governmental development we may distinguish between three stands or approaches that seem to take a different view of the functions and forms of public participation: liberalism, managerialism and communitarianism.

The three approaches could, in a rough fashion, be characterized by some catchwords:

Table 1: A summary of approaches to local governmental development

	Liberalism	Managerialism	Communitarianism
Orientation	individualistic	benevolent paternalism	collectivistic
Role of citizens	consumers	customers	citizens
Function of citizen participation	incentives for service producers, adjusting supply to demand	signals of customer satisfaction, impetus for quality improvement	formulating the community will
Means of participation	choice, product information, consumer rights	customer surveys, complaint systems, citizen's charters, community forums, formal consultation	community deliberations, user democracy, devolution
Nature of empowerment	exit, competition	reputation, public respect, comparisons	voice, persuasion

	Liberalism	Managerialism	Communitarianism
Structure	free market, horizontal	decentralization, result units, vertical	municipal and fuctional self-government, vertical/horizontal
Intellectual locus	economics, public choice	management, organization theory	political science, theories of democracy

The liberalistic market oriented approach to local governmental development stresses market-like conditions for service production. Competitive tendering or full in-house competition are used as means for efficient production. Citizens or different representative bodies or agents are given the freedom of choice between producers. A purchaser-provider split is a much used organizational solution and although it is exclusively typical of a market oriented approach, it is also contained within a managerialist approach as well. The citizen as a consumer chooses between service providers. Provider compensation (through vouchers, consumption rights or direct payments) follows choices made. The dependency of providers on consumer choices presumably enhances efficiency and also stimulates quality improvement. In quasi-markets, mechanisms to especially stimulate quality competition can be introduced by way of a combination of purchaser-provider thinking and consumption rights. Outplacing of public services is encouraged and the political role of provider is oriented toward contracting, market regulation and evaluation of services provided. As within the managerialist model, Citizen's Charters can be used to guarantee a minimum standard of services for the public.

The managerialist approach centers around rather independent public production units. These form a decentralized structure in order to make for close contacts to customers. Result units and management by results are typical. Political and managerial control is wielded through result negotiations and result agreements. Net-budgeting guarantees economic independence of production units within the expectations agreed upon. A purchaser-provider split is a common organizational device in order to guarantee negotiation competence and purchaser independence. In order to stimulate cost-awareness internal markets are established. The purchaser-provider split also guarantees that producers are independent and that professional discretion prevails. The public service personnel is empowered and trusted to do its best.

Citizens are looked upon as customers. Market research and customer surveys are frequently used. Within decision making customer boards or forums are used for consultation. Quality evaluations and certification procedures are popular. The general orientation can be called benevolent paternalism since the participatory mechanisms are not intended to result in any real shift of power between authorities and citizens. In the last instance authorities interpret the signals they receive from the public. Hence empowerment is through reputational mechanisms. The pursuit of public respect stimulates deficiently performing authorities to improve their performance. Open evaluations result in comparisons between varying production units or municipalities and these comparisons further stimulate the pursuit for respect. The public and its servants form a partnership around public services.

The communitarianist approach is more difficult to characterize than the other ones. The reason for this is that communitarianist writing seems to be much preoccupied with anti-stands rather than positive solutions. The arguments of the communitarianists are particularly critical of the liberal market approach, but criticism is directed towards hierarchies and bureaucracy as well. In this respect the communitarianist position represents a revival of the radical participatory views of the 1960s and early 1970s.

Differences of emphasis in relation to earlier positions can be found as well. There is now a deep belief in genuine communication and in the possibility to reach consensus and a feeling of community. Within this view decision making ought to involve as many as possible and it ought to be as open and accessible as possible. Hence it is easy to favor small and clearly delimited communities, be they either geographically or functionally delimited. User-democracy and sub-municipal boards with wide discretion and direct public involvement are means to strengthen real democracy. Administrative barriers ought to be low. Problem solving should not be artificially structured through sectoral or agency mandates. The sense of belonging to a community is something which is taken both as an end and as an axiomatic starting point.

In the academic debate the approaches to local governmental development are pitted against each other. Communitarianists stand against libertarianists and both camps are skeptical of traditional bureaucracy and managerialism. From logical, theoretical and ideological standpoints it may well be true that the approaches are strangers to each other. But from a practical point of view academic orthodoxy is not an acute concern. Real programs for local governmental development mix bits and pieces from all approaches. This is an essential message conveyed by the cities within the Bertelsmann network.

Mixing elements from all three approaches also implies that the ideal-typical constructions are broken with. Individual choice mechanisms need not be perceived narrowly as means to more efficient production; they may also be seen as an essential element in empowering citizens, in showing respect for differing individual tastes and predilections. Citizen's Charters may be looked upon as an instrument for consumer rights or as a control mechanism vis-à-vis the independent result units. But charters may as well be seen as an expression of a genuine community stand on the nature of services to be provided within a particular community.

Within immediate personal services, consumer choice and consumption rights may be an efficient way to organize service production and distribution. In other, more collective services, a purchaser-provider organizational mode may be appropriate. In matters involving use of public authority more traditional bureaucratic modes may be the most suitable. In all of these cases some form of customer orientation and customer contracts or Citizen's Charters may be applicable. In matters concerning physical planning or neighborhoods or in matters dealing with local behavioral matters, a more communitarian approach may be practicable. Thus, in reality we face a mix of organizational principles within local governmental development programs, in general and in relation to citizen and community participation in particular.

Although in reality different organizational principles are mixed, it may be true that the resulting blend differs between countries or regions. The British approach has had a bias toward the first, the liberal approach whereas Germany and the Netherlands seem to favor the second, managerial, approach. That has also been the case in Scandinavia, but the rather clear managerial orientation is not as predominant now as it was in the 1980s. Sweden, and to some extent also Finland, have been moving in the liberal direction. Denmark has over many years been stimulating civil participation. Over the last two years an increasing Scandinavian interest in the communitarian perspective has been evolving. It is perhaps symptomatic that the city of Stockholm has decided to implement a far-reaching sub-municipal board organization, amounting almost to a division of the city into independent sub-municipal units. The British communitarian literature also suggests that a shift is occurring in local governmental values.

An overall impression is that the value-pendulum is swinging again toward participatory values. Although the cities participating in the international network have not been studied over time, the many cases submitted suggest a rather wide and varied interest in participatory mechanisms. From the author's Scandinavian standpoint it certainly seems to be true that legitimacy is again a going concern alongside efficiency.

3. Some General Observations on Citizen and Community Participation

The cities within the international network, Braintree (UK), Christchurch (New Zealand), Delft (the Netherlands), Duisburg (Germany), Farum (Denmark), Hæmeenlinna (Finland), Neuchâtel (Switzerland), Phoenix (USA), Québec (Canada) and Tilburg (the Netherlands), have submitted 102 case descriptions on participatory mechanisms used or projects implemented. These have been chosen in order to provide examples of participation within different sectors (hard and soft), different levels (representative, user, individual) and different problem areas. To some extent the cases have been chosen from a "best-practice" perspective within each country and each city. All cases have been included in a case bank. Based on this information, and bearing in mind, of course, the selection criteria, some general observations can be made:

1. All cities have a rather clear policy of citizen and community participation. Public involvement is viewed as an essential ingredient in local policy-making and in policy implementation. A clear statement is the partnership policy of informing and consulting citizens of Neuchâtel. Another example is the mission statement of the city of Phoenix: "To create a vital City, enhancing the lives of residents and citizens through effective leadership, active community involvement, and a dynamic blend of quality government and services." Community involvement is further given a clear justification: "Citizens take ownership of the issues and are intricately involved in drafting and implementing the solutions. The benefits of this approach include a more cohesive and active community, capable of identifying problems and developing meaningful solutions in a timely manner."
2. Citizen participation and community involvement is justified on many grounds. Participatory mechanisms do not have one purpose only, and this is particularly true with regard to general community involvement policy. Participation may be justified from an empowerment perspective at the same time as it is regarded as a vital instrument in quality management. It may further or alternatively be argued that participation stimulates efficiency or productivity of public services. Most of the cases submitted to the case bank are justified on multiple grounds.
3. The community involvement policy and the projects submitted are genuinely local. Participatory mechanisms are usually problem oriented and the problems tackled vary from one city to another. Efforts to strengthen representative democracy through across-the-board arrangements are rare. A clear emphasis of the uniquely local context can be found in the declaration of principles from the city of Québec: "In less populated or more homogenous cities, people's participation in municipal life is facilitated by the proximity of decision making centers. Québec City, however, is made up of fifteen or so neighborhoods, each with different characteristics. Some have long since reached their full development and are in considerable need of renovation and revitalization; others are in the process of being developed; still others belong to the heart of a national capital, an urban hub, indeed to a city which is considered a world heritage jewel. Thus the challenge of en-

couraging participation is much more complex, just as is the management of the city itself."
4. A customer orientation is common to all cities. For many years customer surveys have been carried out and more directed market research around particular services is often carried out as well. There is a clear tendency toward the establishment of local social indicators, i.e. the same items are included in consecutive surveys in order to establish time-series data on customer perceptions of public service performance. The *City Panel Delft* is a well known case. Another case is the general Finnish City survey in which the city of Hæmeenlinna has been a regular participant.
5. If we make a distinction between representative "big" democracy and neighborhood or user-oriented "small" democracy, we may note that the more empowering the participatory mechanisms are with regard to citizens or community groups, the more they belong to the world of "small" democracy. Efforts to enhance representative democracy are mostly informational or directed at more or less formal consultation mechanisms, as seems to be the case in consultation within general planning processes.
6. A majority of the cases submitted concern members of a neighborhood or users of particular services. Although this impression may be an artifact of the selection principles, it nevertheless seems that efforts at an intermediate level are the most common. Not many cases at the micro level, involving just a small group of citizens, have been submitted. The same holds true for macro level examples, city-wide participatory arrangements, although these are more frequent than the micro level examples.
7. A striking feature of many interesting participatory cases is that they are built around the assumption that the problems dealt with cannot be solved unless a wide community involvement can be brought to support them. This communitarian orientation permeates cases that are very different in nature. Some common features of these cases seem to be either that they involve a need to change the behavior of community members or that problem solving in an efficient way is dependent on widespread community consent.
8. Attempts to enhance citizen participation and community involvement

face the same type of problems in all cities. It is difficult to delimit an appropriate constituency. Once this problem has been solved, it is difficult to mobilize participants. Another common difficulty is to present the problem to be solved in a generally intelligible form. Successful participatory efforts as a rule increase public expectations and these heightened expectations may well run contrary to overarching considerations within a representative democratic setting.

9. It seems that most of the community cases that have been submitted represent efforts that have been initialized by the public authorities. There are not many cases that seem to indicate that the efforts are based in bottom-up initiatives. Public authorities have been the main catalyst and planner of community involvement. This is not, however, to say that authorities censor citizen initiatives. Rather the implication seems to be that growing into a genuinely participatory culture is a slow and difficult process.

10. Participatory prerequisites of the kind favored within a liberal orientation, i.e. freedom of choice and consumption rights, have not been often mentioned in relation to the participatory cases. It seems that these empowering arrangements are not conceptualized as citizen participation. Another possibility is that within some of the cities, services that would lend themselves for this mechanism are not run by the municipality. In a Scandinavian context, however, where municipalities run almost all educational, social and health services, choice is usually perceived to be an important participatory and empowering mechanism.

11. There seems, as a rule, to be a considerable gap between actual and potential participation. In only a few instances, especially when the participatory efforts involve mobilizing individuals, has it been possible to actually mobilize more than a fraction of those potentially eligible for participation. Customer surveys and choice mechanisms are, of course, an exception to this rule. In consultation efforts directed toward civic organizations, the match between actual and potential participation is much better.

12. Efforts to provide systematic feedback on community involvement projects are rather rare. To some extent participatory aspects are dealt with in customer surveys, but even at this level a systematic evalua-

tion, at least in any strict sense of the word, is rare. A number of interesting follow-up reports have, however, been submitted with the case material. One such case is the evaluation of local boards for children's day-care units carried out by the municipality of Farum. Another example is the evaluation of the "New Way Trust Skinhead Project" in Christchurch.

4. Citizen Participation and Community Involvement: Some Examples

It is not possible in the space allowed here to go into actual case accounts of the many types of participatory projects that have been submitted for the case bank. Instead we shall attempt to make a rough summary of the types of projects that exist, city by city. The account is not comprehensive, cases that are mentioned seem to this writer to be of a general interest or they are interesting as examples of rather novel attempts to foster public involvement. We shall mention informational and consultative efforts as well as efforts aimed at a more deeper public involvement.

Braintree district council (UK)

Braintree (120,000 inhabitants) is best known for its quality management approach, including Customer Contracts and across the board certification of the council services. The council works, of course, within the general competitive tendering system of British local government.

The overall impression of Braintree's community involvement projects is one of consultation. Several consultative mechanisms exist, for different areas and for civic and business organizations. Cases such as *Braintree District Luncheon Club, Area Community and Leisure Committees* and *Shaping the Future* (general review of council services) or *Parish Council Co-optation to Planning Committees* all are examples of consultative arrangements.

The Charter system, the *Customer Contract System*, is very interesting.

The contracts are mainly aimed at quality management, but integral to them is to foster openness in council affairs and to provide extensive complaints procedures for the citizens. The returns of this complaint system are used for systematic quality work. The quality approach also includes repeated customer surveys.

Two of the cases deal with social housing and a permanent residential area for gypsies. In the first case a more far-reaching consultation is carried out with the tenants. By and large the Braintree participatory approach seems to be a good example of a rather versatile managerial orientation.

Christchurch (New Zealand)

Christchurch (300,000 inhabitants) seems to be very active in community involvement. The city has submitted 21 participatory cases for the case bank. Efforts cover informational projects, consultation and several projects aiming at a deeper citizen involvement, especially within the field of cooperative planning. Issues dealing with the environment and with physical planning are most common among the Christchurch cases.

The city is presently creating a large Internet-based electronic information system. The system is designed to be used by individual citizens or by organizations or companies, at specially provided information points or from personal terminals. An interesting feature of the project is that the information system is particularly designed to help different user categories, citizens, decision-makers or companies.

The *Green Waste Facility* project is an interesting case of consultation. The project deals with developing a facility to reduce green waste going to landfill by composting. Systematic consultation and information efforts have paved the way for acceptance of the project, both at council level and among those who are supposed to use the facility. Other more traditional consultation projects deal with budgeting and general planning. Especially in the case of planning, consultation is comprehensive and takes place in an early initial phase of the process.

The most interesting cases deal with a more communitarian oriented consultation within delimited cooperative planning processes. These projects are either rather small-scale, dealing with matters within a neighborhood or in relation to some park or other service, or they are of a wider scope like the *Cathedral Square Redevelopment Project*. In the latter case involvement is by civic organizations in addition to individual citizens. Another interesting case is the *New Way Trust Project,* a social work project dealing with the skinheads. Within all these projects discussion and interaction seem to be lively and genuine. In many cases the starting point has been a clear conflict of opinion between authorities and citizens within particular neighborhoods, like in the *Shirley Stream Waterway Enhancement Scheme*.

Delft (the Netherlands)

Delft (90,000 inhabitants) is best known for its extensive customer survey, *The City Panel Delft*. This repeated survey represents a systematic attempt to create a social indicator system based on citizen perceptions of the city services. The panel is also used for in-depth discussions in selected groups of respondents around issues that have been singled out among the results of the general panel survey.

The cooperative planning project *Quality Improvement of the City Center* represents a more in-depth consultation with a wide range of concerned parties, individuals, organizations and businesses around an old market place in the heart of the city.

Duisburg (Germany)

Duisburg (540,000 inhabitants) has submitted three cases of community involvement to the case bank. Together these represent a rather comprehensive community development strategy involving in-depth consultation and wide citizen mobilization.

What is particularly noteworthy about the cases, *The Marxloh City Area Project, The District Budget Project,* and *The Marxloh Development Corporation,* is that they cut across sectoral and administrative boundaries and that they aim at coping with a number of "hard" and "soft" problems simultaneously. The first project is a general development project. In the second project funds are distributed to local associations for community work, and in the third project different forms of assistance is offered to local businesses. A notable feature of the development program is that it explicitly deals with ethnic problems.

Farum (Denmark)

Farum (17,000 inhabitants) is a small suburban municipality close to Copenhagen. Community involvement in Farum is marked by the general Danish policy in favor of devolutionary user-participation. Their most interesting cases fall within this tradition, the parent representation within children's day-care facilities, with extensive decision making powers, and old age advisors, educated within a voluntary organizational framework.

On the informational side Farum has made rather substantial investments in the general information to the public and in a new front office for municipal services in relation to its new administration building.

Hæmeenlinna (Finland)

Hæmeenlinna (45,000 inhabitants) has done exceptionally much in favor of citizen participation and community involvement in the past few years. Many of the projects have been inspired by experiences within the Bertelsmann network. The bulk of the Hæmeenlinna efforts is concerned with consultational participation, but there are notable exceptions in a real democratic direction as well and there are also elements of a more liberal orientation.

Within the consultation orientation the implementation of the first *Citizen's Charter System* in Finland ought to be mentioned. This application had essentially to be worked out within the city, since international examples are concerned with a rather narrow range of services. Further a *Charter Complaints Board* has been set up and a thorough campaign has been carried out in order to introduce a new informal complaints system. Charters are worked out not only at a citywide level but within sectoral boards and within singular service providers as well (day-care centers, schools, libraries).

The consultational attempts have been supplemented by an exceptionally wide range of follow-up procedures, participation in the nation-wide City survey, in the 10 year research program *Finnish Local Government 2004*, and the city has just completed its own Hæmeenlinna survey. At the same time different service areas are carrying out their own customer surveys, or they participate in more formalized bench-marking procedures. A notable part of the recent *Hæmeenlinna Survey* was a mental map-type of solicitation of ideas for redevelopment and modernization of the city center. A rough 600 respondents generated more than 5,000 responses that can be used as a starting point for the new redevelopment project. A *Civic Forum* has been set up for organizations within sports and leisure activities. This forum has been accorded powers to distribute support funds to the associations, thus relieving the city of an administrative burden as well as acquiring general associational support for the decisions made.

A new cooperative planning and redevelopment project has been started as a follow-up to earlier and more limited efforts. The new program includes a number of mobilizing efforts that cut across administrative borders, both within the city and between administrative levels. The program can be compared to the Duisburg program already mentioned. Also, as in Farum, the city has parent involvement in schools and in day-care centers, but it is not as far-reaching as in the Danish case.

Freedom of choice between municipal schools, with reimbursement of schools following choices made by families, has been introduced and presently work is being done on a similar system for children's day-care centers. First, however, the centers are working on their particular care-profile in order to make the choice situation more real. An additional emphasis has been on informational efforts, working out information material on municipal services within different parts of the city. The effect of all these efforts has been very substantial according to the Hæmeenlinna survey.

Neuchâtel (Switzerland)

Neuchâtel (32,000 inhabitants) has over the past few years adopted a city wide development program. Within the program a partnership policy has been developed with regard to public employees, the citizens, other municipalities, civic associations and businesses.

Much of the community involvement centers around informational and advisory activities. The city also supports civic associations in varying ways. An interesting example of more demanding consultational involvement is represented by the Youth Parliament. Within this forum young people can air their concerns and make proposals on how to deal with the problems of the young people. Other consultational procedures deal with the creation of a play-ground or with the establishment of a nature path.

Phoenix (USA)

Phoenix (about 1,000,000 inhabitants) is interesting with regard to efforts to improve information and communication with citizens within a representative framework and due to some cases in which public involvement has been pursued in-depth. Concern with criminality and vandalism is important in the Phoenix cases.

The city cooperates with a private cable television station. *The Phoenix Channel 11* broadcasts council meetings and interviews with city authorities. It is noteworthy that cablecasts are produced explicitly from early deliberative rather than from more formal decision making meetings. *The Computerized Public Agenda* is a real time electronic information system providing immediate access for the public to public meeting agendas and final decisions. Representative democracy has further been enhanced through a *Satellite-Early Voting System*. It has been possible for voters to cast their ballot prior to Election Day and in different places, such as shopping malls and grocery stores.

The Phoenix community involvement projects aim at widespread participation, not only with regard to the informational or voting projects, but with regard to projects aiming at direct involvement as well. This is true, for instance, of the projects combating criminality and vandalism. *The Graffiti Buster* program involves neighborhood groups in removal of graffiti and in cleaning up trash. Almost 1,000 groups have been involved in this program. The *Adopt-a-Street* program works in a similar way. *The Neighborhoods Fight Back* program is smaller, but is interesting because it tries not only to mobilize neighborhoods to fight criminality, but also to establish general development programs for themselves. Within these programs a range of urban problems are addressed. The award-winning *Block Watch* program is largescale (1,200 block-watch groups) and involves cooperation between the police and neighborhood representatives, the Block Watch Advisory Boards.

Québec (Canada)

Québec (170,000 inhabitants, 650,000 in the metropolitan area) is especially interesting with regard to several rather thorough consultation arrangements, some of which are novel among the cases reviewed in this paper. A particular feature in the Québec case is that the city approaches consultation based on relevant categories of citizens (young people, homeless people and elderly citizens) as well as based on neighborhoods.

Neighborhood Councils are consulted in matters dealing with zoning and physical planning. *The Advisory Commission on Women and the City, The Advisory Group on Homelessness, The Symposium on the Needs of Senior Citizens* and *The City Pictured by Children* all represent the particular approach to consultation in Québec. The advisory groups are given a clear position both in an advisory role, dealing with formal proposals on the agenda, but also with regard to initializing decision making. The advisory groups draw on several community interests, civic organizations, volunteer groups, private partners and city authorities.

There is, as in Phoenix, a clear concern with criminality. One program is directed at cooperation between the police and local merchants and their associations in order to prevent fraud. *The Community Police Station* program involves local volunteer police stations in close cooperation with the police.

Tilburg (the Netherlands)

Tilburg (165,000 inhabitants) is known for the Tilburg Model, and the city has recently been awarded a best-practice award for its *City Management Model* by the Second United Nations Conference on Human Settlements, Habitat II. The award was given with explicit reference to the comprehensiveness and genuinely consultative nature of the management model. The City Management Model includes a yearly City program which is prepared based on wide local consultation (120 organizations).

The cases submitted by Tilburg represent both ends of the participatory scale, wide consultation around the yearly preparation of a city-wide comprehensive program, and a number of decidedly local development projects around facilities for young people and play-grounds for children. Within these local projects, families concerned are given the opportunity to plan and to participate in the implementation of local facilities. Activities within the city management process and consultation seem foremost to be connected to physical planning, zoning and urban development.

5. Conclusions and Future Challenges

Based on the review of participatory cases within the cities of the International Network for Better Local Government, some additional observations to those already offered in the beginning can be made. The review also raises the question of future challenges in the pursuit of a deeper and more genuine public involvement in local affairs. First we shall offer some additional observations on the participatory cases:

1. A clear impression is that excellence in local government includes a genuine concern with the involvement of citizens and community in policy-making and policy implementation. Although comparisons have not been made to local governments in general, in the countries represented by outstanding cities, it is my impression that the Bertelsmann cities represent a vanguard also with respect to citizen participation. This, of course, is not surprising, given the criteria that were used in the selection of finalists for the Carl Bertelsmann Prize 1993.
2. There is no single model for community involvement, but rather as many models as there are cities. Participatory mechanisms, the substantive concern within community involvement projects, the scope of participatory projects and the delimitation of constituencies or groups concerned all vary according to local circumstances. Participatory

mechanisms and community involvement are not matters for centralized national regulations.
3. Although local circumstances and local concerns vary from one city to another, there seems to exist ample room for diffusion of good participatory practices. The children's picture of their immediate neighborhood is certainly not input to planning processes that is needed only in Québec. Citizen approval of composting is not a problem limited to Christchurch. Convenient voting arrangements may well be a particularly acute problem in Phoenix, but turnout in local elections can certainly be improved in any of the cities concerned.
4. There seems to exist a clear tendency toward early consultation. Citizens are not involved only on a reactive basis, but increasingly on a proactive basis as well. This involves a shift toward more bottom-up oriented approaches to participation. Still, however, the lion's share of the participatory programs are rather of a top-down nature. However, policy-making and implementation culture seem to be moving in the direction of genuine partnership between community groups and public authorities. This shift includes, as in the case of Tilburg or in Neuchâtel or, for that matter, in cases dealing with budgetary and planning consultations, an effort to make the public aware of necessary and strict limitations on what can be done with limited overall resources. Participation is not only about articulation, it is also a matter of aggregation.
5. A genuine partnership culture entails continuity, recurrent consultation and/or institutionalized forums and practices. The Hæmeenlinna campaign for a new complaints system produced an impressive response over the first few months. In the year that followed the total response was only a fraction of that initially received. Continuous input is required in order to establish an ongoing dialogue. Some critical threshold must be passed in order to reach continuous public awareness of the new participatory mechanism.
6. There seems to exist a clear awareness of the fact that public involvement in program implementation often has to be preceded by public involvement in the formative stages of the policy process. Those involved have to realize their common problem and they have to acknowledge the fact that several often contradictory positions have to be reconciled in order to reach workable solutions.

In addition to these final impressions, a few points may be raised in relation to future challenges for public involvement:

1. It seems that cross-sectoral or multi-agency approaches to public involvement are rather rare. They do exist, of course, for instance in relation to comprehensive consultation processes, but even in these cases genuine multi-sectoral analysis is difficult, proposals often being based on sectoral preparations. This poses the challenge to approach clearly delimited problems from a cooperative point of view of all those who are in some way concerned, be they local or state authorities, volunteer groups, neighborhoods or the business community. The problem of unemployment and job creation has not been tackled in many cases although we should assume that local mobilization resulting in the creation of micro-businesses is one of the few roads open to job creation. Hæmeenlinna has recently initiated a neighborhood-based multi-sectoral and cooperative project on local job-creating.
2. It has not been clear from the cases submitted against which criteria success has been actually measured. In quite a few of the projects it is noted that conflicts may be growing between a representative and a direct democratic perspective. Community involvement heightens expectations and it makes differing stands visible. We may, in situations like this, end up with more dissatisfaction on single issues than before. At the same time, however, participants may feel that they have genuinely had a chance to voice their opinion. Thus, simple customer surveys may not be very appropriate tools for evaluation of community involvement. Involvement may foster satisfaction in public services, but it does not necessarily do so and it may even be that it ought not to do so, if satisfaction is measured at the level of actual services provided.
3. In a recent evaluation of the experimental phase in the development of the sub-municipal administrative model in Stockholm, it was noted that interaction between authorities and the citizens within the sub-municipalities did not become particularly more intensive, but the interaction became more immediate to the problems to be solved. Administrative structure is, it seems, intimately connected to the possibilities for and the nature of public involvement. Above all, this points in the direction of a clear division of work between overall rep-

resentative democracy and the directly involved neighborhood or submunicipal level. As far as I have found out from the background material submitted with the reviewed cases, there has not been a clear awareness of this problem of the interrelationship between administrative structure and participatory mechanisms. It may well be that many conflicts around participation arise from a confrontation between weak overall preferences and rather intense local preferences, a situation which might not arise at all if administrative arrangements would be open for the intense local preferences to prevail.

4. Swedish experiences seem further to suggest that purchaser-provider solutions and participatory mechanisms within a purely managerial framework may create estrangement both on the part of politicians and the public. Customer surveys and result negotiations are primarily internal administrative matters and in any case they strengthen the position of the professional personnel. It would therefore seem important to recognize that not only is public involvement in fact often seen from all of the perspectives introduced in the beginning of this review, but also that it ought to be infused with ideas from all three approaches, from liberal, managerial and communitarian approaches.

5. It has often been noted that open participatory arrangements favor the well educated, well placed and already active individuals or groups. This natural selection process seems to have worked in several of the submitted cases. It is noteworthy that very few of the participatory cases deal with genuinely powerless groups or estranged individuals. At the same time it is often problems posed by these groups or individuals that are dealt with within local participatory programs. It is a challenge to integrate powerless or estranged groups the way it has been attempted in the New Way Trust project in Christchurch or in the Hæmeenlinna project on job-creation (the project mobilizes unemployed in a high unemployment neighborhood).

6. We should finally note that despite all the interesting and promising programs on citizen participation and community involvement, it seems that in many nations criticism of and distrust in politicians and public authorities has been growing. The amount of volatility has increased in elections. At the same time interest in politics is continuously high among citizens. All these observations amount to a constant

challenge to integrate citizens into the running of common affairs. This challenge can, in particular, be seen as a challenge to local government, especially to best-practice local governments, the sources of innovation and excellence.

Literature

Adamaschek, B. and Banner, G., 1996 Local Government in Competition. Paper presented to the International Network for Better Local Government, Braintree Meeting, February 5–6, 1996.

Andersen, J. et al. (1993), Medborgerskab. Demokrati og politisk deltagelse. Herning.

Atkins, R. (1992), "Making Use of Complaints: Braintree District Council." Local Government Studies, vol. 18, autumn, 3/1992.

Baldersheim, H. and Ståhlberg, K. (eds.) (1994), Towards the Self-regulating Municipality. Free Communes and Administrative Modernization in Scandinavia. Aldershot.

Burns, D., Hambleton, R. & Hoggett, P. (1994), The Politics of Decentralization. Revitalising Local Democracy. London.

Hill, D. M. (1994), Citizens and Cities. Urban Policy in the 1990s. Guilford.

Jönsson, S., Rubenowitz, S. and Westerståhl, J. (1995), Decentraliserad Kommun. Exemplet Göteborg. Stockholm.

Premfors, R., Sandqvist, J. and Sanne, M. (1994), Demokrati i storstad. Stockholm.

Osborne, D. and Gabler, T. (1993), Reinventing Government. How the Entrepreneurial Spirit is Transforming the Public Sector. New York.

Severijnen, P. (1994), "Local authorities and market research: Market Research Incorporated in the Policy Process of Consumer Oriented Local Authorities," Local Government Studies, vol. 20, spring, 1/1994.

Ståhlberg, K. (1996), Herre i eget hus. 12 debattinlägg om nordiska kommuner i förändring, Bergen: LOS-Senteret, Rapport 9605.

Appendix

Data form used to gather information on citizen and community involvement

Enhancing Community Participation
Data Form

1. Name (identification) of the case: _____

2. Name and address of contact person:
   _____

3. What services/activities is the case concerned with and what volume/scope does the case have:
   _____

4. How would you place the case within the selection matrix, indicate cell number: _____

5. What practices/mechanisms/means of community involvement/citizen participation does the case include:
   _____

6. How many persons are directly and potentially affected by the case (direct users and potential users of participatory mechanism):

   users: _____

   potential users: _____

7. What type of groups/users are affected by the case (i.e. voters, users of service, volunteer organization etc.):
   _____

8. What is the duration of the case (date it started, time it was implemented):
   _____

9. According to which criteria is the case an outstanding one:

   _____

10. What has been the prevailing conceptualization of the case among city officials and among members of the community? If possible, use the matrix below as a point of reference:

	Democracy empowerment	Quality management	Improving productivity, efficiency
City officials	1	2	3
Community	4	5	6

11. What have been the three most important achievements of the case:
    1. _____
    2. _____
    3. _____

12. If you think about the case in two phases
    a) initiation/decision-making phase and
    b) implementation phase, what have been the most important problems/challenges facing the case in each stage:

    a) initiation: _____

    b) implementation: _____

13. In your personal evaluation, have there occurred conflicts between a macro-democratic perspective and a micro-democratic perspective during the implementation of the case? If so, how would you describe these conflicts (political conflicts, conflicts between involved groups, conflicts between central economic interests and grassroot expectations etc.):

    _____

14. What possible documentation exists of the case and is this documentation sent to us separately:
    a) administrative reports/formal documents on the case:

    _____

    attached: _____

    b) systematic evaluations (administrative/scientific):

Public Participation in Municipal Life: The City of Quebec in the North American Context

André Beauchamp, Jean Dionne

Executive Summary 105
Introduction... 106
1. Common Concerns 107
    1.1   Representative Democracy and Participatory Democracy... 107
    1.2   Towards a Diversification of Participation Issues 109
    1.3   A Science But Above All an Art 110
    1.4   The Contact to the Elected Representatives 111
    1.5   Continuity 112
    1.6   Consultation Costs............................... 113
    1.7   Complex Decisions 114
    1.8   Tensions Between Quantity and Quality.............. 115
    1.9   Revival of Elitism 116
    1.10 Tensions Between Political and Administrative Machinery...................................... 117
    1.11 Consulting at the Head of the Decision-Making Process . 118
2. The City of Quebec 118
    2.1   Historical Background............................ 119
    2.2   From Representation to Participation 119
    2.3   The Local Request for Democracy 120
    2.4   The New Participatory Democracy of the City of Quebec 122
    2.5   The Council Consultations 123
    2.6   Women and City Consultative Commission 123

    2.7   Public Participation in the Districts.................... 125
    2.8   The District of Vieux-Limoilou....................... 126
    2.9   The Resources..................................... 129
Conclusion 129
Literature... 130

Executive Summary

While taking stock of their own experience and following discussion with representatives from other Quebec, Canadian and North American cities, the delegates of the City of Quebec formulate some general considerations concerning public participation within Canadian and North American local governments.

Among these general considerations, the authors point out a growing diversification in the subjects and issues calling for public participation. If public participation stems from issues linked to the control of urban development, the spectrum of matters to be decided for which a structured contribution of the population is required is diversifying rapidly. This diversification creates in turn the need for a more varied and sophisticated range of instruments and structures for public participation.

Public participation also brings up the question of reconciling the complexity of the technocratic analysis of problems with a mass approach which is sometimes oversimplified and even simplistic. In order to get round these limitations, the text suggests that we act simultaneously on all fronts, that we set up varied and complementary means to do so, and that we introduce more refined processes when dealing with limited groups and less extensive ones for broader groups.

As concerns referendum the authors state their preference for consultation well before a decision is made. By definition, the results of a referendum represent a choice between two extreme positions, whereas often the best option arises from consensus, from compromises that have been explored, negotiated or discussed.

Finally, the experience of the city of Quebec and the specific context of the province of Quebec are presented, in particular, experiments with district councils and the Women and City Consultative Commission.

Introduction

In the present paper we would like to reflect on certain issues which are linked with public participation. The local communities have to face challenges which are complex and apparently not very reconcilable. These include the modernization of the management and of the organization culture, the embarkation on the technological way, to balance and – if possible – to cut the budgets, privatization of municipal services and to assure the involvement of the citizen. One of our priorities in the city of Quebec is the development and implementation of a policy of public participation.

We could think that what happens in Quebec is not different to what happens somewhere else in Canada or in the United States, and it might even be similar – mutatis mutandis – to things that happen somewhere else on this planet. We often rightly speak about the global village and the globalization of problems.

If we take stock of our own experience and of the countless interchanges which we have with the other cities in Quebec and Canada and taking into account the prevailing trends which can be observed at the moment in the United States, we think it is legitimate to set out some general considerations. Our reflection is especially inspired through our participation in research which was sponsored by the *Canadian Institute of Public Administration*. It dealt with the participation of the citizens within Canadian local governments. This research is led by the *Faculty of Administration at the Carleton University* in Ottawa. Our reflections are also inspired by the regular exchanges which take place within the International Association of Public Participation Practitioners and the Association québécoise sur les études d'impacts (*Quebec Association on Impact Studies*).

Our report comprises two parts: the first part which is titled *Common Concerns*, suggests general ideas on the position of the citizens in local politics. The second part explains the historical context in which the city of Quebec had to act and the options it chose.

1. Common Concerns

1.1 Representative Democracy and Participatory Democracy

There is an unsolved debate between the advocates of a representative democracy and those who are in favour of a participatory democracy. The first ones, who are sometimes called elitist, claim that it is the elected representatives' task to make decisions. If the people are not satisfied, they simply have to beat them in the next election. The others, who are called participationists, tend to maintain that participation is always desirable and useful and that it improves democracy. J.-J. Rousseau, Tocqueville, J. S. Mill and later on G. T. H. Cole can be considered participationists, whereas the elitist, practically in favour of a purely centralized position is represented by Schumpeter (Godbout 1983: 19–45).

The precise reason for such a strong participationist movement in our cities since 1960 is a series of town and country planning decisions which were – often technocratically – taken and which modified the framework of life in the local communities in a way that the citizens felt excluded in their own environment. City centres were chopped up for the construction of motorways, residential districts were destroyed for the construction of office buildings, hotels, ministries, the distribution of land for redevelopment was sometimes changed without real planning.

In a paper which was presented in 1988 on the occasion of the conference "Making Cities Livable," Gianni Longo describes the origins of public participation in a popular mobilization against the great development projects of the 1960s, especially those for the road system.

"The Federal highway programs were big catalysts in getting citizens organized. Every time I go to Baltimore, I am reminded of this fact. There are two segments of the interstate highway which stop dead, unfinished a hundred feet in the air. They were stopped by a group of citizens called MAD-Movement Against Citizen Destruction. They were very confrontational but it was one of those groups that actually has been instrumental in the creation and success of the inner Harbor. As the movement grew the confrontational tactics became more constructive. For example, the Pike

Street Market in Seattle was a very constructive effort in which architects and the citizens joined together to preserve the market, to preserve its use." (Longo 1988: 2)

When the motorway system in the city of Quebec was designed in the 1960s, for example, the population in the region of Quebec was estimated at one million inhabitants until the year 2000. In 1996, there were not even 700,000 people. There are many such examples. The construction of the Spadina motorway in Toronto in the heart of the city has never been finished because, all of a sudden, the popular resistance became too strong. Similarly, the construction of the Ville-Marie motorway in the eastern part of Montreal has never been accomplished.

The era of enthusiastic planners has engendered an initial feeling of revolt amongst the citizens. This movement has progressively changed to a more positive contribution from the citizens to urban planning; it has also changed to a greater openness from public decision makers towards this contribution.

Additionally, the rise of the welfare state highlighted the request for the rights. It became inconsequent or even unjust to take decisions which modify the framework of the lives of men and women in the city without involving them somehow: the right to access to information, consultation, decision, the possibility to stop projects, legal or political recourse. If we looked at it in an extreme way, we would go back to a model of direct democracy in which the citizens themselves take all decisions and the elected representatives would only be executives of the popular will which is at all times dictated by the people. The participatory democracy would then almost cancel out the representative democracy.

"Participation does not always strengthen democracy. It can even restrict the field of representation. This statement goes against the participationist theory and the ideal which both postulate that any participation is necessarily desirable, is necessarily an addition, a supplement for the representative democracy and that it necessarily widens the domain of political representation. If this is true for several cases, it is also wrong for others." (Godbout 1991: 20)

There is in this connection an unresolved tension between the representative democracy and the participatory democracy. The forces and the limits of both have to be determined so that the participatory democracy improves the representative democracy. At the moment, we think that the privileged and conflict-free field of the participatory democracy is part of the public consultation in the area of the development of decisions, without abandoning the elected representatives' power and duty to make decisions.

In France, we observe the same echoes:

"Within the two bounds of improved representative and direct democracy which would have to be reinvented are also to be found the modalities of a participatory democracy which work well – if only the means are provided: municipal councils for the young, participation of the residents in redevelopment and renovation projects, development of local government control in districts, etc." (Patrick Viveret)

1.2 Towards a Diversification of Participation Issues

We observe a diversification of the subjects and issues for which the public participation is employed. If the participation of the public arises out of issues which are linked with the control of urban development, the range of issues on which decisions – for which a structured contribution of the population is required – have to be made is rapidly becoming more diverse today. This diversification creates for its part a need for a more varied and sophisticated array of participation instruments and structures for the public.

Graham and Phillips describe this shifting in research on Canadian cities and towns:

"First, local governments are confronted with the need to undertake public participation in new areas, such as budgeting, economic development, and political restructuring. Although local governments have been conducting public participation as a routine part of the land use planning process for over 25 years, the methods have been tailored to dealing with development issues. The challenge they are now facing is to establish appropriate approaches for engaging citizens in other policy areas.

Second, an emerging philosophy of governance that focuses on citizen and community responsibility has created new expectations of the public. Rather than offering personal opinions, regardless of whether these opinions have been well thought out, it is now expected that the participants offer informed opinions and be willing to make tough choices. This has sparked a greater interest in public participation mechanisms that provide opportunities for deliberation extended over time." (Graham and Philips 1996: 2)

In the city of Quebec, we have implemented permanent councils on the closest level to the citizen: in the district. Thus we believe to meet the needs of diversification of the issues and of a more in-depth treatment of the problems through interested and involved citizens.

1.3 A Science But Above All an Art

Participation and negotiation have one feature in common: They are sciences, but above all they are art. The science in this field makes rapid and good progress. The art of participation, however, has to be learned by doing and is marked by the difficult art of government. It is the result of our failures and of our success, the reflection of our values, the fruit of local history and culture. We do not believe that there is one single and infallible recipe for the implementation of participation. There are rather good and less good ways, there are adequate methods for certain situations and other methods which lead to pernicious consequences.

Those who are in favor of public participation at all costs such as the IAP3 (International Association of Public Participation Practitioners) and IAIA (International Association of Impact Assessment) like to speak about the principle of basis, of shared convictions or rules of implementation. But they also speak about innovations, imagination and experience. Nothing is infallible. The modes are being used up. Tastes are changing. For no obvious reason, good solutions do not help anymore. Art withers away when it becomes routine.

A certain restriction to the public hearings as the only legitimate means of public consultation can be observed in the province of Quebec. This happens probably in the wake of processes which were established by the provincial government 20 years ago in order to assess the impacts of big projects, especially the building of huge hydroelectric dams.

Current research though, which is widely provided with information, speaks rather in favour of flexible and diverse consultation and participation methods while adapting to an ever fluctuating and endlessly variable context according to the nature of the issue, time, circumstances and the concerned public – depending on whether a certain policy or project is examined or whether we want to reach a common vision or simply specify the scope of a regulation.

1.4 The Contact to the Elected Representatives

It is rightly said that the municipal government is above all the place where democracy can be experienced. If a definition and implementation of a policy is important, it is also important not to retreat into the rigidities of a framework which is too strict. In a local community or a middle-sized town, the citizens always have the possibility to assist at the meetings of the council and they can ask questions. Municipal policy is tangible, often it is based on human relations, it has at least a personal touch.

It happens often that a citizen meets up with a town councillor at his place, that he speaks to him on the telephone, that they meet in a restaurant or in the shopping center. This physical nearness is irreplaceable. Besides, isn't it exactly this which makes the difference between the town and the province and the central state?

A councillor must have the possibility to meet the citizens of his district, to speak with them about priorities, to understand the frustrations and fears or to explore possibilities. A public consultation which – under the pretext of neutrality and effectiveness – restricted the consultation only to consultation professionals would with one hand dig a hole, which it pretends to fill up with the other hand. This is especially the case on a municipal level.

1.5 Continuity

Any consultation or non-consultation policy has to do with politics. Thus, it can change if the mayor or the party changes. That is why certain processes and certain behaviours have to be institutionalized so as to guarantee the survival beyond changes of different political parties.

Conversely, however, it has to be recognized that through practice, people learn to use the implemented consultation procedures and thus become more effective. This can also entail a harmful effect: those who come regularly preoccupy the public arena which has been created and the people who come less frequently feel outstripped. Thus, nothing is easy. And still, stability and continunity are better than improvised changes.

Still, consultation and participatory democracy do not go without saying. Just now, we have to sail a stormy sea. How can the financial crises and the necessity to decrease the role of even municipal governments or the privatization of services, for example, be reconciled with a policy which is open for consultation? The current ideological discourse which underlies the ideal of a participation democracy is about rights. The state cannot unilaterally modify the framework of its citizens' lives without taking their opinion into consideration. This "typical-ideal" vision, however, does not always correspond to real life.

The citizen who is aware of his rights often also behaves like a consumer of local goods and services. He often prefers his merely personal benefit to a more coherent solution for the community. Just think of the choice when buying a private car – in view of an integrated transportation policy – or whether to live in the suburbs in contrast to an ideal of more densely populated cites. This is the choice people in North America have to make.

So, the consuming citizen lives next to the committed citizen. The individualistic consumer who is indifferent about the consequences of his action is in close contact with the citizen who is anxious to live with greater coherence. The one separates his waste meticulously, the other leaves his bin liners at night in public parks.

It has to be added that the privatization of certain services must not mean a loss of rights for the citizen nor a loss of participation possibilities. In other ways, it is certainly obliged to guarantee the proposed functions.

There is a tension in this respect between the city and the market which remains to be resolved.

The companies increasingly understand the necessity of the establishment of loyal contracts with their customers and of sharing certain rights. It is interesting to observe that all the Canadian banks are introducing the service of an ombudsman. In Toronto and Montreal, experiments are being carried out which ease access to the banking system for persons with a low income. Hydro-Québec for example, the company which supplies the province of Quebec with electricity, has likewise created a position for a complaint contact.

The efforts which were made from 1991–1992 by the city of Eugene in Oregon are also fascinating. Since it had to cut the budget, the city linked its citizens to this financial operation: is it necessary to raise taxes and at the same time to cut services? And if then, what taxes should be instituted, what cuts should be carried out? The whole difference between an ideologial discourse on values and the concrete budgeting practice and efficiency measures in the service sector became obvious.

1.6 Consultation Costs

Public consultation is not for free by a long stretch. It is expensive with regard to professional services, to popular brochures which are printed and distributed almost always for free, as to the rent of venues, technical equipment ranging from the microphone or the camera up to a computer, reports, studies, expert reports and counter-reports. Certain ideologists who are in favor of the consultation gladly hold the speeches on excellency. They try to multiply all sorts of demands, approaches, information. Is it necessary to send a delegation to Europe if we speak about a local incinerator? And if we speak about salvaging or recycling do we have to send a delegation to Seattle? – and so on.

In the field of environment, superior governments provide specific participation budgets which are destined for non-profit organizations. These subsidies render the payment of direct costs for participation possible (costs for transportation and maintenance, paper, photocopies, etc.) but sometimes also of associated costs, for example for legal or scientific expert reports. Do the same procedures need to be installed on a municipal level? The city of Quebec, for example, accepts only the assumption of transportation and baby-sitting costs. But the question remains to be answered.

How is it possible to make the city a platform where diverse local resources like colleges and universities, private enterprises which often have great competence at their disposal, or volunteer associations can collaborate? As much as we have to take care about rendering participation accessible, above all to those who are less privileged or to a specialized public, a policy which is too generous in the long run might engender some sort of dependence or a parallel bureaucracy.

1.7 Complex Decisions

How can the complexity of the technocratic analysis of the issues be reconciled with a popular approach, which is sometimes simplistic or else reductionalistic? The decisions we are taking must take into account countless political, strategical, technological, economic, historical, cultural and ethical considerations. But the media like to simplify, to lock themselves up in a dual logic, looking for the good and the bad ones. We all have had the experience of being obliged to give an account of a study or a report which comprises 200 pages. And then a reporter comes and points his microphone at you and asks you to summarize everything within 30 seconds.

On the contrary, there are the advocates of a direct democracy who wish that the elected representatives' only right is the execution of the decisions which were made by the citizens beforehand. Aren't these people the reverse picture of another widely spread tendency which is a governing by radar, through opinion polls on public opinion? Floating due to a volatile opinion, the administration might lose the coherence of its decisions, to forget about continuity when it implements a priority or a long-term vision.

1.8 Tensions Between Quantity and Quality

Do we need to aim for masses and be satisfied with relatively superficial opinions when consulting, or aim at smaller numbers and obtain much more developed opinions? I do not think that both are possible. The questionnaire with profound questions chases the multitude. But what is gained by the small group in view of large information and rigorous analysis is lost in view of the representation. The NGOs (non-governmental organizations) have the wind in their sails and they have acquired an immense credibility, thanks to their competence and the commitment to their conviction. Aren't these qualities fragile and precarious, don't they always have to be conquered? Do we have to demand – as it is in certain fields in the case of the United States – that an NGO which asks to participate in a consultation submit its list of official members and its bugdet?

Conversely, technology now permits the use of flexible and easily accessible means. For example, a telephone number can be installed so that everybody can state their opinion on a certain question. The Internet system offers an extraordinary range of possibilities, at the same time for information to flow fast and for a multitude of those intervening to inform others about their opinion or to complete the information at their disposal. And still, the Internet presupposes users with a computer and a modem: in 82 percent of the cases these are men as in the region of Ottawa-Carleton (Graham and Philips: 28). Once again, the democratic ideal is subject to a distortion in favour of the social and intellectual status of a minority.

In order to compensate for these restrictions it seems therefore that we have to act in any possible field at the same time, that is to say, to implement diverse and additional means to establish quality approaches towards a limited public and those which are less refined towards a larger public. But all this does not give us shelter from all sorts of slips, technocratic slips of the consultant or strategic slips of the activists. Hence, vigilance and innovation are necessary.

In the field of technology we like to speak about the establishment of technological security networks. These networks facilitate the circulation of information and criticism, and for innovations it offers the possibility of finding their real field of implementation. We think that in the regional, provincial, national and international area such security networks are indispensable for municipal life. The network which was implemented by the Bertelsmann Foundation has already proved to be a model, since ten cities which are themselves linked to important local networks have the opportunity to exchange information, to compare experiences and to communicate about innovations in order to achieve the best performances.

1.9 Revival of Elitism

Of course, participation has its adversaries. Some criticize it for reasons which could be described as intrinsic because it imposes deadlines, demands resources and makes the processes difficult. There are disastrous experiences like the one in the region of Toronto where despite a stack of studies and consultations a solution for the waste problem could not be found. When a consultation lasts for years it gets stuck. However, there is also still an extrinsic criticism about participation. It derives from the elitist democracy. Without saying it too loudly, its advocates believe that democracy is not made for the people, that it is the task of those with knowledge and capacity and that the good people will follow anyway. These opponents are thus denouncing the timidity of the elected representatives to take decisions and to wallow in a "consultative fogbank."

In an observation of great interest, Graham and Phillips inform us that we are actually witnessing the emergence of a new elite. They say that these people pretend to live according to international standards and that they are completely disinterested in democracy and the living conditions of less fortunate citizens. Whereas the traditional elites willingly get involved in religious, social, charitable matters or even in the defense of personal rights, we are witnessing the emergence of a new class of rich people who are worried about mobility and personal achievement. They live indifferently in Toronto, Los Angeles, Paris or Tokyo according to the market conditions and the modes of their small group to which they belong (Graham and Phillips: 26–27). These people are disinterested in the public cause. They only get involved through lobbying when their own interests are at stake. If the gap between the rich who isolate themselves and the poor who are increasingly marginalized gets wider the challenges for municipal democracy become both more urgent and more complex.

1.10 Tensions Between Political and Administrative Machinery

The reason for a resistance to participation is often the administrative machinery itself. Indeed, administration has its own logic, structures and areas of competence. The experience drawn out of the past 30 years shows clearly that there is a fight between professionals and the citizens who wish to participate. In certain cases, the resistance comes for example from the union machinery which is required to protect the interests of its members from the "caprices" of the public sector: opening hours, anonymity, complaint service. Most of the time the discontent predominates. It is a refusal to share a part of the power: the power of information, of authority and above all of setting priorities. It is rare that the resistance is shown openly. But it manifests itself in a hidden way, so the technocratic machinery comes to contradict the will which is declared by the political authority.

Indeed, in the public sector on a federal, provincial or municipal level it often happens that the technocratic machinery contradicts the declared will of the political authority. A policy of consultation and participation only makes sense if all officials understand and accept the demands. It is not important whether we speak of citizens, consumers or users, whether we speak of services offered by the public or the private sector. The challenges remain the same: taking the best decisions, sharing the power.

Administrators and the administered have a love-hate relationship.

"The relation between the citizens and the representatives is a permanent challenge in any society and is always a reason to cause tensions. While the superiors and the officials are theoretically and really serving the city and its organization, the "beneficiaries" of the city, however, esteem the costs for the services too high. They grumble, criticize, denounce even if they finally obey, pay their taxes, ask for permission and adhere to the regulations. We should mistrust a too optimistic picture which would transform former times into a golden age and the present time to hell, or vice versa. When Lewis Mumford mentions the 4000-year-old cities of ancient Egypt he remarks the following: 'The city becomes a prison whose inhabitants are strictly observed. The city wall and the gate guards do not have to fulfill only a symbolic but an effective and practical role: compared to this our modern cities are incredibly tolerant places. But there are still shortcomings.'" (Beauchamp 1993: 1)

Thus, a challenge of priority for the successful implementation of an efficient and sustainable policy is the change of the officials' conduct and attitudes towards the public. Here, we are speaking about the problems of the enterprize's culture.

1.11 Consulting at the Head of the Decision-Making Process

In Quebec, we have recently had discussions on the implementation of the possible resort to a referendum for the citizens. The referendum is neither complete nor perfect. It is not a productive consultation, even less is it a negotiation about something that would be acceptable for the majority of the citizens. They must have the possibility to assess the impacts and point out all representations which they consider appropriate. The results of a referendum are, by definition, a choice between two polarized positions, whereas the best option often arises from a consensus, explored, negotiated or discussed compromises.

At the moment, we consider the referendum a last resort which is used by the municipal council for major issues for which other mechanisms did not give enough clarity.

2. The City of Quebec

We have briefly described some of our convictions and opinions on participation, its challenges, its limits and its stakes. It is helpful to bring back the experience of the City of Quebec into its context.

2.1 Historical Background

Every city is unique, of course. This applies to Quebec for several reasons. Quebec sees itself as the most ancient city of North America. Samuel de Champlain chose in 1608 for the foundation of a settlement a narrowed part of the St. Lawrence River which the Indians called Quebec. From the very beginning, Quebec was the center of the French colonial authority in America, of what was then called Canada or New France.

The wars and rivalries between France and England very rapidly became wars between the French and English colonies in America. In the year 1760, Canada or New France became a part of England. Ancient New France gained a certain political status and the recognition of its French character. This historical origin explains the fact that today Quebec is still a city which is mainly French-speaking, the capital of the Province of Quebec and foyer of the French culture in America. This also explains the particular role of the State of Quebec within the Canadian Confederation.

Today, the City of Quebec has 170,000 inhabitants and is part of the large region of Quebec which totals 650,000 inhabitants. Its municipal council consists of a mayor, who is elected by universal vote, and 20 councillors, who are elected by their constituencies. The City of Quebec, which hosts the Province of Quebec government, is a jolly mix of old and new. It has kept the vestiges of the French era to such an extent that Vieux Quebec (the old part of Quebec) is now a UNESCO reserve of world historic heritage. But Quebec also has problems like other city centers in North America: the exodus to the suburbs and its tendency to run down city centers.

2.2 From Representation to Participation

The local power in Quebec and in Canada remains modest; it is delegated and rather restricted. The cities are established through the provincial authority which makes sure that municipalities – contrary to natural persons who are allowed to do anything that is not prohibited – can only do what they have been officially allocated by the provincial authority.

These limitations inherent to municipal power, however, must not be used as an excuse for the elected authorities to do as little as possible. Incidentally, the population expects a lot of their local government whose limitations of jurisdiction they misunderstand. While the municipalities in Canada played historically rather the role of managers for practical problems (for services like road maintenance, drinking water and waste water, managing waste, leisure activities – and on a much larger scale – the planning of the municipal territory), the citizens' expectations are taking shape and changing towards a real political problem.

Since 1960, we have thus been witnessing an increasing demand for the implementation of a participatory democracy which would correct and complement the representative democracy. Two requests are often made: more involvement by the citizens and possibly a better distribution of power; a better articulation on the local life in districts or the council which implies the goal to promote local life. This very strong idea refers to notions like territoriality and nearness, which are constituent for the city.

2.3 The Local Request for Democracy

The democratic participation movement seems to be paradoxical. There were revolutions of ideas and societies. A generation of sociologists, workers and social organisers, specialists in political sciences and in town and country planning who were trained in the United States and France imported concepts on "community development," democratic participation and direct democracy. They wanted to implement all this in the working-class districts of big cities, above all in Montreal and Quebec. But on the spot, the first efforts rather failed as if the traditional structure had resisted.

If the cities resist, the provincial state tries on its part to extend the public participation through its interventions in the field of environment and town and country planning, thus a municipal framework could be achieved.

The quest for democracy in the field of environment was very heated. In 1972, a first act on the quality of the environment already established a right to information on the environmental situation and founded a council for environment which is authorized to consult the population on its own initiative. In 1978, the provincial government of Quebec introduced the assessment and impact examination procedure which provides the realization of a study on the impacts of those projects (stated through regulations) which are likely to be ecologically harmful. The regulation also provides the publication of the impact study, a public information period as a right for all citizens or a group of citizens to demand a public hearing on the intended project.

In 1978, the provincial government decided to impose participation methods in the field of town and country planning. Two of four principles, on which the Loi québecoise sur l'aménagement et l'urbanisme (*Quebec act on town and country planning*) is based, have direct effects on public consultation:
– Town and country planning is first of all defined as a political and not only as a technical question.
– Via information and participation, the citizens are included in diverse stages of the elaboration process and in the revision of the instruments used for town and country planning.

For this purpose, the act stipulates that the municipality has to set up a consultative committee for town planning whose members are mainly residents. It gives its opinion on the passing or modification of regulations on town planning, on minor infringements and the protection of the cultural assets to the municipal council. The act also provides for precise consultation procedures of the population which have to be carried out by the municipal council when regulations on town planning are to be modified or adopted. Referendums are also possible on subjects like amendments on the distribution of land for redevelopment or on borrowing regulations. If a sufficient number of citizens sign the register designed for this purpose, the municipal council has to withdraw its regulation project or to submit it to approval via referendum.

The cities of Quebec and Montreal are not subject to this act. They are governed by autonomous charters which can only be modified by the Assemblée nationale de Quebec (*National Assembly of Quebec*). It has to be emphasized that, in practice, the legislator takes the municipal councils' opinion of Montreal and Quebec seriously into account before he starts modifying the charter of one or the other municipality.

The reactions of the municipalities of Quebec to the measures on participation which were imposed through an act by the central authority were in general restrained. The municipalities have had the tendency to adhere precisely to this act. This, however, did not keep them from following their own way.

At the municipal level we had to wait until the mid 1980s, for the change of the municipal council's members through elections. It is finally the representative democracy itself which progressively installs the participatory democracy.

2.4 The New Participatory Democracy of the City of Quebec

For the current municipal council of the city of Quebec, the reorganization of the municipal democracy is a strategic issue of the highest priority. In November 1991, we introduced the policy and the guidelines of public consultations of the city of Quebec. In 1995, we carried out a systematic assessment of this policy and in April 1996, the council adopted its current policy of public consultation.

Our policy is based on the conviction that public consultation is an important vehicle for democratic participation and for the will to involve the public through simple, clear and effective methods – which facilitate the access to preliminary facts and studies, a debate on the principles and values, a presence of concerned groups and social strata, information on the decisions which are taken by the council in the wake of diverse consultations. Through the variability of methods, our policy aims at two traditional objectives of participation: taking the best decisions while guaranteeing information in two directions and debating on principles and values; sharing the power without necessarily mixing up the roles and prerogatives of each protagonist.

We consult whenever we have to make a decision on an issue which has a certain importance or which is controversial and where there is room for maneuver. The general rule is: if issues only refer to a district, they are transferred to the consultative authorities of that district. If the issues are relevant for the population of several districts or for the entire city, they come under the authority of the municipal council which decides on the adequate methods which are to be employed.

2.5 The Council Consultations

If a question is interesting for the whole city or several districts, we ask the population, preferably via a public hearing which is led by a non-judicial hearing committee.

In addition to that, each year the members of the council invite the citizens of their respective district to participate in a public meeting. Councillors present the most important issues and projects they are working on. They receive feedbacks, and comments from their constituencies.

Also, the municipal council established consultative commissions which are forums where the elected representatives, public representatives and citizen groups can explore new questions and make recommendations to the municipal council. There already exist two commissions: the Commission sur la sécurité publique (*Public Security Commission*) and the Commission Femmes et Ville (*Women and City Consultative Commission*). Two further commissions are intended: one for the economic development and another for the environment.

The public consultation policy also intends the use of referendums on a major issue for which the use of other instruments of public consultation were not sufficient to give an appropriate clarity to the municipal council. We prefer to work at the head of the decision making process – with the population. The referendum is considered a last resort process which is initiated by the municipal council.

2.6 Women and City Consultative Commission

As an example, we would like to mention the Commission Consultative Femmes et Ville (*Women and City Consultative Commission*). In a nutshell, the role of the Commission is to act as a consultant or advisor to the municipal council on everything concerning women and the city.

The commission officially began its work in March 1993. Its first objective was to take stock of the situation and needs of women in the city of Quebec as regards municipal policies, programs, equipment and services.

The commission is made up of 17 voting members. The mayor is automatically the chair of the commission, but can recommend that the municipal council appoint another chairperson. Other elected members of the council must belong to the commisssion, including a member of the executive committee and at least one member who does not belong to the party in power. Citizens are appointed by the council for a two-year mandate and are chosen so as to make the commission as representative as possible of the realities faced by city women. The commission must be composed of at least 50 percent of citizens serving in an individual capacity. The city manager is a non-voting member of the commission. He can recommend the nomination of a city employee as his representative.

The commission generally meets once a month. Within the framework of its mandate, the commission can also initiate public hearings, with the authorization of the executive committee.

The sessions are presided over by the chairperson and support is provided by the Bureau of Public Consultations within the Department of Communications and External Relations. Reports on public meetings are drawn up and made available to all citizens who request them. The members are governed by a code of ethics and have access to the training they need to fulfill their role.

First of all, the commission met with the people in charge of municipal and related services: police, town planning, engineering, leisure and community life, environment, information and complaints bureau, municipal housing office.

These meetings allowed the commission to become acquainted with the municipal administration, to highlight the links that could exist between the activities of these departments and the problem areas experienced by women in an urban setting and to draw up a preliminary report on the needs of women in connection with these departments.

Safety, urban development, housing, economic conditions, transportation, leisure and democracy were at the heart of their concerns.

After this spadework, the commission wanted to hear what women in the city of Quebec had to say, in order to draw up a clear picture of the situation of women and to determine with them the direction of possible solutions. Two methods were chosen in order to reach the largest possible number of women: a series of four meetings in each sector of the city, and a public hearing.

The consultation formula was made to make participation easy and to reach young people, the elderly, mothers – all the women who do not usually take part in the city's public consultations. No preparation or registration formality was required. A free on-site baby-sitting service was organized. Information was disseminated in places where women often go.

During the meeting, the participants could express themselves freely and simply, without a microphone, in small working groups, concerning their experiences and desires in connection with five themes given priority by the commission: safety, housing, transportation and traffic, leisure and community life.

The meetings in each sector were followed by a public hearing that provided an opportunity to present eleven memos. These memos came from organizations or groups of women and covered the entire mandate of the commission, actually going beyond the suggested themes.

This procedure provided the raw material for the report that the Commission on Women and the City presented to the municipal council in the spring of 1995. This report includes 60 concrete recommendations. For the next two years the most important mandate of the commission will be to monitor the implementation of these recommendations.

2.7 Public Participation in the Districts

Our efforts to renew the municipal policy aims also at the twelve districts of the city of Quebec. We intend to create a district council for each district, made up of members who are elected in a district public assembly. The district council is an autonomous legal body which is subsidized and supported by the city. Its mandate is to consult the population of its territory on reglementary issues and on the nature and quality of municipal services. It is equally authorized to take initiatives, to carry out consultations and studies and to put forward new ideas in order to improve the life in the districts. In 1993, the city initiated two pilot experiments in the districts of Vieux-Limoilou and Saint-Jean-Baptiste.

In the other ten districts, we simply installed consultative committees, whose members are nominated by the city council on the recommendation of active groups in each district. These committees guarantee that in their district the policy on public consultation is implemented.

The sphere of activity of the two experimental district councils is much broader than that of the consultative committees which are mainly concerned with town planning.

The two experiments were evaluated positively. The city of Quebec will support the implementation of district councils in the other districts. The district councils will not be imposed. The implementation of a district council will be the result of a formal request signed by at least 300 citizens. Also, a formal vote will be held during a public meeting open to all residents and business people of the district. In the absence of a district council, the consultative committee will remain.

2.8 The District of Vieux-Limoilou

As an example, we would like to mention the district council in Vieux-Limoilou.

At the beginning of its mandate, the district council held two public meetings in order to consult citizens about their needs and concerns. The discussion workshops focused on different subjects such as: urban development, the environment, safety in the neighborhood, community and cultural life and commercial thoroughfares. After these meetings, the neighborhood council submitted its action plan to a public consultation. The priorities adopted aimed at improving leisure activities offered for young people, transforming an abandoned fire station into a cultural center, fixing up back alleys and developing Limoilou's urban heritage. Working committees made up of two members of the district council as well as citizen volunteers were formed for this purpose. We will give a more detailed account of two of the principal themes (giving a face-lift to back alleys and developing the urban heritage).

Among the cases adopted, the project for sprucing up the neighborhood alleys brought together a number of residents. The present condition of the alleys (pavement in poor condition, lack of lighting, not very much greenery) and the possibility of improving them were raised by a good many people.

The committee's mandate was to clarify the legal status of the alleys, the property titles, the existence of a right-of-way and the city's power in this area; to carry out a survey of the present condition of the alleys; and finally to draw up an experimental financial support program for fixing up the alleys.

The mobilization of the population in order to form alley committees was carried out during the public meetings of the council, through articles published in the neighborhood newspaper and by way of radio programs. A document drawn up by the committee was given to people interested in discussing the matter with their neighbors. Two alley committees made up of adjacent owners presented a development proposal to the district council. The latter submitted this proposal to city hall, along with parameters for application of a new subsidy program. The city granted the amount requested and a team of municipal employees are now working on drawing up the program. Five alley committees have already submitted their project and a sixth committee is now being formed.

The heritage committee was created following the demolition of a chapel and a parish hall to make room for the construction of condominiums. A group of residents got together and informed the district council of their disappointment. A committee made up of ordinary citizens, some of whom were experts in history and architecture, took on the mission of sensitizing the owners and the municipal administration to the importance of preserving heritage buildings in the neighbourhood.

An inventory of significant buildings and sites is being carried out. As the person in charge of the project reminds us: "This inventory should be presented in a public assembly for ratification, then communicated to the elected representatives and the different municipal departments." The committee has adopted criteria for choosing buildings and sites: age, state of preservation, originality, uniqueness and significance for the neighborhood. More than 108 buildings, sites or combinations of both have been identified and categorized according to a system based on use and measurement of volume. Slides of each of the buildings and sites listed have been taken in collaboration with students of the local college. These visual documents were used when citizens were consulted in the summer of 1995. A photographic exhibition was held.

The committee completed its document and drew up the recommendations that were submitted for public approval last December. Eighteen recommendations were drawn up, among them:

- to make property owners aware of the interest that their building represents for the neighbourhood and to inform them specifically about support programs for preservation initiatives
- to notify the district council of all applications for permits for demolition or important transformations of these buildings
- to adjust support programs for residential renovation to cover work for "preserving," maintaining or replacing in their original form the following architectural components: openings, railings, outside staircases and porches, cornices and parapets
- To support and supervise the maintenance of trees located on private lots.

At the end of 1995 the district council presented its recommendations to the municipal council.

The power to take the initiative was also exercised through five presentations submitted within the framework of public hearings. The first was presented to the Bureau d'audiences publiques sur l'environnement (gouvernement du Quebec) [*Bureau of Public Hearings on the Environment (provincial government of Quebec)*]. It concerned the coming of a co-generation project (use of steam from the municipal incinerator for the production of electricity). In its presentation, the district council expressed a number of concerns of the citizens of Vieux-Limoilou. It explained how the environment of the neighborhood is already adversely affected by the proximity of a paper mill and of the municipal incinerator. The Bureau des audiences publiques adopted several of the district council's recommendations. In addition, the project will be moved farther east in order to limit its effects on the quality of life.

Finally, four presentations were submitted to public hearings held by the city of Quebec: A Master Plan for a Municipal Bicycle Network, an Advisory Commission on Women and the City, a Development Plan for the Banks of the St. Charles River and an Outline for restructuring a large urban park with local and regional appeal, located near the neighborhood.

In a wholly different area, the district council used its power to take the initiative in order to facilitate dialogue between some citizens and city hall and solve a local problem. Traffic problems were being caused at a crossroads by the narrowness of one of the streets. All those who lived on the street and in the surrounding area were invited to an evening session. Following this meeting, during which courses of action for possible solutions were identified jointly by citizens and the concerned municipal departments, the problem was solved.

On another front, the district council was the first to be consulted by the Department of Town Planning concerning revision of the neighborhood development plan. A general portrait of the neighborhood focusing on the following problem areas was drawn up: environment, transportation and parking, safety, leisure activities and community life, culture, heritage, housing, urban design, commercial and economic development. The neighborhood development plan presents a statement of the present situation. It contains broad orientations as well as related objectives. An action plan is also being developed in line with the orientations of the neighborhood development plan. This action plan includes concrete means to attain the goals, as well as deadlines and costs involved.

2.9 The Resources

The implementation of our participation policy is entrusted to the Bureau des consultations publiques (*Office for Public Consultations*). It comprises five full-time professionals. This office has the mandate to supervise the entire operations which are authorized by the executive committee or the city council. Moreover, we make sure that the varied municipal services grant their support and their competence for the implementation of our policy.

Conclusion

Opting for participation means somehow to live dangerously. It means to maintain an awakened and critical public opinion which will quickly recognise the faults of our decisions. This is a dangerous asceticism. One can only commit oneself with sincerity and convictions. Thus, others prefer the way of secrets, they use the stroke of strength, which means that they inform after the stroke has been carried out; or they are even in favor of a bluff-consultation which pretends that the people are listened to. This is a strategy with a boomerang effect which turns back quite quickly against its initiator.

We think that in the long run and for the benefit of the city, a policy of openness towards public participation is advantageous and appropriate. It is the way of the greatest effort. And above all, it is the way with the highest responsibility.

Literature

Beauchamp, André, Le questionnaire et les publics pour une collaboration fructueuse. Ville de Montréal, Bureau de consultation de Montréal. 1993.

Duclos, Denis, De la civilité: Comment les sociétés apprivoisent la puissance. Paris 1993.

Godbout, Jacques T., La participation contre la démocratie. Montreal 1983.

Godbout, Jacques T. (ed.), La participation politique. Leçons des dernières décennies. Quebec 1991.

Graham, Katherine A. and Phillips, Susan D., Making Public Participation More Effective. Issues for Local Government (soon to be published).

Regards sur la démocratie. In: FORCES, No. 96, winter 1991–1992.

Viveret, Patrick, "Réintégrer la 'zone' dans la ville.". Le Monde diplomatique, p. 29, October 1991.

City of Neuchâtel: From the Reform of the Local Management Structures to the Concept of Partnership

Monika Dusong

Executive Summary 132
1. Reform of the Local Management Structures 133
   1.1 Lines of the Reform............................... 134
   1.2 The Spirit of the Reform 136
   1.3 Towards a City Management Concept................. 137
2. The City of Neuchâtel as a Partner 139
   2.1 Partnership with the Staff 139
   2.2 Partnership Amongst Departments
       and Other Public Entities.......................... 141
   2.3 Partnership with the Citizen-Client.................. 143
   2.4 Partnership with Associations 145
   2.5 Partnership with Business Life 145
3. Conclusions... 146

Executive Summary

Under the pressure caused by the degradation of its financial situation, the City of Neuchâtel has started a reform of local administration structures. However, we had neither a theoretical basis, nor a consultant from outside the organisation to guide our reflections. We chose to resort to the resources necessary for the modernisation process within local administration itself.

To reinvent, as it were, the State structures means to have the courage of systematically calling into question:
– the management concepts,
– the work procedures and methods,
– the organisation.

Management reform necessitates the following additional elements:
1. reflection about the services,
2. definition of quality standards,
3. quest for simplifications,
4. decompartmentalisation among departments,
5. collaboration at every level,
6. effective management tools,
7. decentralised management,
8. coordination.

The reform principles are undoubtedly the same everywhere. You cannot straighten out a burdened financial situation without:
– restructuring,
– re-proportioning,
– the readjustment of certain services,
– the setting-up of management tools,
– a profound change, or even a cultural revolution of the public utilities.

What differs from one public community to the next is the management style, the way of effecting these changes. We must unite forces rather than oppose them, find solutions together rather than impose them, see to it that the process is perceived as necessary, stimulating and status-enhancing for the civil service.

Our will to seek the adherence of the different actors in public life ended up in a political concept, the leitmotiv of which could be *partner-*

ship. It is expressive of the fact that we consider the reform as being everybody's concern.

The basic concept of partnership covers all actors:
- the staff,
- the other public communities,
- the citizens and inhabitants,
- the associations and
- the economic circles.

All the partnership actions integrate at least one of the following criteria:
1. information,
2. advice,
3. consultation,
4. participation, collaboration and
5. integration.

The reform process will, however, take time. We need a sustained effort at innovation and an ever-widening basis of theoretical knowledge. There is no unique solution, no unique method – what matters are the innovative spirit and the reform process.

1. Reform of the Local Management Structures

From 1988, the City of Neuchâtel has known serious financial problems which ended up in the refusal of the 1991 budget by the State Council (Canton executive). Urgent and selective measures allowed a certain upturn. Thus, for example, the maintenance costs were greatly reduced. Obviously, such measures could not be applied in the long run without jeopardising the preservation of the patrimony.

At that time, the economic indicators were significantly deteriorating, since Switzerland was entering a serious recession, the consequences of which will still be felt for several years. At the same time, the Canton, which was itself having financial problems, transferred part of its charges onto the communes. In this unfavourable context it was essential to find the means to cure the finances in a lasting way. To straighten out one's finances and put one's financial house in order can be the fruit only of a joint will of all the concerned authorities. Considering the complexity of the public finances, it requires a vast number of approaches and analyses. Reductionistic and simplistic methods cannot be suitable.

So, under the pressure caused by the degradation of its financial situation, the City of Neuchâtel has started a reform of the local administration structures. However, we had neither a theoretical basis, nor a consultant from outside the organisation to guide our reflections. We chose to resort to the resources necessary to the modernisation process within the local administration itself. This pragmatic step consisted in finding solutions together with our collaborators, and it allowed us to extricate ourselves from the most pressing financial problems. At the same time, it favoured a spirit of creativeness and of innovation within the local administration. Endowed with a greater decision making autonomy, the departments could develop entrepreneurial thinking and take up the bet to test out new methods of carrying out their assignments.

1.1 Lines of the Reform

To reinvent State structures means to have the courage to systematically put into question:
– *the management concepts*
   With its numerous enterprises having a certain autonomy, the local administration forms a real holding company. Where the assignments have some similarity, local administration today is more and more inspired by the management rules of the private sector. This is facilitated by the modernisation of management tools.
   In the light of the economic situation, all the management methods were subjected to a systematic re-examination, whether accounting techniques, subsidies, wage policies or profitability calculations. The introduction of analytic accounting was carried out as a priority in branches having to know their cost prices and it will go on in order to give the departments the information necessary for an effective management.
   The generalisation of internal charges allows today a real analysis of

cost prices and therefore a comparison of the service costs with those of a private enterprise.
- *the work procedures and methods*
  It is just at the moment of setting-up computer tools, that it is essential to seize the opportunity to improve, to simplify and to rationalise the work procedures.
- *the organisation*
  A part-time job has been created for organisation issues. He/She intervenes in support of the concerned employees and on mandate of the various departments looking for possibilities to rationalise work and to increase their efficiency.

The management reform entails the following additional elements:

1. *Reflection about the services* a public community has to provide and about the usefulness of certain tasks:
   - What services do we provide?
   - Who, in the public or private sector, is in a better position to provide them?
   - Who else provides the same services? Can we collaborate?
   - Delegate?
   - Who is the recipient of the services?
   - At what price do we provide them?
   - Who pays and how (tariffs, taxes, assigned reserves)?
2. *To define the quality standards* for all the local administration activities. We must find the right measure. Perfectionism may be very expensive. It is not a matter of providing services at their top level, but at a fair level. The same analysis must intervene as far as the quantity of services provided is concerned.
3. *To seek simplifications* of procedures and organisations. This often is facilitated by providing data-processing equipment. Thus, the administration computerisation was speeded up. The registry office is the only department not yet computerised. However, the project is currently being examinedstudied. It is worth noting that the introduction of new tools is always accompanied by appropriate staff training.
4. *Decompartmentalisation among departments* through data networks and management by project, gathering all the employees concerned regardless of which department they "belong" to.

5. *Collaboration at every level:* state, communes, inter-municipal associations, private associations. The definition of competence centres as well as the task sharing end up in economies of scale and avoiding duplication of effort (e.g. computer agreements with the communes and the Canton, agreements with the SIS [Service d'Incendie et de Secours = fire brigade and rescue department], the health care centre). Sometimes an association is in a better position to carry out a task because it invites the citizens themselves to take a more active part in a cause.
6. *Effective management tools* which permit keeping and checking the accounts periodically such as monthly accounts, weekly lists of overspending, intermediate closings, Management Information System, extractors allowing analyses and simulations.
7. *Decentralised management* of the local administration in order to bring the decision centres close to the employees in charge, allowing them to assume overall management responsibility.
8. *Coordination* and consolidation of the systems in order to guarantee an overall view, a coherent guide-line, a common political will and equal treatment of departments.

1.2 The Spirit of the Reform

The reform principles are undoubtedly the same everywhere. You cannot straighten out a burdened financial situation without:
- restructuring,
- re-proportioning,
- the readjustment of certain services,
- the setting-up of management tools and
- a profound change, or even a cultural revolution of the public utilities.

What differs from one public community to the next is the management style, the way of carrying through these changes. We must unite forces rather than oppose them, find solutions together rather than impose them, see to it that the process is perceived as necessary, stimulating and status-enhancing for the civil service.

Our goal was, and still is, to master in that challenge.

We did not have the impression that we were running the reform in a special way. Only common sense guided our actions. We notice today that our solutions were similar, to a large extent, to those advocated in the various new concepts of local administration reforms. Even if it is undeniable that these concepts contain very good impetus for an in-depth reflection on the structures and the running of the local administration, we think that we must be careful not to apply theoretical models in a doctrinaire way. On the contrary, we are convinced that we must take into account the culture and experience of the local administration.

The best change is the one gaining the adherence of the concerned. The motivation and the stimulation to find specific solutions suited to local contexts are a guarantee for the success of a reform. We favour solutions which save money while developing the quality of the services for our citizens (e.g. the introduction of green waste collection). We seek measures allowing productivity and efficiency gains that make everyone feel like a winner. In this framework belong, for instance, the search for extending our employees' tasks (job enrichment), for in-house training encouragement and enhancing management by project.

1.3 Towards a City Management Concept

In 1993, the City of Neuchâtel was selected to represent Switzerland on the occasion of the Carl Bertelsmann Prize. This participation served as a guideline to a wider and more coherent reflection on the administration structures. Instead of being seen just as an end in itself, this nomination had the effect of stimulating the various reforms under way.

Thus, the members of the city council (government) fixed the priority targets for the whole local administration. It was based on the following findings:

The services of the local administration are often not well known. Whether right or wrong, they all seem of difficult access, and the necessary procedures or formalities sometimes look complicated. Thus it is necessary:
1. to better inform the citizen-client about the local administration services;
2. with respect to public interest, to adapt the services to the users' real needs by optimising the human and material resources available.

During joint seminars with elected council members and department heads, we elaborated the basics for applying participatory management methods.

In order to give concrete expression to these priorities, two lines were retained:
1. fixing of specific targets within the branches and the departments;
2. in order to avoid compartmentalisation, creation of a coordination committee whose goals are:
   - to draw up a list of the experiences made in the branches in order to share them and make them known,
   - to draw up a list of the services offered in order to better define them, and
   - to improve, in a general way, the citizen-client information.

In autumn 1995 we were asked to organise a training seminar for the mayors and the project managers of the Saarland communities, who were also involved in a reform process. The participants' interest was focused on concrete applications of various theoretical concepts.

This event offered an opportunity to group together the different actions coming within the scope of the fixed goals and thus obtain an overall view. At the same time, our department heads became aware that their actions came within a coherent whole. From the synthesis of the actions presented by all the departments a global concept clearly emerged which developed harmoniously around the partnership issue.

The setting-up of a concept facilitates understanding local administration activities. At this stage, we do a summing-up of the situation. It would be wrong to think that this concept will remain unchanged. On the contrary, it is still developing and simply shows our will to continue on this path.

2. The City of Neuchâtel as a Partner

Our will to seek the adherence of the different actors in public life ended up in a political concept whose leitmotiv could be called *partnership*. It is expressive of the fact that we consider the reform as being everybody's concern. The basic concept of partnership covers all actors:
- the staff,
- the other public communities,
- the citizens and inhabitants,
- the associations, and
- business life.

All the partnership actions integrate at least one of the following criteria:
- information,
- advice,
- consulting,
- participation, collaboration, and
- integration.

2.1 Partnership with the Staff

The local administration is the executive arm of the political will. We therefore need this first-rate partner in order to turn this new spirit into reality .

Our interest that the public services recover all their credit is evident. The myth of the civil servant adverse to any innovation must quickly disappear. We prefer to promote the image of the civil servant carrying out his/her tasks competently, in an innovative manner, with an enterprising mind and flexibility.

1. Collaboration with the managerial staff
   In order to get out of financial difficulties, the City Council naturally turned to the department heads and the employees. With them, the City Council wanted to find solutions to the serious problems facing the City. From them, it expected:
   - suggestions for reorganisation,
   - ideas for rationalisation,

- flexibility and ability to adapt,
- financial sacrifices.

2. Tools for human resources management and working conditions for the employees.

   The new part allotted to the civil servants was difficult to play. On the one hand, they had a lot to gain on several levels: in esteem, the extent of their tasks, autonomy and responsibilities. On the other hand, for some people there was a risk of losing some entitlements, of having to quit their routine and of being confronted with more demanding realities than previously. However, a good partnership is one in which both partners are winners. This prompted us to speed up the setting-up of management tools for human resources. Apart from the setting-up of a new evaluation of functions and of the systematisation of periodical interviews with employees, priority was accorded to the improvement of work conditions.

3. Concept of in-house training

   In order to accompany the changes caused by computerisation in an efficient and immediate way, we appointed an in-house trainer for computer office automation (Word, Excel, Access) and created a job of users' assistant job (hot-line).

   Since 1992, the budget devoted to in-house training has doubled. We particularly developed the program of training concerning management and human resources.

4. Working time management

   The employer expects staff to be flexible. In return he must offer the same flexibility, i.e. concerning the job organisation. Various programs were developed together with the staff. We aimed at three goals:
   - to allow people with a family to better meet their requirements both professional and domestic;
   - to take into account the unequal distribution of labour over the year;
   - to create and maintain jobs by various measures of job sharing.

   Optional modulation of the working time
   Possibility to temporarily reduce the annual activity rate, with the guarantee to return to one's initial status.

   Flexible working time management
   The working time management will no longer be carried out on a weekly basis, but on an annual basis, with certain constraints. This pro-

gram allowed the local administration to face up to the reduction of the working time from 41 to 40 hours. Together with a one percent cut in index-linked wages, the creation of 16 jobs and the maintenance of five jobs in the hospitals were made possible.

The maternity and adoption leaves
can be shared with the father, if he also is employed by the City. It is possible to split them up.

The non-paid prolonged maternity leaves
are, as a rule, granted with the guarantee to find the same job or an equivalent one.

Part-time work is encouraged as far as possible.

The choice is offered to take part of the vacations on a *part-time basis:* this will lengthen them and allows parents to fit in the school holidays better.

5-year tailor-made early retirement,
offering the choice of a decreasing activity rate. We thus could fill six jobs prematurely in 1995.

5. Integration of social problem cases

   Certain employees are no longer up to what their jobs demand; psychological problems often play a dominating role in the degradation of a professional situation. In order to avoid laying off these few employees, who would not be able to find another job, a structure aiming at integration rather than exclusion was created.

2.2 Partnership Amongst Departments and Other Public Entities

Often, it is possible to obtain substantial savings through the sharing of resources and a good definition of standards and of the competence centres.

1. Partnership within the local administration

Decompartmentalisation
Through computer networking of all the departments, and the definition of standards and of software, it is possible today to share data bases and to exchange information in a rational way.

Management by project
We group together the experts concerned with the same problem rather than send a project from one department to another.

The amalgamation of different departments is not easy and requires mental adaptation. In this context, we sought methods promoting change. The in-house working parties, interdirectional and targeted at particular projects, well meet the coordination needs. Moreover, the "Softmatch" method is speeding up the movement.

A method of change management: softmatch

The City of Neuchâtel had the chance of being chosen as a partner in the Eureka project, the goal of which is to test participative methods and change simulation. Indeed, the success of a change highly depends on its being accepted by staff. If the employees can participate in the setting-up of a new procedure or organisation, they get more involved in the project and they are more able to accompany the change in a constructive and efficient way.

Total quality management in the Industrial Department

Since 1987, the Industrial Department has committed itself to a procedure of total quality management (TQM), in order to better meet, and at a lesser cost, the expressed and implicit needs of the customers. Setting-up of TQM is effected along five different lines: the quality of the management, staff, environment, product and enterprise.

2. Partnership with other public entities

Systematic search for economies of scale and increased efficiency encouraged us to seek collaboration with other public entities. Two lines emerged:

Definition of competence centres
between the Canton and the City, especially in the computer domain. The City assures the informatics of 54 communes and of the health care domain, it is in charge of the hardware central buying office and of the hardware repair centre, while the Canton is in charge of the Canton communication network and of the printing centre. Moreover, the City of Neuchâtel has signed a collaboration agreement concerning informatization with the other French-speaking cantons as well as with the cities of Lausanne and Geneva.
Services provided as representative
the City assumes several management mandates for the Canton and other communes.

2.3 Partnership with the Citizen-Client

The reform was first started in order to redress our deteriorated financial situation. However, this is not a goal in itself. Reform is useful if it allows the citizens to increase their quality of life in the city. We must strengthen the feeling of belonging and of identification.

Our most important partner is undoubtedly the citizen. The framework defined above is especially well suited to this category:

1. Information

Only recently have public entities been fully aware of the importance of communication and information in general. At every level, people can cooperate better if they know about the projects and the reasons for an action. Our will to improve the information flow, either by the City newspaper, by media, by thematic exhibitions, by open days or by our presence at commercial exhibitions organised in the City, has resulted in a number of activities.

2. Counseling

Citizens sometimes need advice. This is naturally the case when they have personal problems. But advice can also be useful regarding energy savings, procedures concerning various permits, prevention (police and "SIS"), setting-up of budgets for tax settlement, etc. All the departments have created centres for specific counseling.

3. Consulting

Information must not be a one way exercise. Often, it is very useful for the City Council to know the points of view of people who are directly concerned by a project or a measure. The solutions they advocate guide our activities. This is the reason why we have intensified the opportunities given to the citizens and to staff to give us their point of view.

Projects concerning traffic and city planning lend themselves particularly well to this form of partnership. Moreover, a survey made of the quality of reception in the City resulted in accelerating the reorganisation of the registration office, at the premises level and at staffing and training levels as well.

4. Participation, collaboration

We invite inhabitants and certain groups to take part directly in a municipal task. Many actions come within this concept: the campaign led for the introduction of composting, guided tours in the forests, planting by pupils, sport for everybody, Town Hall at disposal for various events, development of the pedestrian zone in close collaboration with the shopkeepers, etc.

5. Integration

This form of partnership is certainly the most advanced. It is aimed mainly at groups of people who risk being left out of a decision process or to be marginalized because of their specificity. Some examples are listed below:
- the creation of youth parliaments highlights our will to take the young seriously and to give them the opportunity to express themselves and put forward their ideas;
- active policy in the employment domain, through integration programs destined for the unemployed and for the young in search of their first job. More than 600 people benefit each year of these programs;
- various aids for non-government cultural circles and for foreigners.

2.4 Partnership with Associations

Missions of general interest do not necessarily need to be executed exclusively by the public agencies. Delegating certain tasks to private actors has been a part of our management culture for quite a long time. It undoubtedly promotes increased participation of the citizens who devote a particular interest to a specific domain.

In this framework it is essential to systematically analyse the new tasks from that angle before the public agencies assume them. Moreover, it is useful to examine if any task might not be carried out by an association in a more effective way and closer to the users.

Collaborations with associations assumes various shapes:
- putting at their disposal premises either free of charge or at favourable terms;
- regular subsidies or deficit guarantee for cultural activities;
- supply of services in kind by furnishing staff and equipment, etc.;
- management mandate delegated to a non-government entity;
- subsidizing in order to favour the creation of places in private nurseries and day-care centres.

2.5 Partnership with Business Life

Promoting the economy represents a clear political priority. In this domain, partnership spirit is particularly important. The means at our disposal to establish a climate of partnership once again take on various forms:
- offering sites at advantageous rates;
- purchase of premises by the City in order to be able to meet business needs as quickly as possible;
- help in finding appropriate premises for a new site or an extension;
- community investments in order to facilitate an establishment (gas, electricity, drainage, etc.);
- management by project, uniting all departments concerned by an establishment, in order to speed up procedures;
- advice when establishing blueprints for district development and buildings;
- simplifying laws and procedures for obtaining permits;
- energy pricing favourable to business;
- investment policy at an especially high level in order to support construction business and civil engineering sectors;
- institution of a special fund in order to allow an additional five million Swiss francs investment in 1993, which maintained about 50 jobs during a whole year in the building industry and civil engineering sectors;
- regular meetings between the City Council and the most important enterprises.

Conclusions

The difficult economic situation and our intention of stabilizing the finances of the City of Neuchâtel have prompted us to implement the reform of administrative structures. Beyond the financial upturn, we aimed at an improvement of the public utilities and at increasing the proximity to the citizens. Together with the staff, whose participation is essential to the success of such a process, we have systematically put into question management concepts, as well as procedures and work methods.

We note with satisfaction that our efforts bear fruit. Even if hard times still await us, we think we have now the necessary tools and spirit to face them. We made a significant step in the desired direction. We are convinced that we are well on our way: our solutions are currently being developed and tested. The process will take some time. To unfold the reform effects in the long run, we need to continue the innovation effort and to widen the bases of theoretical knowledge. We know we have still a lot to learn and to improve.

However, we think that there is no unique method, no unique solution. What is important is the will to carry through changes, to open our minds to new management methods, to dare to question things seemingly well established and unchanged for decades. The method does not matter – it is the innovative spirit that brings the necessary impetus to reforming the administration structures. What matters is the process.

Tilburg: Competition in Local Government
N.G. Maij

Executive Summary 150
1. Introduction 151
   1.1 Sources of Inefficiency in the Public Sector 152
   1.2 Conditions for Implementing Competition
       in Local Government............................... 154
   1.3 Different Forms of Competition 155
2. Using the Market...................................... 156
   2.1 Making Internal Buying Non-Compulsory............. 156
       2.1.1 Undesired Effects on the Demand Side........... 157
       2.1.2 Undesired Effects on the Supply Side............ 157
   2.2 Allowing Outside Selling 159
   2.3 Buying in the Market.............................. 161
       2.3.1 Contracting Out............................. 161
       2.3.2 Compulsory Competitive Tendering (CCT) 166
3. Imitating the Market 170
   3.1 Business Process Redesign 170
   3.2 Financial Incentives............................... 173
       3.2.1 Employees.................................. 173
       3.2.2 Agencies 174
4. Conclusions 177
Literature.. 180

Executive Summary

Governmental organizations are characterized by the influence of politicians. The management style of politicians – sometimes inappropriate – their attention to their relationships with employees and unions to the detriment of attention to the quality of public services, and sometimes their ideological resistance against market competition can stand in the way of improvements by competition.

This paper describes how competition can help to create a better local government. Objectives of competition are (1) increasing efficiency and (2) a better quality of public services. Competitive incentives can be implemented by using the market or by imitating the market.

Using the market is possible when the production of public goods and services by a private provider is a real alternative. The abolition of compulsory internal buying is one way to create competition. A communal department will have to prove its competitiveness in comparison with other providers. Another way to create competition is allowing a communal department to sell outside its internal market. This enables the department to compete on, for instance, regional or national markets with other private or public organizations. It also provides the possibility to strive for economies of scale. Both methods can be used as a first step towards privatization of the department.

Contracting out to private suppliers is also a way to create competition by using the market. Two criteria play a role in the decision whether or not to contract out production. Firstly, efficiency plays an important role. If the production is contracted out to a private monopolist, an increase of efficiency is at least doubtful. Secondly, the strategic importance of a public good or service plays an important role. If a service is vital for the citizens' well-being, high monitoring costs will arise in order to minimize the risk of a failure. These monitoring costs diminish the advantage of contracting out. In the United Kingdom, Compulsory Competitive Tendering is used to increase the efficiency and quality of communal production. This system places communal departments in competition with other suppliers on the market. A study by the Institute for Local Government shows that efficiency increases can be realized.

Imitating the market can be used when there is no real market for the provision of public goods and services. Such a situation can arise from legal restrictions with respect to the supplier of a public service, or by high monitoring costs. Business Process Redesign (BPR) is a modern way to increase efficiency and customer satisfaction with public production, especially in the case of mass production like Social Services. A (public) provider can distinguish himself from his competitors by redesigning his process from customer to customer. Experiences in the Netherlands show increases in efficiency due to BPR. Financial incentives for (groups of) employees can create competitive behaviour. When an employee's performance is closely related to the performance of his/her team, a group reward is preferable.

The cases presented here prove that competition can be an instrument to increase efficiency or quality. It is, however, difficult to draw general conclusions, due to the variety of circumstances under which competition is carried out in practice. Further research which focuses on observed effects on efficiency and quality is needed.

A lack of competition is characteristic for public production. In a private market competition between several players creates an incentive to provide (quality) goods and services in an efficient way. Tilburg has investigated how competition can be implemented in public production, with the aim of increasing quality and efficiency of public production.

The present paper deals with all aspects of competition in local government except comparative performance measurement and benchmarking. These subject-matters are analysed more thoroughly in the paper of the Bertelsmann Foundation "Comparative Performance Measurement – A New Type of Competition between Local Governments."

1. Introduction

Public authorities are often accused of inefficient production of services. In the private sector, in non-monopolistic markets, competition encourages efficiency in a natural way. By introducing competitive incentives in local government it should be possible to increase the efficiency and quality of public production. The subject of this paper is to demonstrate how competition can help create better local government.

Competition in local government pursues the following objectives:
- increasing efficiency;
- improving the quality of public services;
- (better accountability with respect to the production of public services).

1.1 Sources of Inefficiency in the Public Sector

Efficiency

A number of causes of inefficient public production are mentioned in specialized literature. They include the lack of incentives on the organizational level and on the individual level (Stiglitz, 1988).

On the *organizational* level, the lacking threat of bankruptcy is one of the most important factors. This threat limits the losses a manager or a management-team are allowed to incur. In contrast, in many countries a public organization can fall back on a higher governmental authority for grants. In some countries it is possible for a public enterprise or agency to have large deficits over a long period of time. A private firm does not have the same possibility.

Secondly, a public enterprise or agency normally does not face competition. Competition provides a choice for the customer with respect to the supplier of the service. A public monopolist will probably not be as alert to the social costs of an inefficient service production as a public competitor. Besides this, on the *individual* level there are also incentives to produce less efficiently compared to a private supplier. In the first place, the wage structure in private firms is often related to profits (profit sharing, employee ownership), whereas this is not the case in public enterprises. Another difference is that managers working in the private sector aim at profit-maximization, whereas managers in the public sector can be affected by the budget mechanism (Niskanen, 1971). Moreover, a bureaucratic structure (which prevails in most public organizations) is not a very motivating climate for employees.

Finally, firing employees in the public sector is difficult, whereas it is easier in the private sector. The presence of a limit on financial rewards on the one hand and the difficulty of firing employees in public enterprises on the other hand can provoke bureaucratic behaviour.

This theory provides reasons why a public firm could be less efficient than a private firm. There are, however, also authors of a different opinion. Prager (1994) states that the efficiency advantage of the private sector is exaggerated. Job motivation can be created in many ways; it does not necessarily have to take the form of financial rewards (which are mostly higher in private than in public organizations). Besides this, the structure of an organization (public or private) also plays an important role. A separation of ownership and management can cause inefficient production (principal-agent problem). The stockholders of a company will probably strive for profit maximization and maximum efficiency. Managers could for example also strive for more status or a greater market-share. Asymmetric information between those groups creates the risk of differing objectives being pursued.

Empirically, it is not that evident that public organizations are less efficient than private ones. Stiglitz (1988) gives an overview of studies with divergent results. Most of these, however, indicate an efficiency advantage for the private sector.

Quality of services

Besides efficiency, quality is also a major objective in the introduction of competition. Gaebler and Osborne (1992) maintain that competition forces monopolists (public or private) to respond better to their customers' wishes. In other words, competition forces local governments to test the quality of their public goods and services on a regular basis. Monopolies also discourage innovation, whereas competition offers a stimulus in that respect. So, innovation and public evaluation can result in an increase of the quality of public services.

1.2 Conditions for Implementing Competition in Local Government

Implementing competition in the production of communal services requires a number of conditions to be met. Those conditions relate to the local governmental organization as a whole and parts of it.

Decentralization

Decentralization of responsibilities is a necessity. This allows employees on the lower levels of the organization to make decisions. Those workers may be better informed than high-level managers. Bureaucratic behaviour can be avoided, due to shorter decision cycles. The central staff department must be as small as possible to avoid slackness in the organization (Verbon and Van Bussel, 1994).

Integral management

Managers on a lower level of the organization must have the authority to make all relevant decisions for their production processes. This authority enables them to make the right decisions.

Managing key activities

Central management should concentrate on steering its most important activities and not worry about details.

Sound strategic judgment

Sound strategic judgment decreases the risk of high costs in case the expected effects do not occur. Implementing competition (especially using the market) can have large effects on the organization. A clear vision with respect to the entire process is decisive for a successful implementation of competition.[2]

Evaluation of performance

Responsibilities must be defined clearly in order to be able to evaluate the production processes. Output is the basis for the evaluation of the performance of organization units. When the output is compared with the budget (afterwards), conclusions can be drawn with respect to performance. Performance measurement plays an important role in a modern (local governmental) organization.

Effective cost allocation

Effective cost allocation to departments is also a key factor. It is a neces-

---

2 See also the case of GRC Rotterdam.

sary condition to effectively measure the competitive power. The real costs of a department are not only the costs of its own production, but also the accounted costs of services produced by other (supportive) departments. This increase in accountability can have an indirect effect on both quality and efficiency of the production of public goods and services.

1.3 Different Forms of Competition

Competition can be implemented in three ways: between public firms and private firms, amongst private firms and between public firms (Gaebler and Osborne 1992). In this paper, using the market and imitating it are differentiated. Using the market is feasible when the production of goods and services provided by local government is also possible by a private firm (market services). It therefore includes public versus private and private versus private competition. Operating on the market is possible for (local) government by (1) making their own internal buying non-compulsory, (2) allowing outside selling of currently internal services, (3) buying of (supportive) goods and services in the market and (4) offering their own services competitively (like Compulsory Competitive Tendering in Great Britain or Public/Private Competitive Proposal Processes in the United States of America).

Not only with the help of the private sector is it possible to create competition in local government. Within local government itself, market-like incentives can be created. Moreover, competition between local governments can also be developed without interference of the private sector. When the private sector is not used to stimulate competition, the market can be imitated.

Imitating the market can be used when there is no "real" market for the production of public goods and services, due to, for instance, legal limitations with respect to the supplier of these goods and services (public services). In this case (5) Business Process Redesign (BPR), (6) financial incentives for (groups of) employees or departments (e.g. performance related payment), (7) comparative performance measurement and (8) benchmarking, are ways of implementing "market-competition" in the provision of public services.

Characteristic for (local) government is the influence of politicians on the organization. This can render difficult the implementation of more market-like production processes in local government. The main reason for this is the way politicians go about managing government – which may at times be characterized as inappropriate. Secondly, politicians seem to be more concerned about their relationship to their personnel and the unions than about the quality of the services produced for the citizens. Finally, some politicians display an ideological resistance to market competition.

2. Using the Market

2.1 Making Internal Buying Non-Compulsory

Compulsory internal buying can be defined as "the forced buying of a product or service from one communal department (internal provider) by another communal department (internal client)." This may be logical if a (supportive) product or service is needed by several organizational units. Then, it may be cheaper to provide this service within the organization, especially if every department is forced to buy the product or service internally. In particular the provision of supportive products and services within local governments has been made non-compulsory. Examples are internal building cleaning, printing offices and computer services.

Compulsory internal buying includes a risk with respect to the fixed costs and the quality of internal provision. If there is no (or little) work to do for the internal provider, the fixed costs still have to be borne. Production by a private provider does not contain this risk. In addition, the possibility of a decrease in quality due to the lack of competition constitutes a risk for local government. However, compulsory internal buying has the advantage of being independent of the private market, but can have undesired effects on both internal supply and demand (Koppenberg, 1992).

2.1.1 Undesired Effects on the Demand Side

In the public sector, a trend is discernible towards devolving of responsibilities to lower level managers and employees. Local government organizations are divided into a few relatively autonomous organizational units. The managers of these units must have enough autonomy to make decisions, and to buy supportive goods and services. Compulsory internal buying of supportive goods and services entails a restriction of this autonomy. It also provides an excuse for not reaching targets. If the quality of the provided products or services decreases, it might be hard for those managers to do something about it. They can neither turn to another (external) supplier nor force the internal provider to conform to their standards.

2.1.2 Undesired Effects on the Supply Side

The compulsion of internal buying includes an obligation for the internal provider to deliver services. This obligation to buy internally might lead to extravagant requirements on the demand side, because they do not feel responsible for the centrally made agreements about the quality and quantity of production by the internal provider. The abolition of compulsory internal buying also implies the abolition of the obligation to provide the service.

Compulsory internal buying can be beneficial to an organization if the service or product is very complicated and specialization within the organization is necessary. The specialists can contribute to the success of the organization. Compulsory internal buying for those services should not be abolished (Koppenberg, 1992).

Case study: GRC Rotterdam

GRC Rotterdam is an organization specializing in local government information and computer services. It used to be part of the local government of Rotterdam. Compulsory internal buying of computer services at the

GRC Rotterdam was abolished for communal departments in Rotterdam in 1990. The reason for this abolition was the diversity of computer services that were demanded by the communal departments. *GRC Rotterdam* was no longer able to specialize in all those services, whereas they could easily be provided by the market. In the first period after the abolition of compulsory internal buying, *GRC Rotterdam* was "protected" by the "first call, last bid"-mechanism. In this situation *GRC Rotterdam* could adapt its price to the price of the lowest private bidder after the bidding process. However, it was very difficult to enforce this mechanism for "unwilling" clients.

The market on which *GRC Rotterdam* operates is the computer service market for local governments. This market has a turnover of approximately 1 billion guilders (350 million guilders by private suppliers). This turnover consists mostly of custom-made computer services. The suppliers on this market are: *Raet, L+T, K+V Van Alphen* and *Kramers/Iga*.

Most clients of *GRC Rotterdam* did not buy from private suppliers instantly after the abolition of compulsory internal buying. Only the civil affairs department immediately went to *Raet*. It needed a new computer program at the time. The other clients (among others social services, public works, fiscal services, and the local government transport company *(RET)* remained loyal. *GRC Rotterdam* was delivering custom-made services to these clients.

The reasons that *GRC Rotterdam* has survived on this market (according to its director, Ir. H. Bruggeman) are:
1. A major reorganization took place in the early 90s. The number of employees was reduced from 300 to approximately 180. Although this reorganization rendered the organization more conform with the market, it was very costly.
2. Before the abolition of compulsory internal buying, *GRC Rotterdam* had developed a financial system, which was selling very well in the government market.
3. Most of the customers of *GRC Rotterdam* remained loyal.

These special circumstances made a survival on the market possible. The abolition of compulsory internal buying requires a sound strategic judgment of the market, costs of the internal provider, and the opportunities in the new situation. According to Bruggeman, the decision to abolish the compulsion of internal buying in the case of *GRC Rotterdam* can be characterized as lacking good strategic judgment. *GRC Rotterdam* was not competitive in the new situation. This turned out to be very costly for the city of Rotterdam. The costs of the reorganization could have been avoided if *GRC* had been sold to a private organization.

In 1990 (before the abolition of compulsory internal buying) 300 employees were working in the organization. The yearly turnover was 65 million guilders. The customers were mostly communal organizations in Rotterdam. In 1996 only 160 employees were working in the organization. Total turnover on an annual basis had been reduced to 35 million guilders. Still, 60 percent of this turnover were produced for customers in the Rotterdam government. The other 40 percent were produced for customers outside the Rotterdam government.

Since 1 January 1996 *GRC Rotterdam* is 100 percent owned by *Roccade-Civility*, one of the largest suppliers on the Dutch market. Selling *GRC Rotterdam* to this private company has about compensated for the cost of the reorganization. If a clear strategic vision had been available, a positive result could easily have been realized.

2.2 Allowing Outside Selling

When a local government department is too small to produce a communal service in an efficient way, the decision-makers could, instead of simply outsourcing production, also try to make the communal department more efficient. When a department is given the possibility to sell its services outside the communal environment, it can make use of "economies of scale," and its prices can be tested.

A necessary condition for allowing outside selling is the possibility to exactly determine the costs of production. In Germany for instance, local governments use the cameralistic accounting system which makes it difficult to calculate exactly the costs of production of a service (Tartler, 1996).

Case study: Stadsreiniging Tilburg

Stadsreiniging Tilburg (City Cleaning Tilburg) is a part of the *Milieudienst Tilburg* (Environmental Department Tilburg). Its wide range of activities consists of all kinds of cleaning activities by order of the city of Tilburg, other cities and private companies in the region.

Table 1

Cleaning activities	Communal customers
collection of household waste	Tilburg, Berkel-Enschot, Diessen, Hooge- en Lage Mierde, Oost-, West- and Middelbeers, Waspik
collection of (big) waste	Tilburg, Berkel-Enschot, Hooge- en Lage Mierde, Waspik
collection of chemical waste	Tilburg, Diessen, Hooge- en Lage Mierde, Moergestel, Oost-, West- and Middelbeers
mechanical sweeping	Tilburg, Goirle, Berkel-Enschot

Source: Milieudienst Tilburg, IPR Normag

The first reason for allowing *Stadsreiniging* to sell outside the city of Tilburg to other local governments and private companies was to distribute/decrease overhead. An increase of turnover has an advantage in terms of economies of scale. Secondly, the expansion of private companies posed a threat to the organization. Several private companies provide services on the regional market for cleaning activities. The number of these private suppliers is decreasing, but those who are able to hold out on the market are increasing in size. The three biggest providers are *BFI, Van Gansewinkel* and *Waste Management*. Characteristics of those private providers are:
1. rapid growth due to take-overs of small companies;
2. provision of high quality services at a competitive price;
3. access to substantial funds.

It is obvious that these private providers are very strong players in the re-

gional city-cleaning market. Therefore *Stadsreiniging Tilburg* had to improve its position on the market. It started to supply the collection of household waste services to other local governments in the region. An increase of 10,000 in the number of connections was the result. *Stadsreiniging* is now responsible for the collection of household waste at 78,000 addresses. In addition, other activities were carried out for neighbouring local governments (table 1). This increase in scale of service provision made *Stadsreiniging* a more competitive supplier on the market. To maintain its position, *Stadsreiniging* has to work on three issues:
1. Internal effectiveness and efficiency: in the future *Stadsreiniging* must be able to operate independently in an efficient way.
2. Entrepreneurship inside the region: possibilities inside the region to increase its market share must be investigated.
3. Entrepreneurship outside the region: counterbalancing private providers is very difficult for *Stadsreiniging* on its own. Supraregional organizations can do this. Therefore, *Stadsreiniging* will participate in these organizations.

Focusing on these targets will probably result in *Stadsreiniging* maintaining its position on the market for cleaning activities. Permitting outside selling has contributed to the improvement of efficiency in the organization. Because collection of waste is not a public task in particular and *Stadsreiniging* faces good opportunities on the market, it is not necessary to maintain *Stadsreiniging* as a dependent part of the local government of Tilburg. *Stadsreiniging* will therefore be privatized.

Just like the abolition of compulsory internal buying, allowing outside selling can be a phase in the privatization process towards being a competitive, independent supplier of services.

2.3 Buying in the Market

2.3.1 Contracting Out

The buy-in function of communities is getting more important because of decreasing communal income in many countries. Also in the private sector this function is receiving more and more attention (Buter, 1995). In the

Netherlands, for instance, 23 percent of total expenditure of local governments is spent in the market (De Boer, Telgen and Woudstra, 1995). In general, buying goods and services can be more efficient in a competitive market. Such a market creates incentives to provide quality goods and services in an efficient way.

The large volume of goods and services which are bought in the market emphasizes the importance of the buy-in function. A recent investigation of the *University of Twente* in the Netherlands shows that Dutch local government lags behind the private sector in this respect (De Boer, Telgen and Woudstra, 1995; see table 2). The buy-in function is less professionalized in local government.

Table 2: Comparing buy-in policy of local government (l. g.; n = 83) and private sector (p; n = 840):

	l. g.	p
Buy-in is a strategic priority	43%	64%
Works with a buy-in plan	25%	34%
Periodical measurement and review of buy-in activities	45%	48%
Standardized method for supplier evaluation	34%	48%

Supportive goods and services

The products in this category are supportive to the production of the core public goods and services. Some of the products can be tested and compared, because they are already produced. In this case, the buy-in function is not different from the private sector (private companies also buy pencils). Local governments should therefore, like a private entrepreneur, have a market-oriented policy towards the buying of supportive goods and services.

Public goods and services

A local government should decide whether to produce a service or good of a public character[3] by itself, or whether to contract out (if possible) the production of public services to a private supplier (make or buy). The planning and steering remain at the local authority, because local government is responsible for the quality and quantity of public services. As information technology is developing, parts of works which cannot be contracted out totally, can be bought in the market (for example data processing).

Two criteria play a role in the decision process whether or not to contract out production of public services (Kommunale Gemeinschaftsstelle, 1995):

Efficiency

Increasing efficiency means that while output is the same, expenditure can be lower. With respect to this, the local government should take into account the following conditions (Prager, 1994):

Economies of scale

A communal department can be too small to produce a public service in an efficient way. A private supplier who specializes in the production of a product or service will quickly have an advantage due to a larger scale.

Economies of scope

It is not always logical that the activities of a small communal service department are contracted out to a private, more efficient, supplier. Supplying different, not interrelated services by one supplier can also result in cost-savings. For instance, fire protection and vehicle maintenance can be provided by one organization.

Organizational economies

Besides economies of scale and scope, the local authority should also take into account organizational economies. Especially in the case of a large

---

[3] Production with a public character includes production which can only be realized by a (local) government, for example due to legal restrictions with respect to the supplier, or which has typical public good characteristics (such as provision of infrastructure, police services, public health, etc).

community, contracting out can be a very attractive instrument, even if this were not necessary for economies of scale and scope. A communal organization can become too big to be managed effectively. Contracting out can help policy-makers to focus on their most important activities.

It should be noted that a shift of production from a public monopoly towards a private supplier is not always the right thing to do. When only one private supplier operates on the market (which is in a way logical because public production often includes economies of scale, which can only be realized by a monopolist, private or public), an increase in efficiency is at least doubtful (Van der Doel, 1978). That is why sometimes public organizations cannot increase efficiency after being privatized.

Strategic importance

The second criterium with respect to contracting out or not is the strategic importance of the public service. If a public service is vital for the well-being of the citizens in the city, the risk of a failure (for instance bankruptcy) of a supplier must be minimized. This includes high monitoring costs and diminishes the advantage of private production. That is why mostly non-core business is contracted out. Table 3 provides a first impression of services for which local authorities in the European Community frequently use contracting out as an instrument to increase efficiency and/or quality of production.[4] Besides the areas of activity mentioned in this overview, education, urban planning, traffic research and design, environmental research and site development are also activities which are frequently contracted out to private suppliers.

As a result of the various circumstances under which the decision whether to contract out or not is being made, it is difficult to draw general conclusions on the effects. In the United Kingdom the results of competition have been extensively investigated. Therefore, competition in local government in the UK is the subject of the next paragraph.

---

4 Competitive tendering is compulsory in the UK (see also 2.3.2). Countries taking part in this study were: Austria, Belgium, Denmark, Finland, Germany, Greece, Hungary, Ireland, Italy, Luxembourg, Netherlands, Norway, Sweden, Switzerland and the United Kingdom.

Table 3

Activity area:	Countries:
Ground maintenance	Austria, Denmark, Germany, the Netherlands, UK
Recreational amenities	Germany, the Netherlands, Sweden, UK
Cleaning of buildings	Austria, Denmark, Finland, Germany, the Netherlands, UK
Road maintenance	Austria, Finland, Germany, the Netherlands, UK
Street cleaning	Finland, Germany, the Netherlands, UK
Refuse collection	Finland, Germany, the Netherlands, Norway, UK
Waste disposal	Austria, Germany
Canteens and catering	Denmark, Finland, Germany, the Netherlands, UK
Vehicle maintenance	Germany, the Netherlands, UK
Cemeteries and funeral undertakings	Germany
Certain health-care services	the Netherlands
Transport of patients	Denmark, Finland, the Netherlands
School transport	Finland, the Netherlands
Security	Denmark, Finland
Data processing	Denmark, Finland, the Netherlands
Consultant services	Finland, the Netherlands

Source: Council of Europe, The Role of Competitive Tendering in the Efficient Provision of Local Services, 1993

2.3.2 Compulsory Competitive Tendering (CCT)

In 1988 Compulsory Competitive Tendering (CCT) was legislated in the United Kingdom. CTT means that the local governments are forced to subject their service departments (direct service organization, DSO) to competition with other suppliers. The service departments are placed in competition with private companies to achieve a more efficient or effective production of public services. The client (local authority) specifies the work to be done, and invites contractors (private companies and/or the public service department) to tender for this job. The contractor with the best bid (in terms of price and/or quality) is chosen to do the job.[5] The main obligation of local governments is to provide a cost-effective, quality service to the public, regardless of the status of the contractor.

Consumers, too, play a vital role (see figure 1), because they should have a say in the preparation of new contracts, to make sure that mistakes are not repeated.

Figure 1

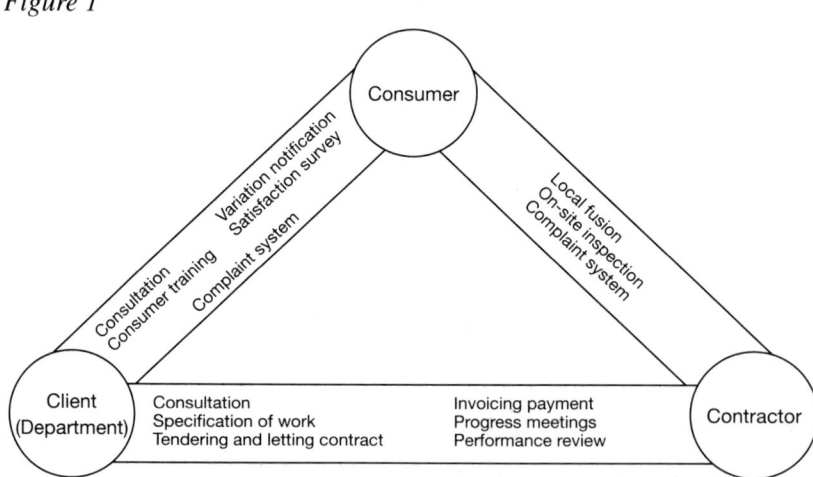

Source: Audit Commission, Realizing the Benefits of Competition, 1993

---

[5] In 1995 only 10 percent of the contracts were not awarded to the tenderer with the lowest price. The reason for this was either technical problems or discounting of allowable not directly related costs.

So far local governments have used tendering for non-core activities[6], while taking into account external economic factors (such as private monopolies) and social goals.

The claimed benefits and costs of CCT are as follows (Parker, 1990):

Benefits:

1. Provision of public goods and services is submitted to competition periodically, lowering costs and maximizing efficiency.
2. CCT enforces the establishing of quality standards and effective policing. This is made possible by the sanction in terms of not being chosen as producer of the public service.
3. The major concern is no longer the inputs of public production but the quantity and quality of outputs.
4. Suppliers, who are not limited in size by the government, can optimize production and achieve economies of scale and scope.
5. CCT also has an indirect advantage: competition leads to increased efficiency, by which both private companies (more profits) and citizens (less tax) benefit.

Costs of CCT

1. Service quality can decline in spite of contractual specifications. Monitoring the contractors is important to make sure that the quality of the production is as it should be according to the contract. It is also possible that the contractor submits a low tender to win a contract, but when the contract is signed hopes to renegotiate prices. This is why a contract should preferably be fixed-price, or at least have a cost-reducing incentive scheme. Price escalation might then be avoided.
2. It is possible that competition is based on public/private wage differ-

---

[6] The Local Government Act 1988 defines as activity areas for CCT besides the activities mentioned in table 4 also *Managing sports and leisure facilities*. Lately also white collar services are being put out to tender (Walsh 1995A).

ences. This might include a reduction in employee benefits, such as sick pay and pensions (some people consider this an advantage).
3. Another disadvantage of public tendering is the opportunity for suppliers not to compete, but to divide the market. In that case the tendering of public services does not lead to an increase of efficiency or effectiveness. It is very important that the market and the bidding process are open and available for public inspection.
4. CCT causes costs for monitoring and negotiating contracts.

Results of CCT

The experience with CCT is not positive in all areas of activity. The *Institute of Local Government Studies* has studied its effects. Table 4 shows the outcome of this study in initial results in savings or cost increase:

Table 4

Activity	Average savings (–) or cost increase (+)
Refuse collection	– 12.4%
Building cleaning	– 20.6%
Other cleaning	+ 2.2%
Catering (education and welfare)	+ 1.5%
Other catering	– 5.1%
Vehicle maintenance	+ 1.8%
Ground maintenance	– 10.2%
Overall	– 7.0%

Source: Audit Commission, Realizing the Benefits of Competition, 1993

Due to competition, the savings are being made irrespective of whether the work is won by the DSO or by private contractors. In general these improvements come from increased productivity (Carnaghan and

Bracewell-Milnes, 1993). Only in building cleaning has the competition probably led to lower wages. Another advantage of CCT is that thanks to the introduction of clear specifications or service monitoring the quality of services has been maintained or improved. The introduction or improvement of standards also had its effect on savings and costs. In general, standards were higher, and therefore real average savings might be higher than shown in the table (ibid.).

In the first years after CCT legislation, the proportion of work won by the service departments stayed constant at around 85 percent of total value, the percentage of contracts won being 70 percent. In 1995 these percentages were 74.9 and 59.5 respectively. The overall average number of contractors (weighted for the number of contracts) was 3.0 in 1992 and 2.7 in 1995 (including service departments).

Consequences of CCT for Local Governments

In response to CCT legislation, the local governments have changed their internal organization and management (Audit Commission, 1989) successfully, according to the figures of bids won. What changes have taken place within local governments?

Culture

Exposure to competition has brought a more commercial and market-oriented approach to the management of local governments.

Organization and Management

The local authorities have to make a decision whether to sell the service departments or use competitive tendering to make them efficient. To avoid conflicts within the organization it is important that the service departments are separated thoroughly from other units, and that they can make their own strategic decisions.

Employment

Personnel policy must also be adapted to the market conditions. Wages and skills of local government workers must be competitive with those of their private counterparts.

Improvement of accounting practices

In order to be able to make a proper choice between the tenderers, the accounting practices should be improved. Poor information on costs has been one of the major problems in preparing for competition (Walsh, 1991). Information technology can play an important role in this.

The results of the research from the *Institute for Local Government Studies* show that CCT can result in an increase in productivity of public services. Proponents of CCT claim that, compared with contracting out, CCT is founded on competition that encourages efficiency instead of the status of the service provider. But of course, contracting out to a private provider on a competitive market can also increase competitive behaviour.

3. Imitating the Market

3.1 Business Process Redesign

The competitive aspect of Business Process Redesign (BPR) is the advantage that can be generated by the way activities are structured, executed and coordinated within the primary process of an organization.

An organization (or a part of an organization) can be considered as a value chain of activities (Porter, 1985). The value chain of a product or service consists of all activities that can add value to products or services during their entire life-cycle. In the value chain an organization can distinguish itself from its competitors by its specific way of organizing the value chain, emphasizing certain chains and processes, and the way the chains interact. BPR can play a role in this. It can be defined as "the restructuring, from customer to customer, of production processes, independently of organization borders, departments or hierarchies." This can have two objectives: on the one hand, the customer value of a service or product (quality) can be increased, and on the other hand cost saving (efficiency) can be realized (Tideman, 1993).

The local government customer value can be increased due to a faster production process. The cost saving can be realized by using information technology in an efficient way, instead of it being a rigid factor within the organization.[7] Processes with mass production in particular are suitable to be redesigned by BPR.

Recently in the Netherlands BPR is being used more often in local governments. Because of BPR being an instrument to redesign homogeneous mass production in particular, the social services are using it to improve their production processes.

Case study: Using BPR in social services in Apeldoorn and Tilburg (Netherlands)

Apeldoorn

The motive for using BPR in the local Social Service Department (GSD) of Apeldoorn was the need to really change the organization instead of just improving the "old" system by a number of reorganizations. Improvement had been used several times, without real change. The strain was getting too big, and there was a broad basis throughout the organization backing a renewal instead of (slightly) improving the production process. For this purpose the department used BPR. The advantages of using BPR were:
– BPR is effective both bottom-up and top-down. Cooperation of both employees who are actually producing the service and management is important for analysing and redesigning the process.

---

[7] Despite large investments in information-technology, in many organizations productivity has not or has hardly improved (productivity-paradox; see for instance Kubeck, 1995). In practice, implementation of information-technology has led in many cases to a rigid production process. Then information technology can be an obstacle for potential improvements of the process.

- BPR is especially effective in the case of repeated mass production which the production process of the department resembled.
- BPR is based on the optimal use of information technology, which can lead to an increase of efficiency and quality of production.
- BPR includes cooperation of advisors, management and other employees.

Several positive changes have been the result of using BPR:
- Process time is shortened.
- Abuse is decreased.
  Because of a better use of information technology, a better decision can be made for each client individually. This increases efficiency and effectiveness of the production process.
- Information is more readily available in the organization.
  Data are imported into the system at the very beginning of a process. This enables the organization to select its customers at an early stage of the process, which can lead to increased efficiency and higher customer satisfaction.
- Interactions with other organizations are improved because of a more efficient use of information technology. Although large investments in information technology had to be made, a yearly net saving of 1.5 million guilders can be realized by the year 2000 and later. Of the 162 people working now in the organization only 135 will then be needed.

Tilburg

In Tilburg, too, BPR was used to make the social services department more efficient.

In the early 90s the department was paying 1.1 million guilders yearly to the central government as a penalty for its inefficient production process. As in Apeldoorn there had been several reorganizations before BPR was used. The employees had become skeptical towards "new ideas" because of the failure of the reorganizations. But after the first results of a test in a small organization unit were positive, there was enough backing within the organization. This human basis is very important for getting better results by using BPR. After the implementation of BPR in the entire department, efficiency went up and no penalties had to be paid any more to central government. The department did not look only at the wishes of the direct users of their product, but also at the demands of an important "client": central government (redesigning from customer to customer).

Using BPR in local government has some divergent characteristics in comparison with its use in the private sector:
- BPR comes with high costs due to necessary investments in information technology. In the private sector the decision whether or not this investment can be made is based on an estimated benefit-cost comparison. The decision process in a local government is more complex.
- Firing employees is more difficult in the public sector.
- Rigid expectations with respect to jobs and careers cause a climate against change (more than in a private organization).
- Using BPR includes a thorough redesigning of the total production process. Part of the process of social departments is determined by external regulations and for that reason is not part of the BPR operation.
- Politicians are not used to formulating their wishes in terms of processes and output. Steering by politicians is often based on interventions. These can lead to disturbances in the BPR operation.

The experience of the departments of Apeldoorn and Tilburg shows that BPR can create increased efficiency, and thereby a rise in competitiveness, in the production of public services.

3.2 Financial Incentives

3.2.1 Employees

Performance-based pay can be used as a way of rewarding the individual or group of employees who is (are) doing his (their) job very well. While in the private sector profit-sharing is a common way to reward the high-performing group or individual, in the public sector, where there is no "profit," part of the budget can be reserved for performance-related pay. The reward of those employees is based on the measurement of performance by management. Performance-related pay is used in the public sector in many countries, particularly at senior levels (Walsh, 1995).

Through these special rewards, competition between employees or groups of employees could be established. An example of this is a civil affairs department with a number of counters. The performance of the separate teams of employees working at a counter are evaluated and compared. This comparison could be the basis for extra pay or bonuses for the team. In Visalia (United States of America), high-performing groups of employees are allowed to keep 30 percent of the savings (or new revenue) they generated (Gaebler and Osborne, 1992).

Several conditions of using performance-based pay can be enumerated (Van der Hoek, 1990):
– The evaluation of an employee must be based on an objective employee-evaluation system. This is a necessary condition for creating acceptance of performance-based pay within the organization.
– Performance-based pay must be an integrated part of the total personnel policy and be congruent with other personnel policies.
– Preparation of the management is also a necessity for succeeding in the implementation of performance-based pay. Managers should be trained to thoroughly evaluate the performance of employees in order to avoid mistakes. A misjudgment of an employee's performance can be discouraging.
– When the performance of a civil servant is closely related to the performance of colleagues, a group reward is preferable. An individual reward might in this case damage the team spirit. In the long term this can have counterproductive effects on efficiency and quality of production.

3.2.2 Agencies

A link between performance and available funds can also be realized on a higher level in the organization. Agencies can receive a budget on the basis of performance. This is called output budgeting. Output budgeting can create alternative efficiency incentives when market competition is lacking. Conditions for output budgeting are (1) the possibility to specify the performance, and (2) the possibility to specify the costs related to this performance. The savings of output budgeting depend among others on the fulfilment of these conditions. An important advantage of output budgeting, in comparison to the use of budgeting by declaration or input budgeting, is to provide a cost-reducing incentive.

Case study: Braintree District Council

The system
Braintree District Council in the United Kingdom has used performance-related pay for employees for several years now. The performance of individual employees is evaluated annually by a Departmental Pay Panel. These panels consist of managers of the department. The performance of an employee is evaluated on the basis of an assessment of overall performance together with his/her success in meeting targets related to the corporate strategy. The evaluation leads to a pay movement; there are no variations in pay levels other than those related to performance. Levels and accompanying criteria are briefly reflected in table 5.

Table 5

Level	Criteria
1. Outstanding performance	Significantly exceeds all job accountabilities; performance is consistently well above the stated performance for the job.
2. Superior performance	Exceeds requirements of job accountabilities; performance is marked by above-average ability and achievement of short term goals with excellence.
3. Fully acceptable performance	Fully meets job accountabilities; performance which is expected from experienced and competent individuals.
4. Incomplete performance	Does not meet all job accountabilities; the need of further development is recognized.
5. Unacceptable performance	Fails to meet minimum job accountabilities; standards of work are consistently below those required.

Source: Personnel Services Department of Braintree District Council, Performance-Related Pay, April 1990

In the first three levels the performance is meritorious. The management can be satisfied with the performance of employees who come into these levels. The fourth level is, for example, used for employees who are new to their jobs, and for that reason not yet performing fully. Unacceptable performance will lead to remedial action.

The financial incentive for an employee depends on the level of his/her salary. In every salary scale there are several incremental salary points. When the performance of an employee is evaluated as outstanding, the salary of this employee goes up by three increments. Likewise the salary goes up by two or one increments in case of superior or fully acceptable performance respectively. No movement in salary will be made when the performance of an employee is characterized as incomplete. In case the performance is evaluated as being unacceptable, disciplinary actions can be made and pay-points deducted. If an employee is at the maximum of his salary scale at the time of his/her performance evaluation, extra payments can be made by way of bonuses.

Some results

Table 6 outlines the results of the performance evaluation of the Braintree District Council employees.

Table 6

Performance	1991	1992	1993	1994
Outstanding	2%	3%	3%	3%
Superior	22%	27%	31%	31%
Fully acceptable	71%	67%	63%	64%
Incomplete	3%	2%	2%	1%
Unacceptable	1%	2%	1%	1%

Source: Bill Bradford, Assistant Director of Personnel Services, Braintree District Council

Most of the permanent office staff of the council (84 percent) feel that a performance-related pay scheme should be retained at Braintree District Council. In addition a large majority (70 percent) consider the award as "fair," taking into account all the circumstances. Disappointing, however, is the fact that only 34 percent of staff experienced performance-related pay in 1994 as helpful in increasing their job motivation. Apparently a financial incentive alone is not sufficient. But, when well integrated in personnel and training/support policies, it contributes to the motivation of employees.

4. Conclusions

Public organizations are often accused of inefficiency. Several incentives are referred to in specialist literature with respect to this. The absence of the threat of bankruptcy and of competition are causes of this inefficiency on the organizational level. On the individual level, the payment structure, the bureaucratic climate and the difficulty of lay-offs differ from private sector conditions. Implementing competition can be an instrument for local government to increase the quality and efficiency of production.

In this paper the effects of a number of competitive incentives are described. A distinction is made between using the market and imitating it. Using the market to create competition is possible if the goods and services provided by local government can also be supplied by a private firm. Imitating the market is a possibility to create competitive incentives, if the production of certain public goods or services by a private organization is not yet a real (political) option. Decentralization of responsibilities, evaluation of performance and effective cost-calculation of departments are necessary conditions for implementing competition in local government.

A first step towards total independency for certain (supportive) departments can be the abolition of compulsory internal buying. In this case the department will have to improve its efficiency and/or quality of production. If the department survives on the market, it can be sold to a private provider or otherwise become part of the private sector. Decisive for the result of the abolition are (1) the customers' attitude (are they leaving instantly after the abolition or not?), (2) the customer value of the products of the department, and (3) the presence of entrepreneurship (to survive in the market).

Another way to prepare a communal department for market competition is the permission of outside selling. The department will have to be competitive in order to attract new clients. The economies of scale which can be achieved due to this operation increase efficiency and thereby competitiveness.

It should be noted that if the market can efficiently provide the services which a department provides, privatization of the department can save money compared with allowing outside selling or the abolition of compulsory internal buying. These operations can be very expensive due to (necessary) reorganizations.

Buying of goods and services by local government lags behind the private sector in the Netherlands. Like private entrepreneurs a local government should have a market-oriented approach towards the buying of supportive goods and services. The production of goods and services of a public character can be contracted out. This decision to contract out is based on two criteria: efficiency and strategic importance. If the outsourcing of a (communal) product or service involves risk, monitoring costs can be high, and therefore contracting out could be more expensive than in-house production.

In the United Kingdom local government is obliged to expose its service departments to competition with private suppliers. The major objective of this forced competition is to increase the efficiency of providing public goods and services. According to a study by the *Institute of Local Government Studies* this efficiency gain is indeed realized. Other studies show different outcomes (Whitfield/Escott 1995). Recently compulsory competitive tendering is also being used for the provision of white-collar services.

Within local government(s) itself market-like incentives can be created by imitating the market. Business Process Redesign (BPR) is a modern way to increase efficiency and customer satisfaction of public production, especially in case of mass production like Social Services. A (public) provider can distinguish itself from its competitors by redesigning its process from customer to customer. Experiences in the Netherlands show increases in efficiency due to BPR.

In addition, financial incentives for (groups of) employees can be a way of creating competitive behaviour. An objective employee evaluation system is a necessity for creating acceptance within the organization. When the performance of an employee is closely related to the performance of his/her team, a group reward is preferable. Individual rewards might in that case damage the team spirit. Output-budgeting for agencies can create alternative efficiency incentives when market competition is lacking.

Competition has been shown to be an effective instrument to increase quality and efficiency of public services in the cases described in this paper. It is, however, difficult to draw general conclusions due to the variety of circumstances under which competition materializes in practice. Some factors which can influence the decision whether or not to use competition are:

Complexity of services

In the Netherlands, for instance, competition by public tendering is being used less in the public works sector as the complexity of services increases. Development in information technology opens the possibility to buy *parts* of public production processes (which cannot be contracted out totally) in the market (for example data-processing).

Organizational factors

Are the organizational conditions met, like decentralization of responsibilities, integral management, evaluation of performance and effective cost allocation? Is competition within a local governmental organization accepted by its employees and by the politicians?

Market conditions

Are there enough private providers on the market to create competition? Is it possible to create competition between (comparable) local governments?

Further research on using competition in local government, focusing on increased efficiency and quality that were observed, will be helpful in evaluating the instrument and knowing when it best can and should be used.

Literature

Audit Commission, Preparing for Compulsory Competition, HMSO, 1989.
Audit Commission, Realizing the Benefits of Competition, HMSO, 1993.
De Boer, L./Telgen, J./Woudstra, A., Inkoopmanagement bij Gemeenten, Openbare Uitgaven nr. 5, 1995.
Boneschansker, E./de Groot, H., Verzelfstandiging van Overheidsdiensten: wanneer en hoe?, Openbare Uitgaven, 1992 nr. 3.
Braintree District Council, Personnel Service Department, Performance-Related Pay, April 1990.
Buter, J. I. H., Uw (inkoop)resultaat structureel verbeteren, Controllers Magazine, nr. 5 october/november 1995.
Carnaghan, Robert/Bracewell-Milnes, Barry, Testing the Market, 1993.
Council of Europe, The Role of Competitive Tendering in the Efficient Provision of Local Services, Strasbourg 1993.
Van den Doel, J., Demokratie en welvaartstheorie, Alphen a/d Rijn, 1978.
DorJe, A. G., Gemeentelijk Aanbestedingsbeleid, 1996.
DorJe, A. G., Aanbesteden van GWW-werken door gemeenten, Bouwrecht, nr. 8, augusttus 1995.
Flanagan, Jim/Perkins, Susan, Public/Private Competition in the City of Phoenix, Arizona, Government Finance Review, June 1995.
Haselbekke, A. G. J., Sturen op prestaties en effecten, Overheidsmanagement, 1995/12.
Van der Hoek, J. C., Flexibele beloning bij de overheid, Financieel overheidsmanagement, 1990/12.
KPMG Bureau voor Economische Argumentatie B.V., Ondernemingsplan Tilburgse Reinigingsorganizatie, 1995.
Kommunale Gemeinschaftsstelle (KGSt), Kommune und Wettbewerb, 1995.
Koppenberg, R., Gedwongen winkelnering, een achterhaalde zaak?, Overheidsmanagement, 1992/10.
Korsten, Arno, F. A. S., Excellent management in de Nederlandse gemeente, 1995.
Van der Krogt, M. P. C./van Mook A. H. M., Kiezen tussen kerntaken en uitbesteden, Overheidsmanagement, 1995/4.

Kubeck, Lynn C., Techniques for Business Process Redesign, Tying It All Together, 1995.
The Local Government Management Board, CCT Information Services, 1995.
Niskanen, William A., Bureaucracy and Representative Government, Chigaco, 1971.
Osborne, David/Gaebler, Ted, Reinventing Government, Addison-Wesley, 1992.
Parker, David, The 1988 Local Government Act and Compulsory Competitive Tendering, Urban Studies, 1990.
Pekdemir, U., New Organizational Forms within Municipalities: the Tilburg Model, Municipality of Tilburg, November 1995.
Porter, M. E., Competitive Advantage, The Free Press, New York, 1985.
Prager, Jonas, Contracting Out Government Services: Lessons from the Private Sector, Public Administration Review, vol. 54 No. 2, 1994.
Smith, Peter, Assessing Competition among Local Authorities in England and Wales, Financial Accountability & Management, Autumn 1988.
Stiglitz, Joseph E., Economics of the Public Sector, 1988.
Tartler, Jens, Kommunen als Konkurrenten, Handelsblatt, 16-4-1996.
Tideman, Ir. B, Prestatieverbetering door Business Process Redesign, Lansa Publising BV, Leidschendam, 1993.
Veldhorst, A. M./Kooistra-Kats, J./Silvertand, P. A. G. E., GSD Apeldoorn vernieuwt met BPR, Overheidsmanagement, 1995/12.
Verbon/Van Bussel, Het Tilburgse Model, in P.A. Verheyen (red.), 1992.
Walsh, K., Competitive Tendering for Local Government Services, HMSO, 1991.
Walsh, K., Public Services and Market Mechanisms, Macmillan Press Ltd, 1995.
Walsh, K., Competition for White-Collar Services in Local Government, Public Money and Management, April-June 1995(a).
Whitfield, Dexter/Escott, Karen, Both Sides to the Story of Savings, Local Government Chronicle, 13 October 1995.

Bertelsmann Foundation: Comparative Performance Measurement – A New Type of Competition between Local Governments

Bernd Adamaschek, Gerhard Banner

Executive Summary 185
1. Introduction 187
2. Established Types of Competition 188
    2.1 Open Competition: In-House Service Providers Compete Against External Providers 188
    2.2 Latent Competition: Internal Markets 188
    2.3 Effect of the Established Types of Competition 189
3. A Newcomer: "Sporting" Competition Based on Comparative Performance Measurement 191
    3.1 Comparative Performance Measurement in Practice 192
        3.1.1 The Project of the Bertelsmann Foundation 192
        3.1.2 The Project of the International City/County Management Association (ICMA) 199
    3.2 The Citizen's Charter Performance Indicators: on the Way to Comparative Performance Measurement? .. 201
    3.3 The Potential of Comparative Performance Measurement 202
        3.3.1 Synergy by Inter-Authority Cooperation 202
        3.3.2 Only Winners, No Losers? 203
        3.3.3 Focus on the Organisation as a Whole 203
        3.3.4 Public Interest and Democratic Accountability..... 204
    3.4 Political and Institutional Framework Conditions of Successful Comparative Performance Measurement ... 204
        3.4.1 Use of Performance Boosters 204

      3.4.2 Publicity of the Results 205
      3.4.3 Management Infrastructure 206
      3.4.4 "Meta Organisations" 206
  3.5 Relationship between Comparative Performance
      Measurement and the Established Types of Competition .. 207
4. Outlook 207
Literature 208

Executive Summary

In local government, as everywhere else, competition is the crucial driving force that leads to performance improvement and innovation. At the same time, however, it is also the basis for legitimacy: a local government that provides its services under competitive conditions will not find it difficult to convince its citizens that its services are value for money.

There are various possibilities of how to expose in-house services of local governments to competition:
– open competition with services provided externally through price comparisons or public invitations to tender;
– in the case of internal purchase guarantees: latent competition with services provided externally if the prices of these services are more favourable, the client units are under pressure to perform and the purchase guarantee begins to falter;
– "sporting" competition between the local governments through comparative performance measurement.

The first two types of competition have already resulted in a marked improvement in the performance of local governments in various countries, above all in England, and are on the advance at an international level.

The situation is somewhat different as regards comparative performance measurement. The local governments of any one country are largely facing comparable tasks. However, they often differ very much in the way in which they organise their performance, in the quality they deliver and in the resources they spend to fulfill these tasks. It is therefore expedient to systematically compare the way in which different local authorities provide the same service, identify best-practice authorities and make their methods generally known in order to set off a comprehensive performance competition between local governments. Such a process of fair comparative performance measurement that is acceptable to local governments can be initiated only if elaborate methods and the necessary financial resources are available. This is why the few attempts at using this instrument have been nipped in the bud.

In 1992, the Bertelsmann Foundation, in cooperation with the *German*

Association of Civil Servants[8] and a limited number of municipalities, started a new attempt by initiating a large-scale comparative performance measurement project. Independently of this project, the *International City/County Management Association (ICMA)* set off a comparative performance measurement project in 1995 with similar objectives and using similar methodology and cooperating with a larger number of American cities and counties.

After a brief discussion of these two projects, the paper analyses the potential inherent in comparative performance measurement as one type of competition and outlines the political and institutional framework conditions required to successfully implement comparative performance measurement. It then draws the reader's attention to the internationally increasing tendency to close the "legitimacy gap" by putting local governments under a statutory obligation to account to their citizens for their performance. Such an accountability of local governments can be used as a control instrument by their citizens only on condition that the performance of their local government is compared with the performance of other local authorities. This would be the case if the local governments' obligation to account for their performance were based on comparative performance measurement. A combination of both instruments should therefore be considered.

Comparative performance measurement enables local governments to learn from each other and thus improve their performance. In contrast to the traditional approach to comparative performance measurement, this paper considers it to be a competition strategy. The paper submitted by the city of Tilburg entitled "Competition in Local Government" deals with the remaining aspects of competition at a local level excluding the concept of comparative performance measurement.

---

8 Deutscher Beamtenbund

1. Introduction

Citizens all over the world increasingly ask for a responsive and efficient local government, i.e. a local government that constantly adjusts the range of services it provides to the changing needs and expectations of its citizens while at the same time constantly improving it in terms of quality and costs.

The chances that such a local government system might be established are quite favourable for two reasons: first of all, in many countries there are hundreds, sometimes even thousands of municipalities that are facing comparable problems, are working under similar political, economic and legal conditions and basically need not keep anything secret from each other. Secondly, the web of local governments comprises innumerable pioneer authorities that achieve outstanding performance in a specific field thanks to the commitment and wealth of ideas of their staff. The local authorities of any one country thus have every reason to compare their performance in order to discover the best performance results achieved and, where possible, implement them in their own administration – in other words: learn from each other.

The possibility of inter-authority learning does not only exist at a national level but also internationally. In spite of the considerable differences between the national framework conditions and local government systems, the local authorities of industrialised countries are in fact facing largely similar and often even identical problems. When the Bertelsmann Foundation adopted the idea of an *International Network for Better Local Government* it did so convinced that until then local governments had hardly availed themselves of the potential inherent in international and intercultural learning and thus deprived themselves of a powerful source of innovation and performance improvement.

The central message of this paper is: Competition, which in local government, as everywhere else, is the crucial driving force that leads to innovation, is not only possible between services provided in-house and those provided externally, but also, and very effectively, between the services provided by different local authorities.

2. Established Types of Competition

Competition is based on comparison. It emerges when there is a constraint to constantly compare one's own performance with the performance of external (private or voluntary) providers. If the price and quality comparison proves to be to the disadvantage of the in-house performance, the latter has to be adjusted to the performance provided externally or, if this proves impossible, be left to the external provider.

As a consequence, competition makes use of the forces of the market, which can either be a genuine market or a quasi-market.

2.1 Open Competition: In-House Service Providers Compete Against External Providers

Open competition implies that a local government invites bids for services that have traditionally been provided internally, with the internal provider being one of the bidders. The contract is awarded to the bidder that submits the lowest or lowest responsible bid. This type of market test obviously exerts a severe pressure for improvement on the organisational units involved. This pressure is particularly strong in the United Kingdom, as local governments have been forced by law on a broad basis to put manual services, and recently also white-collar services, to the market test. In all other industrialised countries, the market test is voluntary and still not used to a large extent. However, there is a growing interest in using this type of competition more intensively.

2.2 Latent Competition: Internal Markets

Internal markets aim at using market forces also in areas in which, for political or practical reasons, no contracting out takes place and the service is consequently provided by the local government itself despite the fact that the service at issue is available in the market. The "privileged" internal provider units find themselves put under competitive pressure as soon as the client units themselves, i.e. the internal clients, are under pressure to perform as they are expected to provide a comprehensive range of services with a limited budget. In such circumstances, the clients are highly interested in being offered services by the internal provider which, in terms of price and quality, are at least as good as those offered by the market. They discover ways and means to find out the market prices, even if they do not always succeed in determining the precise price level, and use this knowledge to put internal providers under pressure.

In current practice, most clients are still forced to acquire services exclusively from the internal provider instead of buying them on the regular market. However, there is an increasing trend to do away with this restriction. If this is actually done, the pressure on the internal providers to perform will drastically increase: The internal quasi-market will become a genuine market, and latent competition will turn into open competition.

2.3 Effect of the Established Types of Competition

Apart from the United Kingdom where the vastest experience has been gathered due to its specific statutory conditions (Walsh 1995), the effect of the established types of competition can now be observed to some extent also in other countries.

An administration that intends to create competition has to change its organisational structure and clearly split responsibilities between the client units (the parties placing an order) and provider units (the parties receiving an order). The client units' task is to explicitly define the service they require and identify standards against which they will subsequently measure the service obtained. If necessary, they invite bids, conclude contracts and make sure that the service is adequately rendered. The provider units have to provide the service and in return are entitled to the agreed sum of money.

The in-house providers of services have to know all their costs. They are therefore gradually being moved onto a trading basis, and internal charging and accounting systems are being developed. In addition to this, these units must be given far greater managerial freedom than they are usually granted in administrative practice.

The necessity of a regular monitoring of services by the client increasingly leads to the development of quality assurance systems, as such systems are considered an appropriate means of reducing the client's supervision costs.

As performance measurement is more and more perfected, it is increasingly used to couple outstanding performances with performance related pay.

These improvements in the management area have undoubtedly contributed to the fact that British local government has been relatively successful in the open competition with private providers. The great majority of contracts for simple and manual services has been won by the local government bidder. This applies even more to the value of the contracts. As yet, it is not clear what the situation will be for white-collar services. However, it is assumed that the private sector will be even less successful in this area (Walsh 1995, p. 136).

The more negative effects of competition are:
- The internal management costs of specifying the services, monitoring the way they are rendered and developing efficient invoicing and payment systems are increasing.
- The client-provider split increases organisational complexity. Local government is moving in the direction of a network of relatively autonomous units. It is getting more difficult to ensure coherence of the range of services. The degree of formalisation rises, which is sometimes perceived as an increase in bureaucracy.
- As the provider usually has a more detailed knowledge of the services than the client, there is a tendency of gathering expert knowledge also on the client side, which may lead to double work and higher personnel expenses. There seems to be an increasing awareness of the need to establish formal systems to mediate on differences between the client and provider sides of the organisation.

The understandable tendency to measure what can be measured with relative ease makes some people fear that too much emphasis is placed on the efficiency of services, whereas aspects of common weal and client wishes are neglected. So far, clients or users have hardly ever been involved in the design of local services. The pervasive improvement of complaints systems cannot compensate for this deficiency. In fact, it can be eliminated only if the client or the customer is the focus of attention of local government policy and administration. A tendency in this direction can already be observed at an international level.

The political effect of the introduction of market mechanisms has so far been given relatively little attention. A delimitation of responsibilities among the elected members according to the client-provider pattern is more difficult than it is within the administrative machinery.

The gulf between the need for reliable public planning on the one hand and the often unpredictable market results on the other may cause problems. Contracting out is often practised in the hope for depoliticisation. However, this objective is generally not achieved as the clients or users continue to hold local government responsible for what they perceive as insufficient or inadequate performance. This raises basic problems of democratic responsibility and public accountability.

We may assume that some of the problems observed in connection with the introduction of market mechanisms are take-off difficulties which will be overcome with increasing experience. For this reason, the established forms of competition have to be further developed so that their benefits can be fully used and their drawbacks minimised. It is to be hoped that voluntary competitive tendering will be practised to a larger extent also by local authorities outside Great Britain. Competition is not a panacea; however, it makes local government more transparent and enables it to proceed on the way to better performance with greater confidence.

3. A Newcomer: "Sporting" Competition Based on Comparative Performance Measurement

Competition is not only created on markets on which services are exchanged, but, if underlying conditions are favourable, also on quasi-markets on which performance is only compared. The best example of this are amateur sporting events which spur the participants to aim at a record performance. As mentioned above, the local governments of any one country are largely facing comparable tasks. However, they often differ very much in the way in which they organise their performance, in the quality they deliver and in the resources they spend to fulfill these tasks. Differences in efficiency by a factor of 1 to 5 are not unusual. It is therefore expedient to systematically compare the way in which different local authorities provide the same service, to identify best-practice authorities and to make their methods generally known. If such a comparison includes all local government services of a country, then there is a chance of triggering large-scale benchmarking processes that will lead to improvements in productivity and quality.

The idea of comprehensive comparative performance measurement is so tempting that it has been discussed time and again by local government management experts. And yet such comparison has so far never been successfully implemented anywhere in the world. In fact, in most countries it has not even been tried, mostly on the grounds that the technical difficulties were too big and that it was hopeless to try to convince the many local governments, so intent on their autonomy, to make personnel available for this purpose and share each other's secrets. Only very recently two systematic attempts have been made in Germany and the USA to arrive at a comprehensive comparative performance measurement that may become the basis for a process of continuous improvement in the municipalities involved. *The Citizen's Charter Performance Indicators* in the United Kingdom are using a slightly different approach, which, however, is also very interesting in this context.

3.1 Comparative Performance Measurement in Practice

3.1.1 The Project of the Bertelsmann Foundation

Project structure

In 1992, the Bertelsmann Foundation initiated a comprehensive project with the aim of improving the political and administrative controllability of local government performance. For this purpose, such performance had to be made transparent. This was done by means of comparative performance measurement. The expected result of the project was to obtain comparative information which can serve as a substitute for competition in cases in which open competition does not take place.

The master project is divided into two subprojects. The participants of the first subproject are six medium-sized cities that investigate into the areas of public order, residents' registration, immigration, registry office, social welfare, green spaces and taxes and charges. The participants of the second subproject are five major cities that compare the relatively "soft" service areas of adult education, music classes, libraries, theatres, museums and archives.

There is every chance that such comparisons will, in practice, actually lead to improvements. German local government is currently in a phase of reform that will eventually result in a strong decentralisation of authorities according to the core-periphery principle and a change in the respective rôles of the council and municipal administration. As a consequence, self-controlling forces will be generated in the partly autonomous operational units that will empower them to use information obtained from other municipalities to improve their own work. This reform movement was initiated in 1990 by the *Local Government Centre for Management Studies (KGSt)*, a local authority association that had already developed performance indicators in some service areas. However, a large-scale use of performance indicators, and, in particular, a comparison of performance based on performance indicators, did not take place due to the lack of financial resources.

This is where the Bertelsmann Foundation came into the fore. In cooperation with the *KGSt*, the *German Association of Civil Servants*[9] (a public service trade union) and, above all, local governments, the *Bertelsmann Foundation* designed and financed the development and implementation of comparative performance measurement.

Method

The following brief outline concentrates on the relatively "hard" service areas of the first subproject.

---

9 Deutscher Beamtenbund

The project is controlled by a policy board that mainly consists of the Chief Executive Officers of the participating cities and scientists.

The work done in the individual cities is organised from bottom-up, i.e. with the highest possible participation of the personnel, including elected staff representatives. The goal of this organisation is to win the expert knowledge and approval of those concerned and to counteract, from the very start, any fears that may exist with regard to comparative performance measurement.

In each city, a control group has been established which comprises representatives of the central units (personnel, organisation, finances), the heads of the service areas and the chairman of the personnel committee, and which monitors the project work. In addition to this, so-called expert teams have been set up in each service area, thus ensuring a broad participation of the personnel that is actually responsible for the provision of the services.

The inter-authority work is coordinated by inter-authority expert teams that are made up of subject matter experts and managers from the participating cities. These working groups first developed a tentative list of objectives and performance indicators. They chose a complex performance measurement process indicating for each individual service to what extent each of the following objectives is met:
- overall objective (service mission),
- client satisfaction,
- employee satisfaction,
- efficiency.

The performance indicators developed in discussions between subject matter experts were subsequently tested in the individual cities. The original list of indicators was then repeatedly revised on the basis of the test results.

The perfected performance indicators form the basis of a reporting system that gives a detailed synoptic picture of how the participating cities have performed with regard to the four criteria mentioned above. These reports do not represent any ranking! They rather give a survey of excellent, satisfactory and insufficient results achieved by each individual city in the four target areas. This implies that none of the cities can be a winner or loser down the line. As a consequence, the initial fears of cutting a poor figure when being measured against another city soon disappeared. In most cases, positive aspects prevailed as good performance, which had not been known until then, was made transparent. The synopsis of the performance in the four target areas allowed the management, politicians and public in the individual cities to obtain a balanced picture of the strong points and weaknesses of their own municipal administration.

The strong points and weaknesses are analysed by quality assurance circles formed by the rank and file according to the principle "Self-management rather than outside control". This analysis is immediately followed by the development of suggestions for improvement. The reports that are submitted to the management level and the council not only contain an analysis of strong points and weaknesses but also suggestions for improvement. It is thus ensured that the persons involved do not give too much attention to the mistakes made in the past but rather concentrate on learning from these mistakes and on the best possible control for the future.

In concrete terms, the following reporting system is currently applied: a quarterly report is prepared for each service area, with a detailed report being submitted to the middle management and a summary report being passed on to the top management. Once a year a "management report" is submitted to the council. This report contains comments on the individual services and provides a survey of the planned and implemented performance improvements.

The public and media are informed about the results of the annual reports at an open council meeting. The performance comparison as such, the comments made by the local administrative bodies and the political discussion enable the media to report in a competent way and put politicians and the top management under considerable pressure to improve performance in those areas in which it is deficient.

Other cities and counties are made familiar with the system of comparative performance measurement jointly developed by the pilot cities and with the methods applied and encouraged by the Bertelsmann Foundation to establish "comparative performance measurement circles". Meanwhile these circles comprise about 150 additional local governments. The continuous increase in the number of local governments involved and the ever vaster range of results thus obtained ensure that the idea of the "sporting competition" is spreading more and more in local government.

Comparative performance measurement requires a strong training element. Without it, the participating cities and counties would not be able to benefit from the comparison of their performance. This caused the Bertelsmann Foundation to develop model-type seminars and workshops for the employees involved in comparative performance measurement, the middle management, top management and local politicians.

Effects

A few examples of the effects that comparative performance measurement has had so far are described below. They have been collected in the residents' registration sector in which comparative performance measurement was implemented first.

Opening hours:
The weekly number of hours units stay open to the public were defined as the criterion for client orientation. Surprisingly big variations were observed in this respect. In fact, the number of opening hours per week varied between 18 and 32 hours. The municipalities with particularly short opening hours had in the past rejected all attempts at longer opening hours for fear of higher personnel requirements and thus higher costs. However, a comparison of costs showed that the municipalities with longer opening hours had not necessarily incurred higher costs. They had rather taken organisational measures to reconcile economy and client orientation. Staff members and management in the "weaker" units promptly agreed on longer opening hours, as nobody wanted to be at the bottom of the list. None of the units involved currently stays open less than 27 hours per week.

Test phone calls:
The handling of phone calls when dealing with clients is an important element of service quality. For this reason, phone calls are made at regular intervals in order to test whether the answers given are correct, the operator is friendly and how long it takes him/her to put the caller through from the central telephone exchange to the competent staff member. This pe-

riod varied between 32 and 60 seconds when the first test calls were made. In the city with the worst results the reasons were generally known: the telephone system was antiquated and overloaded, but still the city was not prepared to spend the high amount of money that was necessary to buy a new system. However, when the negative result became known, the employees insisted on improvement, as they did not want to be identified with the poor service. The management finally had a valid argument for the purchase of a new telephone system and was able to carry its point with the council for the acquisition of a new system.

Collection of fees and charges:
The residents' registration units provide a variety of data from the register. Unless the clients requesting such information are exempted from fees, the units charge them for this service and thus receive a considerable revenue. The rate of such revenue is detailed in the performance comparison. As a consequence, the municipal staff members carefully observe the development of this rate. When Deutsche Telekom, a major client requesting information from the register that had previously enjoyed public authority status, was privatised, it lost its privilege of obtaining information through administrative cooperation and thus free of charge. Thanks to the new interest of one city's employees in the revenue of their unit, Telekom's new liability to pay fees was discovered. This particular city collected the fees it was entitled to earlier than any other city.

Reduction of costs:
The decentralisation of responsibility and authority was also connected with the transfer of financial responsibility to the units. Comparative performance measurement details the costs and cost recovery percentages of the organisational units that participate in the project. This has led to interesting results in several of the cities:
– In one city the computer programme had to be changed because fees and charges had been raised by law. In such a case, the management services unit would normally have called an external technician whose bill would then have been paid by the same unit. As this outside service was now to be paid out of the residents' registration unit's own budget, the unit thought of changing the computer programme itself. It thus

saved the money that would otherwise have been paid to the outside technician.
- In the past, certain service units and the personnel department had to go through a constant struggle for temporary personnel. A lot of energy was wasted on filing applications for temporary staff and on protesting against the rejection or delayed acceptance of such applications. One city granted its units a budget item that they could use to finance temporary staff. All the money saved could be kept by the unit. The result was that temporary staff was employed in quite a different way and far less frequently than before.
- Whereas in the past management service units had to fight against a flood of procurement requests of all kinds, e.g. for office furniture and equipment, and the warehouse could hardly stock all the material, the warehouse manager of one city now finds that his warehouse "has never been so empty ." The obligation to finance their requirements out of their own budgets makes the units think twice before they decide to buy something new.

These few examples clearly demonstrate the scope of opportunities inherent in self-responsibility and self-management. As soon as the basic conditions for reasonable behaviour had been created, it was the rank and file of staff members that initiated positive changes. The central support units which, until then, had been responsible for such decisions probably would not even have perceived the chances for improvement. If, in exceptional cases, they had actually detected these chances, the rank and file in the service units might not have cooperated (see subjects above on opening hours, change in a computer programme and procurement). The results achieved not only satisfy the top management and the council but also the rank and file of staff members who now have a much better chance to do work that is evidently successful and useful.

Outlook

In cooperation with the *KGSt*, the Bertelsmann Foundation is currently working towards making comparative performance measurement a modernisation instrument of local government on a lasting basis. This

can be ensured by continuing and/or initiating the following programmes:
- further development and updating of the system,
- management of comparative performance measurement at the inter-authority level,
- software development,
- inter-municipal comparison via Internet,
- improvement and updating of indicators, measuring methods, etc.,
- quality assurance of the data supplied,
- training,
- research.

After a medium-term funding by the Bertelsmann Foundation, these activities would have to cover the costs incurred.

3.1.2 The Project of the International City/County Management Association (ICMA)

At the beginning of 1995, the *ICMA* initiated its comparative performance measurement programme which includes 39 cities and eight counties. In the course of this programme, the following service areas are examined: police, fire, neighbourhood services/quality of life and support services inside administration.

The primary objectives of the project are to:
- improve each participant's ability to regularly assess the performance of major services;
- develop management mechanisms for the monitoring of the four service areas;
- provide performance information on other, similar jurisdictions that can help guide each participant's own efforts and/or permit the identification of "performance gaps" between jurisdictions which participants could use to formulate specific improvement programmes.

These objectives are to be reached by extensive inter-authority cooperation. The organisational structure of the project is very similar to the Bertelsmann project. In fact, it is monitored by a Policy Board which is in charge of a Steering Committee and Technical Advisory Committees

(TACs) that deal with the individual service areas. One distinguishes between the following types of indicators: input indicators, output indicators, outcome indicators and efficiency and productivity indicators.

In the meantime, staff members of the Bertelsmann Foundation have visited the *ICMA* in Washington. Further visits arranged by the *ICMA* to organisations that are dealing with comparative performance measurement and to a local authority that participates in the project have also taken place. These contacts have proved extremely fruitful for both sides. A continuation of the exchange of experience has thus been agreed upon.

From the Bertelsmann Foundation's point of view, the two projects mainly differ with respect to the following aspects:

- The approach of the *ICMA* project leaves competition out of consideration (although the participating local authorities can obviously use the project under this aspect). The term competition does not appear in the project documents.
- The project is primarily interested in the quality (often equated with effectiveness) of local government performance, i.e. how the quality is judged by the clients or customers. This is due to the fact that customer satisfaction is considered to be the primary purpose of local government. As a consequence, interviews professionally carried out with customers are of crucial importance in the collection of data.
- The American colleagues are very much concerned with the definition of the "overall objective" (also referred to as "service mission") of individual services. This definition determines which additional data are required.
- In contrast to quality comparison, and contrary to the approach of the Bertelsmann project, the comparison of costs is only of minor importance. According to the *ICMA*, this is due to the fact that very different cost accounting methods are used, which makes a comparison of costs too difficult.
- Employee satisfaction is of no importance at all in the *ICMA* project.

These differences in the project design, which are partly attributable to cultural reasons, are considered by both partners as an impulse to improve various details of their project. The comparative performance measurement programme is to run until the end of 1999 and subsequently to be continued on a lasting basis by a Center for Performance Measurement that is to be established by the *ICMA*.

3.2 The Citizen's Charter Performance Indicators: on the Way to Comparative Performance Measurement?

The *Local Government Act of 1992* puts British local governments under the obligation to inform their citizens and taxpayers about their performance every year. Such information is to be published in local newspapers. The law charges the *Audit Commission for Local Authorities* with the definition of the indicators on the basis of which local authorities have to measure their performance. As a result, the *Audit Commission* has published a number of performance indicators for most of the municipal service areas. In its publications, the *Audit Commission* points out that performance data tend to be of little interest unless they can be compared with performance data of other local governments. The Commission encourages local authorities to make such comparisons on their own initiative.

The central message of the *Citizen's Charter philosophy* is to improve the accountability of the individual local governments to their citizens. The idea of comparative performance measurement is no integral part of this message. The law does not enforce comparative performance measurement; at best it suggests that such inter-authority cooperation take place. As in all other countries, it could only be achieved by an initiative of the local authorities themselves. It will be interesting to observe whether in the United Kingdom there is a tendency at local level towards taking such an initiative.

It is to be noticed with interest that local authorities in the United Kingdom are under a statutory obligation to inform the public about their performance. Similar obligations exist in Denmark, New Zealand and perhaps also in other countries. The basic idea of such an obligation may also be interesting to those countries that find it difficult to acquire a taste for a central authority imposing binding performance indicators on local government, which they would consider a violation of the right to self-government of local authorities. If the statutory obligation allowed local authorities to define performance indicators by themselves on the basis of inter-authority comparison, such objections would no longer be justified. Such a statutory obligation would strongly promote the "sporting" type of competition between local authorities for the benefit of the citizens and the economy.

3.3 The Potential of Comparative Performance Measurement

Comparative performance measurement has some specific strong points which make it an independent method of performance improvement. It therefore appears beneficial for local government to use it in addition to the established types of competition, i.e. competitive tendering and internal markets.

3.3.1 Synergy by Inter-Authority Cooperation

A local government that uses competitive tendering and local markets does so in isolation from all other local authorities. If it wins a contract it never knows whether a far better performance would still have been possible. But this is of no interest to it, as at that moment it considers the market to be the absolute standard. However, the question whether "we could do better" should be of interest to any local government at any time for the benefit of its citizens. To answer this question far more information is needed than the data supplied by a single public invitation to tender. Such information is made available by benchmarking comparisons, which, however, can be obtained only through the close and lasting cooperation of a major number of modernisation-oriented local authorities.

Objections are occasionally voiced, especially on the industry side, that such a comparison of public authorities would be of no avail as it only compares "lame ducks" with other "lame ducks." This objection can easily be refuted. Every local practitioner knows that among the country's many local authorities there are pioneers in every special field that are capable of outstanding performance. The only problem is that these pioneers are not known – often they themselves do not know how good they are – and that they are only found by chance. Comparative performance measurement makes us independent of such chance. It makes the performance of leading authorities generally known and can thus initiate a process of collective performance enhancement.

3.3.2 Only Winners, No Losers?

If a local department competes for an order without eventually receiving it, it will initially feel like a loser – and then hopefully learn from the misfortune. Cutting a poor figure in comparative performance measurement is a far less grave experience. As the loser aspect is only of little importance, the experience that consists in learning from others how to work smarter can come to the fore. As a consequence, a process of continuous learning and improvement under psychologically favourable conditions can get under way.

3.3.3 Focus on the Organisation as a Whole

In competitive tendering the interest is focused on success as such without paying much attention to how it was achieved. In comparative performance measurement subject matter experts discuss matters with each other which ensures that they will inevitably ask the best of class: how did you achieve this result? In this way, they go deeply into the organisational and motivational conditions of service delivery. At the same time, the internal coherence of the individual services provided by a local authority is brought into focus. This reduces the danger that the improvement of a service which is in the centre of the politicians' and the public's attention is achieved at the price of a general deterioration of the overall performance of the local authority. Whereas competitive tendering directs the spotlight only at the individual service, comparative performance measurement is also interested in the intricate web of processes providing for "related" services and in the performance infrastructure of the entire local authority. It thus makes the local government aware of possibilities of simplifying its production processes according to business reengineering principles. Only a local government that constantly focuses on this aspect will stand a chance of being among the most efficient authorities on a lasting basis.

3.3.4 Public Interest and Democratic Accountability

In many countries, the role and purpose of local government is considered to consist in organising the public interest and common weal in the best possible way at a local level. It goes without saying that the local government is accountable to its citizens for the results of its efforts. Whenever this role of local government has been accepted, it will not be the local politicians' primary objective to transfer as many services as possible to external providers. Their ambition will rather be to ensure that, whoever may be the provider, the range of local services that have been determined on a political basis be rendered to the citizens at the most favourable price and in a way that best complies with their requirements. In many cases, a local government will be able to ensure the common weal component of a service more efficiently if the service is provided by its own staff, as in that case it is not limited to controlling the services by specification and contract monitoring but can, if necessary, use the hierarchical means that continue to exist even in an organisation that has been restructured according to the core-periphery principle. If price and quality are right, this may often be the best solution in the citizen's interest. In-house provision of services also remedies the mentioned lack in clarity in the council's accountability to its citizens.

3.4 Political and Institutional Framework Conditions of Successful Comparative Performance Measurement

3.4.1 Use of Performance Boosters

No local government is able, on its own resources, to continuously keep the range of its services at the highest possible level of efficiency and quality. This is due to the fact that the intrinsic incentives are not strong enough. It is therefore necessary to support the ambition that is to be observed with many employees in every organisation to achieve a good performance by mobilising performance boosters in the immediate environment of the local authority. The most important future performance booster will be the citizens themselves who are asking with increasing emphasis whether the services provided by their local authority are value for money. In the future, local authorities can no longer afford to ignore this question.

As already explained, the market is another important performance booster. A local government that, in agreement with its citizens, provides most of the services itself must be unconditionally willing to constantly measure its standards against the services offered by the external market. What counts is that the management fulfills its task of looking for better alternatives on a lasting basis.

Local politicians may also be considered a performance booster. As they are interested in being re-elected they are anxious to offer their citizens a broad range of high-quality services that are value for money. A local government whose way of operating is traditional, complicated and expensive drastically limits these political opportunities.

If the potential of performance boosters is well orchestrated and combined with the internal incentives offered by a decentralised organisation and modern personnel management, then this is a configuration that will derive optimum benefit from comparative performance measurement on the one hand and benchmarking, which is based on comparative performance measurement, on the other hand.

3.4.2 Publicity of the Results

The best concept of comparative performance measurement will be worth nothing unless it is implemented and used for improvements at the local level. There is no denying the fact that local managers are sometimes tempted to keep the knowledge gained to themselves and "file" it. In this way, they save themselves trouble and disputes with their employees. Even top management and local politicians sometimes have the feeling that they are opening themselves to unnecessary political problems by participating in comparative performance measurement. The major players in the local arena must be willing, of course, to put their performance to the test.

In this respect, we can learn from the British example. A statutory liability for local governments to publish performance data would prevent the results of comparative performance measurement from disappearing in a drawer. If local governments were put under a statutory obligation to compare their performance and account to their citizens for the results they have achieved, this would not be an encroachment on local autonomy but only a more precise expression of the general democratic accountability that already exists.

3.4.3 Management Infrastructure

The management infrastructure to be created for successful comparative performance measurement is the same as that required for competitive tendering or internal markets. The administrative machinery has to be strongly decentralised according to the core-periphery principle, and the autonomised operational units must be held responsible for the results of their work. This requires that they be given far more leeway in handling resources. Contracts on budgets and results have to be concluded between the management and the operational units. Finally, an informational infrastructure must be created that makes local government activity transparent. The cost of each service must be known, which requires a well developed management accounting system. This can only be realised by means of advanced information and communication technology. And eventually staff management must be radically different from the practices that are still used in the traditional hierarchical organisations.

3.4.4 "Meta Organisations"

At present local authorities, left on their own, seem to be unable to initiate comprehensive comparative performance measurement and keep it going. This applies to local authorities in all countries. Obviously meta organisations that contribute commitment, methodology, coordination and funding are needed at least in the first few years. Foundations or local authority associations appear to be particularly qualified to assume this function.

Comprehensive comparative performance measurement is costly. No solution has as yet been found for its funding on a permanent basis. One possibility would be to put local governments under a statutory obligation to account to their citizens for their performance by using comparative performance measurement and funding it.

3.5 Relationship between Comparative Performance Measurement and the Established Types of Competition

Comparative performance measurement and the established types of competition do not exclude but rather complement each other.

Competitive tendering needs comparative performance measurement as a monitoring instrument to identify excessive prices of external providers (which need not necessarily be the result of illegal collusion). Due to the permanent character of comparative performance measurement, it can also be used to ensure that gains through competitive tendering are maintained over time.

The other way round, the strong pressure for change exerted by the open market test may be welcome to help local governments actually implement the improvements identified by comparative performance measurement.

4. Outlook

This paper suggests that comparative performance measurement holds a substantial potential for modernisation and improvement. As a consequence, everything should be done to make the ongoing projects in Germany and the United States successful, i.e. to develop them to become a comprehensive comparison of performance that is implemented and continuously updated by a growing number of local governments. It will still take a few years to ensure this and require a lot of commitment and money. The exchange of experience agreed upon between the Bertelsmann Foundation and the *ICMA* can help to improve the chances of success on this intricate and politically sensitive ground. It would be beneficial to include the British experience with the *Citizen's Charter Performance Indicators* and the experience gathered in other countries that have put their local governments under a statutory obligation to account for their performance into this exchange of experience.

It is to be hoped that the results published will encourage other countries to initiate comparative performance measurement.

As many of the problems that exist at the local government level are very similar in different countries, some of the recommendations for improvement that are derived from a national comparative performance measurement are likely to be of interest to a larger number of local governments. It would thus seem useful to make them available in the Internet.

Literature

No books have as yet been published on the subject of "comparative performance measurement in local government." However, the Bertelsmann Foundation has published a brochure entitled "Comparative Performance Measurement" (Gütersloh 1997) which contains the most important elements of the project. The following books give a comprehensive survey of performance measurement in general:

The Urban Institute/ICMA (eds), How Effective are Your Community Services: Procedures for Measuring Their Quality, 1992.

Ammons, D. N. (ed.), Accountability for Performance: Measurement and Monitoring in Local Government (ICMA Practical Management Series), 1995.

The following book deals with the effects of market mechanisms in the British public sector:

Walsh, K., Public Services and Market Mechanisms: Competition, Contracting and the New Public Management, London 1995.

From a European point of view:

Naschold, F., Modernisation of the Public Sector in Europe: A Comparative Perspective of the Scandinavian Experience (Finnish Ministry of Labour), Helsinki 1995.

Christchurch: Culture Change in the Staff Organisation – An International Perspective

Mike Richardson, Ian Brooks

Executive Summary 211
1. Introduction 215
2. Organisational Culture................................. 217
   2.1 What is Organisational Culture? 217
   2.2 Why are Organisational Cultures Important? 219
3. Organisational Culture in Local Government 220
   3.1 Perceptions of Organisational Culture.............. 220
   3.2 Old and New Cultures in Local Government
       Organisations 223
   3.3 The Importance of Subcultures 223
4. The Causes of Change................................... 226
   4.1 Change Forces...................................... 226
       4.1.1 External Forces 226
       4.1.2 Organisational Forces 228
       4.1.3 Political and Managerial Leadership.......... 228
5. Initiating Change...................................... 230
   5.1 The Importance of a Vision Statement 230
   5.2 Who was Involved?.................................. 232
   5.3 What Was the Vision Setting Process? 233
6. Implementing Change.................................... 234
   6.1 Types of Change 234
   6.2 Mechanisms of Culture Change 236
       6.2.1 Strategy and Outputs........................ 236
       6.2.2 Structural Change 237

	6.2.3 Systems	239
	6.2.4 Changes in Human Resources Practices	239
7.	The Consequences of Change	241
	7.1 Responses to Change	241
	7.2 The Measurement and Duration of Change	243
8.	Future Research	243
	8.1 Service Orientation	244
	8.2 Structure and Diversity of Local Government Organisational Cultures	245
	8.3 The Responsiveness of Local Government Cultures to Planned Change	245
Appendix		246

Executive Summary

We identified a number of important themes or key messages from our research.

Firstly, we wanted to comment on the significance of the very consistent response we received on the subject of what type of culture respondents were seeking to create. Overwhelmingly, respondents told us they wanted to build quality, learning, value-for-money, efficient, customer-focused, decentralised cultures. This demonstrates the pervasive influence of private sector managerialist values in local government, which Hood[10] noted during the 1980s. This uniformity in response may in itself be an important source of change in local government.

Institutional theory[11] suggests that organisations often seek to mimic or emulate each other. Sometimes, and importantly in the public sector, organisations try to acquire legitimacy by behaving appropriately by doing what other organisations do[12]. For example, it may be perceived that "good councils" develop vision or mission statements that stress customer service and quality. Other organisations, seeking credibility and legitimacy, or unsure about how to achieve success, may adopt these practices in form if not always in substance. In this process they are aided by educators and consultants, and by best-practice networks, of which the Bertelsmann network could be regarded as one. They may also be influenced by management fads as managers seek quick and easy solutions to complex problems[13].

The second conclusion we drew was that there is no single "best way" of effecting cultural change. There was just as much diversity in change strategies and mechanisms as there was uniformity in change goals. From rapid structural change spanning a matter of months, to participative, empowering programmes that will take many years, we noted a continuum

---

10 Hood, C. (1995), The "New Public Management" in the 1980s: variations on a theme. *Accounting, Organisations and Society* (forthcoming).
11 See John Meyer and Brian Rowen (1977), "Institutionalised organisations: formal organisation as myth and ceremony". *American Journal of Sociology.* Vol 83, 340–363.
12 W. Richard Scott provides a very good explanation of institutional theory in *Institutions and organisations*, Thousand Oaks, CA (1995).
13 Levinson, H. (1992), "Fads, Fantasies, and Psychological Management." *Consulting Psychology Journal*, 44(1), 1–12.

of successful approaches to change. Each approach has advantages (for example, speed), and disadvantages (for example, increased resistance), and to a large extent the onus is on management to select change strategies and mechanisms that maximise the advantages and minimise the disadvantages in any particular organisational situation. There is no single best strategy. As one person put it, "you have to pick your problem." That is to say, can you live with the disadvantages of the approach you have selected?

When we asked people what they would do differently next time, many answered that they would try and improve communication, and in particular they would spend more time up front communicating the need for change. This communication needs to be more than just a unilateral directive: it requires to be a genuine two-way dialogue[14] that allows different groups in the organisation to feel that they are contributing. This point was well made by Cherry Lucas (Dunedin City Council) who said that one of the roadblocks to change in her organisation was a feeling "that the solution had already been pre-determined". To communicate effectively requires a major commitment on the part of the CEO and management, a point noted by many respondents. As Richard Bowers (City of Scottsdale) said, a lot of work must be put into persuading people that a "commitment to change a process must be in some way connected to someone's dissatisfaction with their performance." Another person described poor communication as "a spanner thrown in the works." The advice we offer is *communicate, communicate, communicate*, seeing communication as a process of dialogue which creates commitment and involvement.

Fourthly, we noted a number of paradoxes inherent in change processes. John Walker (Brent Council) raised a dilemma that faces councils that choose rapid, centrally directed, structural change as their preferred strategy. "There is a tension between encouraging maximum devolution and ensuring conformance to a radical change programme. You cannot si-

---

14 We refer to the importance of engaging in "dialogue" as distinct to "discussion.. We would characterise the difference as follows:
Inquire/learn rather than tell/sell/persuade; Unfold shared meaning rather than gain agreement on one meaning; Integrate multiple perspectives rather than evaluate parts; Advocate to contribute rather than advocate to convince; Inquire to understand rather than inquire to evaluate; Uncover/examine assumptions rather than justify/defend assumptions.

multaneously tell people you are empowering them and instruct them to follow a particular change programme." Even in Hæmeenlinna, where change was much slower, Robert Arnkil commented: "Finding a good balance between centrally driven efforts and further decentralisation needs continuous attention." It is almost as if there is a clash of management paradigms involved. On the one hand there is the current paradigm that emphasises the importance of empowering the work force, and on the other there is a paradigm that emphasises the importance of strong leadership and rapid decisive action to downsize or otherwise make significant efficiency gains.

Consistency would require that if you are going to empower workers then they should have an empowering role in the change process. If through choice or necessity a centrally directed change strategy is adopted, then the evidence suggests that the price is disempowerment and higher levels of resistance. Part of the answer may lie in being very clear as to the boundaries within which individuals and teams are being encouraged to act with autonomy. In Christchurch our aim has become for teams to be empowered, but aligned with the organisation's strategic direction.

In a similar vein it is difficult to effect positive cultural change in an environment where redundancies are occurring, or where services are being lost to private sector competitors through external tendering processes. It is not uncommon for quality programmes to be introduced as part of a package of measures that include downsizing and cost cutting, forced by legislation or financial necessity. Lawler notes that "there has been considerable debate about whether a move toward employee involvement is possible in an environment characterised by downsizing and delayering."[15] The evidence suggests that if the changes do in fact result in more employee involvement and skills development then it is possible to downsize and effect positive change, although it is certainly made more difficult.

Change requires perseverance, energy, and commitment. The daily demands of organisational life continue: change requires additional effort, often over sustained periods of time. There were numerous reports in our

---

15 Lawler, E.L., Mohrman, S.A., and Ledford, G.E. (1992), *Employee Involvement and Total Quality Management*. San Fransisco.

survey of casualties in terms of burn out, exhaustion, heart attacks, resignations, and other symptoms of stress. This sits uneasily with change programmes that have people as their focus. It is difficult for people to feel valued or empowered if work-induced stress levels are rising.

The final paradox we noted was that arising from the common emphasis on teams in many change programmes. In our case it was more acute because our culture statement focused in part on creating a sense of being valued, which is very much an individual motivator. However, other aspects of our change programme have a clear focus on teams, and we are left to address issues such as whether accountabilities and remuneration should be individual or team-based.

Most respondents commented on how slow culture change was. Having an understanding of the culture construct explains why this is so. Cultures are constraining forces that serve to maintain organisations. They enhance and preserve predictability and stability. Remember, anthropologists originally used the culture construct to explain why group behaviour was consistent over time. Thus we should not be surprised to find when we come to study organisational culture change that cultures (organisations) are notoriously difficult to change, or at least change quickly.

This leads us to our next finding. We noted a difference in approach between organisations that consciously set about changing their culture, and those that set out to change their organisation, albeit knowing that their culture would change. Organisations in the first category, including ours, generally took a slower and what might be regarded as a "softer" approach. Often structural change was small or initiated by middle managers rather than driven from the top-down. Organisations that set out to achieve organisational change, on the other hand, were more willing to rely on structural changes, in some cases fairly significant, to achieve their change objectives.

Finally, we are much more aware of the importance of subcultures than we were previously. Organisations consist of multiple subcultures, some of which will align closely to the new culture, and others will not. This has practical implications for managing the change process, and it also raises some interesting questions about the wisdom of seeking to create or impose uniform values throughout an organisation. How realistic is it? There are a number of ethical issues surrounding the use of normative controls to manage organisations better that become clearer when we think about the subcultural value structures that may be quite different to our own.

1. Introduction

The years 1989–1994 saw very rapid change for the Christchurch City Council: amalgamation of councils, a new organisation structure, corporatisation of trading functions, development of corporate planning systems, launch in some units of TQMinitiatives and a large number of other initiatives touching most facets of the organisation.

Significant efficiency gains had been made, partly by all staff working harder, but this source of gain was felt to be exhausted. We wanted to make sure that the continuing changes were consistent one with another and collectively would move the organisation in an appropriate direction. We also considered that despite (or because of) the amount of change there was evidence that attitudes of staff too often frustrated what was thought to be worthwhile initiatives. Perhaps most important was a commitment to pay more than lip-service to a belief that staff could "work smarter'," largely through unlocking their innate potential and creativity. So we decided to give priority to developing our organisational culture.

A statement was prepared that summarised the culture we wanted to move towards. This statement has subsequently been used as a yardstick to test current practices in the council and to determine priorities for all facets of change within the organisation. New practices will only be adopted if they are consistent with it.

Our experience over the last two years has led us to want to share some of the things we have done and learned, and also to learn from the experience of others. The Bertelsmann network provided an ideal means of achieving both aims.

Our primary research interest in preparing this paper was to address the general question, how have councils planned and implemented organisational culture change? In addition to this general question, we also asked

215

Figure 1: A framework for studying organisational culture change

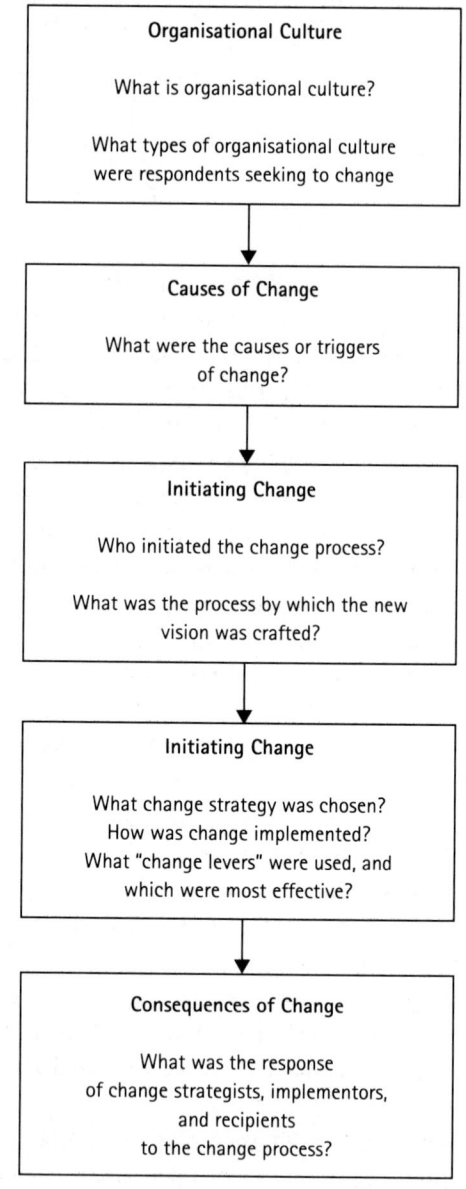

a number of specific questions (see figure 1). Our purpose was more to ask questions rather than provide the "right answer" to often unique and complex problems.

To assist us in our research we renewed our contact with members of a research group in the Department of Management at the University of Canterbury who are conducting research into the process and measurement of organisational culture change. Together we devised an open-ended questionnaire that was sent to councils within the Bertelsmann network. We received 35 replies (see appendix A for a description of respondent councils), which were analysed using qualitative, that is to say, non-statistical, analytical methods. In reporting the results of our analysis we have tried to avoid providing a collated list of all the replies we received. Instead, we have endeavoured to distill and report the most important themes.

We noted two important features of the responses to our questionnaire. The first was the amount of change that local government worldwide has been subject to over the last decade. The popular traditional image of local government as staid and bureaucratic is rapidly changing and our hope is that this paper will assist other local authorities cope with the challenge of organisational change in the future. The second feature was the willingness of councils to critically appraise their own efforts. This openness was much appreciated in the preparation of this paper.

2. Organisational Culture

2.1 What is Organisational Culture?

The organisational culture concept is an offshoot of the culture construct that was developed in the late 19th century by anthropologists in Europe and the United States. They coined the term "culture" to explain the shared behaviours and practices that were specific to particular groups or societies. Culture is a metaphor drawn from the Latin *cultura,* meaning a cultivating. As tilling and cultivating produces regular patterns on the land, so a culture produces patterns of behaviour amongst members of that culture. The concept found its way into organisation studies during the 1930s when Elton Mayo recruited a number of anthropologists to participate in the now famous Hawthorne bank-wiring room studies. This was the first time researchers had systematically studied the social organisation of workers in an industrial setting.

Although Elliott Jacques wrote *The Changing Culture of the Factory* in 1952, it was not until the early 1980s that organisational culture became a popular concept in management literature. At that time American manufacturing was perceived as being in a state of crisis: production was falling as domestic products were replaced by imports, particularly from Japan, and unemployment was rising. American consultants, academics, and managers looked to Japan to try and identify the reasons for Japan's success and, not unnaturally, cultural differences featured prominently in this process of appraisal. In the space of a few years four books[16] were published that introduced and emphasised the importance of having a strong culture with widely shared norms, values and beliefs. The most important of these books, *In Search of Excellence*, is still the best-selling management book ever written. In it, Tom Peters and Richard Waterman repeatedly emphasise the importance of having the right corporate culture and of using values to achieve "simultaneous loose-tight control." An excellent organisation does not rely on tightly constraining rules and procedures; instead, people choose to do what is required of them because they wish to serve the values that they share with those in charge.

Reflecting the concept's eclectic origins, academics have failed to agree on a definition of organisational culture.[17] However, the definition that has attracted the most management interest is that of culture as an organisational sub-system that includes the following: ". . . the common philosophies, ideologies, values, assumptions, perceptions, expectations, attitudes and norms which bind a group together."[18]

---

16 These books were *Theory Z: How American Business Can Meet the Japanese Challenge* by William Ouchi (1981, Reading, Ma.), *The Art of Japanese Management: Applications for American Executives* by Pascale and Athos (1982, New York), *In Search of Excellence: Lessons from America's Best-run Companies* by Tom Peters and Richard Waterman (1982, New York), and *Corporate Cultures: the Rites and Rituals of Corporate Life* by Terrence Deal and Allan Kennedy (1982, Reading, Ma.).
17 Alvesson, M., and Berg, O. (1992), *Corporate Culture and Organisational Symbolism*, Berlin. The authors devote three chapters to defining organisational culture.
18 Kilmann, R.H., Saxton, M.J., and Serpa, R. eds. (1985), *Gaining Control of the Corporate Culture*, San Fransisco, p. 5.

We find this definition useful. Our own culture statement has headings such as the "CCC way of doing things" and the "CCC way of working together." For us it has become increasingly important to use our culture statement as a normative framework not just when planning new programmes but in thinking about all our day-to-day interactions in the workplace.

2.2 Why are Organisational Cultures Important?

During the 1980s and 90s the growth of organisational culture as a management concept was influenced by TQM and the quality movement generally, and by the shift away from manufacturing towards services in western economies. TQM has been described as being primarily a process of culture change[19] wherein the development of a quality culture is the key to achieving quality. In the burgeoning services management literature there is a strong emphasis on developing and managing a service culture.[20] Service production cannot be standardised and subjected to the same rules and procedures as manufacturing, often because of the variability introduced by the involvement of customers in many aspects of the service delivery. Bureaucratic rules and procedures are of less value in service industries such as local government: in fact they often work against effective service delivery. The best way for management to exercise control and ensure quality is to develop a culture that enables employees to exercise discretion within the boundaries set by shared norms and values. In this way bureaucratic controls are replaced by normative controls. Axioms such as "do it by the book" no longer hold. Managers are interested in organisational culture because they believe that there is a link between it and their organisation's performance.

Studies suggest that this relationship operates in a number of ways:
1. The most common argument is that organisations with "strong" cultures perform better than other organisations. Strong cultures are said to exist where management and staff share consistent values and

---

19 A quality culture "is at the heart of the TQM theory and philosophy" (Chopin, J., 1991, *Quality Through People*, Bedford: IFS Publications, p. 326).
20 See for example, *Service Management and Marketing* (1990, Lexington, Ma.) in which the author, Christian Gronroos, devotes a chapter to managing a service culture.

norms. Cultural strength influences organisational performance in three ways. Firstly, it contributes to goal alignment – everyone works together towards a common end. Secondly, strong cultures are said to produce high levels of motivation. People like their work and put more into it. Finally, strong cultures provide a normative basis for control which means that fewer restrictive bureaucratic controls are required.
2. Next, it is argued that what is important is not having a strong culture, but having the "right" culture. A good culture is one that fits, one that is strategically appropriate for the environment the organisation operates in. The better the fit, the better the performance.
3. The third group of theories suggests that organisational cultures can be a source of sustainable competitive advantage. If an organisational culture can be created that is unique, that others cannot imitate, then that culture is said to provide the only real opportunity to create a truly sustainable competitive advantage.
4. Finally, it has been suggested that organisations that have adaptive cultures, cultures that adapt to the continually changing needs of stakeholders, are the only organisations that will be successful over time. This perspective is critical of the strong and right culture arguments. Strong cultures are said to constrain organisations, and cultures that fit today may not fit tomorrow. What is needed are cultures where the strongest values relate to the need to be adaptable in a changing environment. While these theories have found widespread acceptance amongst managers, we should note that there is little or no evidence to support any of them, even though they may "feel right."

3. Organisational Culture in Local Government

3.1 Perceptions of Organisational Culture

Respondents were asked to explain what they understood by the phrase "organisational culture," and to describe their organisation's culture as it was when they began their change programme. The common theme that came through the responses was that "organisational culture is the (usually) unwritten set of norms, values, beliefs and assumptions that guide the thoughts, attitudes and behaviour of members of an organisation."

Organisational culture was colloquially described as "the feel of the place," "the softer dimension," "the way we do things around here," "our organisation's personality," and "our ways." Some respondents described organisational culture in more holistic, embracing terms: for example, Robert Arnkil of the City of Hæmeenlinna in Finland described it as an "overall concept describing the vision, basic values, goals and personnel involvement of the organisation into a business idea and working principles" rather than as something an organisation has. Other people described organisational culture as those things that an organisation holds as important, thereby giving it the status of a corporate ideology or philosophy that spells out how business should be conducted.

Bruce Anderson, CEO of Auckland City, asked in his response, why focus on organisational culture? Can cultural change really be thought of any differently from other changes in the organisation? This is a useful question to ask. If one adopts an anthropological perspective the answer is no; organisations are cultures, and by definition to talk of culture change is to talk of organisational change.[21]

The table shows how, if we take the anthropological view of organisations *as* cultures, everything about organisations is part of their culture.

This wider view of organisational culture was taken by Tharon Greene of the City of Hampton. He included the "internal architecture in terms of organisation structure, job design, and systems as they relate to the organisation's values" in his definition of culture.

While this view is valid, we take the perspective that organisations *have* cultures in the same way that humans have personalities. Two Councils might use similar systems, but "feel" very different as places to work. In this way, cultural change can be thought of as being distinct to structural or other forms of change. Culture can be viewed as just one sub-system of a total organisational system.

---

21 See Ann Jordan (1995), "Managing Diversity: Translating Anthropological Insight for Organisational Studies". *Journal of Applied Behavioural Science*, Vol 31, Issue 2, 124–140, from which the table is taken.

Table 1: Universal Components of Culture and Organisational Culture

Culture	Organisational Culture
Patterns of subsistence	Type of technology
	Division of labour
Religion and magic	Values, goals, ceremonies, myths
Economic system	Reward system
Political system	Organisational structure
	Leadership behaviour
	Power, politics, and conflict management
Language and communication	Communication
Social structure	Informal organisation structure
Art	Organisational artifacts; dress, logos, etc.

We accept in Christchurch that any changes to the organisation are affected by and will themselves affect our culture. Therefore we analyse current structures and practices and any proposed changes from a cultural perspective to identify whether or not they are aligned with our desired culture. Our approach sees structures, systems, strategies, etc., as contributing to culture, and so changing them is a means of achieving culture change. We believe that by being explicit about the culture we want, we can use our culture statement as a framework for testing the acceptability of current practices and proposed changes. That is to say, are they aligned to the culture that we want?

The importance of always acting in ways that are consistent with our cultural values is a lesson that we constantly relearn. One management action that is inconsistent seems to do more harm than half a dozen that are consistent with our culture statement. Initially we saw it as important to consider our cultural values in making "significant" decisions, but increasingly we have recognised the need to apply them to all our activities and behaviour.

3.2 Old and New Cultures in Local Government Organisations

Respondents almost uniformly described their organisation's culture prior to implementing change as bureaucratic, hierarchical, centralised, inflexible, internally focused, and lacking accountability. Just as consistently, the desired cultures they were seeking to create were described as customer-focused, decentralised, value-based, quality, learning, empowering, dynamic, adaptive, results-oriented, or accountable. This consistency is a reflection of the extent to which public administration, including local government, in OECD countries has been, since the mid 1980s, heavily influenced by managerialism.

Hood[22] refers to the influence of managerialism in the public sector as the "New Public Management" philosophy. It embraces the belief that, at least from the standpoint of management, the differences between the public and private sectors are not generally significant; hence public and private organisations can, and should, be managed on more or less the same basis. There is a shift in emphasis from process accountability to accountability for results; devolution of management; a preference for contestable provision of services; the introduction of private sector practices and systems; the use of monetary incentives; and an emphasis on cost-cutting and efficiency.[23] The responses we received confirmed the dominance of the managerialism paradigm in local government. That is not necessarily a bad thing because councils that are run more effectively and efficiently have a greater opportunity to deliver more or better service.

3.3 The Importance of Subcultures

It would be a mistake to think that most organisations have only a single, unitary homogeneous culture.[24] In fact, most organisations comprise mul-

---

22 Hood, C. (1995) (see n. 1).
23 Boston, J., Martin, J., Pallot, J., and Walsh, P. (1996), *Public Management: The New Zealand Model*. Auckland.
24 Although many popular management books promote the development of strong homogeneous cultures, the better view is that organisations contain many subcultures or "multiple cultural configurations" as Mats Alvesson (1993), *Cultural Perspectives on Organisations*. Cambridge describes them. For a good discussion of subcultures, see Harrison Trice and Janice Beyer (1993), *The Cultures of Work Organisations*. Englewood Cliffs, NJ.

tiple subcultures, which can be described as distinctive clusters of cultural forms shared by identifiable groups of people within an organisation.[25] Subcultures seem to emerge from face-to-face interaction and are often based around such variables as organisational sub-unit, occupation, profession, gender, class, and ethnic or national background.

Markku Takala and Osmo Saarelma of the City of Espoo pointed out that their council does not have "an obvious uniform culture"; different parts of their organisation, they say, have developed in different ways and now have their own subcultures. Likewise, Don Siddall described how the Toronto City Council has many cultures, rendering the Council similar in nature to a holding company.

Subcultures are noticeable where councils have been amalgamated. Tony Beynon reported that the amalgamation of two councils into the Gold Coast City Council brought together two very different cultures. It was actually the desire to develop a new culture for the amalgamated entity that triggered his council's organisational culture change programme.

Culture change programmes often have as their aim that everybody in the organisation should share a core set of common values or beliefs. But the wisdom and ethical correctness of seeking such organisation-wide cultural consensus is increasingly being questioned. Some see culture change or control programmes as having overtones of George Orwell's *1984*, while others such as Joanne Martin[26] distinguish between behavioural conformity – which a change programme may deliver – and ideological commitment, an often unattainable goal of management.

Research suggests that change efforts that recognise subcultural differences are more successful than approaches that treat the organisation as having a single integrated culture.[27] There are a number of reasons for this. Communication and information are very important during a change process, but some subcultures near the periphery of an organisation may have better access to, or even block, communication. The result may be that varying levels of resistance are generated. Similarly, change may ad-

---

25 See Harrison Trice (1993), *Occupational Subcultures in the Workplace*. New York.
26 See Joanne Martin (1992), *Cultures in Organisation: Three Perspectives*. New York, especially Chapter 6. Martin discusses culture from three different perspectives: the managerial, single-culture perspective; the organisations-as-subcultures perspective; and the social construction of reality perspective.
27 See above.

vantage some subcultures at the expense of others, throwing them into conflict with each other. Subcultures will have their own perception of what the proposed changes mean for them.[28] Change is more likely to be successful if management has an understanding of those perceptions. And it is inevitable that subcultures will be aligned with the proposed culture to differing degrees. One would expect those subcultures that are more closely aligned to be less resistant or even supportive of the change, while the converse is equally true.

This is an important issue for us in Christchurch. We are pursuing the notion that it is possible to implement a culture that holds good right through the organisation, and yet we are very aware of differences between its parts. Can, for instance, art gallery professionals and a drainage repair gang be expected to buy into the same set of values? Should customer service mean the same thing for library staff as for the planning enforcement team? We are not certain of the answers to questions such as these but we continue to work on the premise that we can have different emphases in parts of the organisation but still achieve overall alignment. Currently we are employing a "leadership development programme" as a catalyst for change throughout the organisation. As this programme "cascades" through different Units, thought is being given to tuning it to best meet differing needs and subcultures. In our view the biggest challenge arises within units that must win their work in competition with the private sector. For such units the new culture must unambiguously lead to their sustainable competitiveness.

We conclude that the appropriateness of aspiring to a single culture throughout the organisation, and how to accommodate subcultures, are important issues for councils to consider.

---

28 Isabella, L.A. (1990), Evolving Interpretations as Change Unfolds: How Managers Construe Key Organisational Events. *Academy of Management Journal* 33 (1), 7–41.

4. The Causes of Change

Organisations are always in motion, always changing. This makes it very difficult to state with clarity when change begins and when it ends, if it begins and ends at all. The identification and labelling of change is often a political process and it is helpful to ask who has a stake in declaring something to be changed or new.[29] In reply to our question asking respondents to identify the causes or triggers of change in their organisations some took us back to socio-economic changes in the early 1980s; others attributed change to the election of a new council or the appointment of a new CEO within the last twelve months; others to a financial crisis. This suggests that change can be the result of many different influences, can take place on many levels, and that a good understanding of change requires an awareness of this diversity. None saw change as resulting from an internal realisation that "things could be done better," although we in Christchurch, and probably others too, would see this as being an important factor.

4.1 Change Forces

4.1.1 External Forces

We identified three groups of change forces. Firstly, at a macro level there is a group of three environmental forces that has affected local government *as an industry*, at either a national or international level. The first of these is legislative change. Councils in Australia, Great Britain[30] and New Zealand all reported on the impact that legislative change has had on their operations. Here in New Zealand the 1989 legislative reforms (colloquially referred to as "amalgamation") had a radical effect. Central government's

---

29 Kanter, R. M., Stein, B. A., and Jick, T. D. (1992), *The Challenge of Organisational Change*, New York ask this important question.
30 The Warwick University Local Authorities Research Consortium is conducting research into organisational change in local government, and their work has identified changing central government legislation and policy as one of three key change drivers. The other two are socio-economic change and changes in local authority leadership and policies. (Courtesy of Kirklees Metropolitan Council)

final reorganisation scheme reduced the number of local authorities from 828 to 87, and a number of statutory operational requirements were put in place to ensure improved organisational accountability and effectiveness. In Australia reform has proceeded on a state-by-state basis, but with a similar emphasis on amalgamation into economically sustainable units; productivity gains through compulsory tendering of some services; and, in some instances, councils have been replaced by commissioners.

Secondly, there has been a shift in community expectations of local government. Whether this is the movement for less government in the United States, for more efficient local government in New Zealand, or dissatisfaction with the quantity and quality of services in Finland, the message is the same. The public's expectations of local government have been, and are, changing. For example, Seppo Kassi from the City of Kotka reported that the inhabitants of Kotka were no longer prepared to "pay for bureaucracy." Bonnie Snedecker, City of Seattle, noted that one of the triggers of change in Seattle was "higher consumer expectations for convenient, cost-effective service delivery."

In some instances the public mood was captured in media criticism of local government; George Tyler of the Auckland Regional Council noted that his organisation had "been targeted by a long-running series of media commentaries," and in the UK the Brent Council was "ridiculed by the press" before commencing its change programme .

The importance of the public's perception of local government is summed up well by Hans-Juergen Heib from the Heidelberg City Council: "In our democracy the credibility of public institutions is a highly valuable good. The goal of reform in public administration should be to counteract disillusionment with the state and politics through more friendly, more open and more efficient administrative work and to improve identification with the community."

The third factor has been socio-economic change, in some cases caused by rapid growth, but more often by recession or depression. Throughout our sample, financial pressures caused by flat or reduced revenues, in turn resulting from wider economic factors, were cited as a significant force for organisational change. For some councils these pressures amounted to a financial crisis that necessitated rapid transformational change. For others they were exacerbated by the loss or decline of a significant local industry. In some countries central government has been cutting back or withdrawing from the delivery of services, leaving a gap that local government is obliged to fill. Aimee Fortier of the Ottawa City Council noted that this trend was an important contributor to the financial pressures facing her council.

Whatever the cause, many councils found themselves having to cut their cloth according to their means, which meant either providing fewer services, or providing the same level of services more efficiently. For example, four years ago the Toronto City Council set itself cost reduction targets of up to 30 percent per annum for some departments. There was a clear expectation that these targets would be met.

4.1.2 Organisational Forces

The second group of change forces exists at an organisational level, and involves changes relating to organisational size, configuration, and systems. Often such changes relate to environmental changes of the type previously discussed, but the perspective of the person describing the change is organisational rather than industry-wide. Respondents identified a number of such changes, including financial pressure; amalgamation; restructuring; the requirement to participate in competitive tendering; moves to split policy functions from service delivery functions; downsizing and delayering; new decision making systems; new technology; reorganisation based on service delivery rather than function; taking on new functions abandoned by central government and dropping other functions; and shifting resources to service delivery functions.

4.1.3 Political and Managerial Leadership

The third and final group of changes results from changes in political and/or managerial control at organisational level. Local authorities are political organisations, and the democratic process inevitably brings about changes in the constitution of elected councils. These changes may result in different stakeholders or interest groups being represented, and in new policy directions being set. For example, in the City of Tea Tree Gully a newly elected council pressured managers to improve organisational performance in areas such as debt servicing, accountability, achievement of outcomes, and the quality of information flows. The Brent Council's ambitious and successful change programme received new impetus after the election of a new council in 1991 which gave the programme its full support.

A new CEO may bring a new style, new goals and objectives, and new ideas about how the organisation should operate. This is often the very reason that a change in leadership is made. Our survey results contained a number of examples of this. When Frank Fairbanks was appointed CEO of the City of Phoenix he brought with him "a consensus building approach to management" that has permeated the organisation. In Adelaide Ilan Hershman has implemented very significant change in the eighteen months since he was appointed CEO.

Peter Senge[31] has referred to change processes being launched in response to either desperation or aspiration. The former seems to have been more common in local government, with outside forces requiring greater efficiency and effectiveness. It may be, however, that conscious choices about cultural change are more often associated with aspirational change, where the initiative for change has been taken from within the organisation rather than forced upon it from the outside. There is a dynamic for change that has been important in Christchurch which is significant in the context of the Bertelsmann network. This is the power of learning from others, of exposure to ideas, leading to the envisioning of a better way of doing things. The following extract illustrates the importance of this in Christchurch. It is taken from a paper in which I tried to set down the origins of our culture change programme.

"By reason of my training and personal experiences I have always held the view that most people working in organisations most of the time are not encouraged or allowed to really give of their best. Too often the workplace is reduced to a contractual relationship of money for time. As individuals we develop all sorts of strategies to cope in such an environment. There is

---

31 Senge, P., Address to International Symposium on Local Government, Phoenix, USA, December 1994.

however an alternative, and, world-wide, a small number of organisations have managed to genuinely put it into place.

I am talking about 'the way we do things' and 'the way we work together.'

On becoming City Manager I spent six months casting about to find 'off the shelf' programmes which we could implement to begin to develop the culture of the organisation along these lines. In particular I was fortunate in being able to spend a month at the Australian Management School in November-December 1993. I came back from that experience firmly convinced that there were no ready made-programmes we could simply pick up and run with but rather there were a set of underlying principles around which we should develop our own initiatives. Recognising that we had many excellent features in our organisation, the requirement was to modify what we had rather than design something from scratch or pick up some textbook theory. We therefore needed our own set of guiding principles from which we could develop our own programmes."

We have classified organisational change forces into external, organisational and managerial, but in doing so we are conscious of the fact that this trichotomy is not always distinct. For example, if a council is being criticised by local media and the CEO decides that his organisation can and should perform better, is the resulting change the result of external (criticism) or internal (a decision to perform better) forces?

5. Initiating Change

5.1 The Importance of a Vision Statement

In 1987 the editors of *Fortune* magazine wrote: "The new paragon of an executive is a person who can envision a future for his organisation and then inspire his colleagues to join him in building that future."[32] It is tes-

---

32 "Wanted: Leaders who can make a difference.", Jeremy Main, *Fortune*, 28 September 1987, 92.

tament to the influence of managerialism in the public service that a clear majority of our respondents reported engaging in some form of vision setting process, although the subject matter of that process varied.

In a few cases a vision statement had been prepared for the staff organisation (only), with a separate vision statement for the city or district. In most cases, however, the vision statement encompassed both the organisation and the city or district. The City of Scottsdale in Arizona, USA, is an example of the former approach: the organisation is driven by the following values that were adopted in 1991:
– respect the individual,
– value diversity,
– commit to quality,
– be a team player,
– risk, create, innovate,
– listen, communicate, listen,
– take ownership.
And its vision statement for the City of Scottsdale is:

"In partnership with citizens, we shape a livable community that is economically, environmentally and socially sustainable by continuously evaluating the impacts of today's decisions on future generations."

On the other hand, the Kirklees Metropolitan Council adopted a set of core values, summarised below, in 1990 that serves the organisation and the district[33]:
– a thriving economy,
– a flourishing community,
– a healthy environment, and
– core values for service provision, quality, and equality.
Likewise, the City of Hæmeenlinna does not have a separate values or vision statement for the organisation. It has a "business idea" for the City, and works to create an organisation that is isomorphic with that idea, that is, the organisation should reflect the sort of community the council is

---

33 Courtesy of Kirklees Metropolitan Council.

seeking to create. Thus, it seeks to create an organisation that is fair, participative, and progressive.

The vision statement in Christchurch, known as "Giving Value-Being Valued," relates to the staff organisation and is distinct from the elected Council's mission statement and strategic objectives. This separation was seen as important to maximise involvement and commitment from a large body of staff who generally feel distanced from the elected Council decision making processes.

It is important to stress that there is probably no "best approach." It seems to us however that councils should make conscious choices on whether single or separate vision statements are appropriate for them. Further, a comparison of the statements for Scottsdale, Kirklees and Christchurch suggests the desirability of determining the length and detail of statements. In Christchurch we even had long discussions on the appropriate style of language for our vision statement, believing this to be a significant issue. The purposes and "market" for the statement are fundamental issues. This leads to the question of whom to involve in its preparation.

5.2 Who was Involved?

The decision as to whether the vision statement related to the staff organisation only, or to the city or district, influenced both the content of vision statements and the process by which they were crafted. As might be expected, the CEO was actively involved in the process in all of the cases reported to us, although he or she was not necessarily the driving force in the process in every case. Likewise, it was very typical for some or all senior management to be involved. Most respondents reported involving elected members, which is in accordance with our finding that most councils had an integrated vision statement. One would expect elected members to play an important role in determining the vision for the community. Some respondents actively involved their communities in creating integrated vision statements. For example, the Wollongong City Council in Australia sent out 30,000 questionnaires, with a twenty percent return rate, to its citizens. The responses played an important part in drafting that council's vision statement.

Those respondents that excluded elected members were those organisations that had developed a separate organisational vision statement. For example, the Wellington Regional Council involved elected members in the process of creating a vision for the region, but not in the process of generating the organisation's vision statement: it was generated by the executive management team. Three respondents reported using external consultants in a significant way: one city relied on a not-for-profit external agency to undertake its vision setting process, while another used a consultant on a one-on-one basis to work with the CEO to develop the vision, and a third established a task force of respected business people to assist it.

In Christchurch the vision setting process started with 110 staff being involved in focus group sessions followed by 86 staff, half of them self-nominated from throughout the organisation, taking part in a series of workshops.

5.3 What Was the Vision Setting Process?

A "top-down" process was the most commonly used. Once some combination of elected members, the CEO, and the senior management group had generated the vision statement it would then be cascaded down through the organisation, usually by way of workshops, but also through the usual internal communication channels. This cascading approach is a feature of standard TQM approaches and is recommended by Deming, Juran, and Ishikawa.[34] As many of the culture change programmes involved (if only in part) some elements of TQM, this is not a surprising finding. The essentially top-down nature of this type of approach was emphasised to us by one respondent who spoke of the need to "sell" the vision to staff. It does raise the interesting question whether they will be more successful than most TQM programmes, of which two-thirds fail.

A significant minority of respondents employed a more collaborative, participative approach to the process. This was usually achieved by establishing workshops or teams that represented various cross-sections and levels of the organisation. The forty-strong "Ginger Group" set up in the

---

34 See Rosander, A. C. (1989), *The Quest for Quality in Services*, New York.

Christchurch City Council is an example of this type of approach. Ilan Hershman, CEO of the Adelaide City Council, set up "brains trusts" comprising opinion leaders at all levels in the organisation to examine "what is," and "what should be." In other organisations the process was facilitated by involving internal Organisation Development Managers who employed standard OD techniques for gathering information from a wide cross-section of the organisation.

6. Implementing Change

6.1 Types of Change

The primary purpose of our research was to gather information about the different types of culture change strategies that are being used by councils and, if possible, which strategies had proved the most successful. In Christchurch we have tended to characterise change as incremental or transformational, but organisational culture theorists Paul Bate[35] and Peter Anthony[36] suggest that planned culture change strategies fall into four categories, of which three interest us:

1. *The aggressive approach* is power-coercive, imposed, top-down, and usually involves significant structural change. Culture change is planned to occur over a relatively short time frame. This approach is deliberately destructive of the old culture. Its goal is to try to put a new culture in place rapidly.
2. *The indoctrinative approach* is more normative in nature. It typically relies on achieving change through training, education, and development. TQM programmes are the best example of this approach.
3. *The conciliative approach* is based on collaborative problem solving, and win-win organisational development activities that produce emergent, incremental change. This type of change process is often quite slow.

---
35 Bate, S.P., (1994), *Strategies for Cultural Change*, London.
36 Anthony, P., (1994), *Managing Culture*, Buckingham.

We looked for examples of these three approaches in our study. The aggressive approach was used by a number of organisations, usually in circumstances where there was perceived to be some urgency about the need for culture change. For example, the Brent Council aimed to "strike hard and fast" in carrying out a "massive restructuring" which was completed in only six months. In most cases where this type of approach was adopted it was supported by the introduction of TQM or some other quality initiative designed to introduce new values into the organisation.

Of the three approaches, the indoctrinative approach was used most often, but rarely on its own. Where it was used, it was either an adjunct to major structural change, or alternatively it itself entailed some structural and systems changes to facilitate the types of behaviour called for by the new culture. Change strategies that had training and development as their focus usually focused on aspects of quality or customer service, often within the framework of a formal quality programme.

The conciliative approach is usually associated with developmental rather than transformational change, but supporters of this approach say that over time transformational change can occur – it's just that it is much less disruptive.[37] We found fewer cases of the conciliative approach. Our own "Giving Value-Being Valued" programme is one example: it has involved very little restructuring, and much of that which has occurred has been initiated from team leader and Unit Manager levels. Its strategy is to be non-threatening, and its time frame is relatively long. It relies heavily on work groups identifying solutions to their own problems. However, it would be wrong to say that we in Christchurch are looking only for incremental change: at some stage in the process we expect the myriad of incremental changes to have produced transformational change.

---

37 Pondy and Huff studied change in three school districts in the US and concluded that frame-breaking change can occur without having to depart from everyday organisational routines. Pondy, L. R., and Huff, A. S., (1985), "Achieving routine in organisational change." *Journal of Management*, 11 (2), 103–116.

6.2 Mechanisms of Culture Change

Each of these strategies employs different mechanisms or levers to bring about culture change. For the purposes of our analysis we classified these mechanisms into four groups: strategy and outputs, structure, systems and people.

6.2.1 Strategy and Outputs

Local government organisations are attaching increasing importance to planning, and in particular the planning of outputs and service levels. In some countries such as New Zealand this move has been required by legislation, but in others it reflects a general trend to increased accountability borne out of, in many cases, having to do more with less. Most respondents spoke of how they had initiated or improved their planning processes. Such plans not only improve accountability, but they also add legitimacy to a council's operations – planning is something that "good" councils do. Plans can also provide direction for employees during the change process: Marion Macleod, a Commissioner of the Boroondara City Council, described their plan as a "direction and a lifeline" for their staff.

New Zealand councils are required to publish an annual plan which, among other elements must explain:
- the intended significant policies and objectives of the local authority,
- the nature and scope of the significant activities to be undertaken,
- the performance targets and other measures by which performance may be judged in relation to the objectives,
- for each significant activity... the cost, including allowance for depreciation and the cost of capital employed... (Local Government Act, S223D).

This focus on outputs and the cost and standard of services has been a fundamental driver of culture change in local government, although it is not always recognised. For example, the City of Hindmarsh-Woodville has a strategic plan, and each division has a plan that is personalised at an individual level on a voluntary basis. Every staff member has an abridged copy of the strategic plan in the form of a pamphlet, a copy of the divisional plan, and their own plan. The focus in these latter documents is on "customer service, doing it right the first time, providing value for money, and can-do attitude programmes."

A number of other initiatives either flowed from or were made possible by planning. Reward systems have become performance-based, management-by-results systems have been introduced, and performance appraisal and development systems can be anchored in organisational outcomes. We are not sure, however, how widespread such developments are. In Christchurch, the progress towards performance-based systems has to date been only small and we find resistance to change at its greatest in the remuneration area.

6.2.2 Structural Change

One of the main findings of this research is that most respondents reported having carried out some form of organisational restructuring as part of their culture change programme. This finding reinforces the view expressed by Peter Anthony that any "attempt to manage culture without structural change is likely to be at best ineffective and at worst dangerous, that structure is not only a necessary accompaniment of cultural change but that it often provides the best means of achieving it."[38] The scale, method and speed of restructuring varied widely across organisations. Every organisational restructuring is different in its own particular way.

In Christchurch we launched our culture development initiative in 1994 and it was some twelve months later that we undertook a significant restructuring (although it only affected a handful of individuals directly). We had, however, seen massive restructuring during 1989–90 which had in reality made our culture change programme possible. Perhaps structure and culture are analogous to a garden in which the trees provide the structure and flowers the vibrancy. They will often be altered together, but if not, change in one is likely to create tensions leading to change in the other.

---

38 Anthony (see n. 27).

In most cases the restructuring only affected the staff organisation. However, in some instances, such as Hæmeenlinna and Kokkola, it affected the political levels of the organisation. For example, in Hæmeenlinna the number of political boards was reduced from 25 to nine, and the number of lay politicians from 524 to 279, in an attempt to improve decision making processes.

In line with current management thinking, a feature of many restructurings was a move to have flatter organisations with fewer layers in the hierarchy. Associated with this was an emphasis on decentralisation and increased delegation. The extent and method of downsizing varied considerably. Some respondents spoke of downsizing by natural attrition and of promising employees that there would be no redundancies. Richard Bowers, City Manager of Scottsdale, told us of his organisation's "quality promise" that no employee would lose their job through a quality initiative. He described the "absence of fear and uncertainty about job security" as critical in achieving a sense of fair play. The Soest and Bielefeld Councils in Germany achieved lower staff levels through natural turnover rather than redundancies. Like Scottsdale, they decided as a matter of policy early in the change programme that this was necessary to maintain confidence.

On the other hand, other organisations felt the need to move quickly and drastically. One organisation reported downsizing by 90 percent over a short period of time through redundancies. Others still spoke of the challenge of handling downsizing as a result of losing competitive tenders to private sector firms.

Some organisations have restructured to separate policy functions from service delivery functions (e.g., Dunedin City). The Kirklees Metropolitan Council created an Executive Board consisting of the CEO and five senior executives with responsibility for policy development. The old departments have been split into 33 service-based units operating under a number of operational boards to create synergy. The effect of these changes has been to give the authority a "sense of direction, confidence, innovation, and energy."[39]

---

39 Courtesy of Kirklees Metropolitan Council.

6.2.3 Systems

Relatively few respondents mentioned the importance of new management information systems or the (future) impact of technological change, which is surprising. There were some exceptions: for example, Adelaide City is spending AU$ 2 million on a new information system that is designed to revolutionise service delivery. A number of councils spoke about re-engineering some of their systems and processes, but without further information it was not possible to determine the extent to which such re-engineering included technological or information systems changes. This area may be worthy of further research in the future.

6.2.4 Changes in Human Resources Practices

Recruitment and selection
The most powerful illustration of the importance of recruitment and selection as a change technique was the fact that approximately half of our survey reported the appointment of a new, often externally recruited, CEO as either a "cause" or significant contributor to the change process. This was most evident in the responses from the USA, the UK, Australia and New Zealand. In the Nordic countries the concept of strong leadership seems to play a lesser role: in a discussion with one of the authors, Robert Arnkil from Hæmeenlinna commented that leadership, as distinct from management, is not a concept that Finns use. If an employee were to be asked, "Who is your leader?", the response would be, "We are all leaders."

This discussion again emphasised that there are important cross-cultural differences[40] of which we should constantly be aware as we exchange information across international boundaries. Aside from appointing a new CEO, some councils (e.g., Auckland Regional Council and Darebin) deliberately recruited outsiders to key positions made vacant through restructuring or separation in order to introduce new

---

40 For example, Hampden-Turner, C., and Trompenaars, F. (1993), *The Seven Cultures of Capitalism*, New York.

skills, knowledge, and values. Others (e.g,. Boroondara) required staff to apply for their own positions and to go through a formal selection process.

Training and development
Most respondents reported making a heavy investment in training and developing their staff as a means of encouraging new values, attitudes and behaviour. Much of this training has been focused on quality in one form or another such as TQM or customer-focus training, or on management development. It has taken many forms, from in-house workshops cascading down through the organisation, to a major launch to the whole organisation. The Brent Council hired out the Wembley Conference Centre to launch its Total Quality Programme to all 7,000 of its staff: the multimedia show was a major success, receiving a 93 percent success rating from staff.

Demonstrating a major commitment to its staff, the City of Scottsdale currently budgets over US$ 2 million for employee development. That equates to approximately US$ 1,300 per person per year. The City is rewarded by high performance and staff loyalty: annual turnover is a low five percent, and sick leave only two percent. Other organisations, like the City of Hampton, also invest in basic skills development such as literacy training.

Reward and appraisal systems
Many councils reported introducing new or improved performance appraisal systems. In some cases this was linked to performance-based pay systems for management (e.g., Auckland Regional Council, Darebin, Hampton, Gosford and Hindmarsh-Woodville Cities), and in others it was an organisation-wide system primarily aimed at staff development (e.g., Christchurch City). Hæmeenlinna City introduced a management-by-results system early in its change process and there is now a continuous evaluation of key result areas. New systems of appraisal such as 360-degree review are also reported.

In Christchurch we have a continuing uncertainty as to the most appropriate way of linking pay to performance. There is a tension between individual and team-based rewards, and between performance in output delivery and culturally desired behaviour such as teamwork and innovation.

Empowerment
Respondents reported a move to new forms of work organisations such as self-managed teams, employee-involvement teams, and quality improvement teams. Generally there was a heavy emphasis on teams. Many respondents stressed the importance of decentralising decision making and increasing delegation as means of empowering those staff who had direct customer contact. Again, we feel some uncertainty as to the extent and real meaning of this trend. The nature of elected members' accountability to individual citizens, and the accountability of senior managers, inherently provides a constraint to effective delegation to front-line staff.

There is a paradox in centrally-directed change programmes that have empowerment as one of their goals. Empowerment is all about devolution of responsibility and decision making, and yet many change programmes are driven from the top down in a way that is quite inconsistent with the principles of empowerment. We see an answer as being in clarity as to the boundaries of autonomy in such a way as to ensure that all individuals and teams are aligned with strategic directions.

7. The Consequences of Change

7.1 Responses to Change

Both common-sense and theory[41] would suggest that responses to organisational change will vary across an organisation. Accordingly we asked respondents to describe the response of three different groups – elected members, change implementors (management), and the recipients of change, typically the bulk of an organisation's members.

---

41 See for example Kanter, Stein, and Jick (cf. n. 20).

Elected members
Recognising some separation of function, many respondents kept their elected members informed without actively involving them in the change process. Perhaps because most change programmes focused on improved customer satisfaction, which is inherently appealing to the public and thence to politicians, the reported response of elected members was positive and supportive in most cases. In one of the few exceptions however, disagreement between factions of the council and the CEO over the type and scale of organisational change resulted in a very public battle through the local media. In those organisations where elected members were actively involved in the change process, respondents reported support for the change process once its direction had been agreed upon.

Change implementors
The reported response of those responsible for implementing change was generally positive, possibly for the reason put forward by Phil Le Gros of Auckland City, namely, "that they were involved from the beginning." However, in some instances middle management were seen as a source of resistance to be overcome or got around in some way. Quite a few respondents mentioned the problem of "burn-out" or exhaustion amongst their managers as a result of the additional workload imposed by the change process. It would seem that workloads are a major obstacle standing in the way of many change programmes.

Change recipients
Not surprisingly there was a wide variation in the response of other staff to change. In many cases staff met the change programme with skepticism that sometimes hardened to resistance, and sometimes melted away. Councils that involved their staff and worked with organised labour early in the process reported less resistance, while councils involved with significant downsizing or restructuring not surprisingly did meet resistance. Some organisations worked with change resistors, while others simply got rid of those who would not or could not change. The range of responses was as wide as the range of change strategies.

7.2 The Measurement and Duration of Change

Respondents were asked if, and how, they were measuring their change programmes, and how long they estimated their programme would take to implement. Approximately one-half of the sample reported that they were measuring their progress, using a variety of methods such as:
1. customer or ratepayer satisfaction surveys;
2. employee satisfaction, climate, or culture surveys on an annual or bi-annual basis;
3. reporting of organisational performance indicators such as profit, the rate of increase in rates or taxes, the volume and quality of services provided, and goal accomplishment;
4. peer review;
5. content-analysis of media coverage;
6. benchmarking and inter-organisational comparisons such as the Bertelsmann Prize or the Berlin Science Centre study.

There was a great deal of variation in terms of how long respondents thought it would take to bring about culture change. This finding is unsurprising given the difficulty noted earlier about identifying when change begins, let alone ends. The range of estimates varied between two and 20 years. Without attempting to imply any sort of mean, many councils suggested that change would take between seven to ten years to effect. Accepting that our sample is not a statistical sample, we should be wary of drawing any conclusions other than culture change is a slow process.

8. Future Research

We are working with the Department of Management at Canterbury University on various aspects of organisational culture change. Three streams of future research in this area have been identified.

8.1 Service Orientation

Service orientation is widely recognised as a powerful force and a competitive imperative in organisations today. Organisations possessing a strong service orientation exhibit superior performance as a result of staff at all levels having a greater focus on their internal and external customers. The possession of a service or market culture is believed to make the entire organisation much more adaptable to change through pro-active learning about customers and their changing needs.

Previous attempts to measure service orientation have focused on for-profit organisations and have used the judgments of senior executives as a surrogate for the whole organisation's culture. Within this context, service orientation has been shown to comprise three dimensions, namely the gathering of information about customers; the dissemination of this information throughout the organisation; and inter-departmental cooperation. Additionally, some researchers have suggested that organisations should also have a focus on competitors.

Recognising that the importance of these three dimensions may be different for not-for-profit organisations such as are found in local government, researchers at the University of Canterbury are developing a new measure of service orientation specifically for local government. Our work commenced with a series of interviews to identify the things that people at all levels in a local authority believed were important in delivering excellent service to internal and external customers. This work has proceeded to the stage where we now have a preliminary instrument comprising 43 items. Work in developing this instrument indicates that service orientation in a local government context comprises six dimensions, which we named:
– customer orientation
– staff job skills
– empowerment
– interpersonal support
– departmental functioning
– management attitudes.

The next stage in this work, which began in July 1996, is to administer this preliminary instrument to a large (c. 200) sample of council staff to confirm the statistical reliability of the scales and the validity of these dimensions.

8.2 Structure and Diversity of Local Government Organisational Cultures

The existence of subcultures within organisations is widely recognised, but there is still a tendency for managers to treat their organisations as having a single monolithic culture. If the structure and diversity of subcultures could be measured in some way and better understood, the opportunity exists for better management of organisational cultures.

Researchers at the University of Canterbury have developed a culture survey instrument with twelve dimensions that is relevant to the New Zealand local government setting. Statistical reliability scores for each dimensional scale are high and all items within each scale are relevant and understandable to people at all levels within these organisations. This instrument can be used to identify subcultures within organisations, as well as the attributes of those subcultures.

It was administered to staff of the Christchurch City Council on two occasions in September 1994 and September 1995. Whilst summary results from these surveys have been used by the Council as part of their culture change process, much more remains to be done, including administering the survey again over the coming years to enable a longitudinal analysis to be carried out.

8.3 The Responsiveness of Local Government Cultures to Planned Change

The effect of the presence of subcultures on organisation culture change initiatives has not been studied. For instance, it may be necessary to manage culture change programmes within different subcultures in quite different ways. Using data from the study mentioned above, we propose to examine factors that facilitate and impede change at work group level. If suitable funding can be found, it is proposed to start work on this project in 1996.

Appendix:

Respondent Data

Council	Country	Population	FTEs	Expenditure
Adelaide City	Australia	[not provided]		
Auckland City	New Zealand	314,000	1,780	NZ$ 461 million
Auckland Regional	New Zealand	1,100,000	320	NZ$ 91 million
Bielefeld Municipality	Germany	325,000	6,084	[not provided]
Boroondara City	Australia	150,000	950	AU$ 83 million
Braintree District	United Kingdom	120,000	750	55 million pounds
Brent	United Kingdom	240,000	5,000	250 million pounds
Castrop-Rauxel City	Germany	80,000	850	DM 300 million
Christchurch City	New Zealand	312,000	2,000	NZ$ 332 million
Darebin City	Australia	130,000	750	AU$ 85 million
Dunedin City	New Zealand	117,000	1,174	NZ$ 184 million
Espoo City	Finland	186,000	9,889	FIM 4.6 billion
Gold Coast City	Australia	316,000	2,500	AU$ 438 million
Gosford City	Australia	135,000	1,050	AU$ 165 million
Hæmeenlinna City	Finland	44,000	1,920	FIM 1.2 billion
Hampton City	USA	133,000	1,300	US$ 219 million
Heidelberg City	Germany	140,000	2,270	DM 804 million
Hindmarsh-Woodville	Australia	90,000	550	AU$ 43 million
Kirklees Metropolitan	United Kingdom	not provided		
Kokkola City	Finland	36,000	1,700	FIM 850 million
Kotka City	Finland	55,000	3,500	FIM 130 million
Osnabruck City	Germany	335,000	945	DM 661 million
Ottowa City	Canada	319,000	2,300	C$ 325 million
Phoenix City	USA	1,087,000	12,216	US$ 1.08 billion
Quebec City	Canada	172,000	2,200	C$ 320 million
Scottsdale City	USA	168,000	1,512	US$ 201 million
Seattle City	USA	520,000	12,000	US$ 1.5 billion
Soest County	Germany	not provided		
South Glamorgan County	United Kingdom	415,000	10,539	270 million pounds
Tea Tree Gully City	Australia	94,000	375	AU$ 40 million

Council	Country	Population	FTEs	Expenditure
Toronto City	Canada	650,000	6,500	C$ 550 million
Vaasa City	Finland	55,000	3,470	FIM 1.7 billion
Vancouver City	Canada	475,000	7,500	C$ 550 million
Waimakariri District	New Zealand	32,000	180	NZ$ 20 million
Wellington Regional	New Zealand	400,000	355	NZ$ 100 million
Wollongong City	Australia	183,000	950	AU$ 135 million

Braintree: Our Aim is Quality

Tony Bendell, Louise Boulter, Robert Atkins

Executive Summary	251
1. Our Aim is Quality	252
2. Defining Quality – Different Perspectives and Models	253
2.1 Historical Origins	253
2.2 Customer Perspective	255
2.3 Total Quality Management (TQM)	255
2.4 Making a Start	256
2.5 Where do ISO 9000 and Quality Assurance Fit in?	258
2.6 Where are You Heading?	261
2.7 How are You Progressing?	262
2.8 Critical Success Factors and the Cost of Quality	263
2.9 Measuring Processes	264
3. Application to Local Government, a Special Case?	265
3.1 Making TQM Work in Local Government	268
4. Quality as a Way of Life – the Braintree Approach	270
5. Application of Total Quality Management in Local Government World-Wide	277
5.1 Current Recognition	277
5.1.1 Understanding of Specific Quality Tools and Techniques	277
5.1.2 The Extent of Implementation Within Bertelsmann Cities and Timescale	278
5.1.3 Indications of Best Practice	278
5.1.4 The Extent to which Quality Tools/Techniques Have Facilitated Best Practice Across the Bertelsmann Cities	279

	5.2	Concluding Comments	279

6. Future Directions in Quality Thinking Relevant
   to Local Government................................... 282
   - 6.1 But What Form Will Such Change Take?.............. 283
   - 6.2 So What of Quality in Local Government?............ 284
   - 6.3 Can Private Sector Quality Models be Applied?........ 284
   - 6.4 And What Should be Their Focus?................... 286

Literature.. 289

Executive Summary

This report considers the nature of quality and its application to local government. It opens with a discussion of the different perspectives that are available to the quality practitioner, and reviews selected quality models. The advantages and limitations of the models are discussed, in the context of their practical implications. The discussion then focuses on the specific case of quality management in Local Government, demonstrating the limitations of models evolved for the private sector.

This theme of quality in Local Government is developed by considering a detailed case study on the history of a quality improvement initiative. Concepts like continuous improvement, staff involvement, and communication are put into context, and the framework in which they evolved is discussed. Particular attention is devoted to the communications channels, with a full discussion of their shape and purpose.

Building on the detailed case study, the application of quality management techniques is put into a wider context in the next chapter. The Bertelsmann Cities were sent questionnaires in which they could explain the state and status of their quality awareness programmes. The results of this survey are tabulated, and some analysis is attempted. This chapter concludes that the survey was of more value for the issues it raised than for the issues it resolved. Some clear areas of future research were identified, but the initial findings did not present a definite conclusion.

The next chapter puts the practical research into the wider context of quality awareness. Selected readings from a Local Authorities Association Quality Group Seminar are presented to contrast the political view of quality-in-public-service with the academic view of quality-in-general. The general conclusion is that the two are compatible, but that there is scope for further work in aligning them. The main deficiency identified was the lack of a suitable forum for benchmarking and sharing best practice.

1. Our Aim is Quality

This report explores the nature of quality and its application to Local Government. It has been prepared jointly with Professor Tony Bendell and Louise Boulter of the Quality Unit of Nottingham Trent University. Our principal thesis is that "quality management" approaches apply to Local Authorities as to any other organisation, as a method for more effective decision making and service delivery. At Braintree, which provides the case study, the origins of the Council's commitment to quality go back more than a decade, with initial core values:
 – we are customer oriented,
 – we believe in quality,
evolving into a strategic approach seeking to transform every aspect of the Council's services. Much of the message of Braintree Council's experience is simple. Indeed, for a number of years, "quality" in the organisation was synonymous with "continuous improvement," and a culture based on constant, sometimes ad-hoc, changes throughout the organisation. This is still a bedrock of Braintree's approach, with the search for minor "1 percent" improvements (after Jan Carlzon's famous phrase) being a constant source of discussion and debate.

Many people speak of "quality" as though it were a thing in itself, a property that can be measured and specified as surely as length or weight. Other people consider quality to be a step in the process of manufacture; you do the task, and then you "apply" the quality.

There are many different philosophies of quality, each one with its own champion; Deming, Crosby, and Juran have donated names to their methods. Business process re-engineering, ISO 9000 (BS 5750), and "Just in Time", all have their adherents who will be happy to explain why their method is better than anyone else's. They are all helpful tools, and they all have their uses. Unfortunately, none of them are "right" in an absolute sense, nor will any one of them provide your organisation with the panacea solution.

To be of any use, the quality system that you adopt will make you think about your business. A good system helps to clarify processes, and provides a basis for more focused and rational decision making. Quality management is not necessarily about uniformity and adherence to written procedure. This may be appropriate in some instances, but above all, it is about building in a cycle of measurement and improvement. With hindsight, it all sounds very obvious and straightforward, but such an insight has to be learned in a tortuous way.

Our experience over recent years encourages us to share our thinking on quality, and to debate other approaches. The Bertelsmann Network provides an ideal vehicle for this.

2. Defining Quality – Different Perspectives and Models

2.1 Historical Origins

Quality under various names has always been a key issue in Local Government. There is little doubt also that more generally quality has become a buzz-word in the 1990s. Today advertisements, high street stores, and even vans and lorries broadcast that a particular organisation or business, and its services and products, are quality orientated. According to Armand Feigenbaum, one of the American quality gurus who introduced modern concepts of quality to Japanese industry in the early 1950s, quality in the West has now become the single most important force leading to organisational success, and company growth in national and international markets.

The meaning of the word quality is very much dependent upon the context in which it is used, and the perception of the various people who will transmit and receive the message. Indeed, it may often be quite deliberately used ambiguously. It is crucial, therefore, that Local Government and individual Authorities and the staff within them reach a clear consensus and understanding of what quality means for them, otherwise exhortations to "improve the quality of service" will be interpreted in different ways by different people, with the ensuing actions leading to confusion. The word quality can also be applied in a general sense, describing for example the way in which the entire organisation is managed.

The modern use of the word quality and its high profile originated after Japan's defeat at the end of the Second World War. Ironically, it was the Americans who exported the basic concepts of quality control to Japan, and the work of Dr. Edwards Deming and Dr. Joseph Juran laid the foundations for the subsequent revolution in quality in Japan. In Europe and the US the post-war boom was at a height and had created a situation in which the consumer, who had long been starved of essential basic commodities, never mind luxuries, would buy items offered for sale. It was a supplier-led market, and created an illusion within service and manufacturing organisations that they were efficient.

Historically, quality has often been used to denote excellence, goodness, beauty or high cost, for example in a painting, a designer dress, or a Rolls-Royce car. A more useful definition of quality is "meeting the requirements of the customer" and a consequent necessary first step is therefore to define those requirements. Frequently the word "requirements" has been mistakenly equated with "specification," the later often ignoring criteria such as price or delivery, so that quality has been defined purely as a conformance to specification for the service or product itself.

However, "meeting the requirements of the customer" can have several weaknesses. For example, it can overemphasise checking and inspection to ensure that *nothing* outside the agreed published requirements is provided to the customer. This can lead to a rather "hit and miss" type of operation where the only way of protecting the customer from poor service or defective products may be to put a great deal of emphasis on end-point inspection, which is unreliable anyway. An additional difficulty with this approach is that it takes place when the service or product is at its most expensive, this is, when the work is complete. In addition, it is also the most critical time to ascertain whether the "end product" is good enough or not, because the next stage is provision to the customer, and failure will usually mean failure to deliver. Quality should not be "inspected in," but should be designed into the service or product.

Not only are such checking and inspection processes expensive and time consuming, they can create a climate in which quality for the customer is considered satisfactory because it just meets requirements and therefore does not need to be improved. Furthermore, it does not take into account that the requirements and needs of the customer will inevitably change, and that the marketplace in which the organisation has to operate is continuously evolving.

2.2 Customer Perspective

It is crucially important to the success of any organisation concerned with quality to understand what the end customer wants, and to define the needs and expectations of those customers clearly for internal purposes. However, to many people employed within an organisation, meeting the requirements of the customer can seem irrelevant. In some organisations only a small percentage of employees meet customers, so how can they understand and interpret their needs?

Every person within an organisation, whether a secretary, accounts clerk or an operator, has a role to play in improving quality for the end customer, but they often fail to realise this because they are distanced from the end customer. It may be helpful, therefore, if everybody within the organisation can appreciate that they are themselves both an internal customer and an internal supplier. The internal customer is the next person or section or department in line to whom they supply what is necessary for them to carry out their work. If, at any stage, there is a breakdown in these continuous customer/supplier relationships within the organisation, then the quality of the end product or service to the external customer will be less than satisfactory.

2.3 Total Quality Management (TQM)

Early approaches to quality and, in particular, Quality Control and Quality Assurance, focused on the outputs, whether they be service or product. As the markets for products became saturated following the post-war boom years, suppliers began to realise that the customer was looking for a total service, not just the product. Therefore, the need became apparent for non-production departments (such as marketing, design and accounting) also to identify and focus on the needs of the customers. TQM thus aims to encompass, in an integrated way, the whole organisation.

It is of course true that some organisations have treated TQM purely as an internal motivational campaign aiming to improve service to external customers. Others have focused on internal training as a way of motivating and giving people tools to undertake improvement activities. Many have identified that beyond training, teamwork and perhaps the use of statistical techniques there is, in TQM, the quest for the self-improving organisation. While cultural change, organisational change and the use of simple tools, together with a documented quality system such as ISO 9000, all have a part to play, TQM thus requires a refocus and redirection of the organisation. The purpose is to develop a self-improving organisation – that is, one in which the rest position is improvement; one in which if you never did anything else to the organisation again, it would carry on improving!

TQM is a strategic approach aimed at producing the best that is currently available through innovation and continual improvement. It is recognising that each person within the organisation is – or should aim to be – the expert within their particular role or function, and it is that person who has, quite often, first-hand knowledge of the process and therefore ideas on how to improve it.

In organisations that have treated TQM purely as a motivational campaign, we often see posters around the walls exhorting employees to "Get it right first time" or similar. While this objective is highly commendable, it can often appear as an insult to someone who has worked for an organisation for, say ten years and has, as far as he or she is aware, been getting it right first time. The problem usually is that they do not know exactly what the "it" is that they are trying to get right first time, since it has never been explicitly agreed.

2.4 Making a Start

In theory, implementing TQM in an organisation is simple – all we need to do is construct a plan, identify problems and opportunities for improvement, and systematically address them in priority order, reprioritising as the need arises.

In starting to execute this plan, different critical issues will be of a different importance in various organisations, partly selecting their starting point. Frequently there is some commonality in areas such as Local Government, with the need to clarify vision at top management level, communication problems and customer focus.

We can conceive of three stages to the path of TQM. A crucial stage, often neglected, is to start by finding out where you are now. In consequence, it is recommended that at the start of TQM implementation the organisation undertakes initial data collection or undertakes an Organisation Health Check. This may include anonymous questionnaires and independent interviews with all personnel – including heads of function – in order to identify gaps in practices and procedures, inadequate management, poor communication and problems encountered by people in doing their jobs.

Figure 1: Path to TQM

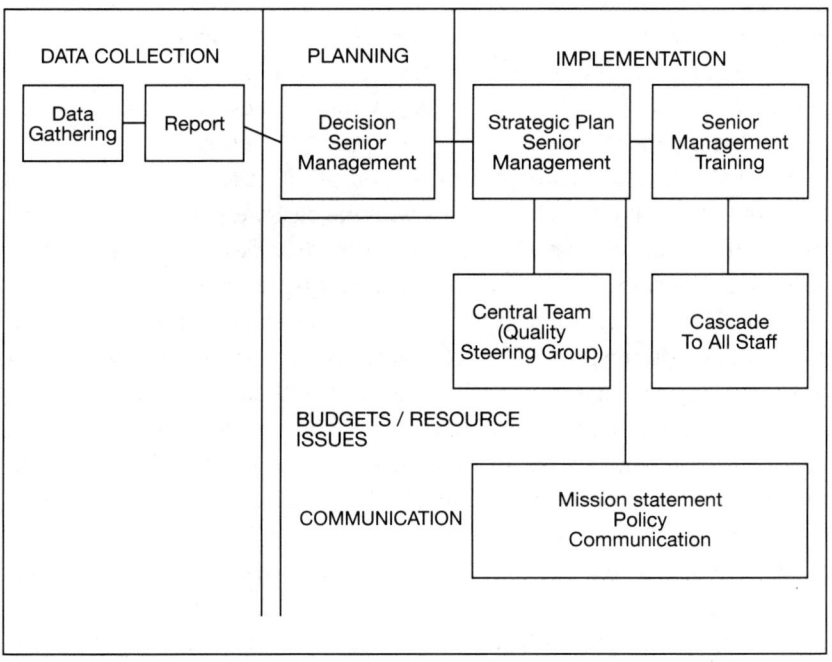

A good way forward at the start of the implementation stage is for a small Quality Steering Group, preferably chaired by the Chief Executive or a Chief Officer and with member involvement, to be established to manage the path of TQM. It will decide resources and monitor, facilitate and remove barriers to progress. This should be followed by basic awareness training and the Chief Officers Group needs to commit itself long term by issuing a mission statement to inform the employees, customers, members, suppliers and other stakeholders of the decided path forward. Experience suggests that a "cascade" model rather than "wall-to-wall" training is to be preferred for TQM awareness.

2.5 Where do ISO 9000 and Quality Assurance Fit in?

The application of ISO 9000 within the public sector in general, and local government in particular is relatively recent, and perhaps may be considered rather incongruous given its origins within manufacturing and particularly engineering industries. Is it just another administrative constraint placed upon employees, or can it assist with the quest for the continually improving organisation?

The International Standard ISO 9000 (with its UK equivalent BS EN ISO 9000, formerly BS 5750), deals with the basic requirements for quality systems to ensure the existence of essential internal procedures, their control and documentation (see figure 2). While the Standard has its origins within manufacturing, it has now extended into all aspects of commercial and administrative life. Not only are service organisations of all types seeking and gaining certification to the Standard, there is also a great interest within public administration. Thus we now have hotels, education establishments, parts of the Health Service, the Police Force and many others, as well as Local Authority Departments and Units, pursuing compliance with the Standard.

Despite the current increase by public and private sector organisations in aiming to achieve certification to the Standard, it is not without its critics. At its extremes ISO 9000 can lead to bureaucratic systems with organisations concentrating on adhering to documented procedures and auditing actual practices against them, to the extent that originality, creative

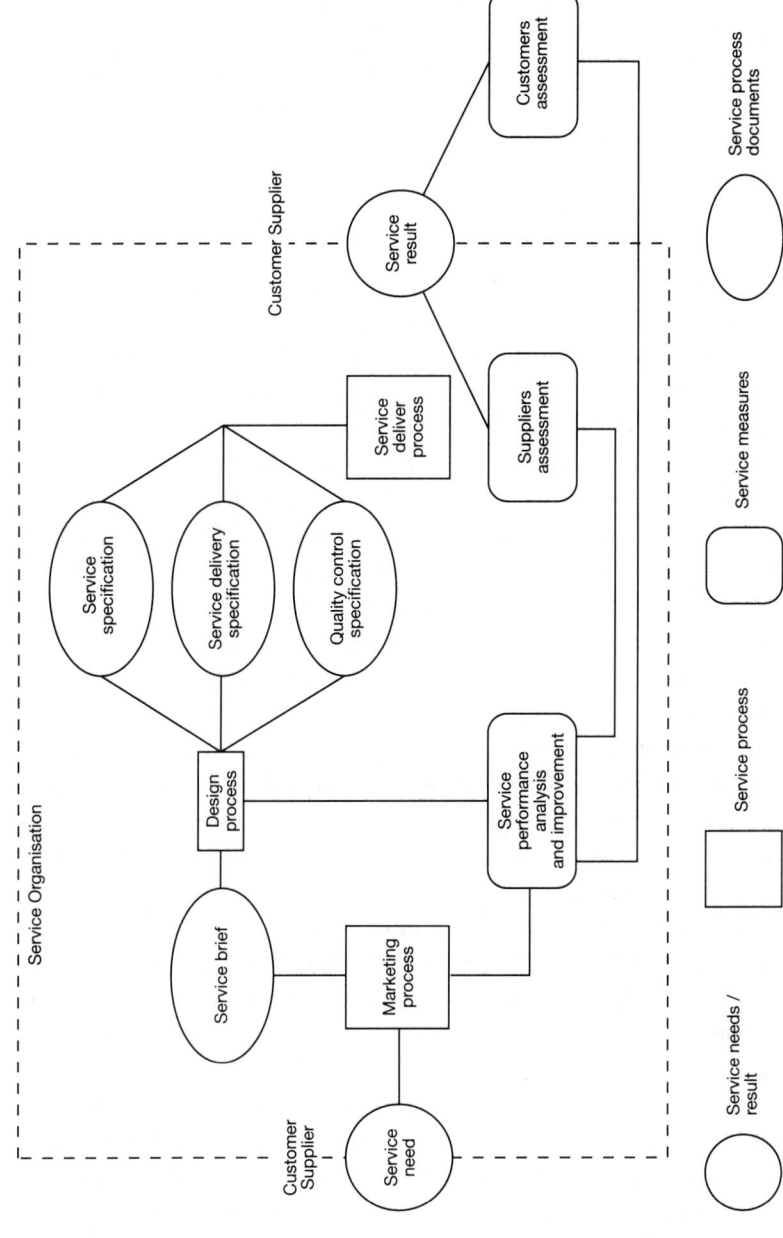

Figure 2: Service quality loop (reproduced from BS 5750 part 8 (1991))

team work, delegated authority and involvement, are stifled. While documentation of procedures and certification to ISO 9000 can provide a key element in the organisation's drive for improvement, the danger is that they are seen in isolation and apart from other initiatives that are required. This can lead to confusion and a too limited view whereby achievement of certification alone is seen as the end point of the improvement process.

As a consequence of today's mass-production, organisations have tended to concentrate upon examining the finished service or product rather than on assuring the quality at creation. This has led to an excessive amount of time subsequently being spent on "fire-fighting," Consequently, too often managers spend a great deal of time studying what is wrong with the actual service or product, rather than looking at what is wrong with the process.

The concentration of effort into detecting defects has a number of serious pitfalls. First, it is very expensive. We typically put our best, most experienced people into the role of supervisor or inspector, rather than use them in the process itself. In addition, we carry out this final inspection at the stage when the service or product is at its most expensive and when the next process will be to deliver to the customer. Failure at this point will almost inevitably lead to the customer being let down, with potentially serious consequences.

In addition, even 100 percent inspection is not foolproof. Any inspection process, particularly that of visual inspection, is fallible, and cannot guarantee that defects will not be missed. Even if we increase the number of inspectors tenfold, we may not improve the quality one iota. While we may prevent more defects being provided to the customer, we may not actually prevent them being generated. Generally, quality cannot be "inspected in," it must be "built in," Furthermore, if the final inspectors miss the problem, the customer is almost certain to detect it. In many cases the customer will receive the service or item only once, whereas the inspectors may see thousands.

Perhaps the most serious problem, arising from too much reliance on final inspection, is that it creates the atmosphere that it is acceptable to make mistakes because someone else is checking. Inspection as a separate operation after the event, reinforces the belief that "quality is nothing to do with me," Why should a clerk, IT operator or cook meet the requirements first time if someone else is checking, and therefore taking the final responsibility?

We therefore need to study the processes by which the customers" needs can be satisfied, to devise ways in which these processes can be defined, measured and controlled. Then we can have some degree of assurance that the service or product will be satisfactory, without relying on detection at the end-point.

Quality Assurance examines the processes by which the service or product is supplied. By establishing a Quality Assurance System, the organisation can demonstrate that it has a process that has the capability of supplying the service or product. While this may not obviate the need for final inspection, it can reduce the level for that inspection. A Quality Assurance System gives the stakeholders increased confidence that the supplier will deliver what has been requested. The definition of Quality Assurance given in ISO 8402: *1986* BS 4778 part one 1987 is: *all those planned and systematic actions necessary to provide adequate confidence that a product or service will satisfy given requirements for quality.*

2.6 Where are You Heading?

It can be observed that many mission statements issued by organisations bear a striking resemblance to each other. This is not surprising, since after all there are only so many ways of saying more or less the same thing. Experience shows, however, that an organisation is missing the point if it merely copies another mission statement. It is the journey towards constructing the mission statement that is important. That is, the mental exercise for the Chief Officers, members, management and staff in terms of disagreeing, arguing and coming to a common conclusion about what the Local Authority is trying to achieve. Typically, the desired vision will be of first class service, value for money, a secure future, good financial performance against budgets, greater creativity and innovation, and may well allude to the harnessing of the efforts of every person in the organisation towards their common aims. But how are these to be achieved? The simplistic answer is only by totally satisfying, and indeed delighting, the customer. While this might seem a self-evident truth, it is still not unusual, particularly in the public sector, to see mission statements, policy statements or quality policies that totally ignore the customer.

Also, there is a need to specify what the Local Authorities require from their sites, departments and units or individuals. It is for this reason that the mission statement or quality policy statement is of vital importance.

2.7 How are You Progressing?

In, say, two year's time, how is the organisation to understand whether it has made progress, and whether there are major barriers and obstacles still to be overcome? Unless performance is measured, at least internally, there will be no monitor of progress towards the mission. At the very minimum, therefore, it is essential that, at all stages of TQM implementation, clear statements and information is provided to everyone in the organisation about:
1. what the aims are, and
2. the current position of the organisation.

Historically, organisational performance measurement has typically concentrated upon outputs and inputs. Examples of this might be weekly service or production figures, monthly financial performance, complaints or costs. This information, while extremely valuable, often comes too late to significantly affect the process to which they relate. This problem has been compounded in many organisations by the fact that measurement has overconcentrated on financial information.

Clearly, some form of measurement is required so that progress can be monitored towards the stated aims of the mission statement. Often in the past, however, measurement has been carried out for its own sake. This has led to a multitude of measurements and measurement methods being employed, particularly at the commencement of TQM initiatives that are unfocused and therefore extremely confusing to those involved. What is required is a unified measurement system that can be utilised for planning, monitoring and driving improvement.

2.8 Critical Success Factors and the Cost of Quality

A unified approach to measurement can be obtained by identifying *Critical Success Factors* (CSFs) for the organisation or department. These represent a small number of key measurable indicators that are such that, if they are showing satisfactory progress towards targets, the organisation as a whole will be perceived as being successful on its path of quality improvement. The Critical Success Factors identified should be directly linked to the mission statement so that as a group they indicate progress, or otherwise, towards the mission of the organisation. This, once again, sets a severe challenge for senior management, since the set of Critical Success Factors needs to be complete in order to convey the total picture. Completeness is essential, since the focus on a selected few will inevitably lead to incompatibility with other desired results. However, they must not be so extensive that they confuse the issues involved and the personnel with the organisation. Typically, Critical Success Factors may include measures of financial performance, cost, satisfaction service, delivery performance, service levels and so forth. For clarity of vision the organisation or Department should seek to limit the number of Critical Success Factors to about six or eight, but certainly no more than twelve.

Having established a clear link between the mission statement and organisational performance by means of Critical Success Factors, each department, section and subgroup of individuals can then begin to identify the measurements that they can contribute to improving in order to help the organisational mission. In order to contribute to improvement in the Critical Success Factors, it will also be beneficial to identify key measurements on particular organisational processes, rather than concentrating solely on functional department or sectorial measurements.

As an alternative to Critical Success Factors the study of the Cost of Quality can provide an initial unification to driving quality improvement in an organisation, and offers a basis for identifying and prioritising projects in a language which can be understood by everyone – that of money. However, it must be realised that while opportunities for improvement can be highlighted by a Cost of Quality exercise, the savings may not always be "real" money. That is, they are not necessarily directly transferable to the bottom line.

2.9 Measuring Processes

Having identified the organisation's Critical Success Factors, we need to look at the organisation's key processes in order to ascertain how given targets on the CSFs can be obtained.

But what is a process? Processes can be defined as the mechanism by which inputs are transformed into outputs. The output may be a service, product, paperwork or materials, which differs from the original inputs because we have added value. For example, the generation of a purchase order to a supplier may well involve several different stages or process steps. Each of these stages, typically, will belong to different personnel or different departments and often no one person within the organisation is responsible for the total process, other than perhaps the senior officer or Chief Officer. Historically, most organisations and especially Local Authorities have been structured on a vertical, departmental or functional model. However, most processes within the organisation flow across the organisation, that is horizontally, passing from department to department or person to person. It is not surprising therefore, that the external customer very often does not receive what is intended. As said earlier, we can liken many business processes to a relay race, with the baton passing from section to section within the organisation. As in a relay race, in real life the problems occur at the changeover points where the baton is dropped.

Identifying key business, or organisational processes, the owners of each process and the boundaries of each part of the process are key elements in the full implementation of TQM. There are techniques available to assist with this identification, such as Process Deployment Flow Charting, but they are not the subject of this contribution. In satisfying this requirement for the clarification and simplification of processes, documented quality management procedures such as ISO 9000 may also have a key part to play, but are not in themselves the key answer.

Various types of measurement can be used in relation to processes. Effectiveness measures how good is the output from the process or, preferably a process stage. One aspect of this is accuracy, is it correct or not and how exactly? Others are reliability, i.e., how many times is it correct? Timeliness, it could be correct all the time, but always late, and if so, by how much? Volume, i.e., it may always be correct and on time, but the customer may only get half the required volume. Other aspects are ease of use of the process or process stage, completeness, capability and efficiency.

While the above aspects of measurement are appropriate at the end of the process, it is more important to use them at the end of each process stage, internally to the process itself. This will assist the organisation to ensure early while the process is running that the outcome to the ultimate customer will be satisfactory. Process measurement can also provide prompt feedback that gives an individual or department the opportunity to improve or compensate for change while the work is being performed, so that they can immediately correct the parameters within their control. Feeding back information in this way directly into the process also enables savings to be made since, for example, employees (hopefully) do not continue to make errors once detected, and resources are not added to an already effective system.

3. Application to Local Government, a Special Case?

There can be no doubt then of the need for the application of TQM in Local Government on a world-wide basis. Whilst there appears to be an on-going debate as to whether Local Government is unique in application and implementation of quality management tools and techniques – what remains an unquestionable certainty is that Total Quality is as directly applicable to Local Government as it is to the private sector – perhaps more so.

However, the application of TQM within Local Government is particularly difficult. There are many reasons that can be put forward to account for this difficulty, perhaps one of the foremost is cultural. Increasing "customer" demands and expectations necessitate that Local Government world-wide move closer to the "real world" in terms of financial accountability, management, quality assurance, and effectiveness. Yet bureaucratic and non-responsive systems remain an unfortunate historical legacy of a bygone era, reflecting a different need in Local Government. The speed of systems, like the speed of life at this time was naturally slower than today's requirements.

This backdrop is one to which the concept of customer service and TQM, the new imperatives, will seem particularly alien and this could make the process of getting TQM established within Local Government very difficult. Staff culture, lack of individual ownership of the work of the process of the administrative function, or the customer relationship, together with lack of responsibility and any concept of client-care or staff empowerment all represent negatives that need to be overcome by the design and implementation of a TQM programme.

As has already been mentioned the systems themselves in Local Government often have a tendency to be bureaucratic and non-responsive. The lack of the incentive of the marketplace for quick response, flexibility, simplicity and the availability of information on short timescales means that introducing this requirement as a "must" within a TQM programme is once again a big step for Local Government. Bureaucracy and non-responsive systems are not just in themselves the opposite of what is trying to be achieved within a TQM programme, they also hinder its introduction, its development and thus slow its progress.

Even where there is the will to transform Local Government towards a culture system and management style that is TQM oriented, technical problems still remain due to the inherent nature of the TQM models currently in use. Such models require adapting for their application within local government. A major orientation of most TQM models is the predominance of the customer in the purpose of the organisation and its infrastructure. In local government this single customer focus is not so clear; it is not just that there are multiple types of customers, it is the fact that even in single transactions Local Government employees could be dealing with multiple customers and stakeholders. A clear illustration of this is demonstrated by the provision of education. In this particular transaction who is the customer? Is it

- the pupil?
- the parent?
- the community?
- the central or local Government?
- the taxpayer?
- the potential employer?

In an attempt to solve this difficulty there has been the introduction of the stakeholder concept. Stakeholder models can now be found in many different aspects of public administration world-wide. For example, Royal Mail identify their stakeholders as: customers, employees, shareholders and the community, whilst other public sector organisations have added suppliers to this list.

A problem, however, remains in that these generic stakeholder groups have a tendency to be somewhat unfocused in themselves. The community is by its nature a very large and inhomogeneous group, with divergent opinions on divergent issues. Lack of focus is what is trying to be avoided with TQM, and so much has to be done in the attempt to clarify. Even when this is done, down at the operational level in the process of Local Government, there may still be a problem. Staff must have very clear priorities in respect of their dealings with the various stakeholder groups so that the organisation can be focused towards their various purposes for existing in the right proportion. This requires clear policy from the top, as well as clear staff understanding and discussion at all levels.

Another problem linked to the implementation of Total Quality Management (TQM) within Local Government is that in many cases the market itself does not determine the level and extent of services. Many "services" are provided to the end customer sometimes not necessarily because the end customer wants the service, but because there are legislative requirements upon Local Government to provide such services. A typical example of this would be in respect of building regulations.

Decisions may also be taken at a political level, and there may be no limit to the demand for a zero price, or subsidised service. This then creates shortfalls in the availability in service provisions which may appear to the customer as inefficiencies. The consequence here is that confusions can remain in the customers" mind – the "public" – between productivity and quality. This problem is built into the nature of public administration and represents a particular challenge for the staff involved in implementing TQM philosophy and principles.

In addition to this, the Local Government organisation may be a "large" organisation and will consequently suffer from the associated complexity and problems of scale, combined with a bureaucratic management style. The implication of this is that in many instances employees will be removed from the customer. In the circumstances where there is customer interface by "front-line" staff, these individuals will be a long way from decision making and will also therefore be at the mercy of the internal systems. A problem that may be exacerbated further where the Department or Unit also has a large scale technological basis.

It can be concluded then that the potential problems for the implementation of a TQM programme within Local Government are not only many but complex. However, in spite of such difficulties there are indications that Local Government world-wide is rising to the challenge. The Bertelsmann Network for Local Government is but one example of how Local Government is trying to facilitate continuous improvement by exchanging ideas and examples of good practice.

3.1 Making TQM Work in Local Government

Despite all the difficulties most Local Authorities do take quality seriously. In the UK, there is now a Local Authority Associations Quality Group that aims "... to promote quality initiatives in Local Government by exchange of good practice and experience." According to their third survey, 96.9 percent of Local Authorities in the UK (348 out of 359 returning) are involved in quality initiatives compared with 96.5 percent in 1994 and 95 percent in 1993. Moreover, according to the authorities that responded, 53 percent of the quality initiatives implemented have been effective in achieving their objectives.

So how should TQM be implemented in a Local Authority? Whilst various models can be put forward for implementation within Local Government, the first question that needs to be addressed is what level implementation is at: across the whole of the Authority or within a particular Department? The answer will vary with size and complexity of the Authority, but in reality most programmes are Departmentally based, with perhaps coordination at Authority level. The reason for this is partly because Departmental cultures and needs vary. For example, whilst ISO 9000 may be appropriate for implementation within Highways and Planning it may not be appropriate for implementation within Recreational Services.

As in the private sector, TQM should for Local Government, from the very beginning, become part of the "real work" of a particular Department. Commitment from the top – i.e. Chief Officers is a "must" for its implementation. Briefing of, and support from elected members at all stages of the programme is also highly desirable. Total Quality cannot be delegated, but a sensible thing to do as indicated in Section 2.4 is to establish a Steering Group of the Chief Officer and most senior managers within the Department to facilitate the transformation of the Department or Unit. This may also include elected members. Ideally this should be chaired by the Chief Officer, for it is only in this way that TQM can become part of the overall job.

The Steering Group will be able to identify and focus on the mission of the Department or Unit, the stakeholder groups, the intrinsic values and their purpose for existing. All employees Body Single should be involved and therefore take responsibility for the process of quality improvement, although it should commence "top-down" before returning "bottom-up." While employee training will be necessary two important aspects should be taken into consideration. Firstly, middle managers should be adequately prepared for the change in behaviour and attitudes that will be expected and required for them for the programme to be successful. Secondly, cascade training is preferable to "wall-to-wall" indoctrination.

A systematic approach to the quantification of quality improvement within Local Government is also highly desirable, since otherwise the programme can be unfocused. This may be undertaken initially by a Cost of Quality approach or subsequently by the development of Critical Success Factors (CSFs). Both systems represent a unified approach to measurement. Whether by looking at the money that is wasted by doing things wrong and the prevention costs involved – or in the case of Critical Success Factors, identifying a small number of Critical Success Factors on which the progress of the Department/Unit and its mission will be judged. These measures then provide a yardstick for improvement activities within the particular Department or Unit. Priority activities are those which will impact on the measures most heavily.

4. Quality as a Way of Life – the Braintree Approach

The Courtauld Family have been associated with the Braintree District for over two hundred years. They were the biggest single employer in the area, and great benefactors to the town. When they decided to close their factories, four thousand people were made redundant overnight. In a district of only one hundred thousand people, that is an intolerable burden, and clearly the Council had to do something. Resources were limited, and direct intervention was out of the question. The Council decided that the best course of action was to work indirectly, becoming a change agent, a catalyst for investment.

The strategy was quite simple. If the Council concentrated on getting things done in a responsive, efficient and above all, positive way, then the district would be more attractive to potential investors. "Braintree means business" summarised the Council's approach, and to make it easy for people to understand what that meant, the organisational aspirations were summed-up in five core values:
1. we are customer orientated,
2. we believe in the abilities of the individual,
3. we must be responsive and responsible,
4. we believe in quality,
5. we are action orientated.

On their own, these five simple phrases are nothing more than wishes. To convert them into statements of fact, they must be measured against our own and our users' expectations. We found that this led us into a continuous improvement loop in which we would set a standard, monitor our performance, and act upon our findings. By finding out how well we were doing, we could be confident that our service guarantees were both appropriate and achievable. Our model for measuring the quality of our services began to look like this:

Figure 3:

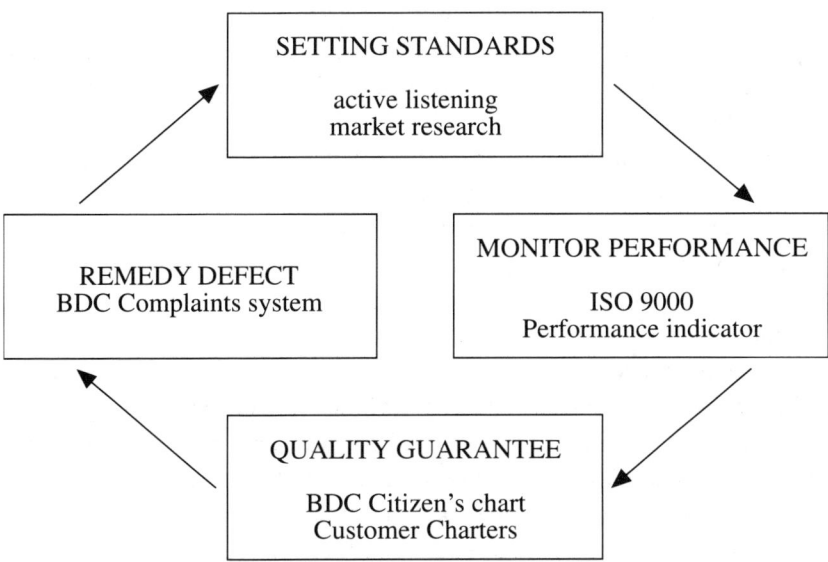

The first step was to make sure that we knew when we got it wrong. We realised that complaints were a valuable source of information and we wanted to encourage them. We had to make sure that people knew how to complain and so our users were given clear guidance about what to do if they were unhappy with our service. A simple form, "I Would Like To Make a Complaint" was produced and made available at all Council offices. The information that it gave us was subjected to a rigorous complaints procedure that analysed individual cases, and then summarised them into categories. Having found out what we had to put right, the next step was not to do it wrong in the first place, and this required a different sort of analysis.

Before you can improve your processes, you must know how well they are doing in the first place. The old adage "If you can't measure it, you can't manage it" is as true for services as for manufacturing. The measurement has to be part of a quality programme that can change the organisation and its culture. In order to do this, the measurements need to fulfill two criteria:

- The measurement must be capable of being influenced. If the parameter is completely outside the operator's control then there is no scope for improvement. That is not to say that such data shouldn't be taken, it might be extremely important but it should not be used as an improvement criterion.
- The measurements should support the work to be done and they must enable the operators to do their work better. If they are not part of the operator's work they will be gathered grudgingly and sparsely. There is a limit to what you can expect quality measurement alone to achieve, it must be linked to the overall business strategy if it is to have a lasting effect.

To appreciate this in action, it is necessary to widen the view of measurement beyond the mechanic's-eye view of process control. In a service industry with an empowered workforce, the most important process is the application of an individual's skill to the task in hand. Therefore, the key process measurement is the performance of that individual. In recognition of this, Braintree introduced a system for performance appraisal in 1987.

Performance appraisal is a thorough and honest assessment of an employee's work. It enables that organisation to explain its needs and goals whilst allowing the individuals to explain what they will need to achieve those goals. This routine examination of individual goals helps the organisation to stay on track. As the needs of the organisation change, the employees are told, and in turn they can explain the consequences of the change as they see them. The benefits of this communication are twofold. It gives the employee an opportunity to see how their work contributes to aims of the organisation. It gives the organisation a way to link an individual's performance into the planning cycle. The whole process runs around a measure – change – measure loop with the management of change at every step. This was to become a key element in the structure of the organisation.

Within this structure, the Council Committees consider their policy, and what will be needed to convert it into strategy. They specify what they will need to know, and the Officers gather the necessary information. This is used to formulate the Corporate Strategy that is used to set targets throughout the Council. Each Committee will use the service strategy headings to set itself targets. Once decided, these targets will become the Draft Annual Plan for the following Council year. There follows a period of negotiation as the requirements of each committee are matched to the available resources. Once the conflicts have been resolved, the goals are incorporated into the Annual Plan: set targets with fixed achievement dates, or ongoing targets with fixed review points.

The Directors receive strategic targets from Members at their Performance Appraisal Panels. They assume the responsibility for determining how those targets will be designed to meet the Annual Plans. They decide which targets they should address themselves, and which they should delegate. Tasks that have been delegated may be allocated with or without a specified method, depending on the skill level of the recipient. In some cases, part of the target may be identification of new procedures, processes, or knowledge. In others, these might be allocated as a separate target.

Although this is a complex and involved process, it is hard to see how it could be simplified without compromising the democratic review of the Council's operations. Given that the operation cannot be simplified, then particular care must be taken to ensure that it runs smoothly.

In 1990, it was decided that the best way of monitoring, and improving the organisation was to formalise it into a recognised management system. This was to be a substantial undertaking which would involve all of the staff in the description and documentation of the Council's operations. A new communication network was needed to coordinate this effort, and so we established the Quality Improvement Teams and Quality Officers. This is how the network is described in our Quality Policy Manual:

"Each Department has a Quality Officer who is responsible for the promotion, understanding, practice, and implementation of the quality management system within that department. They also have specific responsibility for management and disposition of the quality documentation within that Department. The Departmental Quality Officer has a nominated deputy whose role is to support Departmental Quality initiatives awareness, and to deputise in the absence of the Departmental Quality Officer.

Collectively, the Departmental Quality Officers form the Corporate Quality Improvement Team, who exist to promote best practice in quality

management techniques throughout the organisation. This team receives quality targets and determines how to address them:
- whether as corporate or departmental targets
- where to look for best practice
- make officer nominations as appropriate.

In addition, the Corporate Quality Improvement Team receives proposals, reports and issues from staff, or other team meetings. The Chairman of the team places any other point of interest on agendas.

Each Departmental Quality Officer chairs their respective Departmental Quality Improvement Team, and briefs them on matters discussed and decisions taken by the Corporate team. Every section within the Department is represented at the Departmental meeting, and the section representative will provide the links between Departmental quality meetings and their respective section meetings.

These teams assist the Departmental Quality Officers in driving and guiding quality initiatives within their Departments. For targets cascaded down from Corporate team, the Departmental teams will identify the individual staff and sub-teams to address them and monitor progress, reporting back to each meeting. For improvements and suggestions passed up from the Sections, the Departmental Teams will accept, monitor and assess the financial, or other benefits."

The formal management system that was chosen was BS 5750, and the Quality Improvement Teams were to play a crucial role in its development.

At the time BS 5750 was considered to be the standard management system for all organisations. The option of designing our own system was considered but dismissed. While there is no reason why the organisation could not produce its own management system, there seemed little point. A unique system could not be used to make inter-organisation comparisons, nor would it have the advantage of extensive testing. It was clear that BS 5750 had several significant benefits. It was: an internationally understood system that was well known to the general public, an independent check on the fit between written and current practice, a guide to the elements that a management system should have. Above all, it is a constant reminder that documentation, practice, and records must be kept up-to-date. It is a public commitment to maintaining a system to an agreed

standard, and subjecting that system to external scrutiny. In general, it provides a reasonable specification for a management system provided two things are remembered:
1. It is a specification, not a blueprint. It merely lists all the elements that a "good" management system should have, it says nothing about what form they should take.
2. It is nothing more than a measuring system. It is an efficient, and well thought-out tool for measuring how well an organisation is doing. Measurement must come before change, and BS 5750 ensures that the measurements are gathered in a systematic way. In analogous manner, the possession of a ruler will not make for a better carpenter, but the lack of a ruler will make for inferior carpentry.

To correct the many misconceptions that have grown-up around BS 5750, it was revised in 1994. At the same time, it was reissued as an international standard ISO 9000, and it is by that name that it is now known world-wide. For all that the 1994 revision has helped, the existing standard still shows its engineering origins and assumes that if the process is right, everything else follows naturally. By concentrating on process and product control, the existing standard places too much reliance on the here-and-now, without considering what is being done to ensure future success. Unless great care is exercised, the specification becomes more important that the job itself. If the best that can be said to an unhappy customer is "well, it meets the spec," then clearly the customer focus has been lost, and there is more thought required somewhere. Such behaviour negates any attempt at continuous improvement by concentrating on "how good does it have to be?", rather than "how good could it possibly be?".

Given the formality and prescriptiveness of ISO 9000, and its dependence on specifications and procedures, it is not surprising that it tends toward bureaucracy. Assessing the system over-emphasises the detection of what has gone wrong, rather than building on what has gone right, and there is a tendency to evolve a system that satisfies the external assessors. The operators then take care not to play with it, because they now think that it is "right" and they fear non-conformances. Sometimes, this is not a bad thing. Areas that undertake repetitious work with casual or part-time workers might value the continuity that the fixed system provides. However, if the intention is to encourage Total Quality Management through the empowerment of an educated workforce, then the intention and the system will be at odds.

There must be control, and ISO 9000 provides the ideal framework for this. Within that framework, the operatives need the freedom to be creative and get things done. That freedom is only possible if the employees are trained to know what is expected of them and how that is to be achieved. The remedy to blind obedience is empowerment, and it is through the "Investors in People" standard that this is addressed.

If you consider that ISO 9000 looks after the effectiveness of today's systems, then Investors in People looks after the strength of future systems. This integrated approach to management systems is appreciated by many organisations who like the idea of looking ahead, but find prioritisation difficult. The combination of systems is a useful way of balancing today's imperatives with tomorrow's needs. It is not enough to say that an organisation is doing all right now. To add real value, a management system should also consider what is being done to secure tomorrow's success as well. Our management system will take us from "How can we prove we have done nothing wrong?" to "How good can we be, and how do we know?".

To summarise, there are many systems and initiatives available to the organisation that wishes to do something about its quality of service. No one scheme will provide the answer because, as the quality guru Phillip Crosby pointed out, quality is a process not a programme. Quality is not something that you do, it is what you do. Braintree has built a quality improvement programme out of many different philosophies, choosing the appropriate steps from each. None of the steps have been revolutionary, or innovative. Individually, they have all been seen before. What is different about Braintree's approach is that they have been applied in a steady and systematic way. We recognise that quality is a journey, not a destination, and at all times our aim must be to define and improve good service practice.

5. Application of Total Quality Management in Local Government World-Wide

One of the fundamental objectives and purposes of the Bertelsmann International Network for better Local Government was to build a core group of highly motivated Local Government representatives that are committed to the improvement of Local Government and to the idea of intercultural and international learning. With this in mind the authors of this particular Section decided to survey the Bertelsmann Cities. A questionnaire was sent to each of the ten Cities so that an overview of what has been undertaken to date in respect of Total Quality Management (TQM), not only in terms of its understanding, but also in respect of its application and implementation across the Bertelsmann Cities could be gained (see end of this section).

From the ten questionnaires that were sent, six Cities responded. An analysis of the returned questionnaires follows.

5.1 Current Recognition

5.1.1 Understanding of Specific Quality Tools and Techniques

It is very evident that there is not only a good theoretical understanding across the Bertelsmann Cities of specific quality tools and techniques such as Total Quality Management, ISO 9000, and Benchmarking.

There is also a certain commonality in respect to the definitions put forward by the respondents. One specific example of this commonality is illustrated by the definitions respondents put forward in respect of Benchmarking. Different respondents defined it as being:
– comparisons, internal and external measuring performance and outcomes to establish Best Practice;
– comparing your performance (and ways of achieving good performance) with meaningful Benchmarks. They can be internal or external and more or less directly related to your work – as long as they are meaningful in terms of Best Practice, excellence, interesting innovations, etc.

- comparisons and measures with other organisations with the aim of seeking Best Practice;
- a process whereby an organisation compares its products, services and methods with other leading organisations.

5.1.2 The Extent of Implementation within Bertelsmann Cities and Timescale

All of the Bertelsmann Cites that responded to the questionnaires are implementing various quality tools and techniques. A reasonably clear insight as to the specific quality tools and techniques individual Bertelsmann Cities are implementing together with the period of time, where respondents have indicated the period of time over which specific quality tools/techniques have actually been implemented, has been tabulated (see figure 4).

The tabulated analysis also indicates those Bertelsmann Cites that have implemented quality tools and techniques "other" than those set down by Question 1 of the survey. What can be concluded from respondents" replies is that most of the "other" quality tools/techniques that Bertelsmann Cites are implementing are country specific including:
- Investors in People (IIP),
- the Dutch Quality Award,
- the Finnish Interpretation of the Baldridge National Quality Award,
- the Baldridge National Quality Award.

5.1.3 Indications of Best Practice

Across the Bertelsmann Cities, there are indications of Best Practice which may hopefully present some learning opportunities for the members of the Bertelsmann Network. The examples of Best Practice that the Bertelsmann Cities put forward have been tabulated (see figure 4).

5.1.4 The Extent to which Quality Tools/Techniques Have Facilitated Best Practice Across the Bertelsmann Cities

It was hoped that a conclusion could be arrived at in respect of how instrumental specific quality tools and techniques are in relation to facilitating Best Practice within the Bertelsmann Cities. Unfortunately, it was difficult to arrive at any conclusions since many of the respondents either misunderstood the question that was posed in relation to this area, or indicated that it was difficult to quantify since their quality initiatives were still in early stages.

5.2 Concluding Comments

The questionnaire addressed the following areas:
- current recognition and understanding of specific quality tools and techniques,
- the extent of implementation within Bertelsmann Cities and the period of time over which they have been implemented,
- examples of Best Practice within Bertelsmann Cities in respect of quality tools and techniques, and
- the extent to which quality tools and techniques have facilitated Best Practice within Bertelsmann Cities.

From the six Bertelsmann Cities that responded to the questionnaire it can be concluded that theoretically at least there is a commonality in respect of recognition and understanding of specific quality tools/techniques across the Bertelsmann Cities. As far as implementation is concerned respondents are at different levels of maturity in respect of their individual quality programmes. In addition to which not only have respondents implemented various quality tools and techniques, all but one of the respondents have implemented quality tools/techniques that are country specific.

There will hopefully be some learning opportunities across the Bertelsmann Cites in respect of the examples of Best Practice put forward by respondents. Whilst an overview of Best Practice across the Bertelsmann Cites can be gained by looking at figure 4, the examples put forward will certainly require further research and investigation.

Figure 4:

City	Indications of Best Practice, Examples Put forward by Bertelsmann Cities
Braintree District Council United Kingdom	Investors in People Performance Appraisal Strategic Planning Methods
Christchurch City Council, New Zealand	Culture Statement Climate Survey Systems and Quality Management Plan
Delft Local Authority, The Netherlands	Market Research Dutch Quality Award Model
City of Hæmeenlinna, Finland	Quality Work in the Field of Day care Citizen Participation in Town planning and Renovation of Tenant Housing Integrating Key Results with Quality Thinking
City of Phoenix, USA	Internal & External Customer Focus
Ville de Quebec, Canada	Benchmarking; since 1988, a set of performance indicators has been defined to assess our results and efficiency throughout mid and long-term periods. Results are also compared with those of other cities from their own metropolitan region, and with those cities of a similar size within Canada. Indicators address the following areas: – Public safety – Transportation – Sewage – Waste management – Leisure services – Public libraries – Taxation levels – Staff productivity

Figure 5: Analysis of Questions 3 and 4

City	Total Quality Management	ISO 9000	Benchmarking	Statistical Process Control	Quality Function Deployment	Others
Braintree District Council United Kingdom	Yes 12 years	Yes 4 years	Yes 2 years	No	No	Process mapping Investors in People
Christchurch City Council, New Zealand	Yes 4 years	Yes	Yes	No	No	Best practice programme
Delft Local Authority, The Netherlands	No	Yes	Yes	No	No	The Dutch Quality Award Model
City of Hameenlinna, Finland	Yes	Yes 6 years	Yes 6 years	No	No	The Finnish interpretation of the Baldridge National Quality Award
City of Phoenix, USA	Yes 6 years	No	Yes	Yes	No	Baldridge National Quality Award
Ville de Quebec, Canada	Yes 2 years	No	Yes 8 years	No	No	No

6. Future Directions in Quality Thinking Relevant to Local Government

The common trends that we have identified in the development of Local Government include a possible continuation of a movement towards Local Authorities being managers, controllers or contractors, of largely contracted out services to local people against nationally set standards. If this is so, it will have major implications on what quality will mean in the Local Government context. If Local Authorities are largely contract managers and consumer protectors, the search for quality needs to be seen somewhat differently than if they are directly involved in service delivery or major policy determination.

This builds on the historic administrative role. As Sir Ivor Jennings put it, writing in 1959:

"The reason is – though it may not be satisfactory to the pure democrat – that local government is not concerned only with major questions of policy. Its function is rather that of honest and experienced administration. Provided that there is security for the determination of matters of policy according to the wishes of the electorate, so far as they can be ascertained, the major requisite is that the members of local authorities shall be competent administrators. In local government the members of authorities take many administrative decisions which in the sphere of national government would be taken by paid administrators.

Modern commentators vary in their views of such trends:

... it is helpful to distinguish three trends
1. Ideas of the appropriate size of the public sector will shift further, so that governments will be expected to do less, not more.
2. Instead, governments will increasingly be expected to achieve their aims by regulation, not provision.
3. What remains within the public sector will be much more subject to market discipline than at present."

(Hamish McRae, The World in 2020)

6.1 But What Form Will Such Change Take?

"Both the UK and US are seeking ways of improving the performance of the public sector. In the UK the process is 'top down': central government functions, including tax-collection, are being hived off to semi-independent agencies. This project, called the 'Next Steps' programme, was intended to revolutionise the central government bureaucracy in much the same way that privatisation had revolutionised the public utilities. If Next Steps works it may well become the blueprint for reform with other governments, just as privatisation has been imitated elsewhere. In the US the process is 'bottom up': various states and cities are conducting experiments to try to inject a business-style culture into public-sector activities. If initiatives like these are successful then the public sector can rediscover much of its self-confidence, and eventually that will be recognised by voters.

After all, the state can do some things right: both Japan and the UK, where the state has a large influence on the allocation of that spending, spent less than half what the US does on health in terms of a proportion of GNP, yet seem to achieve better overall health care.

If countries decide that they cannot face a radical restructuring of their public sector, then they must find other ways of improving their own performance within the existing organisational structure, or face the fact that what are now thought of as core functions will be hived off.

There is, of course, a third and altogether less attractive option: to accept poor quality public services for the people who cannot afford to buy their way out, while the better-off use their wealth to insulate themselves. This may happen, but it is not a way to stay rich. Countries which choose this option will find it hard to remain competitive in the next century. Their workforce will be worse educated, have poorer health and quite possibly greater social problems than the workforce of countries which maintain decent – and efficient – public services."
(Hamish McRae)

6.2 So What of Quality in Local Government?

"I do not think it is possible to consider quality without thinking about what the service is for, what is its nature. It is vital to think about and be clear about the underlying values and to make the connection between these and the services that you are trying to provide or procure, or to buy, purchase or commission.

... Finally, there is a question, a reasonable question – is quality a fad? I hope very much that the answer is no.

... The new bureaucracy of quality charters and procedures, the short term approach, piecemeal policies, 'cream-skimming,' all lead to the tendency to try and do the easy bits especially at the expense of the 'difficult' bits. It means you will fulfill your targets, but has major implications especially for equalities. Then, if consumers, citizens and front-line staff are to be involved and committed to quality, we need to open up the dialogue, to become more honest and open and give better information.

But against this is the problem of so called commercial confidentiality. This seems to be closing down the debate just when, in the pursuit of a locally democratic approach to quality, it needs to be opened up.

For quality in public services, and in local governance in particular, the key issues are values, making connection and starting from the citizen question. I think if you then take a skeptical eye to all that is being said about quality and bring your own solutions to it, from a democratic point of view, then local government has a real chance to lead the public sector in getting quality to work."
(Lucy Gastor, Local Governance and Quality)

6.3 Can Private Sector Quality Models Be Applied?

"What I think we have to do in the delivery of public services is not take the worst practices from the private sector. There are many good practices in the public sector, the public sector ethos for example which I think does exist. I think we also have to learn from the private sector but not taking the worst practices. We must take the best practices, looking at what's happened in the best companies in the private sector, looking at the way they approach the production of the good or the provision of their service. Looking at how they motivate their management.

Looking at how they build relationships between their management and staff. Looking at how they develop new methods of production which encourage people to participate, encourage people to make suggestions. Looking at ways in which loyalty is built up in the company. Companies like Nissan don't produce cars with a big stick battering the workers in the North East from their plant in Sunderland. They treat the workers as civilised people and they say to the workers, whether they believe it or not is a different matter, but they say to the workers, and I think they do believe it, we want you to be part of our operation, we want you to feel loyal to us, we want you to feel committed to us. We're not going to lie to you and say there can never be redundancies. If no one buys cars, then we have to do something about the level of output, but if we do have to the fact is that we can face that decision together and we want to face it in a way which is as reasonable as possible. There will be constant rewards in the good times and we also want to try to share a little bit of the rewards with you. I think that's the approach we need in the public sector as well. I think ... we need to have the carrot approach to the efficient delivery of services in the public sector. We need to give management in the public sector more initiative.

Politicians in a democratic system have to decide what the political priorities are. If you like the quantity of services to be provided and broadly speaking the level of quality. But the way in which those services are delivered, the levels of efficiency that are involved in the delivery, is something which I think should be given more attention. It doesn't get councillors off the hook, but it should concern the work people, whether they be managers or workers in the provision of those services. They should be looking for new initiatives, they should be looking for things like teamwork. They should be looking for how they could diversify, how they can make suggestions to the councillors who are the political decision makers in their area, or what new service can be provided, or how services could be provided more effectively."
(Doug Henderson)

6.4 And What Should Be Their Focus?

"Quality initiatives are not without pain, cannot be without pain of course. There are going to be difficulties for all concerned. Once operating successfully, I believe that quality initiatives can make a great difference to local authorities, in particular in terms of boosting the morale of those concerned. There is nothing like having the knowledge that you are producing good quality services for boosting the morale both of the councillors and indeed of the officers concerned. The question really is what do we mean by quality and how do we measure it? That's the difficulty. I think for my Party certainly, the important thing about quality is producing really top class services for the public. It's the public in the end who matter most. The priority is to make sure that at every level of our local authorities there is embedded a real feeling of public service, a wish to do what is right and best for the public rather than for oneself. It's perhaps a rather more unselfish mode of life than one finds in many great organisations, but it is something which is very valuable and which perhaps local authorities can engender within their staff more than any other area of our national life."
(David Rendell)

But, "the public" or "citizen" are ambiguous terms. Local Authorities must meet the often conflicting and competing needs of numerous stakeholder and lobbying groups. In pursuing quality, they must find new ways of working together with these divergent groups.

"Seeking ideas on involving local business in a meaningful way, I think that's well worth considering. I just recently set up a partnership in one of the towns in our district and we have involved the local business community in that partnership together with the police and all the other organisations that I'm sure that you're familiar with and with whom you all work. It's going to be quite interesting, we've only had two meetings so far, we've actually set up working groups, and I think the business community have a considerable contribution to make. The whole idea of this is that we're all equal partners, not being dictated to by the local authorities, we're not setting the agenda, the partnership itself decides on that. What we're aiming to do is instead of the usual method of consultation (which

is that we think up ideas and then go out and consult), the ideas are going to come from the partnership, back to the local authority for them to consider. Consultation, if you like, in reverse."
(Councillor W.A.L. MacKay)

In the UK, and elsewhere in the World, the political agenda has focused around the relationships between Central and Local Government. The management guru, Charles Handy, sees this in terms of the "disappearing middle," and an opportunity for community involvement and local citizenship:

"Twin Citizenship implies that we are citizens of only two states. It should in theory be many more. I am a citizen of my town, then of my region, then of my country. Above and beyond that comes the trading bloc or the larger federal state and beyond that, why not, the world. Theory, however, does not always sit easily with psychological reality. Most of us seem to be capable of only two levels of loyalty in any one area of our lives. The ends of the chain, therefore, often get dropped and the centre levels get squeezed out. 'I am a Scotsman first,' my friend said, 'and then a European, I don't feel British at all.' Only those countries which are, like my Ireland, small enough to be tribes, do not get squeezed between the tribe and the federal union. Businesses which try to put another layer of loyalty, often a geographical one, between the operating company and the corporate centre, can end up confusing and weakening the sense of citizenship.

Governments, in their turn, have to decide which layer to omit in dispensing health, education or welfare to their citizens. If they insist on retaining the central control while delegating delivery to local units, the intermediary levels will only get in the way and will atrophy. Either the national government has to shed its power to the intermediary level, retaining only the roles of service and advice-provider, with money allocated according to formula, or it turns the intermediary levels into optional resource centres for the units to draw on if they wish.

A more interesting example of the disappearing middle in government is by David Osborne and Ted Gaebler in their book 'Re-inventing Government.' They want to see more of the ownership and control of public-service institutions passed out of the hands of bureaucrats and government professionals into the hands of communities and individuals. Citizen groups, neighbourhoods, volunteer organisations would be authorised, and, where necessary, be centrally funded, to carry out many of the local activities of government. If that were to happen, whole layers of administration would be unnecessary.

The new executive agencies in Britain are a step along this route. These are autonomous entities charged with the delivery of government services, ranging from the Benefit Agency to the Central Office of Information. When they are truly autonomous, the federalism of government services will be well established. At present, the British Treasury is still reluctant to let go all the strings. The pay and the grading and the number of staff, for instance, are centrally controlled. There cannot be a true feeling of local citizenship when you cannot determine your own staffing levels. Nor is the monitoring of technical details a substitute for the second and bigger loyalty which will be essential if the old traditions of the Service are not to get lost in the new proliferation of independent bodies.

Federalism is not easy. There can, however, be too many definitions of local citizenship. The State of California is fast becoming bogged down in too many layers of government. It is hard to know where real responsibility lies, what with school and hospital boards, local communities, the state and the federal levels, and the continuing experiment with direct democracy whereby the voters can vote to make specific propositions into law. Too many layers of citizenship end up as a bureaucratic nightmare, be it in a corporation or a country. More of the middle needs to disappear.

National parliaments in Europe's larger countries, which are themselves federations of tribal regions, know that they are likely to be squeezed out if and when Europe becomes a fuller federation. Understandably, they do not relish the thought. It is not nice to be a disappearing middle, even if a greater cause requires it. It is not only national parliament which faces this dilemma of the disappearing middle; layers in organisations have been collapsing for a decade at least, not least because those organisations are reorganising federally, even if they do not always call it that or recognise it as such. In the federal structure, hierarchies are limited and local; you relate to people in the wider organisation because their role is relevant to your needs, not because their status in the organisation requires it. Forget the hierarchy, use the network.

I listened to the chairman of a large French supermarket and hotel chain

explaining his federal, devolved organisation to a skeptical Spanish audience who were still hooked on hierarchy. 'Please explain to us,' one of them eventually asked in some frustration, 'to whom does the manager of the store in Lyons report?'. The chairman clearly did not understand the question: 'Well,' he said, 'if it's a question of distributions he will go to the expert who is, I think, in Marseilles, but if it is a purchasing problem the right person is in Paris.' 'Yes, but who is his immediate boss?'. 'There isn't any one person whom he would call 'boss.' ' You could see the mystification on the faces of the Spaniards who live in a partially federal country but do not yet run their organisations federally. Twin citizenship needs no middles."
(Charles Handy, The Empty Raincoat)

In a faster moving world, quality in Local Government requires networking, benchmarking of practices and processes, mutual learning. Such networks are still strangely absent. The UK Local Authorities Associations Quality Group in March 1995 identified that there was no existing forum/network for inputting the considerable UK Local Government's quality experience into even a European framework. The Bertelsmann Local Government network has made a start. Much more needs to be done. Benchmarking practices are being used increasingly in the public and private sectors to improve services and products and to make them World Class. It is crucial that Local Government does not fall behind.

Literature

Braintree District Council Quality Policy Manual Revision 3.
BS 5750 pt8 (1991); British Standards Institute.
BS EN ISO 9001 (1994); British Standards Institute.
BS 7850 pts 1 & 2 (1992); British Standards Institute.
Lucy Gastor, University of Bristol, Local Governance and Quality, Local Authority Associations Quality Group Seminar, March 1995.
Charles Handy, The Empty Raincoat.

Doug Henderson, Labour Party Spokesperson on Citizens Charter, Local Authority Associations Quality Group Seminar, March 1995.
Sir Ivor Jennings, The Law and the Constitution.
Councillor W. A. L. MacKay, Local Authority Associations Quality Group Seminar, March 1995.
Hamish McRae, The World in 2020.
David Rendell, Liberal Democrats, Spokesperson on Local Government, Local Authority Associations Quality Group Seminar, March 1995.

Farum: Strategic Planning at the Local Level in a Decentralized Public Sector

Palle Mikkelsen, Leif Frimand

Executive Summary	292
Introduction	293
1. Principal Considerations	295
1.1 Legal Framework	295
1.2 The Framework for Local Political Activities	297
1.3 The Fiscal Policy Question	300
2. The Danish Model for Local Decisions	302
2.1 The Structural Frames	302
2.2 Unequal Geographical Conditions	306
2.3 Coordination between Central and Local Government Finances	306
2.4 The Structure of Incentives	306
2.5 The Strategic Planning Process	307
2.6 Experiences from the Past with Respect to Planning	309
2.7 The Requirements of Future Planning	311
2.8 Problems	312
2.9 The Requirements of the Political System	315
3. The Municipality of Farum	317
3.1 The Past	317
3.2 The Change	318
3.3 The Vision of Farum 2004	320
4. Perspectives	323
Literature	325

Executive Summary

This is the story about how an ugly duckling in the municipal landscape has been transformed into an attrative municipality. The story is about the municipality of Farum.

The article contains a discussion of the rules of games of the Danish local self-government system. The aim is an understanding of the framework of the self-government within which the development of Farum has taken place. Local governments in Denmark act within the limits set by the legislation responsible for the major parts of the social welfare activities including for instance services for children and elderly people, primary schools, environmental protection together with many cultural and leisure activities. Actually, local authorities in Denmark are responsible for more than $^2/_3$ of the public services. This does not mean, however, that the execution of the tasks is always taken on by the authorities themselves. There is a tradition of cooperation with the private sector within all service areas and this cooperation is growing.

Chapter 1 contains a number of general considerations. The legislative scopes are described with the background in a discussion of central/decentralized division of powers. As the Danish society has developed with a high degree of local self-government section 2 and 3 give principal viewpoints on the local political activity and the fiscal policy issues arising from this model.

Chapter 2 is a description of the decision making process in the Danish model including the organizational structure, the geographical conditions and the economic rules of games in the cooperation between the central government and the local governments.

Chapter 2 also comprises a discussion of planning processes. Against the background of historical experience, the argument is in favour of a process in which politicians as well as administrators are participating in a mutual dialogue. This agreement has been reached through experiences over many years with the use of planning.

Chapter 3 is about the results of the municipality of Farum. It is the story about a change from economic chaos to success. From a position among the ten most tax-expensive municipalities Farum has moved to one of the ten municipalities with the lowest tax rates and at the same time with a service level higher than the average in comparable local governments. This is a transformation which has received a growing support from the local electors.

The process has been successful due to a strong political management with the courage to implement their visions. An acceptance of adjustments has been reached in the organization. The process has also demonstrated that the strategic planning must be related to precise political objectives and the political leadership must be to ready to participate on all operational levels so that decisions are followed up. The process has shown how important it is for local politicians to have detailed knowledge about the actual performance of local administration.

Introduction

According to general economic theory welfare society in a democratic version implies that a relatively large share of the total demand is directed towards services produced by either the private sector on market conditions or by the public sector. The concrete division of labour between the private and the public sector is often founded on historical traditions and/or political preferences.

At the national level, the Danish version of welfare society is characterised by a large public sector whether measured by taxes or public employment/public expenditure as a share of the total economy. At the same time it is also characterised by a strongly decentralized division of public functions and responsibilities. Municipalities and counties are responsible for the predominant share of public sector activities, and a considerable part of the total tax burden in the form of income taxes as well as property taxes are determined by elected local politicians.

For the same reason the model offers rich opportunities for variations in local service levels and quality as well as local tax burdens. This leads to a high, democratic attention being paid to the local political level, a colourful local debate and a high voting rate in elections for the municipal and county councils.

The concrete example in this article is built upon experiences regarding the utilization of such a local political scope of action concerning considerable welfare services. The example shows the possibilities for exploiting this scope when clear political signals are given with regard to the wanted development of a local area – concerning service level and quality of service as well as financing. It also emphasizes the importance of political signals which create possibilities for a democratic control of the political promises. In addition the model shows how it is possible to combine an elected, political leadership with an administrative management system with the aim of executing the decisions made by the mayor and the majority of council members.

Together with the choice of the concrete way of financing, the public sector activities in the form of services and income transfers are the most important means in all the western welfare models to attain the wanted results with respect to allocation of resources in society.

Politicians have to mark out the general and principal guidelines for setting priorities, the resources to be used and the distribution of the results. This is the classical role of politicians. No distinction in this connection is made between politicians acting on the national, regional or local level. The roles are identical.

However, in a welfare society with a high degree of decentralized execution of public functions this concept is not feasible without modification. At the local and the regional level it is decisive for democratic sustainability that the elected local politicians are able to and actually do follow up on their decisions at the same time as they are held accountable for local priority making and its consequences through the democratic process.

In contrast, the question of equity, for instance personal income distribution, must by and large remain the responsibility of the state/national political level even though several aspects of equity are attached to many local decisions.

It is possible to take into consideration the equity issue in spite of the various demands made for a decentralized public sector model. This is for instance the case regarding the claim that the authority to make political decisions should be closely connected to a simultanous demand of local co-financing via a local tax base. The politically decided supply of services has to be visible to the citizens at the same time as the chosen quality and the implied local financial burden must be noticeable.

One-way information of the citizens/the users by the local political and the administrative level is not sufficient. Local politicians are required to communicate. In other words, there is a need for a current dialogue between the inhabitants and the elected politicians. This kind of cooperation with the local politicians facilitates a maximum of congruence of local preferences and the political decisions about service level, composition of services and financing. Consensus is obtained at a qualified level, and the democracy as well as the mutual understanding of needs and conditionalities are strengthened.

1. Principal Considerations

1.1 Legal Framework

Politics is basically a question concerning the distribution of power and influence. Therefore, the division of influence between central and decentralized levels inside the public sector is a very important issue.

In this connection it is not decisive whether the public sector comprises a smaller or larger part of the overall economy. It can be said that political power generally speaking is more concentrated in a society with a relatively large public sector and a little less concentrated in a model society, which presumes, for instance, compulsory or voluntary participation in insurance schemes or membership in clubs, etc. to cover some of the basic welfare needs.

Apart from the size of the public sector itself, the power of the political system is also decisive for the distribution of influence between the politicians on the one hand and the professional administrators on the other hand. This is the case whether the non-market sector is smaller or bigger in relation to the overall economy.

The extremes in a local self-government model are represented on one hand by a legislation consisting of detailed rules for the size and composition of services and on the other hand a legal framework giving more principal guidelines for local services.

Outside these extremes – but within the legally determined limits – there is usually an area in which the decentralized authorities are free to take initiatives including doing nothing. In several countries, decisions about needed innovations concerning tasks like tourism or business development are up to local initiatives.

Aside from areas like these, which in this connection are of smaller interest, it is the distribution of power within a general framework which is the relevant topic for a debate on local self-government. This also forms the background for the following reflections.

The mentioned extreme with centrally fixed norms and standards concerning the services and the stated conditions for allotments does not in itself set the degrees of freedom in a model for the public sector. The Danish model, for instance, comprises on the one hand a local distribution of activities according to legislation and on the other hand services for which only the principal guidelines for the execution of local decisions are laid down in legislation. Theoretically, this implies the combination of deconcentration and decentralization in the same model. But of course the local level of decision making is only of importance in an area where there is scope for the execution of political decisions.

For illustrative purposes, we might mention that old age pensions, child benefits and early retirement pensions are not decided by the local authorities, but are administered by the decentralized system. In Denmark, it is thus the municipalities which take care of the actual payments, and complaints or questions concerning calculations have to be directed to these authorities in the first place.

The fact is that a deconcentrated system is chosen in spite of the obvious opportunities for implementing central payments in a country with only five million people. A major reason is the political wish to make use of the local level as much as possible as the way of access to the public service system.

Furthermore, it is often the case that legally fixed services must be considered in connection with other kinds of services and income transfers in a comprehensive public welfare system. This is an area and a task where local decisions really are useful. The combination of legally decided income transfers in connection with services, which are evaluated locally, in principle offers the opportunity of delivering exactly the combination of income transfers and services which is preferred locally.

Thus, the organizational combination of decentralized and deconcentrated activities is quite advantageous to the users. In principle, this combination is implemented in the Danish model and has been a major argument through the structural and financial reforms of the public sector since 1970. The citizen gains access to the public services via the municipality where he lives. Concerning services delivered at the regional level, correspondingly the county is the entrance to the public sector.

In this connection, it is worth mentioning the often prevailing inefficiency and lack of effectiveness of the Danish model in areas where it has not been possible for various political reasons to implement this principle. Employment services is the most important central administrative function at the local level, and this function is carried out by local offices which are disconnected from the local government system organizationally and with respect to personnel. But it is the municipalities which have to find solutions to the problems arising, when the state employment service fails to offer "real" work but instead must rely upon the social security system or all sorts of job creation programmes.

Division of authority often frustrates users and makes them think that in the public sector one hand does not know what the other is doing although it ought to be experienced as one system by the users. Such a division also creates confusion about the precise address for placing political responsibility for the missing mutual connections.

A uniform decentralized access to the public service system is thus a desirable objective with regard to obtaining efficiency and effectiveness and at the same time contributing to a clear and well defined address for praising or whipping the political system on the election day.

1.2 The Framework for Local Political Activities

As equity considerations are based on national points of view almost everywhere, most income transfers and the criteria for distribution are national responsibilities. As mentioned, this however does not necessarily lead to organizational separation from other kinds of public service areas. Public services often comprise considerable variations with respect to local policy decisions. That holds true for the complexity of services as well as for the specific service level chosen.

The same way of thinking is to be found in the further delegation of responsibilities from municipalities to users in the form of establishment of governing bodies for schools, kindergartens, residential homes for elderly people, etc. or in the form of involvement of clubs and utilization of other kinds of voluntary efforts. This contributies in creating commitment with respect to the development of local tasks and in widening the understanding for local initiatives. At the same time, the model makes it a relatively simple matter to raise attention for cases or topics that are considered to be neglected at the local level.

As an illustration the Danish legislation on primary schools might be mentioned, which gives the municipalities both the formal and the actual responsibility for the provision of services within the rather wide frames given by national law. At the same time the municipalities are given full financial responsibility. They thus finance the public primary schools 100 percent and furthermore pay about 90 percent of the costs, if parents choose to make use of an alternative private school. The remainder is financed either by the parents or through other sources of income of the private schools.

It is up to the local politicians to determine the number of pupils per class and the number of lectures at a given grade within a broad national framework. The teacher/pupil ratio is an important local decision. The same is the case concerning the overall school structure because the choice between smaller or bigger schools is up to local decisions. Correspondingly, wide possibilities of variations exist in relation to educational methods where boards of the schools have some influence.

There are often great differences between the challenges in a local area with respect to the overall school structure and educational policy. Boards must therefore be enabled to make concrete adjustments. The boards consist of representatives of teachers, pupils, parents and municipalities elected for a four-year period. This, of course, results in differences from school to school and from municipality to municipality with respect to educational methods and the actual implementation of the national primary school law.

At the same time, the municipalities have to face the fact that parents may choose private schools, if none of the public schools meet their wishes. In other words, parents may choose and are informed about differences. With respect to functions, this situation resembles a private market but without use of prices. A wide range of choices in this area is combined with certain desirable results as to equity and with the basic point of view that primary education at a certain standard is a "meritorious good" in that education and knowledge of the individual benefits society as a whole.

More and more municipalities have lately allowed for a freer choice between the public schools within the municipal area in order to encourage and stimulate parents to take a stand concerning the specific services and educational methods offered as well as to initiate greater consciousness regarding the external image of individual schools.

Besides offering opportunities for implementing a general framework at the local level, the decentralized model in principle facilitates the abolition of inter-sectoral barriers due to different laws or traditions. It is a common observation that decentralized testing of various models for fulfilling tasks often leads to a consensus about crossing rigid sectoral divisions at national level. Thus there is a tendency to emphasize differences between opinions, as they are transformed into national questions. At the local level it is often easier to reach more pragmatic solutions.

Even within the confines of a relatively small country you often find substantial differences concerning the role of the public sector. Such differences might touch upon the freedom of municipalities to decide on the implementation of tasks or the degree to which private firms can be involved in carrying out tasks based on a contract with the municipality. Of course, there also are differences regarding the extent and composition of local government functions.

In a decentralized model, different ways of financing tasks are also subject to general reconsidering, for instance concerning purchase, leasing, borrowing, taxes/duties, user charges or maybe use of liquidity. These reflections basically concern the more fundamental choices about how to finance public tasks in general. But a decentralized model leaves plenty of room for relevant local viewpoints. Therefore it is important to involve the local politicians.

1.3 The Fiscal Policy Question

In many countries, the extent of decentralization in the public sector is often restricted by worries related to fiscal policy consequences. Naturally, such worries are usually voiced by the Ministry of Economic Affairs.

It is, however, possible to combine considerations concerning the necessary management of fiscal policy with a high degree of decentralization, and it is furthermore possible to build in local or regional liberty of action. But of course a number of conditionalities have to be met, and a number of "rules of game" have to be followed by the various actors.

No responsible government can renounce its faculty of organizing the overall fiscal policy. In an EEC setting it is even more evident that overall fiscal policy must be determined at the national level.

Even in a decentralized public sector model you often find that the levying of taxes is centralized. The level of income taxes as well as indirect taxes is in these cases determined by the national parliaments. A part of the collected revenue is afterwards distributed to the decentralized authorities – its size depending on the degree of decentralization. Often, distribution is carried out in the form of reimbursements of local expenditure. The local authorities can make their arrangements and have parts of the expenditure covered by the central government.

In practice, in some models reimbursement will depend on central government having accepted beforehand to reimburse either a certain percentage or fixed amounts. Other models imply automatic reimbursement, i.e. the shares of local expenditure to be reimbursed by the state are set by law. Central management of course is strongest when acceptance by central authorities is demanded to get reimbursed for a local activity.

Irrespective of the form, financial allocation by reimbursements can be developed into a rather effective management tool from a fiscal policy viewpoint – apart from automatic reimbursements. The reimbursement is, as a general rule, a necessary condition for the execution of a certain activity. The possibilities for fiscal policy management on the expenditure side are thus closely connected with the reimbursement arrangements.

At the same time, however, any reimbursement system implicates to a large degree a central setting of priorities concerning public activities – the factual degree of central decision making depending on the actual organization of the reimbursement system. Such a centralized priority making may be desirable for national political reasons, but whatever the reasons this will mean restrictions on the local political decisions/activities. At the same time national priority making most often implies standardized allocations irrespective of local differences in demands/needs.

First of all, worrying about these consequences for the setting of local priorities led to exploring new ways in reorganizing the Danish public sector. The aim was to reconcile the possibilities of managing general fiscal policy with a higher degree of local self-government in the setting of priorities concerning public tasks.

The biggest challenge for a coordinated fiscal policy of course is freedom at the local level to levy taxes. The more this freedom is made use of, the greater the challenge.

The usual form of this model allows local authorities to utilise but very limited tax bases. Often, they comprise only taxes on real property or various kinds of fees.

Decentralized tax financing might, however, also imply a considerable imposing of income taxes. In that case, the degree of decentralization is usually high, though as mentioned this financing method is not a necessary condition for a decentralized model. With local income taxes a division of the tax base between central and local tax authorities is made. The desired fiscal policy effect in this model has to be ascertained by a system of agreements between the different levels of the public sector. There are not necessarily any restrictions in the freedom of action regarding fiscal policy.

This model with its sharing of rights to impose taxes offers the great advantage of making possible a combination of the responsibility to spend and to finance at local level.

It is not possible from a fiscal policy viewpoint to set up precise guidelines for a division of the right to impose taxes. Neither is it possible to find the "right" division starting from local democratic considerations. Any considerations in this respect must be purely political, and the result will usually deviate from country to country depending on national traditions. In this connection, it should also be remembered that a local right to impose taxes will naturally lead to local differences.

An evaluation of the Danish experiences regarding local rights to levy taxes on income as well as real property easily leads to the conclusion that the local share of the total taxation should be of a considerable magnitude in order to obtain a high degree of local political attention. In this case, local taxation is considered so important by citizens and politicians that it works as an incentive for aiming at the highest possible efficiency in performing local tasks.

2. The Danish Model for Local Decisions

2.1 The Structural Frames

An analysis of the strategic planning process at the local level in Denmark can only be complete if it covers both local conditions and the more general framework for local activities, including the national level. This is especially the case, where such frameworks differ significantly from conditions in most other countries and contribute to a special form and content of the strategic planning process.

There is no doubt that – with respect to functions and organization – the Danish model differs a lot from those of most other countries. A number of factors can be mentioned in this connection. The public sector constitutes a considerable part of the total economy. About 30 percent of the GDP (Gross Domestic Product) concern the production of public services, and about two thirds of the total income creation depends on public finances.

Against this background, the fact deserves attention that more than two thirds of the public services are delivered by local authorities, counties and municipalities, and that the setting of priorities takes place under the responsibility of elected local politicians.

However, this does not imply a lack of frameworks for local self-government. As mentioned above, the frames are for instance defined by laws or by agreements between public authorities. Furthermore there can be other kinds of restrictions on the local freedom to act, for instance in the form of labour market agreements about salaries and other working conditions.

The decisive factor for the strategic planning process at the local level is, however, that in principle the frames are expressed in general terms thus leaving room for flexibility and the use of local judgement and decisions. In this connection, it is important to underline that a precondition for creating satisfactory leeway for managing local tasks is the absence of great geographical inequalities regarding the economic basis. That is the background for the different Danish arrangements for equalizing differences in tax bases and needs for expenditure. The aim is that the local variations in tax burdens should reflect corresponding differences in service level (and efficiency) instead of differences in economic opportunities. Generally speaking, the local level responsible for the decisions should also be responsible for the economic burdens attached to the dispositions.

The financial frames for local decisions are in principle formed by municipal and regional taxes and fees on the one hand and by block grants (general financial aid) and – as far as legally provided income transfers are concerned – by reimbursements on the other hand.

It is deliberate that grants from central to local governments are not earmarked for certain purposes. As already underlined, the important principle behind this way of thinking is that the local and regional authorities are better able to judge the needs and preferences of the local population and to react on changes than central government. Ear-marked grants and reimbursements by the state can furthermore aggravate obstacles or barriers for priority setting according to local needs. Such grants and reimbursements thus restrict flexibility and adjustments across existing institutional settings.

Considerations along these lines are reflected in the comprehensive reforms in the public sector implemented in Denmark from 1970 onwards. (Major parts of the reform complex are shown in the box below.)
- The Amalgamation Reform, 1970, about 1300 local governments reduced to 275, 25 counties reduced to 14
- Reform of the intergovernmental fiscal relations between the different levels of the public sector, 1970 onwards, change from reimbursements to block grants
- Reform of the division of responsibilities between the levels of authority in the public sector, 1970 onwards, decentralization of tasks/functions

- Reform of the physical planning system, 1974 onwards, systematic physical planning/planning of the use of geographical areas
- Reform of the sectoral and overall economic planning system, 1970 onwards, formalised establishment of a comprehensive basis for decisions
- Coordination of finances of the various levels of the public sector, 1970 onwards
- Reform of the budgetary and accounting system in the public sector, 1970 onwards, budgeting covering four years, division according to functions and types of resource use, EDP, coordination between state, counties and municipalities.

2.2 Unequal Geographical Conditions

It is often mentioned as an argument against the local right to impose taxes, that the tax bases vary locally and thus from municipality to municipality. That problem, however, can be solved as the experiences of many years with the Danish model show.

But the local needs for expenditure represent a problem. It is difficult – if not to say impossible – to define precise functional relationships between local and personal needs and the resulting public expenditure. There are also problems with finding suitable criteria that express expenditure needs and are not at the same time affected by the current political decisions.

The provision of a given sum of money on a varying tax base will result in different local tax rates. Everything else being equal, such differences will present an incentive to move to places with the lowest tax rates, resulting in the emergence of so-called tax shelter municipalities. The most wealthy move first, simply because they stand to gain the most from moving.

However, in this connection it should not be overlooked that in a long-term perspective the total gains from moving are relatively modest. That is of course caused by the tax rates being capitalized in the prices of real property, so that the differences in personal income after tax and house expenditure often are moderate and thus altogether do not work as stronger incentives to mobility. In the short run on the other hand, considerable yearly fluctuations in the local taxes can have rather remarkable effects on disposable income and local authorities usually try to avoid such fluctuations.

Irrespective of the capitalization effect the Danish experiences show the need for a certain equalization of tax bases. There may be a difference between the metropolitan area and the province or between country and urban municipalities. In the Danish model it has been necessary to implement a certain equalization of the tax bases even within the metropolitan area. Geographical equalization has over time consisted of a system with central government grants built on the size of the local tax base and an inter-municipal equalization, where, for instance, municipalities with a relatively high tax base are paying to municipalities with a tax base below the average.

The other reason for varying local tax burdens is the variations in expenditure needs. These variations are also to a certain degree equalized in the Danish system. By the way, it should be mentioned that an amalgamation of municipalities seldom helps to solve problems of this kind, because the variations in needs often cover a larger geographical area – as for instance a major part of a region.

Equalization according to criteria expressive of "objective expenditure needs" is closely linked with the scope and composition of the functions being taken care of at the local level. With local tasks comprising the running of primary schools, town development, environmental protection and social welfare services like day-care institutions for children, home help, housing and nursing homes for elderly people, tax assessments etc., it is a necessary condition for the acceptance, that reasonably equal possibilities for solving the tasks exist.

As already touched upon, equalization here aims to create a certain degree of homogeneity as far as the so-called "objective expenditure needs" are concerned. The equalization makes up for some of the differences caused by the fact that in some municipalities there are many elderly people needing care while other municipalities have many children needing places in schools, day-care institutions or the like. Municipalities with expenditure needs below average pay to municipalities with expenditure needs above average. A wide variety of criteria expressing needs is used, the criteria often being debated.

As is the case with the system of equalizing differences in tax bases, the model of equalizing expenditure needs works via block grants (general financial aid). Each municipality knows before the agreement on the budget and thus before the decisions on the tax levy for the coming year are taken, how much money in the form of block grants should be delivered to or is received from other municipalities and how much is received from the central government.

2.3 Coordination between Central and Local Government Finances

For more than twenty years there have been negotiations between the government and the associations of local governments. These negotiations take place in springtime. The main point on the agenda is defining the budgetary frames for the coming year. The demands made on next year's fiscal policy form the basis for these frames, including the following.

It is important that the general framework for the local governments is set for the sector as a whole and not for the individual municipalities and counties. The purpose is to allow for local flexibility. A need for expansion in one place can be met by reductions in another municipality and therefore does not disturb the fiscal political consideration.

During summer and autumn the local governments are able to consolidate their budgets with a high degree of backing by this agreement. Based on the information about the budgetary decisions made by the local governments before the middle of October, national government is able to calculate the financial effects and if necessary adjust the central government budget.

2.4 The Structure of Incentives

The public sector in a welfare society will always consist of a considerable number of agencies. In the model described here the acting politicians are divided according to differences in their points of view regarding the necessity of public services and the level of tax-burden. In addition, geography also causes different interests.

The structure of incentives is very important for the result and thus for the ability of a decentralized public sector to function in accordance with far-reaching consequences of political governance. Political responsibility vis-à-vis the electors is diminished if there are many ways of shifting political responsibilities between public sector agents and if each one of them is acting on behalf of his own interests. The electors cannot be expected to be able to see through the complex system which makes up the public sector.

One method to reduce the unavoidable conflicts in a decentralized public sector with many agents is to shed light on the cross-sectorial interests. The elected politicians have different interests. To illustrate this phenomenon one might mention the difference between the wishes of the Ministry of Finance and the other ministries' want lists. In this context, it contributes to an open political discussion if local governments are able to express their opinions on, e.g., the costs of new legislatory initiatives, especially when their opinions are based on a closer knowledge of the actual performance of the tasks.

Besides the more open discussion about the consequences of a new or changed legislation you will often find differing opinions on the financing of public services. The equalizing effects are of great interest and they are often related to the choice of financing. It is important that such deliberations are made in an open discussion.

The Danish experience proves that a dialogue and an open discussion between the different groups of interested persons and/or organizations with regard to public activities contribute to a greater interest of the public in what is going on. This is due to clearly defined responsibilities in relation to the electors.

2.5 The Strategic Planning Process

There is general agreement on that the public sector reforms have resulted in better structural conditions for an extensive local self-government within general frameworks. This is the case in spite of the fact that from time to time restrictions on or interferences in the system are imposed, for instance in connection with the yearly negotiations between the government and the municipalities as part of the general economic policy.

A fundamental question is therefore, if and to what degree the extant opportunities are exploited. This question is of special importance regarding form and content of the strategic planning process.

At present, relevant strategic planning in the public sector is very urgent. It touches upon questions of public sector functions in relation to the private sector as well as questions of the internal mode of operation of the public sector. Conditions for democracy, welfare, equality before the law, management of resources and equity are also included as are subjects concerning efficiency/effectiveness and the relationship between politicians and civil servants.

Internationally, the relevance of the topic is underlined by the collapse of the centrally directed Soviet system and by the failure of the public sector in many countries to function according to public expectations as the generator of a development process.

Generally speaking, questions have been raised concerning the effectiveness of large systems. There are many examples of huge systems tending to "bog down" in slow and bureaucratic procedures and thus displaying built-in tendencies to restrict the implementation of even the best intentions.

But also in the well-established democracies, goal achievements and optimal organization of planning processes as well as obtainable results are subject to intensive discussions. Among other reasons, this can be attributed to the intensified debate on trust/distrust in the political systems, the participation of the citizens in completely new forms of organization and communication as well as the increasing internationalization, including, in Europe, the EEC issue and the division of labour between the EEC and the national, regional and local levels in each country.

At first glance it seems paradoxical that the question of decentralization in many countries should be emphasized by this development. But it apparently touches something fundamental concerning the form of expression of democracy and the mode of operation of the public sector, which naturally must be very important for relevant strategic planning at the local level. The discussion of public planning is furthermore made relevant by the rapid socio-economic changes, which themselves have caused many disappointments concerning planning – at least that part of planning dealing with the ability to predict such changes and to prevent negative consequences.

The growing distance between the planning process and the political decisions deserves particular attention in this connection.

Some important questions can be summarized as follows:
- How are the political visions/wishes being transformed into active and proactive strategies leading to the wanted goals and results?
- Which demands should be met by the political administrative system in order to make it optimally fitted as generator for a sustainable mobilization of resources and thus the development process – given a certain division of labour between the public and private sector in a market economy?
- Which elements should be included in the political visions – what kind of expression should they take – if the chances of optimal implementation are to be improved?
- How can implementation of the political goals and visions by the administration be secured in the best possible way?
- How are these goals and visions made visible in the administrative organization?
- What conditionalities are needed for the relationship between politicians and civil servants to yield optimal results?

Planning up to now has not given satisfactory answers to most of these questions. Many of them are also far-reaching by nature. A major problem is, however, that even much simpler questions have not been satisfactorily answered. If better results are to be achieved in the future the demands on both form and content of planning must be changed. Consequently, the analysis of the causes for this lack of fulfillment until now is an important basis for the debate on future planning.

2.6 Experiences from the Past with Respect to Planning

In Denmark very good possibilities for evaluating the practical results of planning exist. In the wake of the public sector structural reforms from 1970 onwards, planning systems along standardised guidelines were established for the service sectors, the physical infrastructure, the use of geographical areas as well as the public income and expenditure.

The basic idea behind the municipal planning systems was to replace central directives via detailed rules and reimbursements by a more general planning framework for management. This was to give more flexibility, fewer sectorial bindings and increased local liberty of action. An improved national economic management was to be obtained by closer connections between decisions on different sector areas and levels of authority – also concerning the use of land and the economic consequences. The principle of better agreements between decisions and economic burdens was at the same time to be maintained.

Planning in itself did not, however, become an effective tool for solving urgent national economic problems like, for instance, with the balance of payments, employment, growing public expenditure or the increasing tax burden. Planning in itself did not in any way render superfluous the political decisions on priority setting and management.

It was even negative in that the planning systems very often did not contribute to improving the basis for political decisions. An important explanation was that the systems became diffuse, very technical, detailed and complicated. The planning bureaucracy and a lot of red tape threatened to overshadow the positive sides of planning. This contributed to planning often being alienated from the political process with serious consequences for mutual confidence.

Solving the diversified local priority problems was restricted by the standardised planning procedures, while local authorities felt that they did not get sufficiently relevant feedback from the complex work of collecting information nor for planning and sending it to the central authorities.

It was furthermore displeasing that the planning bureaucracy seemed to emphasize the existing organizational and operational structures, which inhibited exactly that adjustment and adaptation of resources to changes in needs and that search for untraditional solutions – often across sectorial barriers – which were asked for in the efforts to manage the public services. The plans often could be characterized as mere desiderata lists.

On the whole, the evidence of Danish local level experience shows that it is very important to avoid creating a cumbersome bureaucracy when developing and maintaining planning systems. The more formalized the procedures become, and the more technical, detailed and complicated the organization of the planning process, the greater the risk for an alienated planning bureaucracy which at the same time fails to achieve the main purpose of planning – to reach optimal results from the public efforts with the least possible use of resources.

In this connection, however, it is important to emphasize one fact: it does not follow from this that planning is unnecessary. It is widely accepted that a systematic general review of possible choices and consequences is necessary. This holds true for areas like education, health, social welfare, etc. and with regards to coordination and finances. But the experiences from the past unambiguously point towards the conclusion that the intentional purposes of planning – establishing an optimal basis for political decisions – are not automatically obtained. Besides avoiding the pitfalls described, optimal planning also demands precise definitions of the roles of the different actors, not least the roles of the politicians.

2.7 The Requirements of Future Planning

A relevant strategic planning process must be related to present political goals and be based on an active and proactive process with supplementary relationships between politicians and administrators. Otherwise it will not be possible to reach the political objectives – maybe even expressed as visions – under constantly changing conditions. The current rapid changes in socio-economic and political conditions must necessarily be taken into account.

For this reason alone, relevant planning can not amount to simply establishing a "plan." Relevant planning systems in the 1990s must consist of flexible, continuously adjusted and precise information tools, which can form a suitable basis for the necessary selection between different political goals and means for the solution of urgent problems, for instance in relation to the environment, education, health or employment. In Denmark, this is to a high degree emphasized by an intensified discussion of both positive and negative consequences of involving the institutions and the users in the decision making process – a development to a large extent caused by a growing involvement of citizens in the closer community.

Against the background of the local differences in wishes and needs, a relevant planning system evidently must be flexible in the sense that it is able to support the decentralized decision process while recognizing the special local conditions. What with the diversity of problems and possibilities, something similar ought to be obtained concerning the form and content of planning. Only then can planning satisfy the complexity of needs, including the wishes for decentralized solutions.

Relevant planning at the local level today is to a large extent a question of testing limits, frames, modes of operations and the possibilities for action within the given organizational and economic framework. The narrower the limits, the more important is the testing. Identifying bottlenecks and barriers to changes and adjustments are only examples of such a testing. But testing risks to be meaningless and alienated, unless it takes place in a proactive process involving politicians as well as administrators in a mutual, interactive way.

The need for locally adapted solutions and flexibility is naturally also emphasized by the cross-sectorial nature of many urgent problems. Problems connected with social welfare, employment, education, the environment, traffic, energy, health, the labour market or the economy in general, etc. respect no sector limits.

Generally speaking, the possibilities of using planning as a tool for increased mobilization, both with respect to the utilization of resources and the democratic process, can only be exploited, if the mentioned requirements of a future planning system ares fulfilled.

2.8 Problems

Some problems connected to strategic planning at the local level arise because the division of responsibilities between the different levels – central, counties, municipalities – is not so well defined as the "pure" model presupposes. The division lines drawn between responsibilities and tasks of different public authorities (and geographical between different municipalities) can always be discussed. For instance the functional segregation of nursing homes for elderly people, which in Denmark is the responsibility of one level – the municipalities – and the hospitals, which are administered by another level – the counties – may cause many problems. Something similar is the case as far as "overlapping" responsibilities in the social welfare area are concerned, for instance in connection with fulltime placement of children and young people in institutions.

The essential principle of harmony between the power to make decisions and the economic responsibility needs to be modified if it is to solve the problems arising from the necessity of cooperation between several public authorities in the solution of many public problems.

Despite the reform of the division of public sector tasks following relatively clear principles implying that connected tasks should be executed by one and the same public authority at one level (state, county or municipality), the Danish system shows examples of this principle not being implemented with consequence in all areas. To illustrate this the labour market institutions are often mentioned because central government offices for employment exchange at the regional level and responsibility for vocational training do exist side by side with county responsibility for the remainder of the secondary school system.

This lack of consistency raises further demands on coordination at the local level, where the problematic consequences of the inconsistency and incoherence first show and lead to extra and unnecessary demands on strategic planning.

It often causes problems of coordination in some parts of a country if the municipal structure and division of tasks in bigger townships – often metropolitan areas -are not based on the same principles as in the rest of the country. In Denmark the principles behind the geographical division between municipalities and counties were general and clear, but in practice they were never implemented in the Copenhagen area, causing a number of problems.

Generally, however, it seems to be the continued uncertainty about the limits/frameworks for the local self-government which causes the biggest problems for the strategic planning at the local and regional level. In this regard, examples of lack of consequence and consistency abound.

Many examples demonstrate the difficulties of Parliament and central government to act consequently with regard to local self-government. It is, however, exactly the fundamental idea behind local self-government, that variations in the chosen methods and rendered services are visible – the philosophy as mentioned being that local self-government in a decentralized system offers possibilities for quicker and better adjustments to the local needs.

As long as interferences in the tasks of local authorities are of a more general nature, it can be claimed that this poses no grave problems, as at least in this case there is no interference in the local priority setting between tasks and resource use. An example of interference of this kind in Denmark is the general economic frames established through the yearly negotiations between the state, counties and municipalities (represented by their associations) about the economic conditions, including the block grant system and the system of equalizing some geographical differences in economic bases and needs.

It is more dangerous if interferences take on the form of direct commands, rules or alike in specific service areas. An example of an interference of this character in Denmark could be the central government orders to the counties to reduce the waiting time for certain types of hospital operations, which of course if everything else is the same (for instance unchanged overall capacity) will lead to relatively longer waiting time for other kinds of operations/treatments and reductions in service level in these areas. At the same time such interference belies the general assumption that local priority setting is the best to reflect the local needs. Another Danish example of specific interference is the central government claim to guarantee day-care facilities for children in the municipalities.

Generally speaking, an indirect pressure on the local self-government system is represented by the frequent discussions in Parliament concerning the acceptable variations between the different choices of service levels for specific services in the municipalities. The national political tolerance regarding the freedom of action for the local self-government is not defined once and for all, but is subject to frequent reconsiderations.

Finally the addition of new and unexpected tasks at the local level is worth mentioning. Recent examples might include the problems connected with unemployment and minority groups.

2.9 The Requirements of the Political System

There is no doubt that a decentralized public system like the Danish one puts extraordinary demands on the politicians. The politicians are not only administrators acting on proposals from the civil servants. Amongst other things this also demands a general overview – often across specific tasks – although the working day of a politician is very often marked by demands made on him that he look into specific cases. It also demands that politicians transform vague attitudes into operational goals which achievements and results can be measured against.

At present, the demands on flexibility and the ability to adjust do increase at the local level because of the rapid socio-economic changes. At the same time, however, a tendency to emphasize hindrances and barriers to adjustments has made itself distinctly felt, also because of the growing stress laid on professional and sectorial interests. Especially at the local level, extra strength is also needed to disregard such interests if necessary. However, it is worth mentioning in this respect, that the power behind these interests should not be underestimated irrespective of the degree of decentralization.

Furthermore it should be noticed, that a high degree of decentralization must be followed by more general responsibilities, for instance for marginalized or minority groups. Such responsibilities can not be taken on in a relevant way by only considering parish political viewpoints. The inequalities which might result, if these responsibilities are not met, would rapidly be considered unacceptable from a national point of view.

This problem may be regarded as being affiliated with the model: one reason for that is of course, that it concerns needs which in a local area appear of such a limited magnitude, that it would, for instance, be too costly and irrrational to attach the necessary qualified expertise to the local area. But the portion of public services managed locally in Denmark is so great, that such an argument might well be advanced on quite a number of topics. Generally this points in the direction that the local political system as a whole has to be able to take care of more than narrow local political interests.

Especially in these years, the demands are furthermore intensified by current tendencies in the public pointing towards increasing direct user influence on the size and composition as well as quality of the rendered services and wishes for more possibilities of choice. New ways of organization, changed forms of interaction between the public and private sector, expansion of the market for tender bidding, privatization, etc. are also challenges that intensify the demands on the political level.

The operational mode of a decentralized system depends largely on the politicians having sufficient insight to mark out goals and means in a qualified way and being ready to take responsibility. The operational mode is likewise dependent on the actual possibility of politicians being held responsible, politically as well as personally. This could be important in connection with nepotism and abuse of power or alike. This demand alone would in many places in the world seem completely unattainable.

Another challenge to the local political system is represented by the increasingly articulate demands and wishes from the voters as a natural result of the general increase in the level of education and knowledge. The widening use of modern technology plays a major role in this.

The demand that all Danish municipalities be obliged to inform their citizens on the concrete political choices of service levels in different service areas serves to illustrate this development. It is no longer sufficient to just inform on consolidated budgets or the allocation of financial resources. The public has a claim to receiving information about for instance the decision on the number of pupils in school classes and the local fulfillment of the nationally defined demands concerning the environment.

All in all, these last years have seen a marked development to substitute information to citizens by communication between citizens and local governments. Obviously, this trend implies a considerable intensification of the demands made on local politicians and the necessity for the politicians to clarify their goals.

3. The Municipality of Farum

3.1 The Past

The results obtained by the municipality of Farum during the last decade are rather impressing in the Danish context. The municipality has changed from a status as a traditional and ordinary local government to a position as a modern and efficient firm delivering public services.

Farum is a suburb of the City of Copenhagen. The two city centers are just 17 kilometers apart. Farum now has 18,000 inhabitants. The decade from the mid-60s on was characterized in Denmark by a rapid growth in the public sector activities and in the overall economy as well.

Within the metropolitan area this period resulted in the urbanization of new areas, Farum being one of these. From a kind of village-society the area was transformed into modern suburb.

From a local economic point of view the rapid development of a quite new town came close to a disaster. The name Farum became by and large to be identified with political and economic chaos. The municipality was a place to settle for only a shorter period. Young families moved to Farum demanding all the local government services as kindergartens, schools, etc., but as soon as they were able to move to municipalities with a lower tax-burden, they escaped from Farum. Farum kept the "expensive" inhabitants whereas others moved out as soon as they could afford to.

A vicious circle had been established. The tax-percentages increased every year and raised the number of people moving in and out. The local politicians reacted irresolutely and were unable to stop the drift towards the foreseeable collapse of the municipal economy. Farum became the "ugly duckling" in the flock of Danish local governments.

At the beginning of the 1980s the economic situation in the municipality became so alarming that the Ministry of Home Affairs, which acts as the supervisory authority, threatened to intervene and use emergency measures to dictate the economic arrangements in Farum. To put it bluntly, the municipality was close to being limited in its freedom to look after its own affairs. Examples of this kind are very rare in modern times.

3.2 The Change

Before the threat was turned into reality, a small group of local politicians from a number of political parties realized the danger. In 1983 they succeeded in shaping a small majority in the Council in favour of a plan which could stop the downward movement. Many unpopular but necessary decisions about the economy were taken.

Since 1983 the situation has changed complety. Today the municipality of Farum has an income level higher than the metropolitan area average, the tax-percentage has been reduced year after year, and Farum has at the same time succeeded in establishing a service level of its public service activities which is among the highest in the comparable municipalities in the metropolitan area.

Obviously, a turnaround of this magnitude is not possible unless you have the strong political will to make changes, to try the untried and therefore the political will to produce and implement a strategic planning covering a relatively long period of time.

Among the more visible changes due to this process the following are worth mentioning:
- Each year in sequence, Farum has been successful in realizing the goal set by the political majority in the council to reduce the income and property tax with the perspective of being the municipality in the metropolitan area cheapest to live in by the year 2004. In 1984 the tax percentage was 21.9 percent, in 1996 the rate was 17.2. At the same time, the property tax has been reduced from 19 to 6 per thousand. For the individual taxpayer in Farum these reductions in the percentages have meant an increase in disposible income over the years whereas at the same time the average taxpayer in the country as a whole has experienced a reduction in his personal income after taxation.
- It is a political objective to reduce the debt of the municipality at the same time as the tax-burden is lowered. The debt burden became rather heavy during the 1970s. Compared to the tax basis of the city the debt-burden now amounts to 8 percent compared to 14.5 percent in 1984.
- Higher efficiency at the administrative level has resulted in a reduction of town hall personnel by more than 50 percent in the same period. The political intention in this field is for the municipality of Farum to have

the smallest number of administrative personnel amongst local governments in Denmark with the same number of inhabitants.
- Through its construction and housing policy Farum tries to conserve a demographic structure guaranteeing a steady utilization of public services as for instance kindergartens, schools, and homes for the elderly.
- In order to reach these political goals Farum has used to a very high degree the different ways of bringing unemployed people into jobs again. The municipality was among the first to demand that public assistance for the unemployed must be matched by the willingness to work on their side. In order to justify this demand Farum established so-called production workshops, an idea which was later copied by other local governments.
- Very early on Farum looked for solutions minimizing the costs incurred. Tendering out is used as often as possible.
- A large sum of money has been used in order to prevent traffic accidents, first of all those concerning children. This has been done with an attitude that preventing is better than curing and therefore saves money.
- A goal-orientated effort is made to help families which are not able to take care of their children. The intention is to help such families to solve their problems. By establishing a special consultation center the municipality has cut its expenditure by half and at the same time improved the level of services rendered. The need of separating children from their parents has also been halved.
- The extension of different kinds of services for instance to elderly people is based on the principle that home care is the cheapest and at the same time the best offer from an individual point of view.
- Cultural and leisure time activities of different kinds are widely supplied in the municipality. The philosophy is that the supply need not be supported or financed by municipal means. The number of arrangements can be enlarged to a certain degree by demanding user charges and sponsoring.
- Compared to the average situation of Danish local governments, Farum has a relatively high proportion of ethnic minorities. More than fifty different languages are represented in the primary school system, which altogether has just about 2,000 pupils. It is the stated policy of Farum to try to integrate these minorities and at the same utilise their

cultural values. Therefore learning Danish is an offer to all children in the pre-school years.
- The reduction of administrative staff at Townhall must be achieved by attrition. The employees are offered a job guarantee.
- The overall service level in Farum is relatively high compared to other local governments in the same district. Service level in this context means for instance the number of pupils per teacher, classroom size, the number of lessons, study tours, etc.
- The level of information and communication with the inhabitants of Farum is high. Their socio-economic status obliges the council to have an intensive information policy and to be open for participation in various ways before major decisions are taken.

3.3 The Vision of Farum 2004

The Farum experiences are illustrative of the fact that a model of self-determination is not in itself a guarantee of obtaining the results desired. It is absolutely necessary in order to reach substantial results to have a visionary political leadership that is at the same time able to build political consensus within the council and in relation to the inhabitants in the municipality.

If there is no willingness to make the necessary adjustments, it must in some way be brought about. When one's back is to the wall, the need for change is obvious, but the situation does not guarantee that change is made. In the case of Farum, one's back was to the wall and at the same time, there were some visions about how to change the development in the opposite direction.

A relevant strategic planning process must be related to very concrete political objectives and a selection of relevant means which are politically acceptable. It must be based on an active and proactive process provided through complementary relationships between the administrative and the political level. Assuming this condition to be fulfilled from the beginning, it will at the same time be possible to attain the flexibility which is a sine qua non when you think of the unavoidable changes in the socio-economic and political conditions.

With respect to the Farum experience, the central element in planning in a Danish local government context is the coexistence of two factors: on the one hand, the political facilities exist at local level to offer a broad continuum of public services – as it were, custom-made – in a specified area. On the other hand, communities are at the same time able to make the decisions necessary for reaching their objectives. The economic framework is well known to the council. The local tax percentages have to be weighted against the objectives of the services offered.

The perception of a plan as a framework which helps to reconcile wishes and possibilities can be illustrated by the development of the primary school system in Farum.

The vision of Farum 2004 is based on certain assumptions regarding the development of the demographic structure in the municipality. In a next step the service level in the relevant age groups has to be determined, as for instance primary schools or care for the elderly.

Local governments, however, have no ways of regulating the demographic structure of a mobile population or the birthrate. Since the drawing up of the vision of Farum 2004, a lot of changes have occurred in both areas. The number of births is going up in Denmark. As a consequence the pressure on local institutions like kindergartens and other kinds of day care activites is growing and has now reached the primary school system.

Years ago Farum Council decided to give a guarantee of day care services for children up to school age. This implied that families with children who moved to Farum were guaranteed a place in a kindergarten or similar institutions within a very short time – at this time within 24 hours. The effect of this guarantee was that unexpectedly many families with children chose Farum as a dwelling place.

The growing number of newborn children together with the guarantee has made it necessary to revise the expectations regarding the development of the primary school system in the years up to 2004. In a Danish local government context this means that the politicians have to make decisions about the level of service and the capacity needed, for instance with respect to the number of pupils per teacher, childen per classroom, the number of lectures per class, the number of schools, their size, etc. The decisions about the level of service together with the growing number of children affect of course the expenditure side of the budget and thus automatically lead to a revision of the objectives of tax rate development.

In the case of Farum it has been decided to maintain the service level and at the same time preserve the general target of a reduction of the tax burden each year. This is made possible by the combined effect of more inhabitants in higher income groups and rationalization. Finally, the financial support by central government via a higher proportion of block grants than today – because of the relatively higher proportion of children in Farum – should be mentioned.

The vision of Farum 2004 acts as a kind of framework which can be used as a basis for revising the level of quantity and quality of services in the municipality. It enables politicians to discuss the contents and the effects of municipal activities and at the same time preserve the totality and the breadth of outlook.

There is an effect in the direction towards increased responsibility if the elected members of the local councils consider the consequences on the expenditure side as well as the burden of financing – both in the short run and the long run. These experiences cannot be overestimated.

In our system the political leadership must have detailed information about how activities are functioning in practice. At the same time, this is the precondition of a serious discussion about productivity, efficiency and effectiveness in relation to the solution of concrete problems. It makes no difference whether such debates are taking place in local councils or inside political parties.

A decentralized democratic model is furthermore characterized by people always being able to contact their elected representatives, including the mayor, and in this way to get their wishes included in the local political agenda. The model also implies a political level which takes the initiative and is at the same time responsible for implementation and therefore functions as the link to the inhabitants/users of services.

A plan like the vision of Farum 2004 is a consensus-shaping program of a political majority which reconciles financing of local public service activities and their quantity and quality over a relevant period of time.

Of course, Danish local governments differ widely in what they consider to be more or less important activities. In this respect, differences are due to political points of view but also reflect geographical differences.

The value and importance of local democracy are based on the acceptance of such differences and the subsequent adjustment to local preferences and needs. A high degree of freedom to decide is connected with economic accountability supplemented by great flexibility at the local level. The sequence of implementation measures may serve as an example. Local politicians just cannot argue that lack of money or of willingness at the central government level has caused the lack of local service. The participation in the local elections every fourth year is high. The number of votes are somewhat lower than in elections for the parliament.

4. Perspectives

The international development, especially within the EEC and the East European countries, has highlighted the Scandinavian and especially the Danish model of local democracy. The interest in the Danish model is mainly due to its possibilities of combining local decisions with a corresponding local economic responsibility. To achieve this, it unites local performance according to local preferences with the national political claim of being able to set the general framework for public services and the corresponding wish to formulate a policy of equity and the responsibility of the overall financial policy.

Naturally, the experiences of one country cannot be simply transferred to another. The historical backgrounds differ and so do the cultural ones. It is, however, possible to get inspiration and ideas which could be usable in other countries.

As mentioned above, it is a distinctive feature of the Danish model that it unites local adjustments of needs with local financial means. The result is local differences with regard to the level and amount of public services but inside the framework set by a national legislation.

In Europe at the moment we are facing a growing interest in regional and local affairs. The backdrop might be the growing attention for and the political process towards integration and at the same time the breakdown of barriers between national, regional and local areas. There is no contradiction, however, between strengthening the overall level and at the same time revitalizing the local level concerning decision making there. In today's Europe, local and regional values are seen as worth preserving. Integration is a good thing, but local identities should not disappear. The challenge in the light of this tendency is to find a balance between the indubitable advantages of easier and more direct exchange between localities, regions and states on the one hand and the preservation of their distinctive features on the other hand.

Even in a relatively small country like Denmark, it is a fact that people are thinking in different ways and that the needs regarding public services are varying. The model seems to be able to govern the entire public sector in accordance with national preferences and at the same time allow for local and regional adaptations. Of course this model cannot be copied wholesale. But the experience with the finding of solutions in this way is without doubt usable in other places.

The relationship between the overall interests of the national state and the local preferences are an important topic also outside the EEC. There, it often causes conflicts which could even lead to military confrontations. Undoubtedly, finding an acceptable balance between national interests and the wishes or needs for local adaptations is a very sensitive problem all over the world.

The Danish experience shows that a sustainable solution must be based on a learning process covering several years because of the unavoidable changing of balances of power. And this holds true both with regard to national interests and to the relations between national and local interest.

As another experience from the implementation of the Danish model one has to mention the importance of providing local public services in accordance with a local decision made by personalities elected from amongst local citizenry. On the other hand, the local population must at the same time be able to identify the politicians responsible for the choices. It is confusing and leads to a reduction of the interest in local government matters if the electors can no longer discern who are the politicians responsible for a certain result.

In a period where we are talking about the "Europe of the regions," it is extremely important to find the means necessary for preserving local differences – whether they have to do with regional particularities or with local specifities as is the case with the municipality of Farum.

Literature
(In English)

Local Government in Denmark. National Association of Local Authorities, Copenhagen.
The Regional Level. Counties in Denmark. The Association of County Councils in Denmark. Copenhagen.
Brixtofte, Peter: Influence and Responsibility in the Public Sector, in: Carl Bertelsmann Prize 1993. Democracy and Efficiency in Local Government, Vol. 2, Gütersloh, 1994.
Knudsen, Tim (ed.): Welfare Administration in Denmark. Copenhagen 1991.
Mikkelsen, Palle and Steenstrup, Jens Erik: Performance and Democracy in Local Government. The Case of Farum. Farum 1993.
Mikkelsen, Palle and Steenstrup, Jens Erik: Public Sector Reforms in Denmark. Copenhagen 1985.
Mikkelsen, Palle: People Empowerment: Trends in Denmark, in: Decentralization of Government, ed. by Maurice R. O'Connell. Dublin 1994.

Christchurch: Strategic Planning in Local Government – A Practitioner's Perspective

Mike Richardson

Executive Summary 328
1. Implementing Strategic Planning. 329
2. Effectiveness not Efficiency 331
3. Identifies Outcomes............................... 331
4. Recognises Uncertainty 332
5. Involves Interested Parties....................... 333
6. Evaluates Options 334
7. Identifies Council's Role 335
8. Specification of Outputs 336
9. Developing a Funding Policy. 338
10. Long Term Financial Planning 338
11. Perspectives 339
Appendices 340

Executive Summary

The following paper is based on the experience of Christchurch City Council and adopts a pragmatic approach in developing and implementing strategic planning. Strategic planning is seen as an approach to problem-solving and as a process open to evolution, which must not be imposed on an organisation like a definite blue print. A number of central elements may be defined which contribute to this process of strategic planning.

Strategic planning is concerned with outcomes, i.e. with the effectiveness of a city council's activities. Efficiency is no issue in this context. Annual citizens' surveys may serve to measure and, if necessary, to influence the effectiveness of services provided. Planning must precisely define the city council's main objectives, with long term objectives being of particular importance. At the same time, however, their relevance to short term decisions is to be taken into account.

It also must be acknowledged that an organisation like a city council exists in an ever changing environment which it never can completely control or have knowledge of. Keeping in mind these limitations, the community and its environment must be continuously analysed. Essential data relate to the qualitative and quantitative development of inhabitants, economic trends and changing attitudes. This process also ought to involve the different groups of stakeholders. To correctly identify them is fundamental to the success of strategic planning. In addition, tools like market surveys may be utilized.

Strategic planning will result in different alternatives that have to be assessed regarding their respective merits. A public sector organisation like a city council must base such an assessment on which procedure will procure the greatest net benefits to the public. In this, a planning balance which juxtaposes costs and benefits will prove helpful. At present, Christchurch is elaborating guidelines for the evaluation of large-scale projects. Also, strategic planning contributes to clarifying a council's role with regard to particular objectives. The spectrum of roles ranges from that of leading agency as provider of services to monitoring and influencing. In this respect, city councils enjoy great freedom of decision.

Budget planning as well will have to undergo a change, so that estimates allow to clearly discern what outputs a community does purchase with its money. In order to achieve this, the accounting structure needs to be modified: the structure of cost centres must, by and large, be related to categories of output. Another important tool are time sheets, which are at the same time less sophisticated. Such a clear identification of the respective costs also facilitates budgetary planning of the individual service sectors and thus permits long term planning and searching for alternative funding.

All in all, strategic planning represents a method of defining and then reviewing the major objectives of the city council. It determines the way in which resources can best be allocated today and in the future to achieve these goals. The most challenging thing about strategic planning is not making the instruments work but rather the fact that it makes us confront difficult decisions. Thus, strategic planning is not for the timid, but then nor is local government in the 1990s – whether elected members are concerned or professional staff.

1. Implementing Strategic Planning

This paper is titled to emphasise that the views are personal (although it owes much to both management and elected member colleagues). It adopts an approach which is intended to be pragmatic, perhaps in contrast to the majority of literature available on strategic planning which is generally theoretical. It includes a number of hot tips, intended to reflect key points learned from my own experience in strategic planning. It is unashamedly biased towards the experience and progress to date of the Christchurch City Council, simply because that is what I know and understand best. Strategic planning is an approach and a process, it is better not to think of it as a finite plan, although elements such as objectives need to be clearly set out if they are to provide guidance and a point of reference for decision making.

A lot of mystique surrounds the term "strategic planning." For the purposes of this paper I will liken strategic planning to an orchestra. There is a wide range of instruments which can be used to develop strategic planning. At the one extreme some Councils may use them all and have a symphony orchestra (symphony orchestras sound excellent but are not cheap). Other Councils may find it more appropriate to use fewer instruments and have a chamber orchestra or simply a quartet. You can get a pretty good tune out of a four piece band, although you will never play a sophisticated piece of music which has many parts.

Some of the characteristics of a good orchestra are that the instruments are individually well tuned, they work well together, they learn from mistakes and so improve performance and they have a conductor who understands how the instruments relate together.

I do not believe that there is a "right way" to tackle strategic planning in local government. There is however a wrong way: and that is to envisage a blue print plan imposed on an organisation from the outside.

However tackled strategic planning must be the foundation for the objectives and performance based management processes required in our annual plans.

This leads me to Hot Tip No. 2: strategic planning should develop out of current practice, fashioned to suit the particular needs and context of your Council – don' t try and buy an "off the shelf" blue print.

And so to Hot Tip No. 3: strategic planning needs commitment from elected member and senior management level, an individual to drive/facilitate development of the instruments (the conductor) and it must draw in managers throughout the organisation so that they can clearly see how it relates to their day to day activities.

Sections 2–10 briefly review some of the elements which can contribute to a strategic planning process, identifying some of the several instruments which can be used to introduce them. Readers who are wondering what happened to Hot Tip No. 1 will have to keep reading.

2. Effectiveness not Efficiency

Strategic planning is concerned with outcomes (effectiveness) and not efficiency. It is not a management review and should not be concerned with questions of the best means of service delivery. Rather, it is concerned with measuring the environment. It is concerned with the outcomes achieved rather than the outputs which Council delivers. I like to distinguish between performance measures which will assess precisely whether we are achieving stated outputs, and performance indicators which will give us a broad picture of whether we are effectively achieving what we want for, and in, the community. To give an example: a Council may open a Tourist Information Centre on time, operate it to budget and achieve specified performance standards. Performance measurement would tell us that the output has been successfully delivered and the Centre is running efficiently. It may be however, that tourist numbers have remained stagnant and average bed nights per visitor have fallen. These performance indicators would suggest that the initiative is not being effective in achieving the desired outcome of increased tourism.

An instrument that may prove useful in addressing effectiveness as distinct to efficiency is an Annual Citizens' Survey. We have carried out a survey in Christchurch for three years running, asking the same questions each year about the extent of resident participation in and satisfaction with Council services; this focuses on the effectiveness of our services rather than measuring their efficiency. Repetition of questions provides performance indicators which track changes in Council's effectiveness from year to year (see appendix 1).

3. Identifies Outcomes

Strategic planning must make clear and keep to the fore the Council's key goals or desired outcomes. Again this recognises that specific projects and programmes are only of value in so far as they contribute to these outcomes. So, strategic planning is not about service delivery standards nor service delivery methods (although these issues are important for other purposes). It is probably because the outcomes sought by a local body are many and varied, whereas those sought by a business are very much simpler, that strategic planning proves such a challenge in the public sector.

The Christchurch City Council has included a set of strategic objectives in its 1993-94 Annual Plan (as have some other councils). This lists 34 externally focused objectives grouped under three headings: the city's people, the city's physical environment and the city's economy. A further eleven objectives set down what is desired to achieve for the Council as an organisation (see appendix 2).

Developing strategic objectives obviously requires a focus on the long term but it is essential that the objectives have clear meaning in guiding priorities for decision making in the short term. This is well illustrated in the Business Plan recently developed by the Palmerston North Enterprise Trust Board.

4. Recognises Uncertainty

Strategic planning acknowledges that an organisation, whether public or private sector, exists in an ever changing environment over which it has at best partial control and concerning which it never has perfect information. As issues and circumstances change so should priorities and programmes.

Reflecting this reality, strategic planning traditionally analyses the Strengths and Weaknesses internal to the organisation, and the Opportunities and Threats which are external to it (known as SWOT analysis). In local body parlance this identifies the need for another of our strategic planning instruments, monitoring of the community and the environment.

Monitoring should include an understanding of demographic trends, not simply changes in overall population numbers but more particularly in household numbers and household types, issues of population aging, changes in dependency ratios and perhaps in ethnic groupings especially in those districts which are seeing significant immigration from overseas.

Monitoring of economic and employment trends is also desirable, albeit rather more difficult. Recent years have shown that fluctuations in investment and performance of industries such as kiwi fruit, forestry and timber processing, professional services and commercial property and tourism have had profound local effects.

Environmental monitoring has become a statutory requirement under the Resource Management Act (Section 35) – arguably this requirement extends to monitoring of demographic, social and economic factors. The Building Act also requires monitoring of hazards and risks so that information on these can be provided on PIMs.

Attitudes also are changing. A car manufacturer would certainly understand that the market changes and it will not be easy to sell a car model which is five years out of date (unless it is a VW Beetle!). There are clear parallels for local bodies. For instance attitudes towards environmental values have changed greatly over 20 years and considerably over five years. This is evidenced in issues associated with road widening and removal of trees. I would ask whether attitude to and therefore evaluation of travel time delays, which are fundamental to Transit New Zealand's benefit cost calculation, have been altered by the advent of cell phones, as well as sophisticated in-car sound systems.

Hot Tip No. 4: don't neglect monitoring, but ensure it is well focused. It is our essential R and D expenditure.

5. Involves Interested Parties

Strategic planning acknowledges that as issues are identified it is important to have consultation with and secure the involvement of interested parties, who may be referred to as "stakeholders."

The extent to which this becomes critical in developing an effective strategy is likely to depend on whether the strategy relates to a function for which Council is the sole or principal provider of a service (e.g. water supply) or a function for which Council is simply one of many players (e.g. economic development). In the latter instance the correct identification of the stakeholders and their involvement in the strategic planning process become fundamental to success.

Even in traditional areas of Council activity however strategic planning should recognise that the views of our customers are essential. This gives us our next strategic planning instrument: the market survey. Market research tools, surveys, focus groups, etc. can add a number of subtle variations to our strategic planning orchestra. Again, it is essential that such research is focused to gather only information which is clearly relevant to Council's decision making. Avoid the "if it moves we will measure it" syndrome.

6. Evaluates Options

Strategic planning often uses techniques such as brainstorming or visioning, these have been employed in Christchurch in workshop sessions with elected members. Having identified objectives, and perhaps evaluated their robustness against alternative scenarios of the future it is important to use some form of evaluation technique to compare alternatives. Generating alternatives and selecting between them with specific regard to cost and benefit is a key element of strategic planning.

In the private sector evaluation centres around investment appraisal techniques aimed at identifying the best rate of return on competing investment proposals. In the public sector evaluation must identify the courses of action which produce the greatest net public benefits.

There are many instruments which can be used to undertake such evaluation. The planning balance sheet remains a highly useful technique. It can be thought of as a clear and systematic statement of effects, both costs and benefits, with some of these expressed in dollar terms, others in numerical form and others still in words. At present for example we are using this to evaluate the cost to the community (not just to Council) of a range of urban development options for the city.

At the present time we are seeking to develop a framework for the evaluation of capital works proposals and operational programmes and identify the extent to which they will contribute towards strategic objectives which the Council has adopted. To give an example, there may be alternative road proposals which achieve the same benefit cost ratio using Transit's evaluation method, but one may have a greater impact on access to a major employment centre while the other may have benefits principally in improving amenity in a residential neighbourhood. Recognising such differences does not itself produce an answer as to which proposal is better but it does clarify the outcomes and inform the decision making process.

7. Identifies Council's Role

Strategic planning can be used to clarify a council's role with regard to a particular objective. As discussed in Section 6, being clear as to the role of Council and of other stakeholders can be critical to developing an effective strategy. For each of the Christchurch City Council's strategic objectives a role is identified. These range from that of leading agency (provider/funder), through joint leading agency (provider/funder along with others) and support role (where the Council must rely on others to initiate), to a role of monitoring and influencing (where the Council may promote or facilitate, often by organising or securing financial support but will not itself be a provider or funder; see appendix 2).

Every Council should determine the extent to which it will limit itself to involvement only in those services which it is required to provide by statute. The framework above may be a useful instrument for determining the extent of its involvement in functions which it "may" provide.

Perhaps the best example in recent years of a change in role definition is with regard to economic development where an increasing number of Councils see themselves as having a monitoring/influencing role while some go further into joint provision of programmes and services.

Being clear as to the Council's role with regard to a particular objective will often enable particular proposals or programmes to be ruled out of consideration at an early stage and I believe provides a sounder framework for decision making than some of the traditional arguments which are based on the identification of core services and peripheral functions.

A further possible strategic planning instrument is the preparation of a strategy and programme which is for the district rather than the Council. At the present time for instance the Christchurch City Council has an arts and cultural policy (with programme initiatives) and is currently developing a more formal economic development strategy. Both of these require the explicit involvement of other agencies, the explicit definition of the Council's role in achieving them and a recognition that the Council is simply one of many players, albeit perhaps uniquely placed to take a leadership role in the community.

8. Specification of Outputs

We have moved a long way from the traditional Estimates process for preparing our annual budgets. The nature of the Estimates process was that costs were assembled on the basis of inputs such as staff salaries and wages, office costs, materials etc. In so far as rentals, plant hire rates, depreciation, cost of capital and other overheads were fully allocated the capital works programme included in the Estimates would be presented on the basis of outputs. Generally however large parts of Councils' budgets told us that the cost of roading would be $X and of town planning would be $Y but it was not clear what outputs were being purchased by the community for these global sums.

It is absolutely essential to the philosophy underlying our annual planning and annual reporting process that we move to an output process, that we move to an output presentation for our plans and budgets.

Hot Tip No. 1 – output presentation is difficult and time consuming but is the most important single instrument of strategic planning for a local body to implement.

There are two main ways of moving towards output budgeting. The ideal way is to achieve this through the accounting structure. The first and easy step is to ensure that the structure of cost centres is broadly related to categories of output. To give an example, within the Christchurch City Council's Environmental Administration Unit there is a section which deals with processing of planning (resource management) applications and planning enforcement. Although this is only one section of staff there are separate cost centres for applications and enforcement with staff time, office costs, etc. being apportioned between them. The time spent within the applications cost centre is further subdivided using time sheets between answering enquiries (a rate funded activity) and processing resource consents which is fully cost recovered other than 27 precent of the time which is devoted to contesting appeals.

We hope to structure a chart of accounts so that all costs can be allocated in two directions: one way to reflect input costs based on elements of the Council's organisational structure and the other way to reflect outputs based on services delivered to the Community. Possibilities for achieving this are under review at the present time.

The second, less sophisticated way of estimating the cost of outputs is by analysis of time sheets. This assumes that all staff complete time sheets which allocate hours spent to projects and activities defined on a clear output basis.

Use of time sheets which allocate hours spent by all staff on an output basis are a key instrument for strategic planning, as well as for other management purposes. Time sheets were unpopular when introduced but have gained acceptance.

Before leaving the subject of output accounting I would stress that there are significant issues as to the level of aggregation at which outputs are identified which need to be carefully worked through and are likely to take some time.

9. Developing a Funding Policy

One of the advantages of clear specification of outputs is that they can be costed and this facilitates development of a funding policy for each output. This is the approach envisaged by the NZLGA's Working Party on "Principles and Guidelines for Local Revenue Systems" whose discussion paper was released in December 1992. When outputs have been specified it is possible to consider the extent of private and public benefits deriving from each. There are probably no right answers to such an exercise as for many services arguments can be made as to the relative importance of such benefits and whether availability of a service provides benefit even if a household does not use it.

Particularly for those Councils which face funding difficulties for major infrastructure renewal or upgrading I suspect that such an exercise will reduce the extent to which some existing outputs are rate funded and result in more revenue raised from user charges in a way which is clearly justifiable, if less than popular.

Hot Tip no. 5: using outputs as the basis of a funding policy may be a key to identifying non rate revenue sources of income and of justifying new/additional user charges.

10. Long Term Financial Planning

The identification of alternative sources of funding for particular services can lead to the projection of alternative mixes of revenue for Council services in the future. It might well be that reducing the dependence on ratepayer contribution for many of Council's on-going services will prove one means of funding major elements of infrastructure. It is certainly fundamental that funding of on-going programmes and capital projects are treated in a similar fashion with the inter-relationship between them recognised. Long term financial planning allows projection of other sources of Council revenue such as dividends from trading activities, proceeds from sale of assets, etc.

A simple long term financial model which may look anything from three to 20 years ahead can readily be developed on a spread sheet and is a powerful instrument in the strategic planning orchestra. Once such a model is developed it is then possible to test the implications of different scenarios such as variations in interest rates and examine the implications of funding programmes from revenue or from borrowing.

At the present time it would seem that the Auckland City Council has gone further than most authorities in its development of long term financial planning scenarios. Much less work has been done in Christchurch; this illustrates well the approach advocated at the start of this paper: that Councils should develop those instruments which suit their particular circumstances and needs.

11. Perspectives

Strategic Planning is no more than a process for defining and then reviewing the major goals and objectives of the Council and determining the way in which resources can best be allocated today and in the future to achieve these goals and objectives.

The most challenging thing about strategic planning is not making the instruments work but rather the fact that it makes us confront difficult choices.

When I was discussing strategic planning with Roger Paine, Chief Executive of Cardiff City Council and until recently president of the United Kingdom's SOLACE (Society of Local Authority Chief Electives) he made the observation that a likely outcome of any strategic planning process is to increase the number of bids for Council expenditure as new areas are identified where a considerable community benefit can be achieved for dollars spent. In practice such identification drives Councils towards reconsidering traditional priorities and making difficult decisions about long accepted services and levels of service.

So I would conclude that strategic planning is not for the faint hearted – but then as most readers would agree, nor is local government in the 1990s at either the elected member or professional/managerial levels.

Appendix 1

Extract from Christchurch City Council Draft Annual Plan 1993-94

(B) Quality of Service: Survey of Residents Demonstrates Continuing Satisfaction

The City Council exists to provide services to its community. One of the ways of assessing whether or not it is doing a good job with each of the services it provides is to ask the opinion of the people of Christchurch.

For this reason the Council commissions an Annual Survey of Residents. This survey is designed and undertaken by the Department of Statistics, thus ensuring its impartiality. In each of the last three years the Department has carried out around 800 interviews in households throughout Christchurch, a sufficient number to give a very high degree of statistical accuracy.

Most of the questions in the survey relate to the extent to which households use Council facilities or services and how satisfied they are with them. Variations in performance, changing expectations as to service standards, and patterns of use are obtained from Survey results.

Many of the performance indicators in this Annual Plan are taken from the survey completed in February 1993. They represent targets to meet or exceed in the coming year.

As part of the survey residents were told of the cost on their particular rate bill of various Council services. They were asked whether the City was getting good or poor value for money on this amount. The results of this are summarised in the adjoining graph for 1991, 1992 and 1993.

Changes from any one year to another of more than 3 percent may be regarded as significant.

Over the period of the survey residents across the board are voicing continuing satisfaction with the value for money provided by the Council as a service organisation.

The full survey report details high satisfaction rates with these and other Council services. Most satisfying perhaps, is the fact that 92 percent of residents are themselves satisfied with Christchurch as a place in which to live, work and spend time while only 4 percent have the contrary view.

Residents Attitudes to Value for Money for Rate Dollars Spent on Major Council Activities

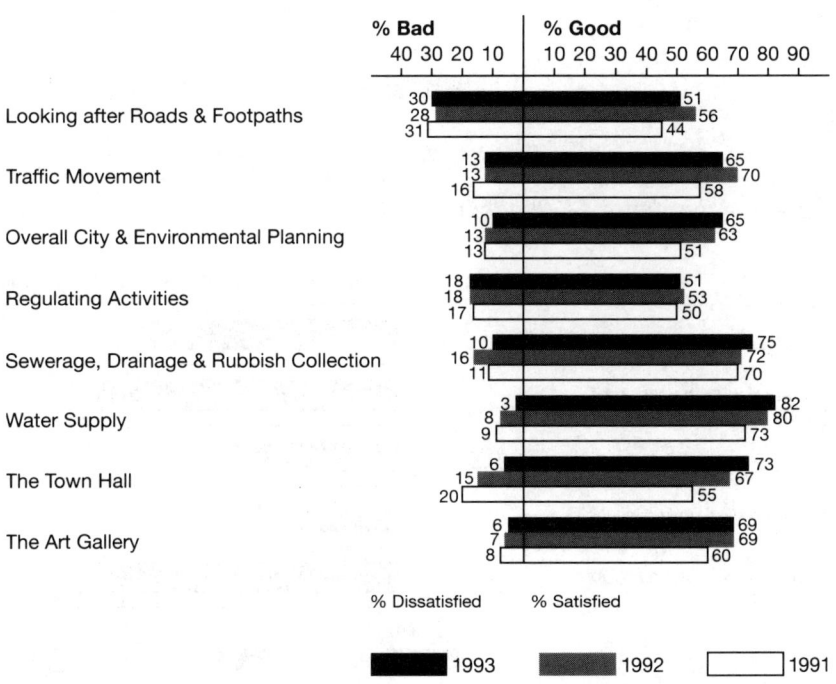

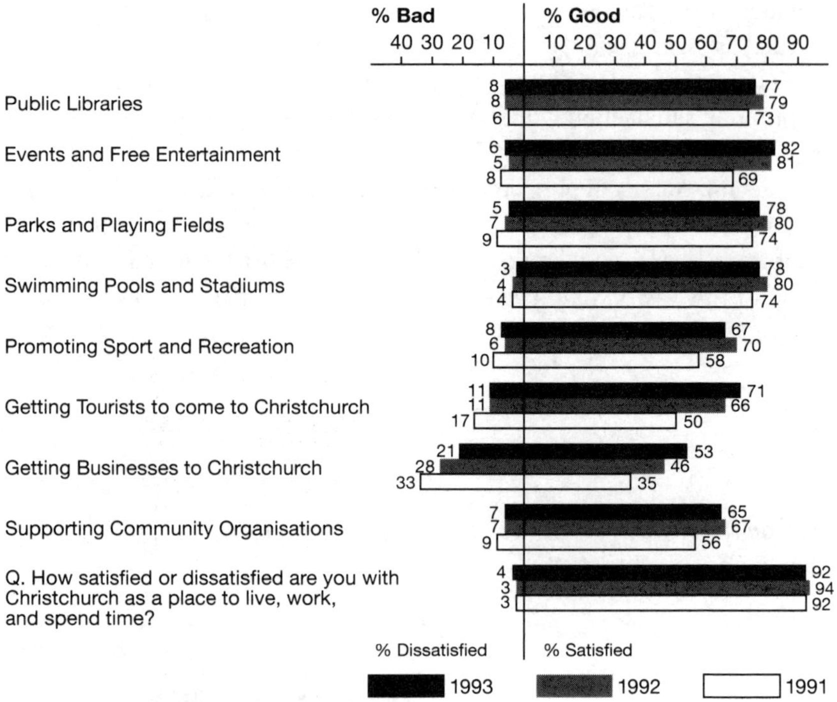

	% Bad	% Good		
	40 30 20 10	10 20 30 40 50 60 70 80 90		
Public Libraries	8 / 8 / 6	77 / 79 / 73		
Events and Free Entertainment	6 / 5 / 8	82 / 81 / 69		
Parks and Playing Fields	5 / 7 / 9	78 / 80 / 74		
Swimming Pools and Stadiums	3 / 4 / 4	78 / 80 / 74		
Promoting Sport and Recreation	8 / 6 / 10	67 / 70 / 58		
Getting Tourists to come to Christchurch	11 / 11 / 17	71 / 66 / 50		
Getting Businesses to Christchurch	21 / 28 / 33	53 / 46 / 35		
Supporting Community Organisations	7 / 7 / 9	65 / 67 / 56		
Q. How satisfied or dissatisfied are you with Christchurch as a place to live, work, and spend time?	4 / 3 / 3	92 / 94 / 92		

% Dissatisfied | % Satisfied

■ 1993 ▨ 1992 ☐ 1991

Survey of Residents – A Random Sample

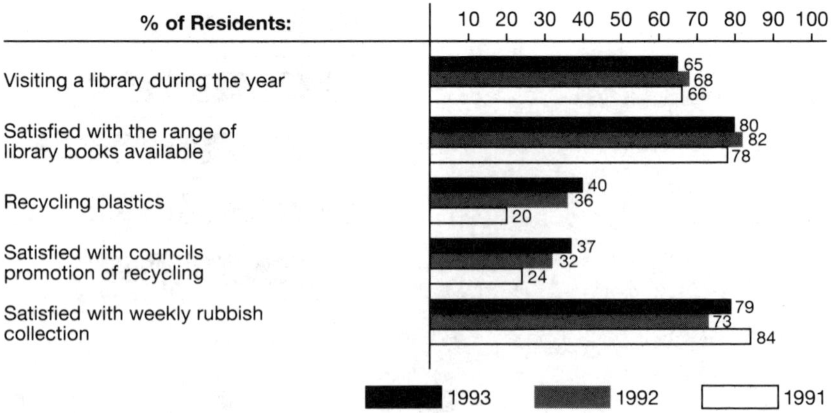

% of Residents:	10 20 30 40 50 60 70 80 90 100
Visiting a library during the year	65 / 68 / 66
Satisfied with the range of library books available	80 / 82 / 78
Recycling plastics	40 / 36 / 20
Satisfied with councils promotion of recycling	37 / 32 / 24
Satisfied with weekly rubbish collection	79 / 73 / 84

■ 1993 ▨ 1992 ☐ 1991

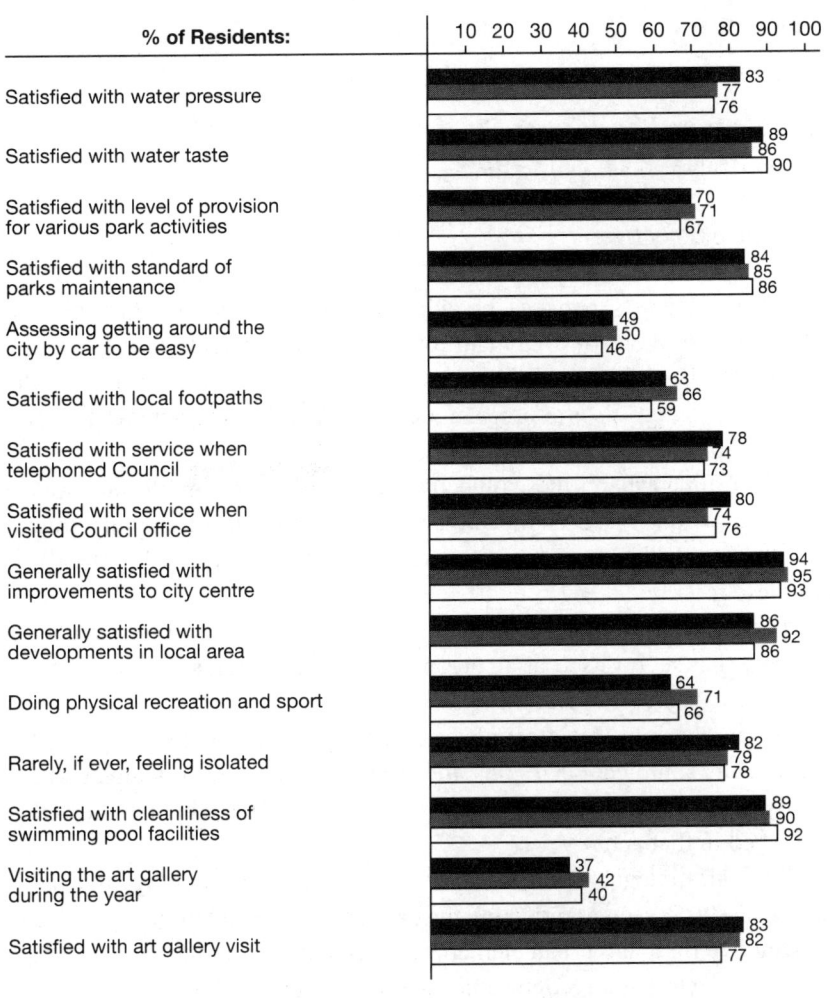

Appendix 2

Extract from Christchurch City Council Draft Annual Plan 1993-94

Strategic Objectives

The Council exists to make Christchurch as attractive as possible a city for its citizens – those of today and tomorrow – in which to live, work and enjoy life. To achieve this requires a focus, not only for services to the city's people, but also for programmes to safeguard and improve the physical environment and our city's economy.

The Council shares these objectives with many other public and private agencies. Alongside each objective therefore is an indication of the role(s) the Council believes it appropriate to play and the ways it will give effect to these roles.

In Section D of this statement of strategic objectives are the aims the Council has set for itself as an organisation – the features which will characterise its style of operation.

In the pages of this draft plan describing the Council's proposals for each of its significant activities, the strategic objectives to which that activity contributes are indicated as well as the reasons why the Council is engaged in that activity.

Several strategic objectives refer to The Unique Identity of Christchurch. This is seen as reflecting the existence of and relationship between distinctive rural and urban elements and aspects of community life which give Christchurch a recognisable Identity – one which sets it apart from other cities. The Council will direct its activities and encourage other public and private agencies to both respect and add to this identity which is made up of:
- rural elements – the rural areas of the plains, the Port Hills, the Estuary, waterways, wetlands and the coastal environment;
- urban elements – a centralised, compact urban form with a defined and strong central city and a radial roading network;
- the contrast between these urban and rural elements;

- amenity elements – many metropolitan and local parks, pleasance areas, formal public gardens, amenity trees and private gardens contributing to a recognisable Garden City character;
- social and cultural elements – cultural and leisure activities, events and festivals which are uniquely "Christchurch" in origin or character.

Key

Possible roles in bringing about a strategic objective:

- *Leading Agency* – the most influential player
- *Joint Leading Agency* – several major players
- *Support Role* – lesser player supporting other lead players
- *Monitoring/Influencing Role* – seek mainly to influence other players
- *No Direct Influence* – but have spinoff or indirect effect on an objective

Means of expressing these roles:

- *Provider* – carry out using own resources
- *Funder* – invest in, grant finance to, or contract others to provide
- *Regulator* – develop and enforce rules governing procedure or behaviour
- *Promoter/Facilitator* – encourage progress or existence of, often by organising or securing financial support
- *Advocate* – express support for or recommend publicly

Strategic Objectives

A The City's People

Personal Safety

A 1 A city in which:
- the sense of personal safety is maximised;
- the risk of physical injury for residents and visitors in everyday life is minimised.

Public Health

A 2 A city in which the risk of exposure to unhealthy living and working conditions and their adverse effects are minimised and within national and international standards or guidelines.

A 3 A city acclaimed for its healthy lifestyles reflecting such things as high rates of participation in healthful activities and low levels of occurrence of stress related diseases.

Education Facilities and Services

A 4 Enhanced learning, communication and participation reflected in appreciation of the ideas and experiences conveyed by written and recorded language, and the visual and performing arts.

A 5 Informed attitudes and changed behaviour which enhance the city's quality of life and environment.

A. The city's people

1 Joint leading agency
   – various; up to provider

2 Joint leading agency
   – various; up to provider

3 Support role
   – mainly promoter/ facilitator and minor provider

4 Joint leading agency
   – various; up to provider

5 Major support role
   – provider and promoter/facilitator

Social Well-being and Community Development

A 6 Ensuring that sufficient resources are available from appropriate sources, through social assistance if necessary, to enable residents to provide for their basic individual and family well-being.

6 Mainly monitoring/ influencing and minor support
   – various; up to minor provider

A 7 Funding and provision of social services within Christchurch:
   – comprising an equitable share of national resources;
   – accessible and responsive to the community's varying needs;
   – delivered in an equitable and efficient manner.

7 Mainly monitoring/ influencing and minor support
   – mainly advocate and some promoter/facilitator

A 8 A strong sense of community at local and city levels reflected in:
   – high proportions of people identifying with focal points or meeting places in their environment;
   – high levels of participation in community groups activities and issues;
   – wide ranging expression of community pride.

8 Joint leading agency
   – various; up to provider

Housing Provision

A 9 The provision of access to quality, affordable housing appropriate to the needs of present and future households.

9 Support role
   – various; up to minor provider

Arts and Culture

A10 Wide ranging opportunities for residents and visitors to increase their participation in and enjoyment of artistic and cultural activities.

10 Joint leading agency
   – various; up to provider

A11 Improved understanding and respect for the contribution of the many different cultural traditions present in Christchurch to the quality of its social life.	11 Support role – promoter/ facilitator
A12 The Unique Identity of Christchurch enhanced by particular recognition of Canterbury's heritage and contemporary artistic and cultural expression.	12 Support role – various; up to provider

Recreation and Leisure

A13 Wide ranging opportunities for residents and visitors to increase their: – participation in affordable and accessible sport and recreational activities which are responsive to current and emerging leisure preferences; – experience and enjoyment of the garden city element of the city's Unique Identity.	13 Joint leading agency – various; up to provider
A14 Enhanced personal enjoyment from the ideas and experiences conveyed by written and recorded language, and the visual and performing arts.	14 Support role – various; up to provider

B The Physical Environment	B. The physical environment

Air, Water and Soils Quality

B 1 Maintenance and enhancement of: – the quality of the city's inland and coastal waters;	1 Joint leading agency – various; up to provider

- air quality in the city, including eliminating any health hazard posed by winter smog;
- the horticultural production potential of high quality soils in the city;
- land susceptible to soil loss through erosion.

Significant Natural Features and Parkland and Rural Amenity

B 2 Maintenance and enhancement of the special values of significant natural features, such as the Port Hills or the Estuary, and improved opportunities for their appreciation and enjoyment.

2 Joint leading agency
   – various; up to provider

B 3 Enhancement of the contribution of open space and landscape elements to the Unique Identity of Christchurch.

3 Joint leading agency
   – various; up to provider

Built Environment Amenity

B 4 A form and direction of development and redevelopment of the built environment which:
- maintains and enhances the Unique Identity of Christchurch;
- provides for a wide variety of living, working and leisure activities throughout the city in a manner which maintains or enhances people's enjoyment of amenity values.

4 Joint leading agency
   – various; up to provider

B 5 Enhancement of the central city's contribution to the Unique Identity of Christchurch with large numbers of residents and visitors enjoying its attributes.

5 Major support role
   – various; up to provider

Heritage Features

B 6 Heritage values of significant and representative sites, buildings, places, areas and other taonga of Christchurch maintained for the benefit of present and future generations.

6 Joint leading agency
– various; up to provider

Natural Hazards

B 7 Adverse impacts for the natural and built environment of actual and potential natural hazards avoided or reduced in accordance with a considered assessment of the risk and consequences of their occurrence.

7 Joint leading agency
– various; up to provider

C The City's Economy

Business Activity and Employment

C 1 Growth of the business base of Christchurch leading to an increase in the number of jobs in the city.

C 2 Employment in Christchurch increased to a level at which it is not of significant concern to the community.

C 3 Increased purchasing and investment in Canterbury by existing firms and new investors.

C 4 More and longer length of stays and increased spending by visitors to Christchurch.

C The city's economy

1 Minor support role
– advocate and promotor/facilitator

2 Minor support role
– advocate and promotor/facilitator

3 Support role
– promoter/facilitator

4 Support role
– promoter/facilitator

C 5 Highly positive local, national and international attitudes towards Christchurch as a place in which to live and do business reflecting:
- recognition as a business and visitor friendly city;
- an active, lively city full of diverse attractions and events;
- sustained high levels of business and consumer confidence in Christchurch;
- acclaim for the city's quality of life and Unique Identity.

5 Joint leading agency
 – regulator and promoter/facilitator

C 6 A skilled and adaptable business base, including the labour force; able to meet the present and future needs of their markets.

6 Minor support role
 – advocate and promoter/facilitator

Utility Services

C 7 A continuous supply of sustainable energy to efficiently meet demand at prices which are locally, nationally and internationally competitive.

7 Monitoring/ influencing
 – funder

C 8 A continuous supply of essential utility services for existing consumers and for property protection at unit costs comparable with those obtainable from similar organisations or alternative suppliers.

8 Leading agency
 – various; up to provider

C 9 Ready availability of extended utility services at competitive supply costs to meet the reasonable service demands from new or expanding users.

9 Joint leading agency
 – various; up to provider

Transport and Communications

C 10 A continuous supply of land, sea and air transport, and telecommunications services for moving people, goods and business information to and from Christchurch:
- responsive to the needs of business and travelers;
- at nationally and internationally competitive standards of quality and price.

10 Monitoring/ influencing
- advocate and funder

C 11 Sustained availability of the roading network and passenger transport within Christchurch, and especially in relation to the city centre, which provides for:
- personal mobility at levels of service satisfactory to the community and consistent with the Council's objectives for the physical environment;
- movement of goods at levels of service consistent with efficient business operations.

11 Joint leading agency
- various; up to provider

Commercial and Industrial Property

C 12 Ensuring development and redevelopment of significant premises, sites or facilities where it is identified as strategically important to the city's economy.

12 Support role
- various; up to provider

C 13 A regulatory framework providing for a wide range of business location opportunities at least cost, consistent

13 Leading agency
- regulator

with reasonable standards of health and safety and appropriate environmental controls.

D The council as an organisation

Elected Member Representation and Decision making

D 1 Successful Council performance in:
  – advocating the interests of the Christchurch community, especially in its relations with other public sector agencies;
  – striking a balance in its actions between the interests of democracy, effectiveness and efficiency;
  – ensuring the effective implementation of its policies.

D 2 A high level of accountability in decision making reflecting:
  – decisions made by elected member forums where representation is drawn from the community of interest matching that affected by these decisions;
  – ample opportunity for the views of those affected to be made known prior to decisions being taken;
  – decisions are made as soon as practical and the reasons for them readily obtainable.

For all these strategic objectives for the Council as an organisation it is the leading agency and the provider

D 3 Elected members properly equipped for and advised on the decision making process and the significant implications of recommended decisions including:
- the long term financial implications of both service development and annual budget proposals;
- the costs and benefits to the wider community and to users of projects and programmes.

Treaty of Waitangi Principles

D 4 Maintaining a means of consultation mutually acceptable to the Council and tangata whenua which gives effect to the principles of the Treaty of Waitangi that are applied by statute to the policy, procedures and operations of the Council.

Human Resources

D 5 To be a Good Employer which is staffed by people with the skills and motivation necessary to achieve high quality service delivery.

Service Delivery Approach and Arrangements

D 6 Acceptable levels of customer satisfaction with the accessibility, quality and range of the Council's service delivery from its service points, on the customer's property and in their communications with the Council.

Financial Management

D 7　A revenue policy which identifies the long term role and fair and efficient mix of all forms of income necessary to fund services provided by the Council.

D 8　Management of financial resources and liabilities so as to:
– maximise income and minimise expense consistent with a generally conservative approach to risk taking;
– facilitate the operation of trading activites;
– maximise trading activity returns to the Council and the value of its investment consistent with the purpose in making that investment.

D 9　Accounting procedures which are:
– consistent with generally accepted accounting practices;
– complying in all other respects with external financial reporting requirements;
– enable the true cost of the goods and services produced to be accurately determined.

Corporate Organisation and Support Services

D 10　A corporate structure which:
– enables the efficient implementation of the Council's decisions and its statutory obligations;

- responds innovatively and quickly to legislative change and advances in management practice.

D11 Internal provision of services:
- which are cost efficient in their use of resources;
- only where unit service costs are, or are likely to become, competitive – at similar levels of quality or reliability – with those obtainable in comparable organisations or from alternative suppliers.

Delft: The Use of Information and Communication Technology by Local Authorities – An International Perspective

Piet Severijnen, Arre Zuurmond, Mirjam Kalverda, Joy Ramsamoedj

Foreword.. 359
Executive Summary 359
1. In Search of a New Balance 360
    1.1 Developments in Information and Telecommunication Technology: New Possibilities 361
    1.2 Developments in Local Authorities: Higher Demands 362
    1.3 Aim of the Research Project 363
2. Research Question..................................... 363
3. Theoretical Considerations 364
    3.1 Developments in the Use of Information and Communication Technology..................... 364
    3.2 Administrative Perfectionism Perspective.............. 365
    3.3 Democratic Perfectionism Perspective 367
4. Research Methodology 370
    4.1 A National Study.................................. 370
    4.2 An International, Quantitative Comparison............. 371
    4.3 Three International Comparative Case Studies 372
5. The Use of ICT in Delft: A National Study into Four Areas of Information Supply 372
    5.1 ICT and a Council Information System................ 373
    5.2 ICT and the Basic Registration of Real Estate 374
    5.3 ICT and a Public Information System................. 376
    5.4 ICT and the City Panel Research 377
    5.5 Concluding Remarks............................... 378

- 6. The Use Of ICT in an International Perspective 379
  - 6.1 The Administrative Point of View 379
    - 6.1.1 Survey Response 380
    - 6.1.2 Functions of the Information System 380
    - 6.1.3 The Administrative Perfectionism Perspective 381
  - 6.2 The Democratic Point of View 385
    - 6.2.1 Survey Response 385
    - 6.2.2 ICT Applications 386
    - 6.2.3 Aims of ICT Applications 387
    - 6.2.4 Effects of the Implementation 387
    - 6.2.5 An International Perspective 388
  - 6.3 Overall Orientation 389
- 7. Three Case Studies 390
  - 7.1 Kent County Council 390
  - 7.2 The City of Antwerp 393
  - 7.3 The City of Bologna 396
  - 7.4 Some Concluding Remarks 400
- 8. Back to the Future 400
- Literature 401
- Appendices 403

Foreword

Delft, a knowledge based city

The City of Delft has adopted a strategy based on the fact that knowledge based industries play an important role in the local economy. The motto is: "Delft – knowledge based city." The scope of this motto goes beyond the use of information and communication technology (ICT) and has as a main objective to create a healthy local employment situation.

The local authority of Delft wants to use recent developments in the field of information and communication technology to achieve these goals. Being a learning organization, Delft wants to learn from experiences with respect to the use of ICT by other local authorities, both in the Netherlands as well as in the rest of the world.

Membership in the "International Network for Better Local Government" motivated and enabled Delft to carry out a world-wide research project into the use of information and communication technology. The results of this project are to be used to improve the democratic functioning and the service delivery of the organization.

This paper, in which the outcomes of the research project are described, is the result of a collaboration between the City of Delft and the Erasmus University of Rotterdam. The authors want to thank all the local authorities that were willing to participate in the surveys and hope that they will also benefit from the experiences of their colleagues from all over the world.

Executive Summary

The contribution of the City of Delft to the "International Network for Better Local Government" is a paper on the use of information and communication technology (ICT) in local authorities. The paper reflects the results of a number of research projects which are based on the following theoretical notions.

Local authorities can have three reasons to use ICT. The first and most traditional is to reduce costs. The other two, more recent ones, are to improve the quality of services and the democratic relationship with the citizens. Local government should strive for an optimal balance between these three aspects.

The general research question is formulated as follows: Does information and communication technology play a role in the improvement of the quality of local government, and what are the conditions to achieve this? To answer this question two perspectives are to be distinguished: the administrative perfectionism perspective and the democratic perfectionism perspective.

Firstly, the use of ICT in four different information systems was investigated on a Dutch national level, based on the two perspectives mentioned above: to what extent can the local authority organization of Delft learn from experiences elsewhere with respect to a council information system, a citizens information system, a real estate information system and market research?

An international quantitative survey was carried out using two different questionnaires, each based on one of the perspectives mentioned above. Subsequently three case-studies were carried out in local authority organizations, one in England, one in Belgium and one in Italy.

The main conclusion to be drawn from the results is that *service delivery* is the most important reason for local authorities to introduce ICT, not *cost reduction or* improving *the quality of democracy.*

Related to this conclusion is the fact that most local authorities concentrate on the administrative perfectionism perspective, i.e. perfecting the internal organization.

1. In Search of a New Balance

Information has become an important resource for organizations. As such, it is a new production factor next to capital and labor. This has made it possible to change the "production function" of local government.

Until recently, information technology was mainly used to reduce costs, by replacing the production factor labor by the production factor information. However, information and communication technology can be used for more than just cost reduction. It can also be used to enhance the quality of services and/or to improve the (democratic) relationship with the citizens.

The sharp fall in costs of informatization continually forces local government to choose between these three values: do we cash in (reducing the costs), shall we enhance the quality of our services, or shall we create a more democratic local community? The challenge is to realize a high performance on all of these three values at the same time. In fact, optima will have to be found and be balanced for all three values (Snellen, 1995).

Some local authorities have already started on the road towards a fully balanced use of ICT. To learn from their experiences, this project looks for examples of best practices of ICT use by local authorities.

1.1 Developments in Information and Telecommunication Technology: New Possibilities

The developments in information and communication technology create new possibilities, not only with respect to cost reduction, but also with respect to service delivery as well as democracy.

For the perspective of democracy, developments in communication technologies are most important. The rise of personal computers and networks, the electronic highway and Internet being their most appealing representatives, has cleared the way for more interactive communication. Open conversation is now possible by means of computers. On Internet, news groups are created by people from all over the world. They join forces to further their cause based on common interests or hobbies.

For the perspective of service delivery, developments in data processing (information technology) are most important. This concerns the creation of a collective data infrastructure. The information systems that were developed up to now, were to a high degree isolated: each department had its own data system and consequently its own information. Every department collected all its own data, even if other departments already had that data at their disposal. This not only caused high cost (cost of double data collection and double data entry) but also a bad quality of the available data: one single department simply is not capable of collecting all the relevant information itself and keeping it up-to-date. As a consequence departments may perform poorly with regard to the services they deliver. The creation of a collective information infrastructure makes it possible to enhance the quality of service.

Information technology and communication technology are now blending. Hence, in this paper the term ICT is used: information and communication technology.

1.2 Developments in Local Authorities: Higher Demands

For some time now local government bodies have been subject to great internal and external pressure. Modern municipalities need to meet higher demands than ever before. The following examples that lead to these higher demands can be mentioned:
- Local authorities tend to adopt more businesslike and consumer-oriented attitudes for many of their activities.
- The marketing of products and services of local authorities has become a major issue.
- Citizens have become more critical of the functioning of local government and require elected politicians to account for their actions. Local authorities are faced with emancipated citizens.
- The model of representative democracy does not seem to function the way it theoretically should.
- Many local authorities have gone through or are in the process of major reorganization.

These developments, which cannot be viewed as separate from one another, bring citizens, politicians, managers and professionals into new relationships with each other. Such situations demand changes in governmental organizations and the rethinking of resources at the disposal of local authorities. Among these ICT takes an important place.

1.3 Aim of the Research Project

Both the developments in information and communication technology, as well as the developments in local government force local authorities to rethink their structure and strategy. The aim of this paper is to find out whether local authorities do respond to these developments and challenges. Do they make use of the new possibilities of ICT to cope with the higher demands of their citizens?

2. Research Question

Central to the research question is the notion that citizens play two roles with respect to the local authority. The first one is the role as citizen with a deliberative and communicative function in discussing public affairs. The second is the role as a client, receiving services and products from their local authority.

Over the last decades, ICT has been mainly used to reduce costs. In view of ICT developments (the new possibilities) on the one hand and more critical, emancipated citizens (higher demands) on the other hand, local government should go beyond cost reduction as a motive to use ICT. To be able to deal with this situation (where citizens want to be involved in the political decision making process and also demand high quality services and products), two alternative strategies can be discerned, the enhancement of the quality of (two-way) communication relationships between the citizens and local authority and the enhancement of the quality of service rendering. This research looks at these two strategies. The general purpose of the research project is to answer the following question:

Does information and communication technology play a role in the improvement of the quality of local government, and what are the conditions to achieve this?

In relation to the distinction made above, the following sub-questions can be formulated:

- Is information and communication technology only used for cost reduction?

Or:
- Do the implementation and the use of information technology influence the quality of the internal local authority organization to enhance service quality?

Or:
- Does the use of ICT influence the quality of the existing democratic relationships between the citizens and public administration?

To answer these questions, attention is first paid to some theoretical considerations (chapter 4). Chapter 5 describes the various research methodologies. The results of the research project are laid down in chapter 6 (Dutch examples), chapter 7 (international quantitative survey) and chapter 8 (qualitative case studies of best practices). The paper concludes with a brief look into the future.

3. Theoretical Considerations

3.1 Developments in the Use of Information and Communication Technology

Information has become an important resource in organizations. Many management decisions are based on information. That is why it is important for all organizations to be able to gather and process information in the most efficient and effective way. Information and Communication Technology (ICT) can help here. ICT has become a real hype during the last decade, mainly as a result of the many advantages it offers. Nowadays it is almost unavoidable for organizations to introduce ICT.

ICT has an important impact on most public and private organizations. ICT can for example change the organizational structure. With the introduction of ICT in the organization, the departments or people who are responsible for managing this new technology can get a better grip on the rest of the organization simply because the organization becomes more transparent. Top management can monitor every action of the employees. The opposite however is also possible when employees get more grip on the organization because of the introduction of ICT. For example, if the employees of the information technology department have more expertise and knowledge of the used technology than the managers, they could (and will) profit from this situation. These examples are only one side of the possible impact of ICT. What will happen in a specific situation, is not so much determined by the technology. Actual ICT developments are strongly determined by the dominant power coalition in an organization, and the perspective on information technology that is supported by this dominant power coalition (Kraemer and King, 1989).

This technology can also influence the relation between the organization and its clients. ICT is capable of changing the way the organization and its clients communicate in terms of speed, reliability and efficiency of the communication.

In this research project the way in which these changes have taken place and the impact they have on local authority organizations are under consideration.

As explained above, ICT can have two possible kinds of impact on organizations. This is also true for local authorities. Paul Depla (1995) distinguishes two perspectives determining the influence of ICT on local authorities. The first is the impact on the internal organizational structure. The second is the impact of ICT on the relationship between the local authority and its citizens. These are two theoretical notions which Depla respectively calls *"vervolmaking"* – which can be translated as the administrative perfectionism perspective – and *"vermaatschappelijking"* – which can be translated as the democratic perfectionism perspective. These two perspectives, which form the theoretical basis of this research project, are discussed in the following paragraphs.

3.2 Administrative Perfectionism Perspective

According to Depla (1995), local authorities fail to provide for their citizens. He considers this failure to be partly an internal, organizational problem. Local authority organizations desperately need to be restructured in order to perform better. It is assumed that ICT can play an important role here and that the implementation of this technology can improve the quality of government (Brussaard, 1992). In many local authorities around the world ICT is used to improve the internal work procedures and processes. An important reason is the increased amount of external information to be processed implying more efficient processing. This is also the case with respect to the information transactions between departments within the organization. Professionals have to know, for example, at any point in time what the important policy issues are. This is why information (technology) is an important resource.

Some local authorities use advanced systems, for example, to connect different data sources in order to generate the information they need. These data bases can contain information about various subjects, e.g. population, domiciles or taxes. They do not have to be located in the same physical space. The system, then, is capable of connecting the data bases *as if* they were in the same physical space. Many employees can use this "virtual" data base at the same time. In this way ICT can be used to perfect the gathering, exchange and use of information within the organization.

Cooperation between employees in the organization, in this case the local authority employees, is another aspect that can be improved by the implementation of Information and Communication Technology. This can be done in various ways. An example is the e-mail function that makes communication between departments cheaper and easier, even if they are located in different buildings.

This means that the daily work of the employees in the local authority can be improved by the use of ICT. It can be done more efficiently, that is putting less strain on the resources of the organization.

The administrative perfectionism perspective means that the local authority focuses on a more perfect internal organization. A more perfect internal organization is one that uses its resources more efficiently and effectively. Important resources like information, time, personnel and money are scarce. That is why they have to be well managed. At local authority level this can be transformed into an organization capable of performing its (core) tasks with a minimum of resources and a maximum of output. The main objective of this perspective is to render the existing internal procedures, social communications and daily practices more perfect.

How do we recognize the administrative perfectionism perspective? How can it be implemented within local authority organizations? To do this, indicators have to be created. Using these indicators it is possible to find out to what extent an organization has realized the administrative perfectionism perspective.

- A first possible indicator is the focus of the information application. The application can focus on improving the internal work processes and procedures or on improving the interaction between citizens and the organization.
- A second possible indicator is the use of information and its importance. Every organization has information relationships and therefore there are flows of information. An important question is which relationships are stressed, internal or external ones?
- Another possible indicator is a change in internal work processes with respect to efficiency. Have the internal work processes become more or less efficient after the implementation of ICT?

These indicators show whether one can speak of an administrative perfectionism perspective in the local authority organization. They were used to develop questionnaires for this research.

3.3 Democratic Perfectionism Perspective

The democratic perfectionism perspective contrasts with the administrative perfectionism perspective. In the latter, the focus is on ICT that makes internal work processes more perfect, in order to provide products and services in an effective and efficient manner. The democratic perfectionism perspective focuses on administrative legitimacy: to what extent is there a healthy and vital relationship between the local authority and its citizens?

The aim of ICT that focuses on the democratic perfectionism perspective is to try to persuade the citizens to get back into the democratic arena and to contribute actively to political and administrative processes. This should lead to a reallocation of societal tasks.

ICT means an enrichment of the instruments that politicians and the governmental organizations have at their disposal (Zuurmond, 1994; Frissen, 1989). Until the arrival of information technology, communication was restricted to the provision of information by government. As seen above, researchers are convinced that the new technology has features that enable other information and communication relationships between local government and its citizens.

Some of them (Schalken and Tops, 1995) show great disappointment about the present use that politicians and local authority employees make of the possibilities of ICT. Network technology in particular offers new opportunities for a change in local democracy, because it facilitates new information and communication relationships between the various actors.

Not everybody, however, is enthusiastic about this idea. It could for example decrease the importance of political parties. For some, political parties play an essential role in the political process. Others have doubts about the possibilities of ICT to stimulate citizens to participate in democratic decision making.

Most authors see either only positive or negative effects of ICT on governmental organizations. The effect of ICT on democracy is either a more direct democracy (one that resembles the ideal of ancient Athens) or an Orwellian society (where political and organizational control and surveillance prevail).

After a few decades of experience with ICT, it is recognized that its influence is not simply good or bad. A lot of theories say that ICT can strengthen existing practices. Dutton and Kraemer (1978) say, for example, that ICT is used to reinforce existing power structures in organizations. Zuurmond (1994) states that local authority employees can use ICT to strengthen the lead they already have in the possession and the strategic use of information.

This reinforcement theory can also be applied to the democratic perfectionism perspective of local democracies. International research offers the opportunity of comparing local democracies in the participating countries. An interesting question is whether the way in which ICT is implemented changes the relationship between the actors in society. In other words, do applications exist that are directed at the democratic perfectionism perspective? Another question is if there is a difference between countries in the application of the new technologies. Not all local democracies are alike. Three different views on democracy can be distinguished that should be seen as points on a continuum, not as either/or situations (Edwards, 1992; Depla, 1995).

Representative democracy – responsive democracy – direct democracy

1. Advocates of *representative government* think that it is superior to other democratic models because there is room for discussion and opinion building. Democracy is therefore shaped by a representative multi-party system. The role of citizens is rather small: they elect the politicians who stay in office for a certain period. These politicians represent the citizens' views on political matters during that period. The citizens can express their opinions again, next time elections are held. The focus of ICT is more on given (one way) information than on (two way) communication.
2. *Responsive government*: Representative democracy is, however, beset with some important problems. It is often stated that there is a large gap between elected members and electorate. Politicians' standpoints are less and less in line with the opinions of the electorate. In a responsive democracy the legitimacy of decision making depends on the extent to which the political discussions take into account the debates that take place in society. ICT can strengthen this form of democracy because it offers opportunities for a debate in which both local government officers and politicians as well as citizens take part. The use of, e.g., opinion polls can also enhance the degree to which the public debate and the political debate are aligned.
3. Local democracy can be judged against the ideal of *direct democracy*. The touchstone for the quality of democracy is the opportunity it offers to take into account the wishes of the population in government policy. In this view, the role of local government is restricted to supporting the decision making by citizens. Only if citizens cannot take care of certain matters themselves, is there a task for government. ICT makes time and place irrelevant for decision making. That is why more direct forms of democracy seem to get an opportunity. Citizens can for exam-

ple express their opinions about current issues, directly from their living room, using ICT.

If ICT has an influence on local democracy in the sense of the democratic perfectionism perspective, there should be a shift on the continuum from the left to the right. Existing representative power structures will then have to be abandoned. Politicians and local authority employees have to change their traditional roles because their relationship with the citizens will change. If more opportunities for discussion and cooperation between government and citizens are created, a more responsive government will arise. If situations are created where citizens can actively influence the political decision making process a more direct democracy will come into being.

The scope of this paper goes beyond ideas and single observations. Its aim is to try to find out, through both quantitative and qualitative research, what the possibilities and effects of ICT on democratic relationships are.

4. Research Methodology

This research project consists of three parts. The first part is an investigation into the use of ICT by Dutch local authorities. Secondly, a quantitative international inquiry into the present situation with respect to the use of ICT was made. The third part consists of in-depth case studies, carried out in three local authorities. Two of them were selected from the international quantitative survey.

4.1 A National Study

In the first part of the research project the use of ICT in Delft was analyzed, in comparison with other Dutch municipalities. Four different possible local authority ICT applications were chosen:
− council information system
− real estate registration system

- citizens/public information system
- city panel research.

For the inquiry into each of these areas a case study design, using expert interviews, was adopted to assess the quality of the use of ICT in Delft, compared to other local authorities in the Netherlands.

4.2 An International, Quantitative Comparison

For the gathering of the international quantitative research data, two different questionnaires were used, one concentrating on the democratic perfectionism perspective, the other on the administrative perfectionism perspective.

The first questionnaire was sent to four different departments in every local authority: the personnel department, the finance department, the real estate department and the registry office. Thus the units of analysis were single departments. These questionnaires ask questions about the use of information systems, applications, work procedures and products of these departments.

For the democratic perfectionism perspective the unit of analysis was the local authority as a whole. This questionnaire concentrated on questions about democracy, elections and information systems.

All members of the "International Network for Better Local Government" were asked to supply names of local authorities in their respective countries that have experience with ICT applications. The same question was asked of colleagues of related universities.

This approach resulted in a list of 82 local authorities in 11 countries (see appendix 1). These 82 authorities were asked to give the names of the heads of the four departments mentioned above. This resulted in a list of 280 possible respondents for the administrative perfectionism perspective part of the research. A total of 139 questionnaires was returned, which is a response of 49.5 percent.

Concerning the democratic perfectionism perspective, the unit of analysis was the local authority as a whole. Thus the possible number of respondents was 82. A total of 35 questionnaires was returned, a response of 42.7 percent.

4.3 Three International Comparative Case Studies

Finally, three municipalities were selected (using the information of the international comparative questionnaire) to be studied in-depth. The cases were selected because of the predominance of either the administrative or democratic perfectionism perspective, or of both. Antwerp, as the first case, has a strategy of marked decentralization, using the newest information technology. With this strategy Antwerp tries to realize a high level of citizen responsiveness. Antwerp thus seems to concentrate on an administrative perfectionism perspective. Kent County Council was selected because it combines the democratic with the administrative perfectionism perspective. Finally, Bologna was selected, because it has an advanced use of information technology from the democratic perfectionism perspective point of view.

5. The Use of ICT in Delft: A National Study into Four Areas of Information Supply

Essential in this first part of the study are four individual research surveys, carried out by the department of public administration of the Erasmus University of Rotterdam. In four areas the municipality of Delft faces problems that are related to information supply. Firstly there is the question whether and how the elected council members can make use of an automated information system. A second issue addresses one type of information supply which has been in use for years, but which has reached a critical point because of its development towards a corporate facility within the decentralized organization structure: the basic registration of real estate. Subsequently an investigation has been made into the extent to which ICT can play a role in supplying information to the public. This first part concludes with a look at the possibilities offered by information technology to support the City Panel market research project.

5.1 ICT and a Council Information System

To examine the possibilities to introduce a council information system in Delft, the existing council information systems of Tilburg, Voorburg and Zoetermeer were selected for in-depth study. These three systems have the following characteristics in common: a data bank storing councils' agendas, council reports, committee reports, by-laws etc. Next to this there is a number of additional functions, differing per municipality. Voorburg, for instance, uses e-mail. Zoetermeer has realized links with a number of external data banks.

In the three municipalities interviews were carried out with councillors about their experiences with respect to the information systems. In general the council members were satisfied with the systems. Important for them is the possibility to have access to the system from their study at home by means of a personal computer and a modem. Those who can do so, use the council information system more frequently and were also much more satisfied. Most councillors think that council work has not changed substantially but experience the system as a useful resource. A number of councillors think that council work has changed politically: they think that their policy proposals have improved, that they have a better insight into the administrative organization and that they are able to locate information much faster. There are, however, also disadvantages: the mass of paperwork has not decreased, and people can not contact the councillor by phone when he/she is connected to the system via telephone modem. A second telephone line could offer a solution here.

It is concluded that in practice the council information systems appear to be very strongly inwardly directed, at the individual functioning of elected members. It is nonetheless striking that the councillors tend to promote democratic involvement of the citizens: it is felt that the citizen should be more involved and the system should be accessible to the citizen. But almost all councillors interviewed think that the system will not bring the citizen closer to local government. On the basis of the survey it was recommended that, when implementing a council information system a first step should be to determine the motivation for, or objectives of the system.

From the results it is clear that council information systems can play a good role in the administrative perfectionism perspective: facilities such as e-mail, and a data base with information such as council agendas and minutes are a first step.

If the council members also experience problems in the representative, external role (towards citizens and third parties), then the council information system should have a different set-up. Then the contents of and the access to the system will (in the long term) have to be tailored to groups of citizens and institutions. In practice this means that citizens should have access to the system and external information sources should be opened up to councillors. After all the councillors will then not only use the information system for their internal communication, but also for their external relationships.

To involve the citizen (and third parties) more in decision making it is, in the light of the democratic perfectionism perspective, also thinkable that not only finished decrees are stored in the system, but that these should be made accessible at an earlier stage of the decision making process. This can be done by putting concept proposals in the system, making political wishes public at an early stage and/or setting up a platform for discussion. In such a case, the council and the collegium of mayor and aldermen might be taking a vulnerable line. It might even become impossible to bring politically sensitive matters to a good end, because publicity can always disrupt the sometimes necessary peace. On the other hand the advantage is that at an early stage citizen involvement can be encouraged, which in itself enhances the quality of the decision making process. Moreover, ideas and suggestions can be generated that improve the quality of the final policy decisions and implementation.

5.2 ICT and the Basic Registration of Real Estate

The application which is considered in the second part of this investigation is the basic registration of real estate information. A few years ago the municipality of Delft opted for a "decentralized structure." Characteristics of this model are a great independence of the various major service departments, integrated responsibility of the heads of departments and sections, and decentralized resources so that each department can adapt its staff work as much as possible to the individual situation. Departments are accountable for product/resources combinations which are agreed upon with the responsible politicians. This autonomy means that each department has to be automated in a different way. There are no standard data definitions. Exchange of information becomes difficult and therefore multiple data entry often takes place.

At the moment a so-called "Basic Registration of Real Estate" (BRRE) is being developed. This is a project which enables the various major service departments to exchange digital information about buildings and other property. Basic registration stands for the principle of standard definitions, single data entry and multiple use of data. Graphic applications will be made possible. This makes it possible for policy information, if need be from different departments, to be projected onto one, single map. The basic registration is an initial impetus for a joint use of information which can prevent the same job being done twice. Moreover the quality of all separate registrations can be improved.

Delft however has problems realizing this project because of its decentralized structure:

1. Each department is accountable for its individual achievements. This entails that those departments that are currently undertaking extra work for the BRRE are in principle not rewarded for this. Costs are made for a project concerning the entire municipality which are not repaid. This steering principle causes a concentration on the individual departmental interests. The interest of the council as a collective is less well served.
2. The BRRE goes beyond individual departments and has far-reaching organizational consequences. The decentralized structure of Delft with its emphasis on independence of departments sometimes hinders the development of the BRRE. Problems often can not be solved because people cooperating in building the BRRE lack formal authority (which rests with the separate divisions). Subsequently it takes much deliberation to come to an agreement, which can seriously slow down the project.

5.3 ICT and a Public Information System

A public information system is a computer system which can contain many thousands of pages with information for the citizens. The system is accessible from various physical locations by the public, for instance through a computer with modem and/or through a combination of telephone and television. It is quite possible to have electronic information pillars. The public can retrieve information by typing (a combination of) numbers or letters. The page with the information appears immediately. It is also possible to make use of (municipal) services through the system. At the same time specific questions can be answered or more detailed information material (e.g. brochures) can be provided.

It appears from experiences in other municipalities that once a public information system is set up properly, advantages can be realized for both the organization of information within the municipality as well as for the quality of service to the citizens. Computerization of information on the one hand streamlines the internal organization of information: everywhere in the local authority organization the same information is available. On the other hand, the quality of service delivery to the citizens and the democratic processes are improved because for having access to information the citizens no longer depend on the physical location of the desired information (system).

The conclusion is that it does not suffice to concentrate on only one of both advantages (administrative or democratic perfectionism perspective). Internal organization and external service-delivery/democratic processes should go hand in hand. The quality of services provided to the citizen can improve only if the internal organization of information has been streamlined. It is necessary therefore that the public information system is very much alive in the organization: municipal support for electronic communication (internally as well as with the citizen) is necessary for the success of the project. The responsibility for keeping the information up-to-date must be put as close to the source as possible.

A second lesson concerns the "trigger departments." From the "AGI project" in Groningen it can be deduced that the use of all information services of a public information system increases when certain, often consulted, interesting pieces of information are offered. In Groningen, for instance, there is a vacancy section in the system, but the supply of houses can also be attractive. This implies that the public information system must contain more than merely municipal information, which incidentally fits the democratic perfectionism perspective.

A third lesson is supplied by the city of Amsterdam: there the public information system is also directly accessible for all local authority employees from the "start up" menu. Still, every single department is responsible for its part of the information, whereas the central information unit performs only a final check. This structure makes for a good, up-to-date information supply.

A last lesson can be learned from Tilburg. There a distinction is made between as to how broad a public should be reached, how detailed the information needs to be and how much interaction is necessary in the supply of information. An example may illustrate this: opening hours should be widely known, but need little interaction; newspapers and cable network messages suffice. In the supply of information about for instance earlier council decisions much more detailed information is needed, but (probably) the audience to be reached is much smaller: then, providing an Internet link to these council data may be an adequate means of providing that group of customers with the relevant information.

5.4 ICT and the City Panel Research

The City Panel is a market research project which examines wishes, opinions and ideas of Delft citizens about their local authority. Once a year a survey is carried out in which various questions about the municipality are put to the citizens.

The Delft City Panel has also been included in the ICT research project. The central question here was if information technology can be of significance to the City Panel (as far as set-up, data gathering and usage of results are concerned).

In the City Panel project four stages can be distinguished: formulation of questions, gathering of data, data processing and presentation of the results. Up to now, information technology is only used for data processing.

The City Panel is above all motivated by the administrative perfectionism perspective: its goal is to evaluate services provided and to establish a link between the providers of services and products and the clients. However, up to now it has not been made clear in how far the results of the City Panel are being considered in new policy making processes.

In this perspective, information technology offers some more unexploited chances. One possibility lies in providing the results digitally to a broad platform within the municipality. This should be done in such a way that the political and administrative organization will be able to combine the results with other information (possibly on the digital maps). Also during the data collection stage, information technology can play a more important role, for instance through the use of "computer aided interview" techniques, or using the television cable network. Thus the data can be collected and analyzed much faster, and the information will also be available at an earlier stage. Moreover, more surveys can be carried out per year. However, the gap between citizen and government will not be bridged this way, because there is no real interaction between citizens and local government.

From the democratic perfectionism point of view, questions of a more political nature should be introduced. A full automation of the City Panel offers the opportunity to ask questions regularly and at short notice. This makes it possible to add questions that are politically hot issues at the moment, when decisions have not yet been taken. This way the council really makes itself more accessible to the citizen.

5.5 Concluding Remarks

What can be learned from this first empirical investigation? First of all that the distinction made between the internal, administrative perfectionism perspective and the external, democratic perfectionism perspective is useful to analyze informatization processes. If a municipality opts for the democratic perfectionism perspective, its information systems and its information architecture will have a different growth process. The accessibility of information, the timing of the information disclosure, and the content of the information are important questions to be answered.

A second important conclusion is that the two perspectives are not mutually exclusive. In some cases the two perspectives are even mutually dependent: to realize good democratic relationships, the administrative processes have to be perfect.

A third conclusion is that in most cases the administrative perfectionism perspective is dominant. The Dutch municipalities that were visited in this part of the research mainly focused on service delivery. They did not introduce ICT to reduce costs. Instead they tried to realize new services, or they tried to enhance the quality of existing ones. In no case was ICT introduced with a view to realizing a more responsive democracy or other forms of direct democracy.

6. The Use of ICT in an International Perspective

This part of the paper concentrates on the results of the international quantitative research into the state of art of ICT use by local authorities. In the following, the two perspectives will be dealt with separately.

6.1 The Administrative Point of View

The main question of this part of the survey was: Does the implementation and use of information technology influence the quality of the internal local authority organization to enhance service quality? To answer this question, it is important to consider it more closely. What is meant by information technology, what is meant by the internal local authority organization?

In this particular case, *information technology* means the information system that is used by a particular department. Respondents were able to choose the most important information system within their department, and all the questions referred to this particular system. The implementation and use of an information system is often considered a very critical event in an organization. That is why the situation before the implementation of the system was compared to the situation afterwards. The research concentrated on perceptions of ICT influence. The researchers did not visit the departments themselves, and therefore they were not in a position to gather "objective" data to check these perceptions.

The internal local authority organization consists of all the formal and informal relations between organization members, together with all the information flows within the organization (as well as between the organization and other organizations), the internal work procedures and the work processes. The quality of the internal local authority organization, therefore, reflects the condition of these relations, flows, procedures and processes.

For this survey four departments were approached in every local authority organization. Two of them (the financial and the personnel departments) are responsible for important resources. It is assumed that these departments use information systems that will support the internal procedures and processes. The other two (the real estate department and the registry office) are departments that interact with clients and deal with information about citizens and property.

6.1.1 Survey Response

139 questionnaires were returned (which is a response of 49.5 percent), coming from 11 different countries. The various departments are represented as follows: 38 financial departments, 40 personnel departments, 27 real estate departments, and 34 registry offices.

6.1.2 Functions of the Information System

The main functions of the chosen ICT applications range from word processing to research. In the financial departments accounting is the main function (42.1 percent). For the personnel departments word processing is regarded to be the main function (23.1 percent), and this is also the case for the registry offices (22.6 percent). Registration is considered the most important function within the real estate departments with a score of 25.9 percent. Some of the other functions mentioned are control, transaction processing, administration, providing information and forecasting.

In most of the cases (44 percent) the department itself was responsible for the choice of the system, while the (central) information technology department was responsible for the implementation (in 59 percent of the cases). In 54.7 percent of the cases, the information system used is a standard one, i.e. a system that can be bought in any (specialized) software shop. For only 18.7 percent of the departments was the information system especially designed. Most systems are not older than ten years. There is an average use of data bases, spreadsheets and e-mail by the different departments. Graphical and statistical software are two types of applications that are not used very often. Word processing remains the most frequently used type of application.

6.1.3 The Administrative Perfectionism Perspective

The central question in this part of the research is whether ICT is only used for cost reduction, or whether it is also used for the enhancement of the internal organization quality (and consequently the service delivery).

Cost reduction

With respect to cost reduction, the research concentrated on changes in the number of employees (Full Time Equivalents, FTE's). After the implementation of the information system the number of FTE's may change. In only 6.5 percent of the cases did the number of FTE's increase. In 48.6 percent of the cases the number of FTE's decreased. This decrease is largest for the registry offices. In Denmark and Germany the decrease was the largest, while in New Zealand the respondents accounted for the largest increase (33 percent).

It is also to be noted that the internal work processes, according to the respondents, have become more efficient (94.6 percent).

Main focus of the application

Respondents were asked to give information about the main purpose of the ICT application. Two possibilities were given in the survey. The information system can be focused at the interaction between clients and the department or it can be focused at the internal work procedures and work processes. In 87.1 percent of the cases the main purpose of the system is to support the internal work procedures and work processes. Looking at the distribution among the departments in the different countries, no important differences were found.

Employee satisfaction

An important issue is employee satisfaction with the information system used. The respondents could answer on a scale from 1 to 10, where 1 stands for not satisfied and 10 for satisfied. For all departments the averages are around 7.5, except for the registry offices, where the average is 8. So, in general, the employees seem to be satisfied with the system.

Service delivery

The administrative perfectionism perspective can also be measured by the possible change in the *number* of tasks carried out by a department. In 62.3 percent of the cases the number of tasks increased! This is quite interesting, because theoretically the number of tasks in an organization should decrease after implementing and using an information system (the information systems taking over some of the tasks). In the Canadian local authorities, most of the respondents (75 percent) consider the number of tasks to have increased. In Austria the smallest umber of respondents (42.9 percent) give that answer. In short, this means that municipalities do not only introduce ICT to reduce costs. Introduction of new information systems also implies new tasks. Possibly, when the information system takes over most of the common tasks, employees have more time left to spend on new tasks.

Another indicator is the change with respect to the *contents* of the tasks. There does not appear to be much change after implementing the system. About 77 percent of the respondents say that some tasks had changed. In 11.5 percent of the cases all the tasks in the department changed. This is especially the case in the Netherlands, where almost 36 percent of the respondents answer that all the tasks in their department had changed. In the United States the same answer is given by 21.4 percent of the respondents. Concerning this indicator nothing can be said in particular, except for the Netherlands.

Quality of the internal procedures

The last indicator is the improvement of the internal procedures and processes. 98.5 percent of the respondents say that the internal procedures and processes were improved by the information system. Only in Denmark and the United States is there one respondent that considers the internal procedures and processes not to be improved.

Quality of the departmental products

The departments' satisfaction with their own products is also considered. Did this satisfaction change? Again respondents could voice their opinion about the situation before and after implementation, using a 10-point scale. The largest difference between the average before and after implementation is to be found in Germany. The difference here is a positive change of 3.6103. In other words this is the largest (positive) change in satisfaction after implementation. The smallest difference is found in the Netherlands, with a 0.9285 between both averages, also towards a greater satisfaction. All that can be said for now is that the implementation of the information system, with respect to the satisfaction with the departments' products, has had the greatest impact for the German respondents. In the Netherlands this impact is the smallest.

Effects of the information system on the organizational structure

In some cases the respondents reply that the departments are given more autonomy in carrying out their tasks by using the information system. There is also some impact on the use of information and information sources. Again, respondents could score on a 10-point scale. This time 1 represented independence of data and 10 represented dependence on data. For the item "using data supplied by other departments from within the same local authority" the average changes from 7.2411 to 7.3000, which indicates a very small shift towards greater dependence after implementation. This is also the case if the departments use data from other (private or public) organizations, but the change after implementing the information system on using data and dependence is negligible.

Other departments (in the same or other organizations) also use data generated by the departments of the respondents. According to the respondents, they have become more dependent (a rise from 7.4250 to 8.6742) on the respondents' departments after the implementation and use of the information system. This can also be related to the fact that the respondents' departments begin to use more information from other resources with the new system. More possibilities have been created by the information system to make use of (or share) already gathered data.

Concluding remarks regarding the administrative perfectionism perspective

What can be learned from these results? First, that not cost reduction but the enhancement of the quality of internal work processes was the main focus of using information systems. Only in 12.9 percent of the cases did the ICT application focus on the interaction between the citizens and the departments involved. In many cases, with the introduction of ICT, new tasks are assumed by the departments under consideration. In general the evaluation of informatization is positive. Respondents are satisfied with the information systems. They think that the quality of their procedures and processes as well as the quality of their products is improved by the introduction of information systems.

There is only a slight change in the organizational structure as a result of information technology. The mutual dependence of the different departments has grown because of the information systems. Interestingly enough, the dependence of the departments investigated on other departments has not changed as much as the dependence of other departments on the departments investigated (maybe dependent organizations will not agree with this). Possibly this is due to the fact that very central information systems (basic registrations and resource systems, such as finance and personnel) were analyzed.

6.2 The Democratic Point of View

This part of the survey concentrated on the influence of ICT on the relationships between citizens and local authorities. It is important to distinguish the several possible relationships that can be influenced, for citizens play two different roles in their relation with local government.

On the one hand citizens participate in the democratic process, among other things by voting. On the other hand they are clients of the local authority organization and depend on the delivery of products and services. In the first role the citizens deliver an input into local government by stating wishes and demands. In the second they are subject to the output of the local government organization. The resulting roles for local governments are that of a political body or of a service provider. The relationships within the local administration can also be influenced by ICT. The possibilities for interaction between politicians and local authority employees can influence the quality and the implementation of political decisions, or the availability of up-to-date policy information for politicians.

6.2.1 Survey Response

For this part of the paper, questionnaires were sent to the Information Technology managers of the selected local authorities. This questionnaire consisted of two parts, firstly a general part regarding the local authority as a whole and the overall view on information technology. In the second part respondents were asked to answer a set of questions on the three most important ICT applications that influenced their relationship with citizens. The questionnaire was filled out by 35 respondents. This makes the response rate 42.7 percent. Information was received about a total number of 88 ICT applications.

6.2.2 ICT Applications

The table below gives an overview of applications available to participating local authorities and which in their opinion influence their relationship with citizens.

Of these applications, 43 (48.8 percent) are used only for internal procedures, that is, they are only accessible to local authority employees or politicians. The other 45 (51.2 percent) are also available to external actors.

	#	%		#	%
Internal	**43**	**48,8**	**External**	**45**	**51,2**
office automation	8	18,6	public information system	17	37,9
registry office	8	18,6	Internet	10	22,2
financial	6	13,9	library	7	15,5
social security	4	9,3	electronic service delivery	4	8,9
taxes	3	7	information system for the council	3	6,6
GIS	3	7	other	4	8,9
other	11	25,6	–	–	–
Total	43	100 %	Total	45	100 %

6.2.3 Aims of ICT Applications

The reasons of local governments for implementing the applications were measured using a number of statements that could be valued on a 10-point scale. There were three types of statements:
- the influence of ICT on the relationship with citizens,
- the improvement of internal policy procedures,
- other statements, namely "to keep up with technological progress," "centrally enforced" and "to make implementation cheaper."

The highest average scores were found in the last category. The reason "to keep up with technological progress" had the highest average, namely 6.68. The score on the statement "to make implementation cheaper" was also high, namely 5.57. When concentrating on the interaction with citizens through communication, a distinction concerning the direction of the communication has to be made. Communication from the local government directed towards the citizen is regarded as more important than communication from the citizen to the government: "To give better information about the government" had an average of 6.38, which is in sharp contrast to the proposition "To know what is on the minds of citizens." That statement scored an average of 3.74. Thus in most local authorities a one-way vision on governmental communication prevails.

The statements concentrating on the citizens' role in the policy process all received a lower score than those concerning the improvement of the internal functioning of local authorities. Of these statements, "to know what is on the minds of citizens" scores highest with (only) 3.74. The statement about trying to involve citizens in the various stages of the policy process, respectively in decision making, implementation and the evaluation of policies are given even lower ratings.

6.2.4 Effects of the Implementation

The effects of the applications were measured by attributing a score to a number of statements (see appendix 2) on a scale from 1 to 9, where 1 stands for diminished, 5 stands for no change and 9 stands for augmented.

An effect discernible in all countries is the possibilities for local authority employees to inform citizens. The average score was highest for this effect (compared to the others), namely 7.26, with very little deviation between the different countries. The possibilities for politicians to inform citizens showed less improvement (6.63), as was the case for all statements about the relationships between politicians and citizens. The number of contacts between citizens and politicians hardly changes. All scores are between 5 and 6, with an exception in the case of the Netherlands. Here, the Dutch score an average of 6.5.

The changes for local authority employees are more clear. The awareness of local authority employees of the citizens' needs and the number of contacts between local authority employees and citizens have both changed. The first averages 6.24, the second 6.23.

Local authority employees benefit from the use of ICT in their communications with each other (6.37). For politicians there is hardly any change, as no improvement is found in the quality of the communication (5.37). The communication between local authority employees and politicians is also hardly influenced.

6.2.5 An International Perspective

A few countries gave a high number of external systems used. In the United States and Canada 66.6 percent of the systems are externally oriented. The United Kingdom scores 64.7 percent. Finland and Denmark also have rather high scores, respectively 41.6 and 42.9.

An interesting statistic is the number of public information systems: eight out of 17 came from the United Kingdom, five from the United States.

The applications named by local authorities in New Zealand, the Netherlands, Austria and Germany were mostly internal systems.

When looking at the overall change due to the use of ICT, there are clear international differences (see appendix 3). New Zealand and the United States, Canada and Finland show a high degree of change concerning all statements.

The quality of services has improved in all countries, most of them indicating an average of 7.5. However, New Zealand, the United States,

Switzerland, Germany and Belgium are most extreme. The client based orientation can also be found in the statement about the services being in accordance with the clients' wishes. New Zealand, the United States, Switzerland, Belgium and Germany again are high scorers, but the Dutch also are above average. The access to information on services has changed more than the access to political information. The countries that have a high average score on the first also have a high average score on the second. These countries are New Zealand, the United States, Finland, Belgium and the United Kingdom. As for political information, Canada is to be added to the list. New Zealand, the United States, Canada, Finland, Belgium and Switzerland all have high scores for the possibilities to express one's opinion about services and about politics. Switzerland and Belgium show a higher score on politics, the others on service.

6.3 Overall Orientation

For the influence of Information Technology in general a few statements have been posed in both the administrative perfectionism perspective and the democratic perfectionism perspective questionnaire (see appendix 3). There were 174 respondents from all local authorities relating to this issue. Respondents could attribute a score on a scale of 1 to 10, where 1 stands for diminished, 5 for no change and 10 for augmented. The major conclusion to be drawn is that political orientations are far more difficult to implement than are service orientations.

The largest improvement ICT has made possible is on the quality of services (7.23). Second comes congruency of services with the wishes of clients (6.65). The access to information about services has also improved. We can conclude that citizens possess better information about services, and local authorities have a better picture of their clients' wishes. Strangely enough, this improved picture does not coincide with an increase in the possibilities to express their opinion about services. With 5.63 that has hardly changed. Access to political information (5.88) and possibilities to express opinions about politics (5.4) also show only a small change. In general, local authorities think they have become more responsive, the average on that proposition being 5.95.

It can be concluded that, on the whole, ICT concentrates on the local authority as a service provider. The (internal) quality of services and the provision of information (one way) to citizens about services have been improved in most cases. The influence on political aspects is much smaller. Here also, the provision of political information to the citizens is more common than the possibilities for citizens to express their opinion. However, a change is in the air.

7. Three Case Studies

7.1 Kent County Council

The Kent public Information System: a quest for the efficiency optimum

In Kent there are two ICT applications that influence the relationship between the county council and the citizens: "Public Information" and "Kent Access."

"Public Information"

This application consists of information about county and district services. Also a lot of information related to leisure is available, for example weather forecast, news, train timetables. Communication is possible via about 40 terminals using a viewdata system. These can be found in libraries and public buildings spread all over the county. A "dial in"-service is also available. This system has been operational since 1993.

"Kent Access"

For this application about 1,000 computer terminals will be installed in libraries, public buildings and in the streets. Among these are a small number of multimedia terminals fit for CD-ROM and Internet. Internet users can also connect to this system through their personal computer at home. The system gives access to information on a broad scale. The infrastructure is developed in partnership with private organizations, like British Telecom, libraries, museums and with other authorities. The initiative for these two applications came from Kent local authority employees. Library personnel in particular has been very influential.

Background

Kent County Council can best be characterized as being a representative democracy. There are no possibilities for citizens to participate directly in the political process or to participate in the development of local policy. No consultation takes place. Political influence on the development of the two initiatives mentioned above has been very small. The role of politicians is limited to the final decision making. According to the interviewees, politicians in English counties are volunteers. They get paid for their expenses only. There is nobody for daily governance, and most local authority politicians are retired people, who do not have enough knowledge and expertise with respect to ICT.

Targets

The purpose of the system is in the first place to reduce costs. ICT is perceived as an opportunity to maintain quality in the county at a lower cost. At present, local authorities in England are forced to do anything they can to save money. ICT is especially helpful to avoid the duplication of information. Local authority employees feel that they should have the knowledge and that they needed to explore ICT applications because they had to build up expertise. Also, the county sees ICT as an important stimulus for economic development.

There were no objectives quantified, when the system was implemented, but only qualitative targets were formulated:
1. to provide information about services,

2. to provide information of a general nature,
3. to make information of all departments and authorities available in one system, and
4. to get a strategic position as an information provider.

Procedure

The initiative for both systems came from local authority employees. Especially those who had a lot of contacts with citizens knew what their needs were. The other departments only slowly became enthusiastic. Only after the profile of, for example, World-Wide Web had become more distinct, did they see its potentials.

When the "Public Information" system was started, technical possibilities were smaller than they are now. Because not everybody appreciated the choice of a viewdata system, inconsistencies resulted. Also, other local authorities had other information systems. When cooperation between local authorities became necessary, technical problems arose. These problems can now be solved by the new "Kent Access" system. All participating partners agree on the more advanced technologies now available.

The purchasing costs were shared by different authorities and organizations. The updating costs are mainly paid for by the county council. Plans exist to share these costs as well in the future.

There was no organizational change necessary, especially because of the small scale of the "Public Information" system. ICT is mostly additional, not directed at changing the organization. Possibly, after installing about 1,000 terminals for "Kent Access," there will be a cultural change. No organizational changes however are intended.

One thing did change though. The updating of information used to be the responsibility of the departments. This caused problems with respect to the validity of information, so now there is a special department responsible for keeping the information in "Kent Access" up-to-date.

Effects

For citizens, the "Public Information" system provides a lot of governmental and leisure information. However, about 45 percent of the users consult the terminals for information about leisure activities. It is hoped that the popularity of the leisure pages will make people use the system for council information as well.

Other actors get a chance to provide information through the new "Kent Access" system. An integration of all services should take place. All public sector organizations will be working together, but private sector organizations also cooperate, e.g. British Telecom and the Chambers of Commerce. There are no special functions for politicians, but this will probably change after the next local elections. There is an idea of having minutes and reports available electronically. The political attention for ICT is growing and is expected to increase.

In the future "Kent Access" will play a more important role in the provision of information. This system will gradually take over the functions of the "Public Information System," which will phase out after 1997. Then information will also be available about other local authorities, libraries and other public sector organizations.

7.2 The City of Antwerp

The case of Antwerp, striving for the service optimum

The city of Antwerp wants to improve the dialogue with its citizens. Through the use of ICT a decentralization of departments was made possible. A quick reconstruction of infrastructure, using fiberglas cables, facilitated this development.

All applications that are directed at the citizens are included in the concept of "Antwerp, Intelligent City." This includes an Internet site (The Digital Metropole Antwerp), that will soon be available in kiosks as well. There is a central "unique" telephone number, which gives access to the whole municipal organization. When citizens have a problem, any problem, they do not need to look for the telephone number of a specific department to deal with their problem. They use the one phone number. From there he or she will be connected to the right department. Using the so-called "response card" people can file complaints about services. The city guarantees that these are dealt with within a week. Also, every Saturday there is a television program with information about the city and city services. The so-called Cybercafé is open to all citizens and provides all facilities and guidance for surfing the Internet.

Background

In 1983 the city of Antwerp merged with eight suburbs, increasing the population from about 200,000 people to a total of half a million. This population growth was accompanied by a rise of extremist parties. The local authority feels that this problem was also caused by its failure to communicate with the citizens. The political organization of 55 council members and ten board members failed to provide a healthy contact with the population. The organization at that time had a centralized structure.

Targets

The dominant philosophy in the use of ICT is to develop a dialogue with the citizens. This is determined by the sort of democracy desired: a responsive democracy.

Telepolis

The initiatives for the implementation of ICT come from the informatization department, called "Telepolis," under the responsibility of an alderman. This department, which has the legal status of a corporation, also works for the province of Antwerp. This status gives the department a kind of flexibility, for example with respect to salary payments which otherwise could not have been achieved. In the fast changing world of ICT it gives the department the possibility to hire high quality personnel.

It also has the advantage that new applications do not need the approval of individual local authority departments, thus gaining a lot of time with the introduction. Another advantage is that the department has a business-like relationship with other municipal departments. It is responsible for introducing and supporting new ICT systems. The updating and the quality of the information, however, is the responsibility of the clients themselves. Telepolis sees to it that departments hire the right staff for that job. Of course this corporation is accountable to the city council. It also has a board which consists of high level representatives from all departments involved.

Effects

Local authority employees are the main users of information technology application. The most significant impact of ICT therefore is on the administration. The introduction of ICT has not *caused* major changes in the administration, the reverse is the case: ICT is used to facilitate major changes in the administration, the decentralization of which would not have been possible without ICT. Also, a more professional and formal organization and culture have emerged in which routine jobs have been taken over by the computer.

Politicians have a lot of facilities at their disposal to support their work, but the use that is made of these varies strongly. Politicians are more interested in ICT applications that can create more possibilities for their electorate. Successful applications help their personal image.

Most of the applications aimed at citizens intend to improve and speed up the deliverance of services. This is achieved by the decentralization of services, by bringing them closer to the citizens. The information, however, is still collected and updated centrally. Also, communication with the citizens has been improved. Citizens have the possibilities to send e-mail messages to politicians and local authority employees. There is, however, no formal consultation. There are no applications intended to facilitate citizen involvement in political decision making. The possibilities of access to central information at a decentral level, however, are also valuable for representatives at the decentral level.

Future perspectives

Future plans exist for the cooperation with other actors, especially private organizations. A cooperation with the local university already exists, a cooperation with the Chamber of Commerce is being developed. Antwerp also wants to make its fiberglas infrastructure available to other organizations, but until 1998 Belgacom has the telecommunication monopoly.

For the citizens two developments are important: the first is the idea of an intelligent agent. A computer system should, after a few consultations, be able to know what the preferences of a user are. Another development is the combination of governmental information with other information. In doing so, a kind of information supermarket comes into being. Governmental information that is not very attractive is accompanied by other information, perhaps more interesting for citizens. Citizens logging in for fun are thus also faced with more serious information. As in the supermarket, you want to buy one loaf of bread but return with a bagful of groceries.

7.3 The City of Bologna

Iperbole – from the wall to the world: a telematics networks to talk to one another

Since January 1995 the population of Bologna has had the possibility of using ICT applications for their communication with the local authority. The project, called IPERBOLE (which stands for *I*nternet *P*er *B*ologna e *L'E*milia Romagna), uses Internet for the development of tele-democracy, of two way communication, of a transparent administration, of the right to information as a social service, of interactivity with the citizens and of participation in the decision making process as a condition of the renewal of public institutions.

The idea for this interactive network was born at the university of Bologna. Here a group of philosophy teachers, concerned about democracy and transparency of local government, looked for ways to bring the local authority and its citizens closer together through an interactive public network.

The main purpose of the project was to experiment with the use of ICT in the relationships between local authority and citizens and the internal relationships within the organization. Another purpose was to be able to find out about citizens' opinions, to use the network to obtain and to make information, opinions and suggestions available.

History of the system

1994: Feasibility study, user requirements capture and feedback analysis.
1995: January: project start-up.
Service to the citizens and organizations and setting up of a specific desk charged with providing free accounts, passwords, World-Wide Web basic training, technical assistance, communication with users. End of March: 3,200 individual users; 250 collective subjects private and public, schools and non-profit organizations connected also as information providers; 90 municipal offices connected to e-mail. Some important cities of the Emilia-Romagna region are joining the IPERBOLE initiative, launched by Bologna: Modena, Reggio Emilia, Ravenna, Rimini, Forlì and Cesena have the intention to provide a public World-Wide Web free of charge for their citizens.
1997: For the beginning of 1997 the system is expected to have 7,000 to 8,000 users. To face the problem of citizens' widespread computer illiteracy a number of attended access points will be made available. The IPERBOLE-Internet network will be linked to other World-Wide Web pages to provide users with more sources of information. Connections with other city councils in the metropolitan area, and other public administrations, schools and non-profit organizations will be realized.
1999: 12,000 to 15,000 users connected to the civic network in the metropolitan area.

Who can use the system?

All citizens who have (access to) a computer and a modem can connect to the civic network IPERBOLE, and through this connection to the World-Wide Web of Internet. There is no time limit with respect to connection in the civic network. If one wants to use Internet there is a time limit of 45 minutes for "surfing." The civic network is open to all citizens of Bologna, to associations, schools, and other public administrations at a metropolitan level.

Interaction

To describe the functions of IPERBOLE, four levels of interaction can be distinguished:
1. Providing information.
   Individual citizens and organizations are given the possibility to construct a home-page and give information about any subject. At the moment there are about 100 providers of information. A major problem is keeping the information up-to-date.
2. The second level concentrates on political interaction. Two aspects are worth mentioning here. All citizens have the possibility to contact the municipal organization via e-mail. The other aspect is the possibility to start up so-called news or discussion groups. These latter are initiatives of individuals or groups of citizens to discuss hot issues, in order to put them on the political agenda. Important is the basic philosophy of free access. Everybody can start a group.

   For the e-mail function there is a keyword/message rooting system. At the moment within the local authority organization there are about 90 e-mail addresses, both of politicians and local authority employees. The target is to give ten percent (about 500) of the local authority employees an e-mail address.
3. The third kind of interaction occurs when the newsgroups gather in local bars to prepare for lobbying, to have face-to-face meetings, to form political pressure groups. The philosophy behind this aspect is that a modern politician must value the resources within/of the society.

This destroys the classical power base, and it also means that the citizens must change and take responsibility. A crucial factor in the IPERBOLE system is the answer of politicians. They are not used to responding in this way.
4. The fourth possible interaction offered by IPERBOLE can be summed up as rights and duties. It has to do with the delivering of products and rendering of services by the local authority. There is the duty for example to pay taxes. This can be done by using the so-called Bancomat, plastic money or through cashpoint-like vending machines (sportelli). These can also be used to retrieve documents like birth certificates.

Critical points

One critical point is to be made. This concerns the acceptance of the system by the political and administrative organization. A quite demanding training campaign within the municipality was started for the officers (more than 300 have already been trained) in order to promote the internal use of the "civic network" and in general of communication technologies. To face the problem of citizens' widespread computer illiteracy many public access points to the network (in districts, libraries, youth centers, etc.) were made available. Here, citizens, who do not have a computer at home or who do not know how to work with a computer, are helped by local authority staff.

Some of the key factors for the success of the system are: an efficient system of assistance and training, an always increasing amount of information and services provided, integration and coordination of data, an efficient collection of user requirements.

The costs

The total sum available for the first 16 months of the project was Lit 630 million, including personnel. For 1996 a budget of Lit 800 million is available, while for the future new financial sources will have to be found, possibly through sponsoring. Although it has been stated that the citizens have free access to Internet, it was made clear by all interviewees, that in the end the citizens pay for this project with their tax money.

7.4 Some Concluding Remarks

Comparing the three case studies, a few differences stand out in relation to the theoretical distinctions that have been made:

For Kent County Council one of the main reasons to introduce ICT is cost reduction. Antwerp wants to establish a dialogue with its citizens, whereas Bologna wants to use ICT to experiment with the relationships between local government and its citizens. Of the three Kent is the very example of representative democracy, Antwerp seeks to develop a responsive democracy, while Bologna comes closest to a direct democracy. Both in Kent and in Antwerp, local authority officers, and not politicians, played a significant role in the introduction of ICT applications. The initiative in Bologna came from outside the organization, namely from the university. However one politician (who at the same time is a professor of philosophy) was a driving force behind the introduction within the local authority. Of the three cases, the IPERBOLE system of Bologna is the best example of the use of ICT to enhance the democratic relationships with the citizens.

8. Back to the Future

The following main conclusions can be drawn with respect to the research questions formulated in chapter 3:
- *Cost reduction* is not the main reason for local authorities to introduce ICT applications. No indications for this were found in the national or in the international surveys.
- The most important reason for local authorities to introduce ICT is *service delivery*. Municipalities want to introduce new services or improve the existing services. This means that ICT applications have an

important function in improving the internal organization of the local authority: the *administrative perfectionism perspective* is dominant.
- For most of the local authorities, improving the quality of the *democratic relationships* with the citizens is not a major issue when introducing ICT. The fact that in some cases the democratic perfectionism perspective can be shown to have stood at the beginning, shows that a change is in the air.

In general it can be concluded that information and communication technology does play an important role in the improvement of the quality of local government. However, with the main focus on the internal organization, information technology is still more important than communication technology. Debates in society (an indication for responsive democracy) or even decision making by the citizens (direct democracy) are still a long way off. To achieve this, the classical power base needs to be destroyed. Politicians and local authority employees must value the most important resource in society: the citizens who must face their responsibility.

Literature

Cuilenburg, J. J. van (1993), De maatschapelijke informatievoorziening. In: J. W. van Deth, Handboek politicologie. Van Gorcum, Assen 1993.

Depla, P, (1995-a), Vernieuwing van lokale Democratie: vervolmaking of vermaatschappelijking. In: Vraagstelling, voorjaar 1995, p. 133 t/m 146.

Depla, P, (1995-b), Technologie en de vernieuwing van de lokale democratie. 1995.

Dijk, J. A. G. M. van (1992), Informatie- en communicatietechnologie en bestuurlijke vernieuwing bij gemeenten, in: Frissen, P. H. A et al. (red.), Orwell of Athene? Democratie en informatiesamenleving. NOTA, Den Haag, 1992.

Donk, van der W. B. H. J., P. W. Tops (1993, Informatisering en democratie, Orwell of Athene? In: Zuurmond, Huigen et al, Reader Informatisering in het openbaar bestuur. 1993.

Edwards, A. R (1992), Informatization and Views of Democracy, in: Frissen P. H. A et al (red.) Orwell of Athene? Democratie en informatiesamenleving. NOTA, Den Haag, 1992.

Gilsing (1994), Lokale bestuurlijke vernieuwing in Nederland, in: Acta Politica 1994/1, p. 3 t/m 36.

Korsten, A. F. A (1979), Het spraakmakende bestuur: een studie naar de effecten van participatie in relatie tot demokratiemodellen en sociale ongelijkheid. Uitgeverij VUGA, Den Haag 1979.

Kraemer, K. L., King, J. L., Dunkle, D. E. and Lane, J. P. (1989), Managing Information Systems: Change and Control in Organizational Computing. London/San Francisco 1989.

Laudon, K. C. (1977), Communications Technology and Democratic Participation. Praeger Publishers, New York 1977.

Leijenaar, M. H. (1993), Lokale politiek, in: J.W. van Deth, Handboek politicologie. Van Gorcum, Assen 1993.

Severijnen, P. C. A. (1994), Local Authorities and Market Research, Local Government Studies, Vol. 20, No. 1 (Spring 1994), Frank Cass Publishers, London.

Severijnen, P. C. A. (1994), Delft: Marktforschung für Kommunen, in: Herman Hill (Hrsg.), Die begreifbare Stadt, Köln, 1994.

Snellen, I. Th .M. (1995), Informatie-communicatietechnologie en democratie, in: Wijsgerig perspectief 36 (1995/96)-1.

Snellen, I. Th .M. (1996), Informatisering en inconsistenties van de democratie, in: Christen democratische verkenningen 1996, nr. 1.

Snellen, I. Th. M. and Zuurmond, A. (1996), Lokaal bestuur en informatisering: zoeken naar nieuwe optima (notitie aangeboden aan het gemeentebestuur van Rotterdam).

Thomassen, J. J. A. (1979), Burgers in twee gedaanten(rede) Enschede, 1979.

Tops, P. (1994), Moderne regenten, over lokale democratie. Amsterdam/ Antwerp, Uitgeverij Atlas, 1994.

Tops, P. W. and Depla, P. (1993), Vernieuwing van de lokale democratie: een ordening in de discussie, in: Acta Politica 1993/3.

Veld, R. J. In 't (1993), Dynamische Bestuurskunde, Rotterdam 1995.

Veldheer, V., De betekenis van de lokale overheid voor de inwoners, in: Beleidswetenschap 1995/1 p. 24–39.

Zuurmond, A., De burger als citoyen: informeren of communiceren? Concept-artikel voor I&I 1996.
Zuurmond, A., Hofstede R., Moolenaars R., Muermans J. and Rodenhuis, J. W., Van kennis delen wordt iedereen wijzer, Rotterdam 1995.

Appendix 1

The local authorities per country

Finland

1. Hæmeenlinna
2. Kuusamon Kunta
3. Tampereen Kaupunki
4. Seinajoen Kaupunki
5. Joensuun Kaupunki
6. Oulun Kaupunki

New Zealand

7. Christchurch
8. Auckland City Council
9. North Shore City Council
10. Wellington City Council
11. Dunedin City Council
12. Manukau City Council

Canada

13. Quebec
14. Calgary
15. Toronto
16. Ottowa
17. Vancouver

United States

18. San Diego
19. San Bernardino
20. Seattle
21. Orange County
22. Dade County
23. Bellevue
24. Portsmouth
25. Eugene
26. Austin
27. Phoenix

Austria

28. Kapfenberg
29. Linz
30. Salzburg
31. Wels
32. Graz
33. St. Veit/Glan
34. Innsbruck
35. Klagenfurt

Netherlands

36. Roosendaal
37. Voorburg
38. Hoogvliet
39. Emmen
40. Tilburg

41. Almelo
42. Groningen
43. Brunssum
44. Haarlem
45. Delft

Germany

46. Duisburg
47. Köln
48. Düsseldorf
49. Bochum
50. Dortmund
51. Fürth
52. Unna
53. Heidelberg
54. Osnabrück
55. Essen

Great Britain

56. Braintree
57. Manchester
58. Edinburgh City Council
59. Swansea City Council
60. Highland Regional Council
61. Newham County Council
62. Cheshire County Council
63. Kirklees
64. Kent County Council
65. Hampshire County Council
66. Nottinghamshire County Council
67. Oxfordshire County Council
68. Hertfordshire County Council
69. Powys County Council
70. Birmingham

Denmark

71. Farum
72. Næstved Kommune
73. Holstebro Kommune
74. Struer Kommune
75. Skive Kommune
76. Slangerup Kommune
77. Odense
78. Aalborg
79. Ballerup
80. Hals

Switzerland

81. Neuchâtel

Belgium

82. Antwerp

Appendix 2

Could you please indicate what the effect of the use of this application was on the items listed below: diminished, no change or augmented?
- the awareness of local authority employees of the services the citizens want;
- the number of contacts between local authority employees and citizens;
- the possibilities for local authority employees to inform citizens;
- the costs of deliverance of services and products;
- the communication of local authority employees with each other;
- the awareness of politicians of citizens' needs;
- the number of contacts between politicians and citizens;
- the possibilities for politicians to inform citizens;
- the communication of politicians with each other;
- the communication between politicians and local authority employees.

Appendix 3

Could you please indicate what the effect of the implementation of information technology in your local authority is on the following items (in the citizens' relation with the local authority): diminished, no change, augmented?
- the quality of service;
- the accordance of service with the clients' wishes;
- the access of citizens to information about governmental services and products;
- the possibility for citizens to express their opinion about governmental services;
- the access to information about political processes;
- the possibility for citizens to express their opinion about political preferences;
- the responsiveness of government to the wishes of citizens.

Human Resources Management in the City of Duisburg

Winfried Lappé, Elke Holzrichter, Günter Grygiel, Gabriele Nakonz, Robert Tonks

Synopsis with Seven Theses 409
1. Concepts and Strategies for Human Resources
   Management 410
   1.1 New Framework Conditions for Municipalities 410
   1.2 Human Resources Management and Personnel
        Development 411
2. Human Resources Management in Municipalities 417
   2.1 From Personnel Increase to Personnel Reduction
        in the Context of the Budgetary Crisis and the
        Modernisation of Administration 417
   2.2 Differences in the Framework Conditions
        for Personnel Management between the Public
        and the Private Sector 418
   2.3 Personnel Development Concepts and Single Measures
        Integrating the Results of the International Research 419
3. Practical Example: Strategic Personnel Management
   (Human Resources Management in the Municipality
   of Duisburg)... 428
   3.1 Basic Understanding 428
   3.2 Personnel Development............................. 430
        3.2.1 Strategic Planning 430
        3.2.2 Instruments of Personnel Development........... 431
        3.2.3 Main Focus of Operative Personnel Management .. 434
        3.2.4 Current Developments........................ 436

4. Success Factors of an Efficient Human Resources Management within Changed Framework Conditions 438
   4.1 Networking 438
   4.2. Long-Term Political Perspectives 438
   4.3 Prevention of Disadvantaging 439
   4.4 Avoiding Demotivation Processes................... 439
   4.5 Decentralised Personnel Management 440
   4.6 Standardised Framework Conditions for Public Administration 441
   4.7 Subsidiarity of External Consulting 441
   4.8 Regular Efficiency Reviews........................ 442
   4.9 Orientation towards the Customers and Citizens 442
Literature... 443

Synopsis with Seven Theses

1. In view of the economic and social framework conditions, personnel management in German municipalities has undergone a fundamental change in the past ten years. This change manifests itself in three stages. The first stage was marked by the optimisation of *personnel management*. The second phase comprised a personnel development which primarily means *qualification*. In the third stage the emphasis was put equally on both *measures for staff cutbacks* which are accompanied by instruments for personnel development and instruments for a *modernisation of administrations* and for a consolidation of the budget.
2. In the course of this process, *new instruments* have been developed. They currently make up the focus of personnel management: personnel participation, personnel controlling and reductions in staff which are socially acceptable.
3. For the time being, personnel management in public administrations is still subject to *particular framework conditions* of the public service law, the civil service law and the budget law. In contrast to the private sector, they restrict considerably the flexible implementation of personnel management coordination instruments.
4. In connection with concepts for personnel development, the activities clearly exceed the classical form of training and advanced training: procedures of staff assessments, selection procedures of executives, achievement incentive schemes, staff discussions, flexible working hours and quality management prove themselves as independent instruments which are – now also for administrations – highly relevant. The development of these instruments is based on principles of *motivation, training* and *participation*.
5. Since the beginning of the 1970s, the municipality of Duisburg has been intensifying and networking its activities in the field of personnel development and organisation development. Since the beginning of the 1990s, these activities were made to serve a *comprehensive citizen-directed modernisation of its administration*. About twelve action fields – which are marked by a strong participation of the staff – are the operative basis.

6. At the moment all measures for a personnel management are nationally and internationally within the *area of conflict between centralised and decentralised discharge of duties:* After a successful networking of instruments which have so far been isolated, those activities in the field of personnel management which are of fundamental and coordinational relevance for the organisation and those which can be assumed on a decentralised basis, have to be redetermined. Next to the strengthening of decentralised units, emphasis must also be on the adherence to quality standards which are centrally determined and controlled.
7. In the future, important success factors for an efficient human resources management are a stronger networking of measures for personnel development and organisation development, a specific activation of the in-house know-how of the staff, as well as an intense promotion of their motivation. *Regular efficiency reviews* in accordance with a comprehensive *quality management approach* serve to find out the customers' needs and level of satisfaction. It sets the actual standard for a successful personnel management within a modern services' management.

1. Concepts and Strategies for Human Resources Management

1.1 New Framework Conditions for Municipalities

The economic, political and social framework conditions for the private economic sector, for public administration and in particular for the activities of municipalities have become extremely unstable and prone to crises. The ongoing economic recession linked directly with decreasing demand, increasing unemployment and a lower tax revenue are leading to an increasing burden on the social net and a scarcity of financial resources in municipalities. Additionally, the advancing technological development, with its ever shorter innovation cycles, places higher demands on the qualification of the employees. The qualitative demands on municipal services made by employees on the one hand, and the citizens on the other, are also increasing.

The current reactions of municipalities to these changes concentrate on the general modernisation of administration and, in particular, a consolidation of the budget. The requirements resulting from that have to be met with new strategies. Required is a modernisation of administration which comprises a new administrative culture and modified forms of organisation as well as a new leadership behaviour and a more comprehensive promotion of employees.

1.2 Human Resources Management and Personnel Development

Due to the described processes of change, the "personnel" plays a crucial role in practice.[42] External requirements (framework conditions for the activities of municipalities) confront internal requirements (by the staff).

In this context the change of values in society emphasises the conditions necessary for the reform process, such as "participation," "autonomy," "responsibility."[43]

Precise definitions

Apart from the generic terms of human resources management and personnel management, this part deals also with the increasingly important "personnel development." Furthermore, taking into consideration the background of an increased interest in concepts for cost and efficiency control, a close look will be taken at the terms of "personnel controlling" and "personnel reduction." In the following, human resources management is practically used as a synonym for personnel management, al-

---

42 This is emphasised in various publications and papers for the private as well as the public sector, cf. Löhr 1995, Klages/Hippler 1991, Doppler/Lauterburg 1995, Thom/Zaugg 1994 and many others.
43 In various surveys among municipal staff carried out by the Sozialforschungsstelle Dortmund (Institute for Social Research) these aspects are clearly emphasised by the employees. Where they are not taken into account by the executives significant negative impacts on job satisfaction, on the assessment of executives and on the process of organisational development and modernisation can be noted.

though the wider definition of human resources management includes not only personnel but also organisational aspects.

Personnel management

Personnel administration and personnel management[44], which began to develop in the twenties, did not have a central function until the eighties. With the development of new technologies and thus the demand for qualification the process of change from a mere *administration* of staff to personnel *management* began. Its importance increased even more due to the new framework conditions described above and the reorganisation and modernisation measures connected with them.

Due to this development the use of the terms human capital and human resources has increased in recent times. Whereas the term *human capital* refers to the achievement potential of the population, economically represented by trained and highly qualified staff, the term *human resources* comprises the achievement potentials (including achievement reserves) of all members of an enterprise or an administration. The achievement is determined by the individual abilities and motivation of the staff.

Human resources management or personnel management are generic terms for diverse tasks referring to personnel which have to be linked to each other, coordinated and directed.[45] These are:
– personnel development (properly speaking)
– personnel leadership
– personnel planning
– staff recruitment and staff selection
– personnel placement
– personnel controlling
– maintenance of staff numbers

---

44 These terms are often used synonymously, although they describe different phases and contents of the field of work.
45 cf. Luczak/Oberbannscheidt/Seiwert, Personalmanagement in der Rezession – Handlungsfelder und innovative Strategien, in: Fortschrittliche Betriebsführung und Industrial Engineering, no. 4, 1994, p. 148 and Gablers Wirtschaftslexikon, 1988.

- redundancies, staff cutbacks
- staff assessment.

The general duty of personnel management is "to ensure on a long term basis the human resources necessary for the realisation of the strategic goals of the enterprise as far as quantity, space and time are concerned and to solve all legal, social and administrative problems linked with the use of manpower."[46]

Personnel Development

Since the beginning of the nineties, personnel development is no longer merely considered as an instrument for compensating deficiencies in qualification. With regard to municipalities this means:

"Personnel development consists of systematically structured processes which make it possible to determine the achievement and learning potential of the staff and to foster these potentials in accordance with the administrative demand, orientated towards practical application and development."[47]

This definition has been incorporated by many administrations into their concept for personnel development. The definition has been extended in connection with the Neue Steuerungsmodell[48]:

"Personnel development in the Neue Steuerungsmodell has to deal with the question as to how personnel development can motivate the staff to both participate in and further the reform process, and to work successfully in a restructured administration."[49]

Due to this widening of the definition of personnel development, a tendency to extend the instruments of personnel development may also be noted.

---

46 cf. Antoni 1988.
47 from the KGSt report 13/1994, p. 9.
48 model developed by German municipalities similar to New Public Management in the USA (translator's note).
49 KGSt draft report "Personalentwicklung im Neuen Steuerungsmodell" of 3rd November 1995, p. 8.

Personnel controlling, code number systems

Personnel controlling – as an instrument of personnel management still in the "experimental phase"[50] – has the task to collect and continuously provide a manageable quantity of exactly defined code numbers for an efficient, demand-orientated personnel information system for planning, coordination and control purposes.[51]

Personnel controlling in the scientific discussion as well as in practice does not have the same rank as the "classical" forms of controlling (production, finances, investments etc.). It is practically applied for an efficiency control and for the support of decision making in personnel management: i.e. cost control, analysis of code numbers and indicators, impact analysis of personnel management measures.

Data for such code number systems are based on
- structural code numbers (sex, age, education etc.);
- productivity of work (overall and achievement-specific output/input analyses);
- personnel requirements (cost-related analysis of personnel placement);
- staff behaviour (fluctuation, absenteeism, job satisfaction, etc.).

It becomes increasingly obvious that quantifiable goals and numbers are only one aspect of the success of personnel management. Therefore, qualitative goals and tasks, apart from merely quantitative code numbers, are increasingly included. In the scientific discussion this development is reflected by an extension of personnel controlling from merely operative to strategic tasks and from quantitative to qualitative aspects.

---

50 Expert literature on this subject has only been available within the last ten years. The use of such instruments also strongly depends on the size of the enterprise: 60 percent of enterprises with more than 10,000 employees have an organisational post for personnel controlling (cf. F. Metz, A. Betzer: Entwicklungsstand und Verbreitung von Personal-Controlling, research project at the University of Karlsruhe, 1993).
51 There is no clear definition of personnel controlling. The ambiguity in the concept often leads to substitute definitions such as "human resources management, personnel planning, personnel information." Cf. R. Wunderer: Personalarbeit in einer immer noch jungen, entwicklungsbedürftigen Disziplin, in: Personalführung. no. 8/1990, p. 512.

Personnel reduction

Personnel reduction is often regarded as the simplest, most effective and fastest way to reduce costs. The consequences for the remaining municipal staff are increased workloads, new tasks and in this context deficiencies in qualification and increased demands on their flexibility. Thus, personnel reduction requires an increase of qualification of the remaining staff. Efficient personnel management in crises must therefore not concentrate exclusively on personnel reduction. A precondition to overcome the crisis is rather a farsighted, strategically developed long-term application of all instruments of personnel management in order to promote the flexibility, qualification and motivation of the employees. With this method personnel costs will be reduced in the long run.

Instruments of human resources management

Strategic personnel management, apart from quantitative procedures, also increasingly includes qualitative measures. The new requirements apply to executives as well as to their staff. Sought are qualified employees in flexible structures as well as forms of leadership which are orientated towards staff and procedures. Qualitative indicators become ever more crucial in personnel management and especially in personnel development: efficient leadership behaviour, Cooperation in the team, achievement through synergies, transparent forms of information and communication, responsibility and participation in decisions, identification and motivation, future-orientated qualification (training and further education).

The instruments and measures for personnel management and personnel development can be divided into person-orientated and organisational/ structural fields of action, which are described briefly in the following.

Fields of action of person-orientated measures

Person-orientated measures aim at individual and group *attitudes and behaviour*. In this context special attention or a superior function is given to the qualification for management tasks and the *improvement of leadership behaviour*. Furthermore, group- and team-orientated approaches, as well as psychologically orientated instruments for individual self-knowledge and self-experience play an important role.

Fields of action of organisational/structural measures

Apart from the person-orientated measures concerning attitudes and behaviour, there are the following instruments for the improvement of structural and organisational working procedures:
- analysis of functions and working procedures
- achievement incentive and promotion schemes
- diagnosis instruments
- staff assessment and staff selection
- orientation and control instruments
- quality and organisation improvements
- development of mission statements.

Supplement: achievement incentives/achievement-related pay

The discussion about achievement-related pay plays an important role in the effort to improve the efficiency of public administration. Monetary and non-monetary incentive schemes are to be differentiated.

Monetary incentives currently meet the limits of legal provisions (salary and collective agreement regulations).[52] Furthermore, numerous methodical questions have to be answered if they are really to lead to a lasting improvement of achievements.

Non-monetary incentives are also significant for municipal staff.[53] Apart from monetary incentives, they can be genuine incentives for rendering human resources more efficient.

---

52 see also Müller 1995, p. 16.
53 cf. e.g. Banner, p. 11.

2. Human Resources Management In Municipalities

2.1 From Personnel Increase to Personnel Reduction in the Context of the Budgetary Crisis and the Modernisation of Administration

For a long time personnel management and personnel development in public administration were not important subjects. In comparison to the private sector, the staff was merely "administrated." Personnel development was equated with an offer of various training courses preparing or accompanying an employee's career, which was ideally supposed to always point uphill.[54]

A long-term, farsighted personnel demand planning was not considered a priority. Until the end of the eighties/beginning of the nineties it was normal to recruit new staff if there were new or changing tasks.[55] The main problem of the municipalities was not personnel reduction but the recruitment of suitable junior and senior staff from training schemes and the labour market.

Since 1992, however, the number of employees in public administration has been decreasing for the first time since the founding of the Federal Republic of Germany. Thus, a change in thinking has been initiated: also in public administration there was a demand for the introduction of *modern methods of personnel management* which correspond to the altered framework conditions.

The "financial crisis"[56] in the public sector, which "accelerated modernisation,"[57] is named explicitly by the majority of municipalities as the

---

54 To this ideal corresponds the division of advanced training into introduction, assimilation and promotion courses which describe the "phases of the professional life" or the "ideal case" of the career of a civil servant, in which "he is trained, has to prove himself and is promoted" (Meixner 1984, p. 46 f.).
55 cf. Keller 1993, p. 37.
56 In a survey carried out by the Deutsche Städtetag (Association of German Cities) in February 1995 almost all (93 percent) the cities questioned named the "financial crisis" or the "necessity to consolidate the budget" as one of the "main reasons for modernisation and restructuring" (Deutscher Städtetag 1995).
57 In 1992 52 percent of the municipalities questioned (in the old german federal states) declared that modernisation measures had been started or planned; in 1994/95 in 90 percent of the cities questioned, in the old german federal states even in 94 percent, a restructuring was taking place or was planned for the very near future (sources: Kühnlein/Wohlfahrt 1995 and Deutscher Städtetag 1995).

initiating and determining impetus of the administrative reforms started at the same time.

Under the pressure to reduce the personnel costs in order to relieve municipal budgets, it is no longer a priority to recruit dedicated and qualified staff for the administration but to *motivate and "foster" the currently existing municipal staff*. The strategies of personnel management and personnel development have to link two postulates: the minimisation of personnel costs and at the same time the maximisation of the training and achievement potential of the (remaining) staff. [58]

The international research has proved that all cities of the network reduced their staff numbers, some of them drastically, in the last five to ten years. Whilst restructuring their organisation, all cities seem to have applied the instruments of "natural fluctuation," which implied increased workloads. Further measures, which were more drastic, were the privatisation of many sectors (Tilburg) and/or the change to other legal forms, e.g. to corporations (Christchurch).

2.2 Differences in the Framework Conditions for Personnel Management between the Public and the Private Sector

In comparison to the private sector the political and legal framework conditions play a more important role for personnel policy in public administration; this refers to the political provisions for the activities of the municipalities as well as to public service law and pay regulations.

1. The personnel policy in public administration has to adhere to many legal provisions such as formal entry qualifications for the different categories and regulations for promotion as well as dismissal (employees with tenure). The scope of action for municipal personnel policy is therefore comparatively narrow.

   These legal framework conditions have recently been criticised for too strongly limiting a flexible and mobile personnel placement, which stands in contrast to the requirements of modern personnel policy.

---

58 cf. Kühnlein/Wohlfahrt 1994.

The efforts currently being made in politics to reform public service law are making only very slow progress.
2. Personnel development in public administration is not only confronted with certain legal and political limitations as far as the organisation and the planning of personnel demand and completion of tasks are concerned, but it also has a special social and political responsibility to the public ("orientation towards public interest"), on the municipal level especially to the citizens. This also touches upon the relations to its own staff.

The public sector as an employer, due to its political self-image, has taken over certain *"model functions,"* from which it follows that a political dimension of the municipalities properly speaking has to be taken into consideration internally as well as externally. This distinguishes it fundamentally from private enterprises.

2.3 Personnel Development Concepts and Single Measures Integrating the Results of the International Research

Both the administration executive and the staff representatives demand the elaboration of comprehensive, "integral" *personnel development concepts*. Therefore, it can be assumed that in many municipalities, especially in the larger cities, plans for the development of a modern personnel management within the Neue Steuerungsmodell or other measures for the restructuring of administration do exist. So far, however, only a few municipalities have developed concepts which are ready for application.

In most municipalities there are *decisions or agreements on comprehensive personnel development concepts* or corresponding *concept drafts*. However, only individual elements have been practically applied or are in a test phase. These elements have not been networked yet and varying emphasis is put on their practical importance in the individual municipalities, since each municipality tries to *find its own suitable way* under its own specific framework conditions.[59]

---

59 KGSt 1995, p. 46.

In most municipalities the budgetary situation also requires "the courage to make decisions and set priorities when scant resources have to be used efficiently."[60] The necessity mentioned here to set priorities in personnel development and to attach different weight to them refers to the target groups on the one hand and on the other hand to the selection of instruments which are to be primarily used.

In view of the current trend the focus is therefore on a selection of *personnel development instruments* which are primarily discussed in the municipalities or are already being used.

The international research demonstrates that the majority of network cities are currently developing an overall concept for personnel management. There are differences as to whether the instruments are to be tested and introduced step-by-step, based on a jointly developed general philosophy, or whether the instruments already in existence for several years are to be more strongly networked in the future.

New participation schemes

Of particular importance in the context of the current restructuring measures are *participation schemes* which aim mainly at reducing the fears and prejudices among the employees which have arisen in connection with the restructuring measures and which are generally regarded as one of the most serious impediments for the success of the initiated changes.[61] Besides they are hoped to ensure that the experience potential of the local staff is taken into consideration and integrated as much as possible into the restructuring process of administration.

The development of new participation schemes as a crucial measure of personnel development has therefore to be seen as a consequence of recognising that the application of measures for administrative reform or for the consolidation of the budget in the municipalities cannot be realised without the active and responsible participation of the employees.

---

60 Lappé 1994, p. 255.
61 cf. Deutscher Städtetag 1995.

This is clearly emphasised in most municipalities.[62]

This also applies to the same extent to the network cities. All of them emphasise that they depend more strongly than ever before on the active participation of those concerned in the development or further development of instruments.

For this purpose the following different instruments are tested in the municipalities both on the national and the international level:
– carrying out of staff surveys,
– new forms of work in teams and groups, and
– quality or staff circles.

As examples of formally regulated participation schemes the *Herne participation scheme*[63] and the *participation concept of the City of Duisburg*[64], developed within the modernisation of administration, are to be mentioned.

In both cities the measures for the restructuring of administration are continuously accompanied by project and work groups. Part of the philosophy of change is that it is not sufficient to merely call upon the staff to participate, but that participation has to be understood as a process which has to be supported and secured continuously.[65]

Achievement incentive schemes

New procedures of growing importance are agreements on *monetary and non-monetary achievement incentive schemes*. They are to contribute to staff motivation. In some municipalities pilot projects have been started which so far have mainly concentrated on monetary incentives.

These are granted for example in the form of attendance bonuses, "ex-

---

[62] "The employees are to be involved in the process because they are to support and contribute essentially to a lasting modernisation process and its results. It is particularly important that not just one group of persons is considered to be responsible for the modernisation of administration (...) but that all employees, executives and staff, are to jointly support the process." (Stadt Bielefeld, 1995: Personalentwicklungskonzept, Draft p. 11).
[63] City of Herne, 1994: "Leitvorstellungen zur Strukturreform der Stadtverwaltung Herne."
[64] Duisburg: "Duisburg 2000, Stadt auf Reformkurs: Herausforderung Verwaltungsmodernisierung, Auftaktbericht."
[65] Most of the employment contracts and Cooperation contracts or framework agreements which have been concluded during the recent years regarding the subject of "modernisation of administration" in general put great emphasis on the issue of staff participation.

tra pay for attendance," additional proficiency pays if a post is temporarily vacant, bonuses if the employee deals with more than a prescribed number of cases, in the form of efficiency bonuses for an increased recovery of money or as a bonus for increasing competitiveness.[66]

Significant for future developments is an employment contract or collective agreement on the "remuneration of special achievements specified in *achievement contracts* in the City of Dortmund." An essential characteristic of this agreement, which was developed on the basis of a two-year pilot project in the social services department,[67] is the form in which the "normal achievement" and the increased achievement of employees are defined.

It is planned to conclude an "achievement contract" on a voluntary basis between employees and the employer/the head of department.[68] A commission still to be established which is to be composed of an equal number of representatives of each party is to ensure transparency and – at least in its approach – an objective determination of the achievements specified in the contract.

Non-monetary achievement incentives, however, have to date hardly been tested. Only in Bochum is there a framework agreement in which it is planned to develop achievement incentives together with the staff in connection with the establishment of a new Citizens' Office.

Some of the network cities have long-term experience with (at least monetary) achievement incentives. Their basis is an accepted and transparent setting of aims agreed between superiors and staff. It seems that the quite positive experiences to date in Phoenix, Braintree and Tilburg are only possible on this basis. The example of Tilburg shows that the form of introduction of such an instrument is of great importance. The programme was started only after a three-year pilot phase, involving the staff representation.

---

66 cf. Reichert and others 1995.
67 cf. Schäfer 1995.
68 "The achievement contract is a voluntary agreement limited to twelve months at the most between employees and the employer/head of department on special achievements and their remuneration." (§ 4 of the collective agreement on "the remuneration of special achievements laid down in achievement contracts in the City of Dortmund," draft).

Flexibility of working hours

In the context of job and staff cutbacks in the municipalities the search for new forms of *flexibility of working hours* becomes ever more important. Different models are being discussed which mainly orientate themselves on the experiments carried out and experiences made in the private sector.

Under discussion are in particular the introduction of new, more flexible part-time models, job sharing, the establishment of flexitime accounts and "models for sabbaticals" (e.g. leaves of several months in set intervals within a certain employment period). Such measures, which have been started in only a few municipalities, have been tested in practice only very warily so far. The same is true for the facilitation of *part time work on the executive level* which is to improve among others the access of women to executive posts. One can expect, however, that in the future more part time jobs will be offered on the whole because – on the basis of a new bill for a reform of public service law – it will become easier for civil servants to work part time.[69]

For some of the network cities flexibility of working hours is a crucial subject in personnel management. They regard it as an important means to increase motivation and therefore productivity among their staff. In future they aim at taking the individual needs of the staff more into consideration as well as extending the services for the citizens. Tilburg, for example, offers "normal" opening hours until 6.00 p.m. (7.00 p.m. on Thursdays) and is assessing whether services are wished for and possible on Saturdays.

Staff talks/new assessment procedures

Due to the general dissatisfaction with the national experiences of staff assessment, which is to be carried out in certain intervals for civil servants as "regular assessment" and which – due to the preset, general criteria and

---

69 This has so far only been possible as an exception. For this reason the vast majority of part time jobs are to be found among employees (female employees in the clerical category) (cf. corresponding details in the Statistische Jahrbuch des Statistischen Bundesamtes [Statistical Year Book of the Federal Statistics Office]).

the tendency towards too favourable assessing – is criticised for being not very explicit, many municipalities are looking for new, more individual assessment procedures. Such assessment procedures are measures of personnel development in as far as they criticise the labour and personnel law, which divide the staff into the three groups of civil servants, employees and workers, whereby a regular assessment is prescribed for civil servants but not for the other groups. These provisions – often explicitly regarded as a limitation – are to be avoided with the development of new assessment instruments.

"Structured talks between staff and superiors" or "talks for staff promotion," in which the work to be carried out, the working situation, individual career plans and personal and professional wishes and expectations are discussed and binding aims are agreed upon, are regarded as an essential part of systematic personnel development in a growing number of municipalities.

There is a very controversial discussion in the national municipalities if and in how far staff talks can also be used as an instrument for assessment or whether to adhere explicitly to the current assessment regulations as the legal provisions.[70] It is, however, indisputable that the staff talks, as a basis for concrete agreements on aims between the staff and the superiors, are considered as binding to a high degree and therefore have an impact on the assessments.

Some of the network cities have already had experience with the practical realisation of staff talks. In all municipalities regular institutionalised talks between superiors and staff take place, which have to be seen in the context of achievement assessment. A "cycle of setting aims and assessing the results" exists in all cities. In Tilburg this character of the talks is most clear. In the first talk the expectations of both parties concerning the professional achievements are discussed, the second concentrates on the joint reflection and the assessment of individual achievements by the superior.

In Haemeenlina and Braintree the staff also assess their superiors. The results are presented to the superiors in feedback workshops.

---

70 H. Lühr, Freie Hansestadt Bremen. Senatskommission für das Personalwesen. Praxisbericht: Personal als wichtigste Ressource der Verwaltung – Ansatzpunkte für eine strategische Personalentwicklung in der Freien Hansestadt Bremen. October 1995.

Tilburg demonstrates a special case. All divisions are assessed regularly by external experts. They assess
– how high the qualification of all employees is on the whole,
– how good the achievements of a group are, and
– which new tasks have to be tackled.

As a result of the external assessment a list with suggestions for improvement is presented. Experiences with this kind of assessment are described as positive. As all employees are assessed in the same way it is not considered to be discriminating.

Analyses of staff potential

With the systemising of staff talks and the reform of achievement assessment there is also a growing demand for *analyses of staff potential*. These serve not only to advise and promote promising staff but also for the recruitment planning for junior executives.

There are as yet, however, only first drafts for concepts.

Selection procedures for executives

Finally, *selection procedures* in public administration are of importance for the future, on the executive level as well as for the training of qualified junior staff. In order to make possible a more targeted selection of suitable executives a procedure is being sought which takes into account technical, leadership and social skills as selection criteria.

With this background several national municipalities are developing "block programmes" – taking as an example concepts from industry – which aim at preparing potential executives step-by-step for their future tasks in two to maximum four-year cycles and at providing the administration management with better arguments as to who is actually most suitable for which task.

Such block programmes include, for example in Duisburg, a three-year series of seminars on "administration management" and "the practice of leadership."

These programmes are complemented in some municipalities by a range of measures for the improvement of leadership skills.

All these measures have the common theme that the participation in these advanced training series should be *compulsory* for future executives.

This does not apply to all network cities. Apart from Christchurch, in all other cities the participation in advanced training courses for executives is not compulsory for internal promotion. However, as Christchurch aims to include *all* executives, there is no need to exclude someone from internal promotion if he does not participate. The subjects offered in the courses range from specific knowledge such as financial management and organisation management (as in Quebec) to a change of the individual leadership behaviour (as in Christchurch).

The question of how to optimise the selection procedures is still a widely unsolved problem in most of the municipalities. In this context the model of "group selection procedures" which was developed in Duisburg – following the assessment center procedure – has to be mentioned.[71] In most of the other municipalities the group selection procedure is not applied as a regular selection procedure because it is considered to be too work, time and costintensive.

There are different procedures for the appointment of executives in the network cities. The majority of them declared that they do not use uniform procedures, except for top political managers, because the departments appoint their executives independently. What the cities have in common are the methods. Almost all of them use prepared interviews. Psychological tests and case scenarios are used very rarely (Tilburg, Quebec, Christchurch). In Braintree, similar to Duisburg, a modified assessment center is used.

Phoenix and Tilburg are unique in the group compositions of persons who take part in the procedure. In Tilburg a team of employees participates "which represents the persons directly concerned." In Phoenix a Citizens' Committee is consulted when politically high-ranking posts are to be filled. The final decision, however, lies with the City Manager.

---

71 For more details see section 3.2.3 of this report.

In-house job markets

The establishment of *in-house job markets/job centres*, which are to contribute to more transparency as to which posts are vacant in the municipality and are hoped to make a long-term preparation for the filling of these posts possible, improve the in-house selection and appointment procedures. This procedure gains importance, especially since the impression exists that there are more and more job cutbacks and that the recruitment of external applicants has been stopped. Two forms of "in-house job markets" are to be differentiated: on the one hand they merely provide more transparent information about vacant posts or posts becoming vacant which do not have to be advertised externally, on the other they can also have the function of advising staff concerned by job cutbacks and to qualify them further for future tasks. Only the second form can be regarded as an instrument of personnel development. In this context farsighted qualifying strategies (retraining), which complement the current programme of advanced training, become increasingly important.

Change in the Understanding of Advanced Training

All instruments of personnel development which are applied in the context of the restructuring of municipalities require appropriate qualification measures which in general only make their implementation and practical use possible. Due to the change from personnel administration to personnel management the (self-)image of advanced training in municipalities has fundamentally changed. This is true for the scope and contents of the training courses offered as well as for their function as an essential part of personnel development and "modernising instrument" which continuously accompanies the administrative reform.[72]

In the following some aspects of the change illustrating the scope of the necessary rethinking process are described:
– New contents of advanced training:
  The spectrum of the traditional offers of advanced training is comple-

---

[72] cf. Kühnlein 1996.

mented by business studies, technology supported information processing, seminars regarding behaviour and information on all aspects of modernisation of administration.
– New forms of advanced training:
The "classical" forms of advanced training mainly organised as seminars are complemented by more flexible, more open forms of learning ("training on the job"), which accompany many of the personnel development measures. On the whole a tendency can be noted towards a departure from centrally organised seminars towards advanced training close to the workplace and accompanying projects, which is controlled decentrally.
– New organisation of advanced training due to decentralised personnel management:
With the new understanding of advanced training as a service function for all units of administration the organisation of advanced training is also changing. If advanced training is understood as a service for departments instead of having a general function, certain responsibilities (such as decisions about the distribution of financial means and the participation in training courses) are given over to the decentralised units.
As an instrument of personnel development professional advanced training is changing in its form and organisation. Since it has the task not only to accompany but to influence *actively and with foresight* the organisational and person-related changes in the restructuring of administration, there is a general change of perspective from a "demand-orientated" to a "needs and future-orientated" advanced training.

3. Practical Example: Strategic Personnel Management (Human Resources Management) in the Municipality of Duisburg

3.1 Basic Understanding

Since the beginning of the eighties, the installment of a strategic personnel management has been promoted in the Municipality of Duisburg. This development is an essential part of a comprehensive *management of change* with which administration and politics encounter the diverse financial and social problems of a far-reaching structural crisis.

In accordance with the basic understanding of this strategy to solve problems and to take countermeasures, the municipality sees itself as a modern public service company which has externally a Cooperative relation to citizens, business life, science and society and which is internally led by an up-to-date and goal-orientated management.

Very early on, the staff of the municipality have already been the focus of the introduced processes of change. The personnel are both creator of changes and those affected by them, thus they represent the potential of success for any public service company. Only if they possess the qualifications and motivation which are demanded, if they participate actively in the necessary reorganisation processes, can the chosen course be successfully continued.

Within the general strategy to tackle the problems resulting from the structural change, the efforts which help to develop a strategic personnel management play an important role – also in times when resources become scarce. The various measures which were introduced for this purpose as well as their linking to a general system will be explained in detail within the following paragraphs.

The set of measures aims especially at
- developing a common basic understanding about the municipality's tasks and objectives,
- securing the fulfillment of tasks according to standardised action principles,
- raising the qualification level of the competence in the technical and social field with a view to the corporate objectives, and
- improving the information and motivation through active participation.

3.2 Personnel Development

3.2.1 Strategic Planning

The municipality of Duisburg possessed favourable conditions for the introduction of first elements of a strategic personnel management. Different single measures within the personnel development and the organisation development had already created an awareness of the necessity of a modern goal-orientated personnel management among many members of staff and the employees' representation.

On this basis, the establishment of a strategic planning started after extended and intense discussions with the administration management, the employees' representation and politicians on the occasion of the introduction of binding principles for the promotion and selection of executives.

The discussion of these principles showed clearly that strategic personnel management remains incomplete if the measures are solely restricted to the executive level. New forms of participation and qualification were sought in order to develop also the learning and development potential of employees at the grass roots level. This led inter alia to the following measures:
- introduction of *quality circles* on a trial basis in some chosen departments;
- questioning of all staff in a survey in order to develop an action catalogue for strategic personnel planning and leadership behaviour.

Dramatic changes in the financial framework conditions from 1993 onwards, which forced trenchant economy measures, caused an adjustment of the strategic personnel planning to this crisis situation. The main emphasis of current and future investments is thus placed on programmes and projects which serve to qualify and retrain staff affected by economy measures.

Another main focus will be the extension of training and advanced training which are both – as central core of personnel development – enriched with decentralised responsibility for resources under the principles of the modernisation of administration.

The *concept of modernisation* of the municipality of Duisburg[73] aims at
- an in-house improvement of the coordination ability, and
- an external improvement of the quality of services, the political ability to make decisions and competitiveness of the municipality.

A coordination and development project was founded as an independent organisation unit to coordinate the measures. It paves the way for the strategic reform decisions made by the administration management.

The basis of these decisions are development processes established in eight pilot areas in which the affected staff have the greatest possible participation. The basis for this are previous developments of the strategic planning and the instrument of staff participation is further developed.

The engagement of management consultants (according to a "payback"-system) and the conclusion of corresponding consultative contracts could be waived.

3.2.2 Instruments of Personnel Development

According to the basic understanding of a strategic personnel management in the municipality of Duisburg, a systematic personnel development has to start at the same time as the selection of personnel and the training.

On this basis, the personnel development programme "Duisburg 2000" describes eleven innovative approaches which fit together like building blocks.

These blocks comprise the following items:

Staff selection in the field of training

A written and oral selection procedure which has been developed in Co-operation with scientists at the University of Duisburg is an instrument of trainee selection. It takes into consideration the necessary professional key qualifications regarding adaptability to changes.

73 Duisburg: Duisburg 2000.

Qualification training

The main focus of the training is to convey key qualifications in the field of social/communicative competence, knowledge of methods/techniques for problem-solving as well as the implementation of certain techniques. For in-house seminars, a special training centre is at the trainees' disposal.

Practical training

The practical training/introduction of new staff to their work is considered as a crucial executive task for superiors. Important instruments are here introductory seminars, a handbook for new staff members and plans for practical training.

Advanced training

The offers for advanced training on an in-house and external basis correspond strictly to the requirements of the respective standards fixed by the corporate objectives. In accordance with the ideal of a public service company orientated towards the citizens, the advanced training conveys technical and interdisciplinary competence, professional key qualifications and qualifications in the field of technology-supported information processing and business administration.

Quality circle/staff circle

Within the framework of the introductory period different (also interdisciplinary) circles have been founded. In their work and during implementation of the results, they are supported through the central personnel development.
    At the moment, the work in the staff circles is intensively and systematically carried out in a modified form within the framework of measures for a modernisation of the administration. In eight pilot sections, members

of staff participate via new forms of teamwork decisively and intensively in the shaping of the processes of change.

Advanced training for executives

The programme of personnel development for executives will be explained in detail in section 3.2.3.

Procedure of personnel selection

The main focus of further development of modern methods of personnel selection is the appointment of posts on the basis of group selection procedures (especially at the executive level) with the support of observers who have been trained specifically for this purpose (see section 3.2.3).

Strategic administration management

Seminars on concepts and strategy are instruments of the strategic administration management. These are led by individual organisation units and departments, and fundamental problems at work are discussed and agreements on certain objectives are made. The results will influence the work of administration management; administration principles and fundamental decisions on the personnel policy are worked out in the framework of annual meetings of the Councillors' conference.

Approaches for the development of an "administration culture"

Efforts are continuously being made to improve the internal and external image of the municipality through different approaches. Regular surveys of the citizens and the staff help to give information on goal-orientated measures. Meanwhile, a new "Corporate Design" has been developed for the public relations department. Internally, the staff newspaper published every other month lends extra impetus to optimise the "administration culture."

All these approaches are completed through intensive measures for the promotion of women, the agreement on an exchange of trainees between administration and private enterprises, current ideas on a new assessment procedure and management of ideas (suggestion scheme).

Every suggestion for reform is developed in a dialogue between all persons involved so as to guarantee acceptance, transparency and the highest quality possible.

3.2.3 Main Focus of Operative Personnel Management

Advanced training for executives

For the municipality of Duisburg, the personnel development programme for executives is a central element of the strategic personnel management.

The participation in the advanced training for executives is announced well in advance before its commencement. It takes three years and is designed for executives of all occupational groups. It is a compulsory precondition for the filling of executive posts.

The executives have three qualitatively equal series for advanced training:
- the series "Administration Management" which paves the way for positions like head of department/institute and head of division (senior management);
- the series "leadership practice" which prepares the participants for posts such as head of subject divisions and team leader (middle management);
- the series "leadership practice for team leaders in day nurseries."

All three series have the following goals in common:
- the imparting of social and executive competence;
- the broadening of special and interdisciplinary key qualifications;
- the updating of cross section knowledge;
- the increase of motivation through participation on fundamental questions;
- the integration of staff members as agents for innovative processes.

Importance is attached in the seminars to large proportions of practical training and to the assumption of transfer and project tasks which are drawn from real life experience in administration.

The advanced training for executives is concluded with an educational efficiency review and an individual analysis of the participants' strong and weak points. A certificate of successful participation is issued.

Procedure of group selection for executives

In the framework of the personnel development programme for executives, a special selection procedure for the appointment of executive posts by the administration management is introduced. This is in accordance with agreed political guidelines and offered parallel to the compulsory advanced training schemes for executives.

Future vacant executive posts within the senior management are, in principle, *advertised on an in-house basis*. Without exception, only those members of staff who have participated or are participating in the advanced training schemes for executives are entitled to apply for a post.

The basis of the job advertisement and of the further selection procedure is a differentiated *requirements profile* which takes into consideration the specialised qualification features and also the definite executive tasks of the advertised post.

For every selection procedure, a *group of observers* has to be appointed in accordance with the administration management and the employees' representation. It is a prerequisite that this group has beforehand taken part in a special *observers training course*.

The applicants who meet the requirements of the advertisement are invited to a *group selection discussion*. Tasks from practical experience with the focus on executive and social competence are set. They have to be solved individually or in a team followed by a discussion in the applicant group. The group selection procedure is led by a neutral presenter. The observers do not take part in the discussion, but only concentrate on their task of observing.

The *appointment decision* is based on the results of the group discussion and on comprehensible observations under consideration of the previous achievements. The decision is made on the principle of consensus. A detailed *feedback* on the results of the group discussion is offered to all applicants.

3.2.4 Current Developments

An essential focus of training and development in connection with the measures introduced to modernise administration is *further education in the field of business administration* for staff working at a professional and executive level. Thus the competence in business administration which is necessary for the Neue Steuerungsmodell can be built up.

A pilot project in the bridge construction section of the civil engineering department is a new *approach for the consideration of permanent achievement incentives within the system of remuneration*. A model has been developed for this section which is founded on proofs of achievement and economic efficiency for individual productivity bonuses. The basis for them is a comparison to offers from engineers of the private sector as to costs and productivity. The first result after experience of more than one year is that with the same number of personnel, the number of accomplished projects has distinctly increased. Further suggestions for achievement incentive schemes are being developed at the moment by the participating groups of employees who are working in the pilot sectors aiming at a modernisation of administration.

The *coordination of economic reorganisation processes* and the permanent efforts of council and administration to create a solid basis for the municipal budget are challenges of prime importance for the management of change in the municipality of Duisburg during periods of structural change. In order to achieve this goal, 1,000 jobs altogether have to be cut in the financial years 1994–2000, in the framework of a *budget consolidation concept* on which the municipality decides through a *task inspection procedure* (cutbacks or change of tasks).

In view of the fact that such a reduction in the number of personnel cannot be achieved only through natural fluctuation, additional measures in personnel policy have become necessary (especially premature retirement schemes, sabbatical leave schemes, part time work, change of jobs accompanied by retraining schemes).

In order to maintain the staff of the municipality as a "potential for success," the objective of the strategic personnel management was to avoid feelings such as a lack of prospects and fear of one's existence and to present the measures for the necessary personnel cutbacks in a way that, on the one hand, an effective budget consolidation can be reached, and that, on the other hand, the staff do not lose their motivation and qualification.

The following essential regulations were stated:
- renunciation of dismissals for purely operational reasons;
- employment of trainees, which corresponds to the municipality's demand and their further transfer;
- financing of qualification programmes to retrain those members of staff affected by economy measures (including their environment).

A special project was founded for the implementation of the qualification/ retraining programmes and a qualification centre was established in order to implement the training measures. The programme comprises opportunities for professional orientation, including the possibility of sitting in on classes, and specific qualification measures for chosen professions (for example jobs in administration, education or nursery).

On the whole, the success of the measures introduced for job cutbacks depends on the participation of the concerned departments. This is why they are accompanied and controlled by *financial instruments*. In this connection *budgets for personnel costs* were introduced as a financial framework. They are autonomously managed by the respective departments. At the same time, this is a first step to the planned conglomeration of the responsibilities for tasks and for resources.

In the framework of the process of *decentralisation of personnel responsibility*, the following fundamental questions are currently dealt with and decided on within a short period of time in the course of the modernisation activities:
- preparation of the departments so that they assume their subject-specific share of personnel development;
- budgeting of a part of the means for personnel development – which, until now, have been centrally administrated;
- compulsory fixing of quality standards for personnel management which must be met by the departments in future.

Now, it becomes clear that activities in the field of personnel development and organisation development in connection with the modernisation of administration can no longer be seen separately from the implementation of the processes of change. They are the main instruments used to shape these activities and a prerequisite for a long-lasting quality management.

4. Success Factors of an Efficient Human Resources Management within Changed Framework Conditions

The success factors of an efficient human resources management have to be orientated towards four relevant development trends which will determine municipal action in administration in the future:
– increasing orientation towards competition (inter-municipal comparison in achievements, privatisation pressure),
– elevated quality standards and enforced quality management,
– increasing orientation towards the citizens or customers, and
– stronger orientation towards achievements.

4.1 Networking

The *networking of personnel development measures* for an integrated general concept is not only a desirable objective but also an essential element of a strategically orientated personnel policy. At the same time one can assume that, up until now, only in exceptional cases could such a general perspective be developed. However, in many cases a widening of the perspective is indispensable for a successful implementation of the intended measures in order to avoid countereffects through isolated measures. This applies above all to the specific linking of measures for personnel development with appropriate qualification offers. Advanced training which corresponds to the needs and is future-orientated can only be attained if it is integrated into the personnel management.

4.2 Long-Term Political Perspectives

On the basis of the limitation to one or several instruments, which is mostly regarded as necessary, their differentiation and evaluation constitutes an essential practical criterion for success. In our estimation, no general "features" could be detected. However, one deciding factor is surely the desired role of the respective measure for personnel development within the whole process of reorganising municipal administrations. That is to say that the choice of those instruments which first of all seem most important must not only be measured with effects which can be achieved within a short-term period. Rather, it must be orientated towards the objective of *permanent motivation* of staff and also the *increase in quality* of administrative work.

4.3 Prevention of Disadvantaging

In view of the objectives of an administration profile which is increasingly achievement-orientated, the danger that "less effective working" staff (groups) are disadvantaged is very real. If, however, personnel development – in the true meaning of the word – follows the purpose of developing, thus promoting all *members of staff* it would really be counterproductive to restrict personnel development merely to certain target groups which are highly competitive, even if it is normal that the employees of those target groups have priority under strategic aspects and are considered as "promoters."

It is a prerequisite for the success of many personnel development measures that those affected are ready to commit themselves and if necessary to bring forth (dependent upon the situation) increased achievement. However, the individual readiness to accept such new responsibilities is not sufficient. Additionally, the provision of *corresponding prerequisites is necessary*. This involves the guarantee of corresponding day releases for the participation as well as specific promotion of such employees or groups of employees who, for different reasons, do not have equal opportunities of taking part in the participation procedure and in other measures of personnel development.

4.4 Avoiding Demotivation Processes

In the course of a modernisation of personnel management procedures which aim above all at an increase in efficiency, motivation and a just differentiation of achievements and where thus the special emphasis is put on good and committed work, practice proves that in the end there are not only "winners."

For precisely this reason it is most important to avoid the impression that personnel development aims exclusively at having ready reward programmes for especially "well-deserving" members of staff [74] because this would increase the *threatening attitude of blocking* by those who are in this sense "negatively" affected. In view of these aspects, the following features may be indicative of a "successful" personnel management:
- presenting the applied criteria openly;
- a transparency of decisions as extensive as possible;
- a joint search for appropriate workplaces or new tasks;
- agreement on "social contracts" which are valid on an interdisciplinary basis.

4.5 Decentralised Personnel Management

The efforts of decentralising personnel management in municipalities are still in their initial phase.

Conceptionally they are marked by two basic ideas of the Neue Steuerungsmodell: on the one hand there are the expectations of the departments to assume an extensive *general responsibility* which includes responsibility for personnel organisation and financing; and on the other hand there are optimisation ideas for the *general coordination* of an organisation, which amount to transferring all resources from all departments to a central coordination unit and to a central service.

The implementation in practice depends at least on two framework conditions: the size of the municipality and the question of how much executive competence is actually to be decentralised.

In this connection, international experience with personnel management which is already decentralised and national experience in current reorganisation processes correspond visibly. Fields such as "personnel management (selection, transfer, etc.)," "promotions" and "personnel development (especially subject-specific personnel development)" are im-

---

74 cf. accordingly also Lappé 1994.

portant for departments, whereas other sectors will in future either be offered by another "central service" or become part of the "central management" because of their general role for the administration as a whole.

The state of art of decentralised personnel management in the Federal Republic of Germany is marked by the work on the description of these new interfaces and the first transfer of jobs (on a trial basis).

4.6 Standardised Framework Conditions for Public Administration

An important assessment factor for "successful" personnel management is the securing of framework conditions, which are necessary especially for an "atmosphere of reform less characterised by fear." In this connection, special demands can result from an increasing *decentralisation* of personnel management.

The transfer of personnel and financial decisions to smaller units does not only promote the autonomy of the lower levels of hierarchy, it also promotes competition and thus internal competitiveness between the departments. If this is not to contribute to the loss of the special responsibility of public employers ("obligation to provide for the welfare of its employees"), decentralisation must be accompanied by *central provisions of certain guidelines which have to be adhered to* (promotion for women, training and advanced training activities, quota systems for the placement of less effective staff, etc.).

All this is especially important with regard to decreasing employment figures and to the necessity to transfer personnel to other tasks and new workplaces. The functioning of the "in-house job market" definitively depends on the readiness of all departments and divisions to accept such common "rules."

4.7 Subsidiarity of External Consulting

Another success factor lies in the subsidiarity of external consulting. Helping to help themselves, on the job training, transfer of know-how have to come to the fore. The most widespread activation of the in-house staff does not only save costs in the medium and long run and render further qualification nearly independent of external problems, it also in the end increases the flexibility of the qualification transfer.

4.8 Regular Efficiency Reviews

In the course of the processes of change, fixed points for efficiency review (for example regular, comparable surveys amongst the staff) have to be introduced. Regular feedback on leadership behaviour, job satisfaction, organisation development, identification with the citizen, citizen satisfaction, quality of the services and the administration's public image should be garnered from the respective groups (employees, superiors, other organisation units, external consultants, citizens).

4.9 Orientation towards the Customers and Citizens

Measures serving the improvement of personnel management and the modernisation of administrations as a whole must not only have in-house effects.

The citizens are the most important criterion of efficiency assessment. The improvement of the organisational structure and the level of job satisfaction, the development of "products" and services for specific groups of citizens as well as the implementation of comprehensive measures for personnel development need to be compared with the resulting improvements for the citizens. Not only are the perception and assumption of the citizens' needs and the services or the improvements in quality a guarantor for a positive public image; for their own achievements, municipalities should also pursue more parallel "marketing" measures, that is to say, public relation activities. But, in view of their current financial crisis, municipalities will probably not be able to make greater investments in this direction. Despite all this, all the available means could be used more effectively for public relation activities which are run in accordance to the modernisation process and which could serve to improve the bad image.

Human resources management in public administration is not an end in itself but a means to an end for an improved orientation towards the customers, job satisfaction and increase in efficiency.

Literature

Antoni, Manfred, 1988: Personalmanagement. In: Gablers Wirtschaftslexikon, pp. 853–856.

Banner, Gerhard, 1994: Neue Trends im kommunalen Management. In: VOP (Verwaltungsführung, Organisation, Personal), Fachzeitschrift für öffentliche Verwaltung, 16.

Bickenbach, Jörg, 1993: Personalentwicklung in der Stadtverwaltung Duisburg. In: Gewerkschaft ÖTV (ed.): Personalentwicklung in der öffentlichen Verwaltung. Hanover, pp. 83–107.

Bieberle, Martin, 1995: Organisationsentwicklung im Main-Kinzig-Kreis. Verwaltungsreform aus Arbeitgebersicht. In: Gewerkschaft ÖTV. Kreisverwaltung Hanau (ed.): Beschäftigtenbeteiligung im kommunalen Reformprozeß. [Documentation of a specialists' meeting, June 27–28, 1995 in Maintal.] Cologne, pp. 25–33.

Bundesministerium des Innern (ed.), 1994: Bericht der Bundesregierung über die Fortentwicklung des öffentlichen Dienstrechts – Perspektivbericht. Bonn.

Bundesministerium für Bildung und Wissenschaft (ed.): Berufsbildungsbericht (passim). Bad Honnef.

Cornelißen, Waltraud/von Wrangell, Ute, 1995: Die Verwaltungsstrukturreform aus der Sicht von Frauenbeauftragten. Ergebnisse einer schriftlichen Befragung der Frauenbeauftragten in Bremerhaven im September 1994. In: Zeitschrift für Frauenforschung. Nr. 2/1995, pp. 39–51.

Deutscher Städtetag, 1995: Stellungnahme des Deutschen Städtetages. In: Mitteilungen des Deutschen Städtetages (Mitt DST), July 24, 1995, Nr. 640/95, pp. 342–348.

Dieckmann, Jochen, 1994: Neue Steuerungsmodelle in den Kommunalverwaltungen. [Paper presented on the occasion of a conference series:

"Verwaltung im Wandel – Anforderungen an eine moderne Kommunalverwaltung," organized by Niedersächsischer Städtetag, March 1, 1994, Langenhagen]. Ms. Cologne.

Dulisch, Frank, 1993: Nachwuchsmarketing für den gehobenen nichttechnischen Dienst. In: Verwaltungsrundschau. Nr. 11/1993, pp. 372–377.

Doppler, Klaus/Lauterburg, Christoph, 1995: Change Management – Den Unternehmenswandel gestalten. Frankfurt/Main.

Gablers Wirtschaftslexikon 1988.

Gewerkschaft ÖTV, 1995: Anstöße zur Modernisierung der Öffentlichen Dienste. Stuttgart, August 28, 1995.

Grömig, Erko, 1995: Verwaltungsmodernisierung und kommunale Fortbildung. In: das rathaus. Nr. 9/1995, pp. 428–432.

Klages, Helmut/Hippler, Gabriele, 1991: Mitarbeitermotivation als Modernisierungsperspektive [Results of a reserach project on leadership and work motivation in public administrations]. Gütersloh.

Keller, Berndt, 1993: Arbeitspolitik des öffentlichen Sektors. Baden-Baden.

Kommunale Gemeinschaftsstelle (KGSt), 1994: Dezentrale Personalarbeit – Der Beitrag der Personalwirtschaft zur Modernisierung der Verwaltung – KGSt-Report Nr. 7/1994. Cologne.

Kommunale Gemeinschaftsstelle (KGSt), 1994: Personalentwicklung: Grundlagen für die Konzepterarbeitung. KGSt Report Nr. 13/1994. Cologne.

Kommunale Gemeinschaftsstelle (KGSt), 1995: Personalentwicklung im Neuen Steuerungsmodell. KGSt Draft Report Stand 03.11.1995. Cologne.

Kommunale Gemeinschaftsstelle (KGSt), 1995: Das Neue Steuerungsmodell in kleinen und mittleren Gemeinden. KGSt Report Nr. 8/1995. Cologne.

Kommunale Gemeinschaftsstelle (KGSt), 1992: Das Mitarbeitergespräch. KGSt Report Nr. 13/1992. Cologne.

Kuban, Monika, 1993: Abschied vom Rasenmäher? Neue Strategien der Haushaltskonsolidierung durch Budgetierung. Beispiel Duisburg: Nach Aufgabenstruktur gewichtete Sparvorgaben. In: Zeitschrift für Kommunalfinanzen. Nr. 7/1993, pp. 146–149.

Kühnlein, Gertrud, 1996: Fortbildung als Modernisierungsinstrument? Personalpolitik und Qualifizierungsstrategien in Kommunalverwaltungen. In print, in: Reichard, Christoph/Wollmann, Hellmut (eds.): Kommunalverwaltung im Modernisierungsschub. Basel et al.

Kühnlein, Gertrud/Wohlfahrt, Norbert, 1994: Zwischen Mobilität und Modernisierung: Personalentwicklungs- und Qualifizierungsstrategien in der öffentlichen Verwaltung. Berlin.

Kühnlein, Gertrud/Wohlfahrt, Norbert, 1995: Leitbild lernende Verwaltung? Situation und Perspektiven der Fortbildung in westdeutschen Kommunalverwaltungen. Berlin.

Kühnlein, Gertrud/Schenk, Thomas, 1995: Das Ausbildungsverhalten der öffentlichen Arbeitgeber auf dem Prüfstand. In: Berufsbildung in Wissenschaft und Praxis (BWP). Nr. 3/1995, pp. 9–15.

Lappé, Winfried, nd: Personalentwicklung als strategischer Ansatz – Leitlinien und Zielrichtungen in Zeiten knapper Ressourcen, Workshop 4.

Lappé, Winfried, 1994: Personalentwicklung als strategischer Ansatz – Leitlinien und Zielrichtungen in Zeiten knapper Ressourcen. In: Bertelsmann Foundation (ed.): Carl Bertelsmann-Preis 1993. Demokratie und Effizienz in der Kommunalverwaltung. Band 2. Gütersloh, pp. 249–268.

Lipphardt, Manfred, 1995: Der Countdown für eine neue Personalpolitik ist überfällig. In: Innovative Verwaltung. Nr. 3/1995, pp. 42–43.

Löhr, Ulrike/Schöneich, Michael, 1995: Verwaltungsmodernisierung und notwendige Änderungen des Dienstrechts. In: Verwaltungsrundschau Nr. 6/1995, pp. 188–193.

Löhr, Ulrike, 1995: Qualifikation angesichts neuer Aufgaben – Verwaltungsmodernisierung sowie Aus- und Fortbildung in den Kommunen, In: der städtetag 1/1995, pp. 8–12.

Luczak, Holger/Oberbannscheidt, Frank/Seiwert, Gerald, 1994: Personalmanagement in der Rezession – Handlungsfelder und innovative Strategien. In: Fortschrittliche Betriebsführung und Industrial Engineering. Nr. 4/1994, pp. 148–151.

Lühr, H., Freie Hansestadt Bremen, Senatskommission für das Personalwesen: Praxisbericht: Personal als wichtigste Ressource der Verwaltung – Ansatzpunkte für eine strategische Personalentwicklung in der Freien Hansestadt Bremen. October 1995.

Meixner, Hanns-Eberhard, 1984: Aus- und Fortbildung in der öffentlichen Verwaltung. Konzeptionen, Verfahren und Instrumente des Mitarbeitertrainings. Cologne et al.

Metz, F./Betzer, A., 1993: Entwicklungsstand und Verbreitung von Personal-Controlling [Research project of Karlsruhe University].

Morgenstern, Vera, 1992: Frauenförderung im öffentlichen Dienst. In: Gewerkschaftliche Bildungspolitik. Nr. 5/1992, pp. 114–117.

Müller, Udo, 1995: Controlling als Steuerungsinstrument der öffentlichen Verwaltung. In: Aus Politik und Zeitgeschichte [Supplement of: Das Parlament. B5/95, pp. 11–19.]

Reichert, Jürgen/Stöbe, Sybille/Wohlfahrt, Norbert, 1995: Leistungsanreizsysteme im öffentlichen Dienst. Stand und Perspektiven der Einführung von Motivations- und Leistungsanreizen in der Kommunalverwaltung. HBS (ed.): Graue Reihe Nr. 92.

Rürup, Bert, 1995: Controlling als Instrument effizienzsteigernder Verwaltungsreform. In: Aus Politik und Zeitgeschichte. [Supplement of: Das Parlament. B5/95, pp. 3–10.]

Schäfer, Wolfgang, 1995: Zur Notwendigkeit der Einführung von Leistungsanreizen im Sozialdezernat – Einstieg und Erfahrungen in Dortmund –. In: NDV Nr. 9/1995, pp. 378–381.

Stadt Bielefeld, 1995: Personalentwicklungskonzept [Entwurf].

Stadt Duisburg (ed.): Duisburg 2000, Perspektiven der Stadtverwaltung – Personalentwicklung. No date, pp. 8 sqq.

Stadt Duisburg (ed.): Duisburg 2000, Stadt auf Reformkurs, Herausforderung Verwaltungsmodernisierung – Auftaktbericht. No date.

Stadt Herne, 1994: Leitvorstellungen zur Strukturrefrom der Stadtverwaltung Herne.

Statistisches Bundesamt: Statistisches Jahrbuch [several volumes]. Wiesbaden.

Sternecker, Petra/Wollsching-Strobel, Peter, 1995: Anforderungen an eine latente Personalentwicklung: Was kommt nach den Hierarchien? In: Gablers Magazin Nr. 5.

Struwe, Jochen, 1995: Lean Administration und Verwaltungscontrolling – Das Instrumentarium. In: Aus Politik und Zeitgeschichte [Supplement of: Das Parlament. B5/95, pp. 20–32.]

Tarifvertrag über die "Vergütung besonderer Leistungen im Rahmen von Leistungskontrakten bei der Stadtverwaltung Dortmund." Draft.

Thom, Norbert/Zaugg, Robert, 1994: Personalmarketing – auch in rezessiven Zeiten? In: Management-Zeitschrift IO. Nr. 4/1994, pp. 72–76.

Wunderer, R., 1990: Personalarbeit in einer immer noch jungen, entwicklungsbedürftigen Disziplin. In: Personalführung. Nr. 8/1990.

Zimmer, Dieter, 1994: Personalentwicklung – zentrale Aufgabe erfolgreicher Unternehmensführung. In: Deutsches Steuerrecht. Nr. 15, pp. 551–554.

Appendix

Members and contact persons of the International Network for Better Local Government

Braintree

Robert Atkins
Director of Housing and Community
Housing and Community Services
Braintree District Council
Causeway House
Braintree Essex CM7 9HB
Great Britain

Christchurch

Mike Richardson
City Manager
Christchurch City Council
Civic Offices P.O. Box 237
Christchurch
New Zealand

Delft

Piet Severeijnen
Onderzoeksmanager
City of Delft
Phoenixstraat 16
2611 AL Delft
Netherlands

Duisburg

Winfried Lappé
Leiter der Projektgruppe
Entwicklungs- und
Koordinierungsprojekt
Verwaltungsmodernisierung
Stadt Duisburg
Burgplatz 19
47049 Duisburg
Germany

Farum

Leif Frimand
City Manager
Farum Kommune
Radhuset
3520 Farum
Denmark

Hæmeenlinna

Robert Ankil
Social Researcher
Social Development Ltd.
Hallituskatu 19
13100 Hæmeenlinna
Finland

Neuchâtel

Monika Dusong
Conseillère communale
Direction des Finances
Ville de Neuchâtel
Fbg de L'Hôpital 2
2001 Neuchâtel
Switzerland

Phoenix

Frank Fairbanks
City Manager
City of Phoenix
200 W Washington Street
Phoenix, Arizona 85003
USA

Quebec

Jean Dionne
Manager Public Consultation
Hôtel de Ville Quebec
Rue des Jardins, Bureau 319
Quebec G1R 4S9, Canada

Tilburg

Hein van Oorschot
City Manager
City of Tilburg
Stadhuisplein 130
5000 T.H. Tilburg
Netherlands

Local Government Center for Management Studies
(KGSt., Cologne)

Harald Plamper
Vorstand der KGSt.
Lindenallee 13–17
50968 Köln
Germany

Professor Gerhard Banner
Vorstand der KGSt. a.D.
Mülheimer Str. 54
53604 Bad Honnef
Germany

Bertelsmann Foundation

Dr. Marga Pröhl
Vice President "State and Public Administration"
Carl-Bertelsmann-Straße 256
33311 Gütersloh
Germany

Margit Sommer
Project Manager "State and Public Administration"
Carl-Bertelsmann-Straße 256
33311 Gütersloh
Germany

International Network for Better Local Government
Subjects for 1996/1997

- multi-ethnic society,
- change management,
- strategic information management,
- securing sustainable development in the local authorities, and
- community participation.